Porter-Bogard Debate

held at

Damascus, Arkansas
March 23-26, 1948

W. Curtis Porter
Monette, Arkansas
Church of Christ

and

Ben M. Bogard
Little Rock, Arkansas
Missionary Baptist Church

Speeches Recorded by Electrical Transcription

ISBN 1-58427-043-8

Guardian of Truth Foundation
P.O. Box 9670
Bowling Green, Kentucky 42102

BEN M. BOGARD
Little Rock, Arkansas

W. CURTIS PORTER
Monette, Arkansas

CAROL CHRISTIAN
Holdenville, Oklahoma
Moderator for Mr. Bogard

JOE H. BLUE
Salem, Arkansas
Moderator for Mr. Porter

PROPOSITIONS

1. The church known as the Missionary Baptist Church is Scriptural in origin, doctrine, practice and name.

   Affirmative: Ben M. Bogard

   Negative: W. Curtis Porter

2. The church known as the Church of Christ is Scriptural in origin, doctrine, practice and name.

   Affirmative: W. Curtis Porter

   Negative: Ben M. Bogard

INTRODUCTION

The Porter-Bogard Debate was conducted in the Church of Christ building in Damascus, Arkansas, March 23 to March 26, 1948. Ben M. Bogard of Little Rock, Arkansas, represented the Missionary Baptist Church and W. Curtis Porter of Monette, Arkansas, represented the Church of Christ.

Each session of the debate comprised two hours with speakers alternating every thirty minutes. During the four days eight sessions were given to the discussion—one session in the afternoon and one at night of each day. The debate was conducted on a high plane, and good attendance, good order and attention prevailed throughout.

The debate was recorded by electrical transcription. A number of men, using their own machines, recorded the discussion, but it was recorded by brother Christian A. Lyles, Fort Worth, Texas, for publication in book form. In addition to his own records he had access to the records of brother J. O. Jones of Memphis, Tennessee.

But publication of the debate was delayed because of lack of finance to put it through. Printing books is an expensive undertaking, and it was hoped that the book could be brought out within a short time. However, the unavoidable delay caused Mr. Bogard to reach the conclusion that we did not intend to publish it. A lady in Memphis, Tennessee, was hired to transcribe the records, but her work was very unsatisfactory to both Mr. Bogard and to me, as she often condensed whole paragraphs into a few words of her own. So the work had to be done over from the first. During this delay Mr. Bogard wrote a series of articles in his paper, The Missionary Baptist Searchlight, concerning his "Long Career As A Debater." In the last installment of that series, published in issue of February 25, 1950, Mr. Bogard wrote as follows concerning the Damascus debate:

> "My 237th, and last debate, was held at Damascus, Arkansas, with Elder Curtis Porter, one of the very best Campbellite debaters now living. His strength is not in his arguments but in his sophistry, which is intended to deceive. He

tries to laugh his opponent out of court, so to speak. His wise cracks, and slurs seem to suit his people and he makes the most of such as that. To debate with him one must be on the alert all the time to prevent him from getting by with such disreputable stuff as that. But his failure has been made manifest in many ways.

"The purpose of the recording machine was to have the debate published in book form and I hoped that the book might be printed, but it was only a half hope—a very strong wish. All who expected the book, some of them actually paying for books in advance, have been disappointed for no book has been published. The Campbellites have the records and therefore I cannot publish it. So there will be no book. Why? Two FULL YEARS have passed and still no book.

"It was a four days debate and my method in debating is to make the debate CUMULATIVE. The first day I lay off my ground and work to cover it. I will allow much to go unanswered the first day so as to build up the hopes of my opponent's followers and they go away very sure that their man is going to win. The next day I tighten up some and make the hearers remember what was said the day before; my own friends are glad and my opponent's followers begin to get uneasy. The third day I go over much of the same things that have been said in the two previous days and show how my opponent fell down on his part, and the fourth day I round up the corners and tie him up hopelessly and as a result come out triumphantly. This method worked well in this debate.

"I have several reasons to believe that they were willing to have the first two days debating published and many reasons to believe that they did not want the last two days published. They sent me a very imperfect transcript of the first two days and requested that I return it. I wrote to them that I was not willing for any of the debate to be published UNLESS ALL OF IT BE published and asked that they send the transcripts of the last two days and then it could all be put together and the book could be published. That was ELEVEN MONTHS AGO and I have not received a word from them yet, and thus we see that they have backed down and out as to publishing the book."

The preceding quotation from Mr. Bogard's articles gives his reaction to the delay in publishing the book. No idea of not publishing the book was ever entertained, but the financial problem held it up. In this introduction I would make no effort to argue the merits or demerits of the book, as it pertains to either debater, but am perfectly willing for the reader to decide for himself. He can make his own decision as to whether my power was not "arguments" but "sophistry" and as to how "triumphantly" victorious Mr. Bogard became as the debate neared its close. But at least every one will be able to see that there has been no "back down" on publishing the debate.

After a long unavoidable delay, brother Lyles offered the records and transcriptions (as far as they had been made) of the debate to me if I could work out some means and way of publication. I decided that it could be done. Accordingly, all the records which had not been transcribed and the transcriptions that had been made were delivered to me on March 31, 1951.

A little more than two and one-half days of the debate had been transcribed by sister Christian A. Lyles. I went to work on the transcription of the remaining records, and within a short time had the work of transcribing completed. Then the complete transcription of the debate was submitted to Mr. Bogard for his correction of his speeches. About that time, however, Mr. Bogard became seriously ill, and within a short time, before he was able to do much of the work of correction, he died of a heart attack, May 29, 1951.

The death of Mr. Bogard, of course, caused further delay in printing the book. But before he died he authorized Mr. L. D. Foreman, Mr. C. L. Jones and three others, whose names I do not have, to finish the work of correction of the manuscripts. Credit, therefore, is given to these men for their work in that respect.

All speakers, as far as I recall, use in their oral delivery many contractions permissible in the English language, as "don't" for "do not," "I'll" for "I shall," "wouldn't" for "would not" and many other such expressions. In correcting the speeches of Mr. Bogard nearly all the contractions of this nature were eliminated. This makes the reading a little smoother, but in no way changes the meaning. So no objection was made to these changes, but this will explain why such contractions appear in my speeches but not in Mr. Bogard's.

During the debate each speaker had his own moderator. Mr. Carol Christian of Holdenville, Oklahoma, was moderator for Mr. Bogard, and brother Joe H. Blue of Salem, Arkansas, was moderator for me. Both men did their work well.

And now after a delay of more than three years, we offer to the reading public, in this volume, the Porter-Bogard Debate. We trust that it will mean much toward the salvation of souls and the glorification of the name of the Lord .

W. Curtis Porter
Monette, Arkansas
August 29, 1951

First Day

BOGARD'S FIRST AFFIRMATIVE

Gentlemen Moderators, Mr. Porter, Ladies and Gentlemen:

It affords me no little pleasure to appear before you today to defend the truth and propagate the principles of our Lord Jesus Christ. I have asked the Lord several times, and I believe He will grant my request, to let me die in the middle of a fight because we are commanded to fight the good fight of faith.

It is a great pleasure to me to meet my friend, Porter. We had a debate once in Oklahoma. It was very pleasant, and I am sure this will be.

Coming directly to the question, let me say that Bro. Porter and I request you to keep yourselves out of the debate. Do not speak up from your seat; do not make any demonstrations like cheering, clapping the hands, or stamping the feet; and whatever you do, do not try to help your man out or help the other man to get out. It is our business to do this debating. If the Baptists had not been willing to risk me, they would not have called me. If my friend's people had not been willing to risk him they would not have called him, so we do not need your help from either side. Keep out of it please, because if you get started in demonstrations, the first thing you know there will be disorder that will hurt instead of help. We are fully able to take care of the situation on each side. Don't you get uneasy about it. Friends, do not start arguments out in the crowd or on the grounds, for you do not know how. If you knew how your people would have asked you to do it instead of calling on Mr. Porter and me. And if you have no confidence in us, start a debate of your own on the side. The very fact that you raise a question out among yourselves shows dissatisfaction on the part of anybody who does it. The best thing to do is to keep perfectly quiet and listen.

The proposition reads very much alike in both my affirmative and Bro. Porter's affirmative: "The church of which I am a member, known as the Missionary Baptist Church, is scriptural in origin, doctrine, practice, and name." I want to emphasize the latter part of this proposition, *it is scriptural in name.* And the one who fails to substantiate that feature will fail in the debate. If I fail to substantiate the name "Missionary Baptist Church" by the Bible then I have failed. If my friend Porter fails to find the name of his church, the one of which he is a member, he has failed. I want that understood to begin with.

The scriptures teach, by that I mean the word of God, the Bible, that no matter where the Bible speaks, that is God speaking. And so we take the scriptures as our all-sufficient and perfect rule of faith and practice. By church, I am using the term church *in its institutional sense*, of course; I do not mean any particular, local congregation, but the church as an institution. We speak of the family as being the cornerstone of civilization. We speak of the eagle as the king of birds—not any particular eagle, but the eagle as a species. We speak of the family in the institutional sense, not in the particular sense. I think everybody will understand that. There might be some individual congregation wearing our name that I would not think of endorsing or trying to defend, but the church as an institution, the "Missionary Baptist Church," of which I am a member, "is scriptural in origin, doctrine, practice, and name."

In order to get at the matter we must first find out when the church began, and what kind of a church it was when it began; and then, by means of those marks of identification, we can locate the church as we have it now.

Our Lord, before He left the earth, said, as we read in Mark 13:31-35, that He is the "master of the house" and would go away and come back again. And He commanded His servants to watch for in such an hour as ye think not the master will appear. Well, what is the house? He left the house when He left the world. We read in I Tim. 3:15, "the house of God which is the church of God, the pillar and the ground of the truth." Then the church of God is the house of God, and He left His house when He left the world and promised to come back again and gave His servants authority and a work to do. The authority He gave them was to "teach all nations," as we find in the great commission, "baptizing them in the name of the Father, the Son, and the Holy Ghost, teaching them to observe all things whatsoever I have commanded you, and lo, I am with you alway even unto the end of the world." So that institution which He left and which He called His church, and which was defined by the apostle Paul as being the house of God, is what He is coming back to *in person* and will be with in spirit always, even unto the end of the world.

The actual beginning of this church is found in Acts 1:21, where Peter stood up and said that one must be chosen to replace Judas who had "companied with us all the time the Lord Jesus went in and out among us, beginning from the baptism of John." Note this company which Jesus was in all the time He went in and out among them *began from the baptism of John.* Note, it did not say beginning *with* the baptism of John, but beginning *from* the baptism of John. John the Baptist was the first Baptist. Why? Because the word Baptist means one who is authorized to baptize. John the Baptist was the first one authorized to baptize; therefore, he was called the Baptist because there was no other one at that time. The church had not begun at that time, but beginning with the Baptist preacher sent from God, the material was prepared, and Jesus organized that material into His church, and said, "Lo, I am with you alway, even unto the end of the world." If my friend could find somewhere in the Bible where it says any kind of a church or institution begins on the day of Pentecost, he would be happy. But I find the exact beginning of the church from Peter's own words, "Beginning from the baptism of John."

We are given the very names of the first members of that church in John 1, beginning at the 35th verse. "Again the next day after John stood, and two of his disciples; and looking upon Jesus as He walked, he said, Behold the Lamb of God, and the two disciples heard him speak, and they followed Jesus. Then Jesus turned, and saw them following, and said unto them, What think ye? They said unto Him, Rabbi, (which is to say, being interpreted, master,) where dwellest thou? He said unto them, Come and see. And they came and saw where He dwelt and abode with

Him that day for it was about the tenth hour." Now here are the names: "One of the two which heard John speak and followed Him was Andrew, Simon Peter's brother. He first findeth his own brother Simon, and saith unto him, We have found the Messias, which is being interpreted, the Christ. And he brought him to Jesus. And when Jesus beheld him, He said, Thou art Simon the son of Jona: thou shalt be called Cephas which is by interpretation, a stone. The day following Jesus would go forth into Galilee, and findeth Philip, and saith unto him, Follow me. Now Philip was of Bethsaida, the city of Andrew and Peter. Philip findeth Nathanael, and saith unto him, We have found him, of whom Moses in the law, and the prophets, did write, Jesus of Nazareth, the son of Joseph. And Nathanael said unto him, Can there any good thing come out of Nazareth?" There are the very names of the members of the company that began with Jesus and stayed with Him all the time "the Lord Jesus went in and out among us" unto that same day that "He was taken up from us." And to that company He gave the commission, "Go ye therefore and teach all nations, baptizing them in the name of the Father, and the Son, and the Holy Ghost, and lo, I am with you alway, even unto the end of the world."

The word "missionary" means one who is sent on a mission. Webster's dictionary will tell you that. We all know that without the dictionary, as for that matter. John the Baptist was sent on a mission. What was that mission? To preach and to baptize. Very well then, he was a missionary because he was sent on a mission. He was a Baptist because he was sent to baptize, and therefore, he was a Missionary Baptist preacher, the only one at that time.

Somebody says, "Who baptized John the Baptist?" "Nobody." "Well," you say, "can a man be a Baptist *now* without being baptized?" "Certainly not." Then how could John be a Baptist not having been baptized?

Let me come at you with another question. When God got ready to create the Baptist church He created the first one without baptism. All since then have been baptized, without exception. Can a man exist without a mother? Why no. Who was the mother of Adam? Nobody. How could he be a man without a mother? When God got ready to create the human race, He created the first man without a mother. So when God got ready to create the Missionary Baptist Church, He created the first one without baptism. All other men since Adam have had mothers. And all other Baptists since the first Baptist have been baptized. So John was a missionary Baptist preacher. Then when Jesus organized the material that John got together, prepared material for the Lord, He told that church in Matt. 28:19-20, "Go ye therefore, and teach all nations, baptizing them in the name of the Father, and of the Son, and of the Holy Ghost: and, lo, I am with you alway, even unto the end of the world."

Since a missionary is one sent on a mission, and Jesus sent His church out on a mission, it was necessarily a missionary church. He sent that church to preach and to baptize, so it was a preaching church and a baptizing church; therefore, the church I belong to is a Missionary Baptist Church, made so by divine authority. We ought to call a thing what it is, and that is what it is. If God made no mistake in naming the first Baptist, the Baptist, and if God made no mistake in sending out on a mission the first Baptist, then we make no mistake in calling the church the Lord sent into all the world a missionary church. And we make no mistake in calling it the Baptist church, the Missionary Baptist church.

I'll drop this thought with my friend Porter, and I hope all of you may remember that missionary means one who has been sent on a mission. A Baptist is one who has been sent to baptize. The Missionary Baptist Church is the only church in the world that even pretends to baptize. I pause a moment to let that go in. The Missionary Baptist Church is the only one on earth that even pretends to baptize. We have church baptism, a church authorized to baptize, a church sent out to preach and to baptize. A church sent on a mission makes a missionary church. Being sent to baptize makes it a Missionary Baptist Church. The Lord promised to be with that Missionary Baptist Church to the end of the world. The world has not come to an end yet, so therefore *He is with the Missionary Baptist Church to this good day.*

Then I come to the marks and characteristics of a church. First of all, a church, in order to be scriptural, must have a scriptural beginning. Now notice the beginning of the Missionary Baptist Church, a company of baptized believers, associating in the faith and fellowship of Jesus Christ, sent out on a mission, and part of that mission being to baptize. And He promised to be with that Missionary Baptist Church clear on down to the end of the world. Let me repeat again, for I want you to remember it, (arguments are not made by noise, but by words) that the Missionary Baptist Church is the only church in the world that baptizes. All the others have their baptizing by individuals—not church baptism, but individual baptism. Bear that in mind. And the Missionary Baptist Church claims authority to baptize because Jesus said, "go teach and baptize."

The Missionary Baptist Church and the Bible Church are identical in doctrine and practice. For instance, in Bible times the church received its own members. Rom. 14:1. Him that is weak in the faith, let the preacher shake him in, or take him down to the creek and baptize him in. That is not the way it reads. "Him that is weak in the faith, *receive ye.*" That was said to the church at Rome. The church did its own receiving. That is why we vote on members coming into our church. The Bible says do it. Somebody says, "How in the world can you vote on a man's salvation?" We do not. We do not believe in church salvation. Salvation is of the Lord, "saved by grace through faith, and that not of yourselves, it is the gift of God." Church membership is a matter of fellowship, and we decide who shall be in our fellowship. That is all we mean by voting. Rom. 14:1. "Him that is weak in the faith, receive ye." Who is to do the receiving? The ones spoken to. Who were spoken to? The church. And that being true, we ask the church to do the receiving. Somebody must receive whoever comes in the church. *Somebody decides that thing.* No man decides who shall be saved, but men decide who shall be in their fellowship. And we, therefore, decide who shall be in our fellowship. *Somebody must decide to baptize whoever is baptized.* He can not force himself on the people.

But with my friend and his people, *the preacher does all the deciding. He does all the voting.* And I have a mighty good friend sitting right out front of me, and I will not call his name, who did refuse to baptize a party who came and offered herself for baptism. He is right over here. (Pointing to a preacher.) If he has a right to decide it, then why hasn't a hundred in a membership a right to decide it? That is all we mean by voting. Somebody decides who shall be baptized and no man could force another to baptize him. Therefore, somebody must decide to receive the one who is a believer and that is either done *by some individual* or done by the congregation. Baptists adopt the scriptural method of having the church to do the receiving.

Another doctrine of the New Testment Church is the doctrine of total hereditary depravity. Now somebody says, "Do you believe that horrible doctrine?" There is nothing horrible about it. It is just a matter of scripture. The Bible plainly says in Rom. 8:7-9, "The carnal mind is enmity against God and not subject to the law of God, neither indeed can be. So then they that are in the flesh cannot please God. But ye are not in the flesh, but in the Spirit, if so be that the Spirit of God dwell in you. Now if any man have not the Spirit of Christ, he is none of His." I hope my friend will note this particular point. "They that are in the flesh *cannot please God.*" Would not God be pleased with anything that is good? Why, surely He would. The things that are in the flesh cannot please God, so there is nothing in a man who is a fleshly man only, to please God with—no good in him. If there is any good in him, I hope my friend points out what that good is, and then he will flatly contradict what the Bible says. "They that are in the flesh cannot please God."

Now there may be a difference here as to what constitutes the flesh. The flesh is *what we are by nature.* It does not mean meat, and bones, fingernails and hair, muscles, nerves; it does not mean meat, but it means what we are by nature. For instance, I think I can give you a good definition from the Bible of what we mean by flesh. And remember that they which are in the flesh cannot please God. What is the flesh? It does not mean the hair and the hide, the meat and the bone, and the skin and the nerves—the meat, like you speak of the carcass of a dead man or hog or horse—not that. The word flesh is used in the sense of *what we are by nature.*

For instance, the flesh has a will. John 1:13. "Which were born, not of blood, nor of the will of the flesh, nor of the will of man, but of God." Now the meat and the bones and the hide and the hair do not have a will. But that thing that the Bible calls flesh has a will. And therefore, it can not be just a carcass or the body.

Next, flesh has a mind. Col. 2:18. "Let no man beguile you of your reward in a voluntary humility and worshiping of angels, intruding into those things which he hath not seen, vainly puffed up by his fleshly mind." Now fingernails and hair and skin and muscles and bone do not have a mind, but the flesh has a mind. So it does not mean a carcass—it does not mean meat and bones.

The flesh has a body. Read Col. 1:22—"In the body of His flesh through death, to present you holy and unblameable and unreproveable in His sight." Now meat and bones are part of the body. The body certainly does not have a body, but the flesh has a body. Therefore the flesh does not mean the body.

Again, the flesh has desires or lusts. I Peter 2:11. "Dearly beloved, I beseech you as strangers and pilgrims, abstain from fleshly lusts." Therefore the flesh can desire, can want, can lust. The fingernails and the hair and the hide and the bones can not have desires, so that shows that the flesh does not mean just the body.

Then the flesh has wisdom. II Cor. 1:12. "For our rejoicing is this, the testimony of our conscience, that in simplicity and godly sincerity, not with fleshly wisdom, but by the grace of God, we have had our conversation in the world, and more abundantly to you-ward." Therefore the flesh does not mean the body. It does not mean fingernails and hair, hide, and muscles and bone. *Flesh means what we are by nature.*

Then the flesh has works. Gal. 5:19. "Now the works of the flesh are manifest, which are adultery, fornication, uncleanness, lascivousness." Now my fingernails and my hair, my hide, my bones do not have works. What can a corpse do lying there in a coffin? Nothing. But the flesh has works. Therefore the flesh is what we are by nature. Let me read it again now. Rom. 8:7-9. "In me, that is, in my flesh, dwells no good thing." In me as I am by nature, my natural condition before I have been born again, dwells no good thing.

Now that forces us to the doctrine of total depravity. What do you mean by total depravity? It means all there is to man is depraved. Of what does man consist? He consists of body. There is nothing good in the body. If so, it is something good that God would be pleased with. There is nothing good in the mind. If so, God would be pleased with it. There is nothing good in my spirit. If so, God would be pleased with it. "In me, that is in my flesh, dwells no good thing"—an utter absence of good, the utter absence of that which is in harmony with God, an utter absence of the love of God. And that is what we mean by total depravity and that came by nature, for we are all the children of wrath by nature. Eph. 2:3. And naturally, therefore, we are in a condition in which we can not please God. The kind of church that believes that is the kind found in the Bible. There are many other things, to be sure, but we can not bring them all in in one speech. And we will go further with these marks of identification.

First Day

PORTER'S FIRST NEGATIVE

Gentlemen Moderators, Mr. Bogard, Ladies and Gentlemen:

It likewise gives me pleasure to be present upon this occasion to enter into this discussion of things that pertain to principles of divine truth. I enter wholeheartedly into the suggestion that Mr. Bogard made regarding your leaving off demonstrations and things of that nature, and of leaving the debate entirely to us who have been chosen for this particular work. Many times people have had the wrong impression of religious discussions, because somebody failed to do what he ought to have done along that line. We simply urge you to let us do the discussing, and you keep out of it; and I'm sure it will go along in a fine way, and there will be no blood shed during this entire discussion. As Mr. Bogard mentioned, we have debated before, and got along just fine; and I'm sure we'll do the same thing now. We'll be able to prove to the people of this community that religious discussions can be had without any knock-down, drag-out, blood-shed, or anything of that nature. You just come and listen and let us present to you the things that we have to say, and then you compare them with your Bibles. Search the Scriptures for yourselves to see just what is the truth of the matter.

Mr. Bogard came, in the discussion of his proposition, to the first point as THE NAME. The proposition says, "The church known as the Missionary Baptist Church is Scriptural in origin, doctrine, practice and name." He said, "I want especially to emphasize the last part of this proposition—that it is Scriptural *in name*." Furthermore, he said, "The one who fails to prove the church is Scriptural in name fails in this debate." Mr. Bogard's failure is already a fact. "The man who fails to prove the church which he represents is Scriptural in name fails in this debate." That is Mr. Bogard's statement; and to that I shall hold him in the discussion as it goes on. I have no doubt that I am going to be able to show you that he has miserably failed, and that failure will be continuous and monotonous, as this debate goes on.

In order to get at that, I have just a few questions I want to submit to my friend. I do not like to follow the plan of giving a long list of questions in order to take up a lot of time and divert attention from the debate, but a few well-chosen questions I want answered will help to focus the issue; and so I'm giving him a few of these at this time that he might have time to look them over as the speech goes on.

1. Is the name "Missionary Baptist Church" mentioned in the Bible?
2. Can a thing be Scriptural in name if not named in the Scriptures?
3. Was John the Baptist a member of the church of the Lord?
4. Was any man who was a member of the church of the Lord ever called "Baptist" in the New Testament?
5. Do you believe and teach that infants are totally depraved?
6. Do you baptize the inner man or the outer man?
7. Is the sinner saved by a living faith or by a dead faith?

I shall appreciate a forth-right answer to those questions when Mr. Bogard takes the floor the next time.

Now, he said he used the term "church" in the institutional sense because there might be some local congregations who would hold to the name "Baptist Church" that he would not be able to endorse. So they might wear the name, and still hold to things that he would not agree with, and, consequently, could not endorse them. But he presented certain things that must be necessary in order to present this matter, that he might prove the statements of the proposition. And the one with which he began was with respect to the beginning of the church—when the church began. First, he introduced Mark, the 13th chapter, verses 31 to 35, in which the Lord was referred to as the master of the house, when He was going away and coming back again. Also, the statement that he "left His house and gave authority to His servants." My friend turned to 1 Timothy 3:15, to the statement of the apostle Paul, in which he says the "house of God is the church of the living God, the pillar and ground of the truth." Now, he reasoned that the house is the church, or the church is the house, and the Lord left His house, or the Lord left His church, when He went to heaven. Consequently, the church was established and in operation during the personal ministry of Christ.

Well, the word "house" sometimes refers to the church in a completed form, or in a form in which it is operating and carrying on. Not always must that be true. Besides, we find another Scripture right along this particular line that shows my friend is entirely wrong about it. The only sense in which He left the house was in the sense of preparation; of course, the work was being prepared, the arrangements were being made, and all of that; and the *material that would constitute the house* was left. In that sense, He left the house. But in Luke 19:12 we have another statement made by the Lord in which He refers to His going into a far country, or going to heaven—just as He referred to it in Mark 13—and declared He was as one taking a journey to "a far country to receive for himself a kingdom, and to return." Now, the Lord *had not received* the kingdom when He went to the far country—He was going to the far country *to receive* the kingdom. Mr. Bogard oftentimes has made arguments to prove that the kingdom and the church are the same, and he will make those arguments again during this discussion. So the Lord went into the far country, or into heaven, *to receive the kingdom.* The kingdom then had not been received. It existed only in the sense, or in the state, of preparation.

Then he said, "I want to give you the actual beginning of it. I want to show you exactly where it began." He turned to Acts 1, verse 21, in which reference is made to the selection of one to take the place of Judas Iscariot, who had committed suicide. And they selected one who had companied with them all the time the Lord went in and out among them, beginning from the baptism of John. He said, "I want you to notice this, and I want to emphasize this fact, that it began *from* the baptism of John." So the church of the New Testament, which my friend says is the Missionary Baptist Church, (though he couldn't prove it if his life depended on it) began there. Because after all, and remember this, *there is not one single hint in all of God's book of the Missionary Baptist Church.* Whenever my friend gives us the passage that speaks of the Missionary Baptist Church, I'll close this debate and go home. Want to tell me where it is, Mr. Bogard? *I'll read it now,* and close the debate. If you will tell me where the Bible mentions the Missionary Baptist Church, or where it says a word about the Missionary Baptist Church, I'll close the debate and go home. The debate will be over. But he said that "the Missionary Baptist Church began from the baptism of John." He said, "I want you to notice now that it was not *with* the baptism of John but *from* the baptism of John." In other words, the Missionary Baptist Church didn't begin in the days of John. He back-tracks from some things he has said in other debates, that are on record, in days gone by. He doesn't want to get into those holes again. So he says, "It began *from* the baptism of John and not *with* the baptism of John." Do you want to take it back, Elder Bogard, or shall I expose you on it? "It began *from* and not *with* the baptism of John." So says Mr. Bogard.

I hold in my hand here a little book. It's entitled "Baptist Way Book." Now, this was written by my opponent, Mr. Bogard. On page 29 of this book, in which he discusses "The Historical Way," he introduces Acts 1:21. Here is what he says, "When did the company or congregation of baptized believers begin?" (That's what he asked us a while ago.) "Peter answers the question in Acts 1:21. 'Wherefore of these men which have companied with us all the time that the Lord Jesus went in and out among us, beginning from the baptism of John,' and so forth." Now, here is his comment: "This passage affirms that certain men'companied' with Jesus and that this 'company' began '*with* the baptism of John'." Do you want to see it, Elder Bogard? "This company," he says, "began *with* the baptism of John." "W-I-T-H," with. And now my opponent said a while ago that it didn't begin "*with* the baptism of John" but it's "*from* the baptism of John." Why don't you revise your Way Book, Mr. Bogard? It "began *with* the baptism of John," he says, in the book. But *now* he says it didn't begin with the baptism of John"—it was *"from* the baptism of John." That's Bogard versus Bogard. He can straighten it out if he sees fit. If he doesn't, why, it will haunt him through the debate.

Well, he said, "John *the* Baptist." Yes, "John *the Baptist* was called 'the Baptist' because 'the Baptist' means one who is authorized to baptize, and he was the first one that was authorized to baptize. Therefore, he was called 'the Baptist'." "John *the* Baptist" because, Mr. Bogard says, "he was the *only one* at the time." All right; John the Baptist was called "the Baptist" because *he was the only one at that time.* If there had been more than one, Mr. Bogard, what would *he* have been called? If there had been more than one at that time, what would he have been called? John *the* Baptist? No. He was called John *the* Baptist inasmuch as he was the only one at that time. If there had been more than one, he would have been "John *a* Baptist," wouldn't he? But the Book said "John *the* Baptist." And Mr. Bogard says that means that *he was the only one at that time.* Well, when the record closes concerning John he was still called "John *the* Baptist." He never had made another, because he was still *the only one when he died,* Mr. Bogard. He was still referred to as "John *the* Baptist." There is not a place in all of God's Book that refers to him as "John *a* Baptist." So there never was another, according to Bogard's own admission. "The Baptist" means "the only one at that time."—the *only one* when he was working—the *only one* when he died. He hadn't made any more. Still "John *the* Baptist." Thank you, Mr Bogard.

Then he endeavored to name the first members of the church. And he gave John 1:35-46. Andrew and Peter, his brother. He went on to talk about the commission being given to this little company. Here are the first members of it; and it constituted a company. And the Lord gave to this company the great commission in Matthew 28:19, Mr. Bogard says. So here's the church, the company. Mr. Bogard concluded that a company couldn't exist without the church existing. He might have something. But listen, friends, it was *to this very same company,* or at least a portion of it, that the Lord said in Matthew 16:18: "Upon this rock *I will build* my church, and the gates of hell shall not prevail against it." The company existed before the Lord made that statement, "Upon this rock *I will build* my church." And that statement was made to *the same company.* So the church hadn't been built, according to the Lord. It had, according to Bogard. You can take your choice.

Furthermore, in Luke 10:9, when he sent out the seventy, some of that *very same company,* during the personal ministry of Christ, he said to them, "Go and preach that the kingdom of heaven is at hand." It hadn't come yet, unless "at hand" means already come. Bogard said that one time in one of his debates, but he has been sick of it ever since. And I don't think he will say it any more—that "at hand" meant already come. So the kingdom of heaven is at hand. Unless "at hand" means "already come," Mr. Bogard, then you're in trouble along that line. So please tell us what that means.

I was really amused at how he proved the name "Missionary Baptist Church." The word "missionary," Mr. Bogard says, "means one sent on a mission." And John was sent on a mission. Therefore, he was a "missionary." The word "Baptist" means "one who was sent to baptize." John was sent to baptize. Therefore, John was a Missionary Baptist. Not *a* Missionary Baptist, Mr. Bogard, but *the* Missionary Baptist, if that is true. Remember he was *the only one at that time.* All right. Then, in the next place, he found the commission given, as he said, to the church. So he had "church." He put them all together and had "Missionary Baptist Church." Here is his proof for the Missionary Baptist Church being Scriptural in name. I can take that very same form of reasoning and prove that the Latter Day Saints are Scriptural in name, Mr. Bogard — that they're a Scriptural church. I can follow that very same sort of reasoning and prove that the Latter Day Saints are the true church. Why, we remember that Peter stood up on the day of Pentecost and preached. He was a preacher, wasn't he? Yes, he preached; so he was a preacher. Now, furthermore, he preached in "the last days," because he referred to the fulfillment of Joel's prophecy as being accomplished that day. "In the last days I will pour out of my Spirit upon all flesh." He was also a saint. Yes, Peter was a saint; and he was a preacher; and he preached in the last days. Therefore, he was a "Latter Day Saint" preacher. It proves it just as conclusively as Mr. Bogard proved "Missionary Baptist Church." You can go somewhere and find the word "church" and add to it, and you'll have "Latter Day Saint's Church." If that was the best I could do, I would take out.

And then he said something more along this line that I want to call your attention to. He said somebody will ask the question, "Well, how could John be a Baptist and never be baptized? Well, when God got ready to make a man, he made a full grown man—he created a man. When God got ready," he said, "to form that first Baptist Church, God created the first Baptist Church without baptism." "God created the first Baptist Church without baptism." And I'll vouch that those are the words he said. He didn't say that God created the first Baptist—he said the first Baptist Church—and the record will show that he did say it. That "God created the first Baptist Church without baptism." All right, Mr. Bogard, will you tell me some of those who were members of that church that had not been baptized? "The first Baptist Church was created without baptism." Did John constitute the first church? All those who accepted his teaching were baptized. They couldn't make up the first Baptist Church, because the first Baptist Church didn't have baptism. There had to be a Baptist Church before John baptized anybody, because, Mr. Bogard says, he created the first Baptist Church without baptism. So I want to know who made up that church? Was it John? Anybody else besides John? Who were the members of that first Baptist Church, that didn't have baptism, which God had created?

Also he tells us that the church became the Missionary Baptist Church when the Lord gave the great commission in Matthew 28:19. All right, before then it wasn't the Missionary Baptist Church—it began that day. Well, the commission the Lord gave in Matthew 28:19 was given after his death and after his resurrection. Therefore, there was no Missionary Baptist Church before Jesus died, according to Mr. Bogard's argument, for it *became* the Missionary Baptist Church *when the Lord gave them the great commission* in Matthew 28:19. That was after his death. Hence, Mr. Bogard will have to see, according to his own argument, there was no Missionary Baptist Church before Jesus died. The first one was made when the Lord gave the great commission in Matthew 28:19. And since there was no Missionary Baptist Church before Jesus died, according to my friend's argument, then I'm still wanting to know who constituted the first one which was created without baptism? I hope that he will have the disposition to tell us something about it.

And, then, here's another statement that is worthy of your consideration. I believe I'll just agree with Mr. Bogard on this. He said, "We ought to call it what it is." "We ought to call it what it is" I believe that. I would shake hands on that, if he'd want to shake hands on it. Yes, sir, I believe the church ought to be called what it is. Did the apostles do what they ought to do? Did Jesus Christ and the apostles do what they ought to do? Bogard says they ought to call it what it is. Well, *if they called it what it is,* and what it was, it wasn't a Missionary Baptist Church, because they never called it that. And since it ought to be called what it is, then they didn't do what they ought to do or else it wasn't a Missionary Baptist Church to begin with. Now, just clear that thing up for us and let us know about it. Did the apostles call it what it was? Did Jesus Christ call it what it was? You say it ought to be called what it is. And you said it is a Missionary Baptist Church; therefore, it ought to be called the Missionary Baptist Church. Well, the apostles didn't call it that. *Did they call it what it ought to be called?* Jesus didn't call it that. *Did he call it what it ought to be called?* Or did they fail to do what they ought to do? Or could it be true that it wasn't that to begin with? Why, that's the truth of the matter, of course. They *did call it what it was.* They called it what they ought to have called it, but they nowhere called it Missionary Baptist

Church. So *it was not that* and should not have been called that. I challenge my opponent, every inch of him, from the top of his head to the soles of his feet, to straighten that out. He will not have done it when this debate has come to a close.

And, then, how about this one? "The Missionary Baptist Church is the only church in the world that pretends to baptize." And he said, "I want to emphasize that. I'm saying it for Porter's benefit, and I hope the rest of you get it." "The Missionary Baptist Church is the only church in the world that pretends to baptize." Well, I'll admit that it "pretends" to baptize, with emphasis on the word "pretends." Yes, sir, I'll agree with Mr. Bogard. The Baptist Church *pretends* to baptize. But pretending to do a thing and doing it are two entirely different things. I deny that it baptizes according to the teaching of the New Testament. I admit the Baptist Church *pretends* to baptize—using your own words. Thank you very much.

Next he came to the characteristics of the church—as the beginning of it. He says, "We have discussed that already." And so have I.

Then to its doctrine and practice. The first doctrine introduced by Mr. Bogard to prove the identity of the Baptist Church with the church of the New Testament (he said they were both the same) is that it receives its own members. And he based it upon Romans 14:1. "Him that is weak in the faith receive ye, but not to doubtful disputations." Here he gives his authority for voting in the church —for voting on members—for those who are to become members of the church. Paul said, "Him that is weak in the faith receive ye." That meant to *vote on him.* Well, I'll just agree that a man must be weak in the faith that would seek membership in the Baptist Church, that this must be the very pattern that my friend is looking for—"Him that is weak in the faith." That's the one to be voted on, according to Bogard's argument. So I'll just agree that if a man is seeking membership in the Baptist Church, he must be one that is weak in the faith. And at least, *in that particular* his passage must apply. "But," he said, "we don't vote on his salvation. Somebody says, 'Do you vote on the man's salvation?' No, we don't vote on his salvation." But you do vote on his becoming a part of the bride, don't you? He does vote on his becoming a part of the bride of Christ—he votes on that. We are going to find out after a while though, before this debate is over, just how much importance he attaches to the bride. How much, therefore, is involved in this matter of voting on a man, whether or not he will become a member of that bride, or a part of that bride? We shall ascertain that as the debate goes on. But somebody must decide who will be baptized, and "one man," he said, "before me refused to baptize somebody." That, of course, is entirely aside from the discussion. Whatever the reason was for refusal—I have an idea it was legitimate—because even John refused some when they came and failed to bring forth the works meet for repentance. He said, "Who hath warned you to flee from the wrath to come?" But that doesn't sustain his idea for voting. He is going to have to have something better than this in order to get his scripturalness for voting men into the church, or whether or not they will become members of the church.

He came to the doctrine of total hereditary depravity. That was a very bad-sounding term, and somebody might think that he shouldn't hold to that old doctrine— that terrible doctrine. He said, "There is nothing so terrible about that." Then he gave us some passages along that line that I want to look at. First was Romans 8:7-9. "The carnal mind is not subject to the law of God," and so on. I want to turn to that passage. I think I know what it says, but I want to turn to that passage and read just a little along here in Romans, the 8th chapter, in order to see just what Mr. Bogard is getting at. Romans 8:7-9: "Because the carnal mind is emnity against God: for it is not subject to the law of God, neither indeed can be. So then they that are in the flesh cannot please God. But ye are not in the flesh, but in the Spirit, if so be that the Spirit of God dwell in you. Now if any man have not the Spirit of Christ, he is none of his." This Mr. Bogard refers to the natural man, or to the man as he is by nature—that he "is not subject to the law of God, neither indeed can be." Mr. Bogard says *he can be* if he has a direct operation of the Spirit on him. If he can get that extra operation of the Spirit, he will be made subject to the law of God. But this says it is not subject to the law of God, "neither indeed can be." You just *can't make it subject* to the law of God. Now, the fact is the words "carnal mind" mean the "minding of the flesh," and that refers to man's living after the flesh; in other words, sin. And sin is not subject to the law of God; and sin cannot be made subject to the law of God. That's the point.

But let me see again about it. He makes a statement along here that there is no good in the sinner—the man as he is by nature. There is not any good in him at all because "they that are in the flesh," Paul said, "cannot please God." That's the man as he is by nature, the person as he is born: he cannot please God; he can't do a single thing that is pleasing to God. Everything that he does is sin. Everything is a sin, according to his position on this matter, because nothing in that man is good. There is nothing but that which is evil. *Everything is wrong.* That's total depravity. That's not all of it. He claims that he is born that way, as you shall find out as this discussion continues. But he said, "What is meant, now, by 'they that are in the flesh'?" Well, we'll see what Paul meant by it. We'll drop back to read verses 4 and 5 to see what Paul meant by *being in the flesh.* He said "that the righteousness of the law might be fulfilled in us, who walk not after the flesh, but after the Spirit. For they that are after the flesh do mind the things of the flesh; but they that are after the Spirit the things of the Spirit." The man, therefore, who is in the flesh, and who cannot please God, is the man who is *walking after the flesh, doing the works of the flesh, following the deeds of the flesh.* That's the man who is *in the flesh* and *can't please God.* And, certainly, nothing of that kind is going to be pleasing to God.

But Mr. Bogard says, "That doesn't mean flesh and bones, hair and toe nails and finger nails and things of that kind; so I'll just show you what it means." He went to John 1:13 and found something about the "will of the flesh"—not being born by "the will of the flesh." Then to Col. 2:18 about the "fleshly mind." So the flesh had a mind. Col.

1:22—"the body of his flesh." So it had a body. First Peter 2:11—"the desires of the flesh." So the flesh had desires. 2 Corinthians 1:12—"the wisdom of the flesh." "Not with fleshly wisdom," said Paul. Then he reached the conclusion that "flesh" does not mean the body, flesh and bones, but it means what we are by nature. Then he added Galatians 5:19-21—"the works of the flesh." He declares all of these things force us to the conclusion of "total depravity." Nothing good. All this forces us to the conclusion of total depravity. Now, what did we find? The will of the flesh; the mind of the flesh; the body of the flesh; the desires of the flesh; the wisdom of the flesh; and the works of the flesh. And those who have these things are totally depraved. Mr. Bogard was very unfortunate in his selection of texts, because one of these passages which he chose referred to Jesus Christ, the Son of God. Didn't you know that, Mr. Bogard?

Mr. Bogard speaks: "Yes, sir."

Porter continues: Therefore, Jesus Christ is totally depraved—and was when he was here—absolutely so. Colossians 1:22, referring to "the body of his flesh," referred not to a sinner, but it referred to Jesus Christ, the Son of God. And these things, Bogard says, including "the body of his flesh" in Colossians 1:22, force us to the conclusion that there is total depravity—that men are totally depraved. If that be true, then it must force us to the conclusion that Jesus Christ was totally depraved. Therefore, there was no good in Jesus Christ. Everything was wrong. Jesus lived a sinful life. Everything he did was contrary to God's will; nothing pleased the Father. Yet Jesus said, "I do always the things that please Him." Mr. Bogard's argument will make him say, "No, there is not anything that I have done that pleases God," because he had "the body of his flesh." That is one of those things that represents us as we are by nature: therefore, inherently totally depraved. Jesus Christ, therefore, was inherently totally depraved—born as mean as the devil, because the devil can't be any meaner than that. My friends, the devil could not be worse than totally depraved. "Totally depraved" means just as depraved as can possibly be. There can't be anymore than that.

If man is totally depraved, that includes Jesus Christ, according to his line of argument. Then that means that all men, and Jesus Christ, himself, were and are just as mean as the devil, for the devil cannot be worse than totally depraved. I shall await for Mr. Bogard to clear that matter up. I don't think he will. *I am sure that he won't.* I think he'll make an effort. I believe he'll try, but I'm just sure of the fact that that's going to haunt him during this discussion. Then he gave us Ephesians 2:1-3—he didn't have time to develop it—we were "by nature the children of wrath, even as others." He connected it with those passages already introduced: John 1:13—"the will of the flesh;" Colossians 2:18—"the mind of the flesh;" Colossians 1:22—"the body of his flesh;" 1 Peter 2:11—"the desires of the flesh;" 2 Corinthians 1:12—"the wisdom of the flesh;" and Galatians 5:19-21—"the works of the flesh;" (one of which applied to Jesus Christ, the Son of God). He declares that Ephesians 2:1 connects with all of this—that we "were by nature the children of wrath, even as others;" and "Jesus Christ, then, was by nature a child of wrath, even as others," because he had his flesh. Mr. Bogard talked about it's not meaning the body; it didn't mean flesh and bones and toe nails and hair, but meant that depraved nature which we have received from our parents. Jesus Christ had it, according to Mr. Bogard. Jesus Christ died upon the cross, a totally depraved man, as mean as the devil—dying to rescue men from the devil, but still totally depraved—depraved just as much so as anything could possibly be. And I want you to keep those things in mind. I see my time is almost gone. I haven't time to introduce more, and that completes the speech that my opponent has just made. Just how much time do I have?

Mr. Blue speaks: "About five seconds."

Well, that isn't long enough to start anything more. So we are going to close right there. I thank you very kindly for your attention.

First Day

BOGARD'S SECOND AFFIRMATIVE

Gentlemen Moderators, Ladies and Gentlemen:

I certainly appreciate the privilege of referring to the speech, if speech it may be called, of my good friend who just preceded me. I had hoped that he would answer, at least to the best of his ability, what I said, rather than pervert what I said and try to answer that.

He gave some questions here:

(1) Is the name "Missionary Baptist Church" mentioned in the Bible? I am going to be perfectly frank, and I want you to do exactly the same with me . If you do not I will show the public how it is. The name "Missionary Baptist Church" is not in the Bible. But when a man makes a picture of a cat, does he have to write under it, "This is a cat," to make men like you understand? If he makes a picture of a horse, does he have to write under it, "This is a horse," to make dull men understand? A thing that has to be named in order to understand what it is, is a poor thing to start with.

(2) Can a thing be scriptural in name if not named in the scriptures? Yes sir. And if you say it cannot you are in a bad fix before you get very far in this debate.

(3) Was John the Baptist a member of the Church of the Lord? I distinctly told you he was not a member of the church, but he was the one who began the work that resulted in the organization of the church.. My friend says, "Well, the first Baptist Church, according to Mr. Bogard, was without baptism." I never said that, awake, asleep, drunk or sober in all my life, and nobody heard me say it. I said the first Baptist was without baptism, just as the first man was without a mother. You did not choose to notice that, but had to pervert by saying that I said the first Baptist Church was without baptism. I gave you the names of the first members of the first Baptist church from the first chapter of John. I gave the time when it was to begin, by what Peter said in Acts 1:21, "Beginning from the baptism of John."

(4) Do you believe that infants are totally depraved? Yes sir. Certainly, we are by nature totally depraved. If infants were not, why not? That is the very thing I am going to prove beyond all question.

(5) Was any man who was a member of the church of the Lord ever called Baptist in the New Testament? They did not need to call them that because everybody could see what they were by the description. You are driving an auto out here and do I say, "Is that a wagon or an oxcart or what?" I have sense enough to know what it is by looking at it. And there it is in the Bible, described clearly, the parts, characteristics, all about it. Do you have to name it to make it that? Now, you are getting into trouble, deep trouble, my friend, just as sure as you are born if you are going to *demand the exact wording of the name.*

(6) Do you baptize the inner man or the outer man? I baptize the whole man, put him all under.

(7) Is a sinner saved by a living faith or a dead faith? A sinner is saved by faith and faith that works, and never fails to work. Your faith is a dead faith, according to your doctrine. I have answered those questions, and I will pass on to the next now.

In Mark 13 I read where the Lord left His house and commanded His servants to watch and gave them authority and work to do, but says Porter, that does not necessarily mean the Lord's church. Well, anyway, I read in I Timothy 3:15, "The house of God, which is the church of God." You find many houses, but here is "the house of God, which is the church of the living God, the pillar and ground of the truth." The *house that Jesus had must certainly have been His house,* and He left *His house* and promised to come back again. Then he read over in Luke where Jesus went away to get or to receive for Himself a kingdom. We are not debating the kingdom question. Do you want to get into the millenium reign of Christ? I will accommodate you. Perhaps we will later on. We are talking about the church now. And Jesus Christ has gone to receive for Himself a kingdom, and by and by the *kingdoms of this world will become the kingdom of our Lord Jesus Christ*—the very thing you deny.

Then he wants to quit the debate if I find the words "Missionary Baptist Church". All right, you are going to have to quit the debate without that. I am going to give you a description of it that every child can understand, without naming it. Now, I hope to make it perfectly plain so that even my friend, who seems to be dull of understanding, can understand it.

The Baptist — John *the* Baptist — was called that because at that time he was the only one, and Bro. Porter perverted that by saying that no other Baptist existed until after John died. He was called John the Baptist before he began to baptize. "In those days came John the Baptist" and that was before he baptized anybody. You do not have to baptize people to become a Baptist. You have to be *authorized to baptize.* Adam was the man until other men came into the world and there were more than one. In Matthew 16:18 he quoted, "Upon this rock I will build my church." Bro. Porter said the church hadn't even been established at that time. Jesus was talking to that same company, bless your soul. "Will build" there does not mean *to start, to begin,* but it comes from a Greek word meaning *"to build up, to edify."* You come out on that a little heavier and I will answer that too.

He said the Latter Day Saints could prove their name just as good as I can mine. Well, perhaps they could, if they are really saints. I deny they are. If they are Latter Day, they would be Latter Day Saints. We are what the Bible teaches; we are Bible Christians and we have a church *with the description, marks, and characteristics* of the New Testament Church. Then we are undoubtedly what we call the Missionary Baptist Church.

Now, he says, "The church did not become Missionary." (Get it. This is going on record for future generations.) "The church did not become missionary until Jesus gave the commission." I wish you would just rise up here—I do not want to get away from the microphone—and shake hands with me on that, that the church became a missionary church when Jesus gave the commission. If so, that was *before Pentecost* and if so, it was the church of our Lord Jesus Christ that He Himself made Missionary Baptist, you being the judge. It said it was sent on a mission. What mission? To go into all the world to preach the gospel to all men and to preach and baptize.

So, according to my friend, it was a Missionary Baptist Church before Pentecost, commissioned to go into all the world to preach the gospel.

Let us see what else we have here. Oh, on the Baptist Church being the only one that even "pretends" to baptize. He quibbled over that. That is unworthy of an honorable debater to quibble. He says here the Baptists "pretend" to baptize. He played on that to divert the attention of the people away from what I said. I will come again.

The church of which you (Porter) are a member does not baptize and doesn't even "pretend" to do it. I think that ought to be sufficient.

Romans 14:1. "Him that is weak in the faith receive ye." Notice how he perverts; it is unworthy of an honorable debater, to pervert. "Him that is weak in the faith receive ye." He said, "I will acknowledge that a person who is a member of the Baptist Church is weak in the faith." Isn't that a wonderful answer for a man of distinction, supposed to be about the best man they could put up to debate, to make a statement like that? God's word said in Romans 14:1, "Him that is weak in the faith receive ye." Porter said that he would be weak in the faith to join the Baptist Church. *They joined some church. They were received by the Roman church.* The church of Jesus Christ received members by vote. Otherwise, how would they? "Him that is weak in faith" let the preacher shake him in? Now, who is to decide? Who is to decide? (What's that? Want to stop? What is wrong? The machine is out?) (Due to failure of a recording machine there was a necessary pause in the speech).

Now we will start farther along. I regret that the machine went out, but the other one is keeping it perhaps.

On the subject of flesh, my friend said that the passage I quoted made Jesus Christ totally depraved. Does my friend not know that the Bible plainly says that He that "knew no sin became sin for us" that we might be made the righteousness of God in him? *He (Jesus) assumed the flesh*—Do you deny that Jesus Christ came in the flesh? The Bible says you are an anti-Christ if you do.

Now coming to the expression of "total depravity." He says that the devil can be no more than totally depraved, utterly ignoring what I said—that we mean by total, the *total man.* Man is not as bad as he can be but the *total man, all there is to a man, is depraved.* Every bit of him, *mind depraved, body depraved, spirit depraved,* all of it depraved, is total depravity. It does not mean the *extent,* as far as wickedness is concerned, in which he can not get *worse and worse,* deceiving and being deceived.

Now he said, according to this doctrine, a man who is totally depraved can not do any good at all. That is exactly what the Bible says, "That in my flesh dwelleth *no good thing.*" I quoted that for you a while ago. The best thing that you can do, my friend, as a sinner, an unsaved man, unregenerate, is to sin. Where is the scripture on that? Take I Corinthians 10:31, which says "whatsoever therefore ye eat, or drink, or whatsoever ye do, do all to the glory of God."

Did you *do anything for the glory of God* before you were saved? If not, then you did not do any good. You sinned every step of the way. Suppose a man pays his debts. *Does he do that for the glory of God?* If so, he is already a child of God. Suppose the man tells the truth. Is he doing that for the *glory of God?* If so, all right; otherwise, he is not doing right in leaving God out. Suppose a man lives a sober life. That is good from the worldly viewpoint but *"that which is not of faith is sin."* And if you do not do that by faith, no matter how much good you may do in the world's estimation, you are *not doing what is right in the sight of God.*

To give you another description now that will clinch that. In Proverbs 21:4, we find these words, "An high look, a proud heart, and the plowing of the wicked is sin." These farmers who go out here to plow—the Bible says that plowing is sin if you are wicked. Why? Because you are *not plowing for the glory of God.* This doctrine of hereditary total depravity takes out all self-righteousness. It knocks the sinner out of saving himself by being good. For *the best he can do,* according to the scripture, *is not pleasing to God.* "In me, that is in my flesh, dwelleth no good thing."

Now I gave the scriptures to show what the flesh is. The flesh has a will, the flesh has a mind, the flesh has a body, the flesh has wisdom, the flesh has desires, the flesh works, and *you know that does not mean the body.* It does not mean finger nails, the hair, the hide, the bones, the muscles. It it bound to mean *what we are by nature.* And so, according to scripture, "we are all by nature the children of wrath, even as others."

That brings us to the point where we must have a new birth in order to be saved and therefore we must have the ingrafting of the word in order to be saved. That is done by the Holy Spirit.

Now, coming to the other. What other marks and characteristics do we have as a church of the Lord Jesus Christ? There is the doctrine of salvation by grace through faith in the Lord Jesus Christ, not by works lest any man should boast. Salvation comes wholly by grace through faith. The grace reaches us through the faith that we have in the Lord Jesus Christ. "The wages of sin is death," Romans 6:23, "but the gift of God is eternal life through Jesus Christ our Lord." Salvation is by grace, through faith, not through obedience.

Then baptism is for those who have already been saved. Acts 10:47, 48. "Can any man forbid water, that these should not be baptized, which have received the Holy Ghost as well as we? And he commanded them to be baptized in the name of the Lord." Who? Cornelius and his household. Who were Cornelius and his household? Those who had already received the Holy Ghost. Jesus said, John 14:17, "Him the world cannot receive."

Then we come to the next mark or characteristic of a New Testament church which is the security of the believer. Romans 8:28, "We know that all things work together for good to them that love God, to them who are called according to his purpose." Salvation makes one safe. When you are saved, you are not left in danger, "but all things work together for good to them that love God, to them who are the called according to his purpose."

In Psalms 37:23, 24, "The steps of a good man are ordered by the Lord and he delighteth in his way. Though he fall, he shall not be utterly cast down, for the Lord upholdeth him with his hand." Salvation is such that when we stumble and fall, when we fail to do right, when we commit sin, we shall not be utterly cast out, for the Lord will pick us up every time.

1 John 2:19 says, "They went out from us." Who? Those who seemingly went to the bad, "because they were not of us. For if they had been of us, they would no doubt have continued with us."

Then the New Testament Church practiced what we call "restricted" communion. The Lord's Supper was restricted to those who had actual church membership. Acts 2:41, 42, "Then they that gladly received his word were baptized; and the same day there were added unto them about three thousand souls. And they continued steadfastly in the apostles' doctrine and fellowship, and in breaking of bread, and in prayers." Nobody took the Lord's supper except those who were actual church members in fellowship in the church.

II Thessalonians 3:6, "Now we command you, brethren, in the name of our Lord Jesus Christ, that ye withdraw yourselves from every brother that walketh disorderly, and not after the tradition which he received of us."

The church received its members. Romans 14:1, "Him that is weak in the faith receive ye." The church decides who shall remain members of the church and they are to withdraw from those who walk disorderly.

Then we have the local congregational church government, under the Lord, of course. The law is given by Jesus. We can not make law. We do not try to make law but, taking the law given in the New Testament, we execute the law as a *democratic* body.

Matthew 20:25, 26 says, "That the princes of the Gentiles exercise dominion over them, and they exercise authority upon them. But it shall not be so among you." Therefore, we do not have ruling elders to decide what shall be done. We do not have a bunch of men to get off to themselves in a corner and tell the congregation what to do. No big "I's" and no little "You's". Let every man have an equal right with every other man. "The princes among the Gentiles exercise dominion over them and they that are great have authority upon them. But it shall not be so among you."

We read in Acts 1:15-26 where the successor to Judas was elected, and it was done by taking the vote or ballot of the people.

I Corinthians 5:13 records how Paul instructed the church at Corinth to withdraw from the incestuous man—not the elders to withdraw from him, but the church to withdraw, "to put away such a man from among you." II Corinthians 2:6 records how the church had received him back after they had administered enough punishment meet for the offense that had been committed.

Matthew 16:18 says, "Upon this rock I will build my church." This means *build up* my church; continue the work of the church; edify the church. My friend erroneously states that this meant the establishing or starting of the church.

Now I am coming back to the discussion, having noticed what he said, about the work of the Holy Spirit in conviction and conversion. A graft is something that is imparted. Take a tree out here, a crab-apple tree, and you graft a winesap into it. So we read in the Bible that we receive with meekness the engrafted word, James 1:22. The Lord put that graft in. No graft ever put itself in. No crab-apple tree ever became a good tree until a graft was put into it. That crab-apple tree could not change itself but was overcome by the graft and brings winesap apples thereafter. "Wherefore, lay apart all filthiness and superfluity of naughtiness and receive with meekness the engrafted word, which is able to save your souls." And a graft never put itself in. Get the point. So the Holy Spirit comes and engrafts the word. "Receive with meekness the engrafted word, which is able to save your souls."

A fine illustration of that is found in Ezekiel, thirty seventh chapter, where Ezekiel was told to go out and prophesy in the valley of dry bones for they were very dry, representing dead sinners. And as he preached or prophesied to the dry bones, there was a movement among the dry bones and God said to Ezekiel, "Prophecy to the wind." And then he did prophesy to the wind, "Come from the four winds, Oh breath, and breathe upon these slain." And there stood up a great host, a great valley of dead men, a valley of dry bones, a figure of how the Jews must be saved by preaching. And when the Jews are saved, it will be by preaching, like to a valley of dry bones.

Revelation 5:9. In answer to what my friend said about babies I read, "And they sang a new song, saying, Thou art worthy to take the book and to open the seals thereof: for thou wast slain, and hast redeemed us to our God by thy blood out of every nation, and tongue, and people." Somebody came from all over the world. They sang a new song. I want to ask my friend if babies would be permitted to sing that song of the redeemed? If they are, then they were redeemed by the blood and it took the blood of Jesus Christ to redeem babies. Else they would all be cut out of the singing in the glory world. I want my friend to notice that. Are babies depraved?

Now Ephesians 2:3. "Among whom also we all had our conversation in times past in the lusts of our flesh, fulfilling the desires of the flesh and of the mind; and were by nature the children of wrath even as others." Common objection to this is, (my friend has not made it yet, but I presume he will), that over in I Corinthians 11:14, 15 it says nature teaches that a man should have short hair and a woman long hair and so he tries to make it out that nature there just means custom, but it is a fact that a man's hair is naturally short and a woman's hair naturally long. A man's hair, if let alone, untouched from infancy, will not be more than eight inches long, not one exception in a million. A woman's hair, if let alone, untouched from infancy, will be twenty-eight inches long on an average. So nature teaches that a man should have short hair and a woman long hair. So that shows that the word nature is used in its natural sense, in its ordinary sense. So we are by nature the children of wrath.

Men and women are born depraved, born on the side of wrong, born to do evil and it is as natural for a child to do wrong as it is for a child to breathe. Then, how does he ever get right? He must get right by the Spirit of God coming into him and be saved by the grace of God, by receiving with meekness the engrafted word, which is able to save the soul.

Now coming to the name. My friend has a name that I want him to write on the board. When he writes the name of his church on the board I will write the words Missionary Baptist Church right under it and give the scripture reference. "It must be mentioned in the Bible," he says. I want that to go in the record. "A name to be scriptural must be named in the scriptures." I defy him to show the name of the church of which he is a member in the Bible. Then that will be sufficient answer to all I might say on the subject. My friend is standing for names. Mark you now, I am going slow on this because I want you to get it. He stands for names. A thing must be named in exact words in the Bible for it to be scriptural. Let that go in good and thick. It must be named in the Bible.

One other thing. My friend objected to our voting people in the church, the only way to get in. Why, he said the Lord added to the church. How did the Lord add? Did He do it by direct work of the Spirit or by the hands of some preacher? If He did it by the hands of some preacher, then what is the difference between you taking a man in, you a preacher, individually voting to take him, and the whole church voting to take him in? Bear that in mind now. I want folks to remember it. He objects to folks voting people into the church. You can not get into any organization without a vote. The preacher takes him into your congregation. The whole church takes him in among the Baptist people which is according to the scripture, Romans 14:1, "Him that is weak in the faith receive ye." Somebody has to decide it. Somebody must say when a man comes into the church. If you say nobody is to decide it a man can just walk in and make himself at home and not a thing done. If somebody has to baptize him, somebody has to decide on that baptizing.

Here is a man who comes up to you, and one did come up to my friend Blue sitting right over here to my right, and wanted to be baptized. Blue refused to baptize him. I have the record on that. I can give the time and place when it happened. Well he said, "The man is not sincere." Why certainly. Who decided he was not sincere? Who decided he was a hypocrite? My friend Blue. All right. Then when the whole church decides that a man is dishonest and not coming with good motives what is wrong with that? "Him that is weak in the faith, receive ye." And whosoever shows faith, receive him. How? In the scriptural way. Baptize him, receive him into the church and start him out on the Lord's work as he should be.

Do not forget that I gave the names of the members of the church, the first ones. I gave the time, "Beginning from the baptism of John." He did not try to answer that. He may do it in his next speech. He quibbles around about whether I baptize the inner man or the outer man. He quibbles about a dead faith or a living faith. He quibbles around about the first church being without baptism. I never said a word like that at all. The *first church* did have baptism. The first individual Baptist did not.

First Day

PORTER'S SECOND NEGATIVE

Gentlemen Moderators, Respected Opponent, Ladies and Gentlemen: I am before you again for the closing speech of this session of the debate, and to deny for the next thirty minutes that which my opponent has been affirming for the past thirty. "The church known as the Missionary Baptist Church is Scriptural in origin, doctrine, practice and name." My friend has expressed astonishment, when he came before you a while ago, at the speech that had been made. I saw that he was astonished. But he referred to it this way: "If it may be called a speech." I'm willing to let the audience decide whether it was a speech or something else. Bogard cannot decide that for you. You decide that for yourselves.

He said he hoped I would—or he *had hoped* that I would—answer what he said instead of perverting what he said. I did not pervert a single thing that my friend said. I gave you exactly what he said. I'm telling you the record will bear me out. Even that statement that he has denied emphatically, during this last speech, of having ever said asleep or awake, is on the record. And it must go into the book, as he said it on the record. It *shall not be changed*—we *will not permit it*. Bogard is wrong. He did say what I said he said—that the "first Baptist Church" was without baptism—because God created it so. He didn't say "the first Baptist." He said when "God created the *first Baptist Church*." And he said it more than once. I took careful notice to see whether he said that or the "first Baptist," and he said the "first Baptist Church." I'm willing to let the record speak for itself as to whether he said it or not.

But I have just a few more questions for him.

8. In conversion, which man becomes the child of God, the inner man or the outer man?
9. Is faith without works living or dead?
10. Are the souls of infants pure at birth?
11. Is there any honor for a child of God that is greater than to be a part of the bride of Christ?

12. When did your people first take the name "Baptist Church" or "Baptist Churches"?
13. Is there any history written before the 17th century that speaks of the "Baptist Church"?
14. Does it not take more to get into the Baptist Church than it does to get into heaven?
15. Can you find the expression "Baptist Churches" in the Bible?

And since that question is upon the very point he was discussing a while ago, before going any further, I'm coming to that very point. I wonder if there is some crayon around here? Here is some right here. Now, my friend challenged me to write something on the board; so we are going to do a little board work just for a minute. I'm going to write something on both sides. Now, here (pointing to left side of blackboard) I'm going to put "Church of Christ." All right. And here (pointing to space beneath "Church of Christ") I'm going to put "Churches of Christ." Over here (pointing to right side of board) I'm going to put "Baptist Church." And here (pointing to space beneath "Baptist Church") I'm going to put "Baptist Churches." All right. Here (pointing to space beneath "Churches of Christ") I'm going to put Romans 16:16. Here (pointing to space beneath "Baptist Churches") I'm going to leave a line and let him put a passage on it.

CHART NO. 1

Church of Christ	Baptist Church
Churches of Christ	Baptist Churches
— Rom. 16:16	———————

Now, then, my opponent has been claiming that his position is the same as mine—that I'm in the same predicament that he is in—because he admitted a while ago that he could not find the name "Baptist Church" in the Bible. He said, "Porter is in trouble when he insists on the name." All right, I'll tell you what I'll do, Elder Bogard. You find "Baptist Church" *or* "Baptist Churches"—I don't care which one you find—I'll take both of them. If you'll find the place in all of God's Book where "Baptist Church" is mentioned, I'll have sense enough to know that if one of them is a "Baptist Church," a number of them would be "Baptist Churches." Or if you will find anywhere in God's Book the statement, "Baptist Churches," in the plural number, I'll have sense enough to know that if a number of them are "Baptist Churches," then one of them would be a "Baptist Church;" and I'll take both of them. In Romans 16:16 Paul says, "The churches of Christ salute you." Will you take both of them because one of them is mentioned? I'll do it for you over here (pointing to right side of board). Will you do it for me over here (pointing to left side of board)? What do you say? Churches of Christ—"the churches of Christ salute you." And, Mr. Bogard, please tell me if a number of them are "Churches of Christ," what would one of them be? Put it down and tell me about it. This debate will come to a close, but he *will not tell me.* I'm going to be on his trail.

And then he came to the questions I asked him a while ago and gave his answers.

"1. Is the name 'Missionary Baptist Church' mentioned in the Bible?" He said, "No."

"2. Can a thing be Scriptural in name if not named in the Scriptures?" "YES." I suppose a thing could be historical in name if history said nothing about it.

"3. Was John the Baptist a member of the church of the Lord?" He said, "No."

"4. Was any man who was a member of the church of the Lord ever called 'Baptist' in the New Testament?" He said, "There is no need to call him that." Why, you said a while ago you ought to call it what it is. You said a thing ought to be called what it is. If they were Baptists, why didn't they call them that? That reminds me: he didn't answer that argument I asked him, or that question I presented to him, in that connection, did he? I said, "Mr. Bogard, please tell us in your next speech if Jesus Christ and the apostles called the church what they ought to have called it?" He was as silent as the tomb about it—not one single, solitary word, not even a look or expression on his face that he had any intention of referring to it. Why didn't you tell us something about it, Mr. Bogard? *Did Christ call the church what it was? Did the apostles call it what it was?* You said it ought to be called what it was. Since they did not call it "Baptist Church," then was it a Baptist Church? If so, then Christ and the apostles didn't do what they should have done. Now, *why didn't you grapple with that?* That's what he couldn't call a speech, you see; that's the thing he couldn't recognize as a speech. Well, we are going to be with him in this matter. And we are going to insist that he answer that; and if he doesn't come clean with it, I'm going to put it in writing and see that he doesn't forget it. Will you remember it your next time, Mr. Bogard? *Please tell us. Did Jesus Christ and the apostles call the church what it was?* You said it should be called what it is. Did they do that or did they fail to do what they should do? Now, this audience has a right to know; and *I'm demanding that you tell them.* "Oh," he said, "there is no need to call them that." He said, "Everybody could see it." I wonder why everybody could see it when there wasn't a word said about it. Mr. Bogard is *seeing things.*

All right. "5. Do you believe and teach that infants are totally depraved?" He said, "Yes." But he said Porter "failed to recognize what I had said and pay attention to the argument that I made—that it's the total man that's depraved." Well, I want to get that up here. I think we have room to write a little more on the board. We'll just put here "The total baby"—since you said the baby was born that way. We'll just put down: "The total baby is depraved." And then, we are going to put beneath that, "The baby is totally depraved."

CHART NO. 2

The total baby is depraved
The baby is totally depraved

Now here (pointing to second sentence) is what Bogard says he believes, because I asked him, "Do you believe that infants are totally depraved?" He said, "Yes." All right—"the baby is totally depraved." And Bogard says that means "the total baby is depraved." Grammarians will laugh at you, Mr. Bogard. In this sentence (pointing to first) we do not have a parallel with this one (pointing to second). Here (pointing to first sentence) we have "total," which is an *adjective,* modifying the "baby," telling *how much of the baby* is depraved. Over in this case, (pointing to second sentence) "totally" is an *adverb* of degree, modifying "depraved," telling *how depraved* the baby is. *They are not the same. They are not parallel.* One is the "total" baby, an adjective, modifying "baby." The other—"the baby is *totally* depraved"—"totally" modifies "depraved." And you cannot have totally, more totally, and most totally. Yes, "totally" is just as mean as the devil, and you can't get away from it, Mr. Bogard. It's that. You have signed your name to the question, or rather given your answer to the question, that you believe *the baby is totally depraved.* And "totally" modifies "depraved," telling *how depraved.* It *doesn't modify "baby."* It *modifies "depraved"*—an adverb of degree, telling *how depraved* the baby it. Now, come and grapple with it. Well, these other answers we'll have for further discussion as other things come up.

Now, then, back to other things in his speech. He said, "No, the name 'Missionary Baptist Church' is not in the Bible." But he said if some one would draw a picture of a cat on the board, why, in order to make Porter understand it (he's dull of comprehension) you would have to write under it and say, "This is a cat." Well, Bogard, if the picture of the cat you drew on the board didn't look anymore like a cat than the Baptist Church does the New Testament Church, that's what you'd have to do. You certainly would. *You'd have to do that.* If it didn't look any more like a cat than the Baptist Church looks like the New Testament Church, you'd have to write under it and say, "This is a cat," in order for me to see it.

Mark 13—"He left his house" and Luke 10 where he "went into a far country to receive a kingdom." He says, "We're not debating the kingdom." Well, you wait and see if we're not. Before he gets through, he'll give you some passages right along that line.

And I promised him that I would quit the debate if he would find the name "Baptist Church" in the Bible. He said, "You'll have to quit the debate without my finding it."

I know it. If I ever quit it, I will have to quit without it. I am just sure of that. If I ever quit the debate, I'll have to quit it without your finding that, because you are *certainly not going to find it.* You'll not find it *in any form.* You'll find neither "Baptist Church" nor "Baptist Churches." If you'll find *either of them,* Bogard, I'll *stop the debate right now* and go home and start plowing for a living. What do you say? *Find either of them!* Can't do it? "No," he says, "you'll have to quit without it." I knew it. I knew it—if I quit, but I am not planning to quit. I knew I was going to have to quit without it when I made the proposition.

He said I perverted what he said about John the Baptist—that I said he referred to his death. No, I didn't say Bogard referred to his death. But I said at the time that John was killed he was still called, in the New Testament, "John the Baptist." And if when he was called "John *the* Baptist" at the beginning of his ministry, he was *the only Baptist* (therefore, called that), then at the *end of his career,* when he died, he was *still known in the New Testament* as "John *the* Baptist;" so there was *still only one.* He was still "John *the* Baptist." No, you didn't say it, but the Book of God says it. And that just ruins your argument. That is what I was getting at. "Oh," but he said, "Adam was *the man*—that is, he was *the only man* until there were others." Fine. I agree with that. And then he became "Adam *a* man," didn't he? All right. "John *the* Baptist . . . he was *the only Baptist until* there were others." Now, then, will you give me the name of some of the others? Where can I find some other Baptists besides John? Will you turn to the Book of God and give me the passage that mentions any other Baptists besides John? *Do it*—and I'll quit the debate. Will he do it? No, he'll not do it. *He knows it isn't there.* Nobody knows it better than Bogard. He would give the last shirt from his back to find a passage like that. *It isn't there!* No other man in all of God's Book was ever called by the term "Baptist" except John. And he was John *the* Baptist. Mr. Bogard says it means *the only one*—at the time—that is, *when he was called that.* All right, at any other time if there were some others, let us have their names; let us have the passage that refers to them.

In Matthew 16:18, when Jesus said, "Upon this rock I will build my church," he says that means to edify—enlarge. Well, in Luke 12:18 we have the same identical expression where the rich man had a great, abundant harvest, and he hadn't room in which to store his goods. He said, "I know what I'll do. I'll tear down my barns and *will build* greater." There is your same Greek word, letter for letter. Does that mean he is going to enlarge his barns?

Oh, he says, "I think Latter Day Saints would be all right. We are preaching in the latter days now." Yes, but I said Peter was a Latter Day Saint. Bogard got away from the thing entirely. Peter was a "Latter Day Saint" because he preached on the day of Pentecost, and, therefore, It was the last days. He was a preacher. He was a saint. So he was a "Latter Day Saint Preacher." And he preached there in connection with the church—was a member of the church. So Peter was a member of the Latter Day Saints Church. That's just as simple and just as conclusive as you have proved the Missionary Baptist Church mentioned in the Bible.

Then, as to the church not becoming a "Missionary Baptist Church" until the commission—he wanted to shake hands with me on that. Well, I didn't say that. I merely referred to your argument. You're the man that made the statement that the church did not become a Missionary Baptist Church until the commission was given. Then do you remember what I asked about that? I asked you, "If the church did not become a 'Missionary Baptist Church' until that time, what kind was it before then?" What kind of church was that church before the Lord gave it the commission? It wasn't Missionary Baptist, because Bogard says it *became* Missionary Baptist Church *when* the Lord gave the commission to it. "Oh," he said, "but that was before Pentecost." Well, suppose it was. What kind was it before he gave it? That's what I want to know. What kind of church was it prior to the giving of that commission? It wasn't a Missionary Baptist Church; *so what was it?* They didn't call it that before that because it wasn't that, and because a thing *should be called what it is.* But after that it became that, and, therefore, should have been called what it is, but it never was. So I guess it wasn't. We want to know more about that. But even that commission—they did not begin laboring under it until Pentecost. So that wouldn't help him out any at all on that!

"Oh, but he made a quibble," Mr. Bogard says, "about the word *pretend.* I said that the only church in the world that pretends to baptize is the Missionary Baptist Church, and Porter just quibbled about it." Well, I just used your word—that's all. I supposed you meant what you said—I didn't know. *I know what you said.* And I know what the word "pretends" means—and you're the man that used it. I didn't. I used the same word that you did with the meaning it has in all standard authorities. I wasn't perverting what you said. And *this audience knows* that I wasn't perverting it. I simply took your word—your very expression—for it. It *pretends* to baptize. "Why, I'll deny," he says, "that the church that you're a member of baptizes at all." And I'll deny that same thing for the one that you're a member of, Mr. Bogard. So it's mutual.

In Romans 14:1—"Him that is weak in the faith, receive ye, but not to doubtful disputations." Again, he said, "Porter perverted." No, Porter didn't pervert. I merely showed this man was weak in the faith, and if that is the authority for his voting in the church, then he is voting on those that are weak in the faith. And I suppose the man would be weak in the faith to seek membership in the Baptist Church which my friend admits that he cannot find in the Book of God. No perversion about that. I just upset his argument there, and he doesn't know how to recover.

But I asked him whether Jesus was totally depraved. He said Jesus was not totally depraved but that he became sin for us, because Jesus came in *the flesh.* And if you deny that Jesus came in the flesh, then you're an infidel, the Book teaches. Why, I believe that. But does the word "flesh" mean what you say it means—that inherent depravity? The word "flesh," you said, meant, in all these passages that you gave, that we are *totally depraved* by inheritance or by birth. And then you said Jesus came in the flesh— the same sense in which you used the word. Then Jesus came totally depraved, according to your argument. It still stands—you haven't touched it. Then, I asked him whether or not man is so depraved that there is no good in him at all. Mr. Bogard said everything that he does is wrong. Why, if he pays his debts, that's a sin; if he is a good moral man, why, that's a sin—everything is sin. Everything he does before he is saved is wrong—everything that he can do is a sin. Does the unsaved man repent before he is saved? Huh? Does the unsaved man repent before he is saved? You say that *everything* the man does before he is saved is a sin. If, therefore, he repents before he is saved, he sins when he repents and is saved by his sinning. Mr. Bogard, when the unsaved man prays to God to save him, is that prayer a sin? Now, you *come on and tell us.* You have said that *everything* that he does before he is saved is a sin. Therefore, if he prays to God, it is a sin; if he repents of his sins, it is a sin for him. Therefore, it is a sin to repent of sin. Will you back up or are you going to stay hitched? Well, you're going to stay hitched, I'm going to tell you. Then to Proverbs 21:4: "The plowing of the wicked is sin." Therefore, he tried to prove that everything was sin. Well the margin reads, "The lamp of the wicked." So does the Revised Version read that way.

Then he came to the idea of the new birth. We must have the new birth—the engrafting of the word. But he got away from that and talked about some other things, and then came back to it presently.

All right. Here we notice now "salvation by grace" as another of the doctrines by which he identifies the Baptist Church. Ephesians 2:8-10: "By grace are ye saved through faith; and that not of yourselves: it is the gift of God: not of works, lest any man should boast." Mr. Bogard says a man is saved *wholly by grace.* Is that a perversion or did you say that? Mr. Bogard must be getting rather forgetful. Mr. Bogard, am I perverting what you said? Or did you say that salvation is *wholly by grace?* Now, if salvation is *"wholly by grace,"* it is not "through faith." If it is through faith, it is not "wholly by grace." The passage says: "By grace are ye saved *through faith."* And salvation is not wholly by grace. "Wholly by grace" means the whole thing is by grace—it's all by grace—nothing besides that. Paul went on to mention faith, and *faith is not grace.* If, therefore, the sinner is saved *by grace through faith,* that is not *wholly by grace.* Don't get up and say that I perverted. Meet the argument.

The next is Romans 6:23, "For the wages of sin is death; but the gift of God is eternal life through Jesus Christ our Lord." Then, Mr. Bogard says that it's a gift of God; and since salvation is a *gift of God,* it is not through obedience. Did you say that, or am I perverting? The record will show that he said it—that salvation is a gift of God, and "not through obedience." Who said that? My opponent, Mr. Ben Bogard. What does the Book of God say about it? In Hebrews 5:8-9, the apostle Paul speaks. And Paul said concerning Christ: "Though he were a Son, yet learned obedience by the things which he suffered; and being made perfect, he became the author of eternal salvation unto all them that obey him." O-B-E-Y, obey. *"Unto all them that obey him."* Jesus "became the author of eternal salvation unto all them that *obey him,"* said Paul. Mr. Bogard says it's *"not* through obedience." Paul says it is. Which are you going to take? The Baptist Church or the church of the New Testament? Mr. Bogard or Paul?

We go to Acts 10:48 and John 14:17—the case of Cornelius. Cornelius received the Holy Spirit, which John 14:17 said "the world cannot receive;" and he received it before he was baptized. Therefore, he was already saved *before he received the Spirit.* That's the argument. Saved before baptism. All right, now, get this. Mr. Bogard says Cornelius was *saved before he received the Spirit* on that day. Well, if that be so, he was *saved before he believed,* because Peter said in the 11th chapter of Acts, "As I began to speak, the Holy Ghost fell on them, as on us at the beginning." Peter, when did the Holy Spirit fall? "As I *began* to speak." Mr. Bogard, when was Cornelius saved? "Before the Holy Spirit fell." All right, then, if Cornelius was saved before the Holy Spirit fell, and the Holy Spirit fell *as Peter began to speak,* he was saved *before Peter began to speak.* And if he was saved before Peter began to speak, he was saved without faith, because Peter said, "God made choice among us, that the Gentiles by my mouth should hear the word of the gospel, and believe." Acts 15:7. So if that proves salvation without baptism, it proves salvation without faith. That proves entirely too much for my friend.

Next I come to the "security of the believer," and Romans 8:28: "All things work together for good to them that love the Lord." He said that when a man is saved, he is not in danger any more. *There is no danger.* Well, in Matthew 5:22 Jesus says that whosoever shall call his brother a fool is "in danger of hell fire." I want to know, Mr. Bogard, is it possible for a child of God to call his brother a fool? *Put it down.* Don't forget it. *Please write.* I'll stop long enough for you to write it down—if you'll just write it down and tell me about it. Don't go to sleep on it. *Put it down, please.* Now, then, Jesus said the man who calls his brother a fool is in danger of hell fire. I want Mr. Bogard to tell me if it's possible for a child of God to call his brother a fool.

Psalms 37:23-24, "The steps of a good man are ordered by the Lord." And "though he fall, he shall not be utterly cast down, for the Lord will uphold him with his hand." If he had just read on a little farther, verse 27 would say, "Depart from evil, and do good; and dwell for evermore." So the promise was conditional. The Lord promised to uphold the man who would "depart from evil and do good." That's the man, he said, who would "dwell forevermore."

1 John 2:19: "They went out from us, but they were not of us." That is, whenever a man returns to sin, that proves he never was converted. That seems to be his idea. If he goes wrong, he never was right. And so, "they went out from us, because they were not of us." Well, he didn't say "they *never had been of us,*" Mr. Bogard. He didn't say *they never had been of us.* The fact is, they were not of us *when they went out;* they had ceased to be of us.. They got different ideas—they held to different theories and different doctrines. So they went out *because they were no longer of us.* That's the point. He didn't say they never had been of us. You'll have to read that again.

And to "Restricted Communion"—Acts 2:41-42. I believe nobody has a right to partake of the Lord's Supper until he has obeyed the gospel. I am certain of that.

Then the "local church government." Regarding the local church government, he said the Baptist Church is a democratic body. Well, I have always heard that a democracy is a government of the people, by the people, and for the people. I guess that must be true concerning the Baptist Church. It's a government of the people, and by the people, and for the people. Is that what you want? That is what we recognize as democracy—if that is what the Baptist Church is—a democratic body.

He said they have no "ruling elders." Well, that just proves they are not the church of the New Testament. That merely proves that it is not the church mentioned in the New Testament, because "they have no ruling elders," he said. Am I perverting? I just get scared about these things —he has charged me with perversion so much that I am just afraid that everything I'm saying is perversion. But, Mr. Bogard, am I perverting? "The church—the Baptist Church," he says, "has no ruling elders." Wonder what the church had in the days of the New Testament? In 1 Timothy 5:17, Paul said, "Let the elders that *rule well* be counted worthy of double honor, especially they who labour in word and doctrine." Mr. Bogard doesn't belong to this same church that Paul and Timothy belonged to, because the church that Paul and Timothy belonged to *had ruling elders*, for Paul said, writing to Timothy, a young gospel preacher, "Let the elders that *rule well be* counted worthy of double honor." Mr. Bogard says the Baptist Church doesn't have that. Well, that just proves the Baptist Church is not the church of the New Testament. I thank you, Mr. Bogard; we are making progress.

Go now to Acts 1:1, or rather Acts, the first chapter, and the latter verses. I didn't make any notice of my time when I started. Just how much time do I have?

Mr. Blue speaks: "A little over three minutes."

Well, I'll hurry right through this then. Here, Acts 1, selecting a preacher. That was selecting a man to take the place of Judas Iscariot; that was selecting an apostle. That was not selecting a pastor for the church, Mr. Bogard.

Then to the work of the Spirit. James 1:21, "Receive with meekness the engrafted word." Bogard said the Lord always put the graft in. No graft can get in by itself. Mr. Bogard, I have one question on that and I pass it until we can have time for further discussion. What does the Lord put the graft into? Will you answer that in your first speech tonight? Into what does the Lord put the graft? Into what does the Holy Spirit put the graft? I want to know. Then we will have some things happening.

Ezekiel 37. He said this is the valley of dry bones which illustrates it. The prophet was told to prophesy to dry bones, and there was a movement among them. Well, then, the prophesying accomplished something, didn't it? It wasn't altogether dead, because there was a movement among the bones. And then he was told to prophesy to the wind, and breath came upon them. He said this proves that "the Jews were saved by preaching." Why, I thought you were trying to prove that they were saved by a direct work of the Spirit. You said the wrong thing. *I'm not perverting.* You said that.

About Revelation 5:9—"Babies redeemed by the blood." Well, the babies were never lost—the babies were never lost.

Ephesians 2:3 and 1 Corinthians 11:14—"Were by nature the children of wrath." And since we are by nature the children of wrath, everything we do is wrong. Well, why not try Romans 2:14 on that? "The Gentiles, which have not the law, do *by nature* the things contained in the law, these, having not the law, are a law unto themselves." All right; here were men who did "by nature" things contained in the law. Were those things in the law good? I'm telling you, friends, they *did by nature* some things contained in the law.

Then he spoke about voting into the church—somebody has to vote. And brother Blue refused to baptize a man who came to him. *I deny that emphatically.* Brother Blue *did not refuse* to baptize a man who came to him. In the incident to which he refers, Mr. Bogard will admit, I feel sure, that brother Blue did the right thing. But in that case it wasn't as Mr. Bogard has represented it at all.

Well, that brings us back to "calling it what it is." I can't get away from that. And the little tract also. I think I have time to mention both of these again. Mr. Bogard says, "The church ought to be called what it is; it is the Missionary Baptist Church; therefore, it ought to be called Missionary Baptist Church." This will haunt him in his dreams tonight if he doesn't get to it in the next session. Mr. Bogard, did the apostles call it what it was? Did Jesus Christ call it what it was? Does the record in the New Testament call the church what it was? It should be called what it was, Mr. Bogard said. But they failed to call it the "Missionary Baptist Church" or any other kind of Baptist Church. Therefore, it wasn't. Or, if so, then they failed to do what they ought to do. Let him grapple with that.

Did you notice how he skipped that little predicament that he found himself in regarding his waybook and this little church that began there in Acts, the first chapter, "beginning *from* the baptism of John?" He said, "Now, that means *from* the baptism of John—that doesn't mean *with* the baptism of John." I picked up the Baptist Waybook—the little book written by Mr. Bogard . . . (time called) . . . Thank you, Ladies and Gentlemen.

First Day

BOGARD'S THIRD AFFIRMATIVE

Gentlemen Moderators, Mr. Porter, Ladies and Gentlemen:

I regret the little confusion this afternoon on account of the machine going dead. That frustrated all of you, got your attention somewhere else, and got me just a little confused about where I was, waiting for the machine to get ready again; but I trust that there will be no such interruption in the future. We are making splendid headway, considering we have only had two hours of the debate.

It is a pleasure to respond to what my friend said this afternoon, because I am sure that the further we go the clearer it will be in your minds. What may seem confusing at first sight will be perfectly clear as we go further along in the discussion.

Mark you, I made this statement to begin with, and I want you to hold it in mind, and I am going to make you remember it by repeating it again and again, for our Lord repeated and He is certainly a good example as a teacher. I am not above repeating it, because people do not get what you say the first time you say it. Therefore, we say it over and over again that somebody may learn. I started out this afternoon by saying the church of our Lord began *from* the baptism of John. I quoted some scripture to prove it; I quoted some scripture over in Acts 1:21-22 where Peter said somebody must be chosen to succeed Judas who has companied with us. How long? All the time that our Lord went in and out among us. Beginning when? Beginning from the baptism of John. So the company that companied Jesus, His company, began back there with the material made by John the Baptist. I think people can very easily remember that. Then I went to the first chapter of John and read the names of the first members of that company. My friend, up to date, has not responded to that. He may do it later. But there is really no response to be made, for the simple reason that their names are given and they constituted the company, and the company of baptized believers was composed of the believers that John had made ready for our Lord. And they stayed with Him all the time that He went in and out among us beginning from the baptism of John until that same day that He was taken up from us. I think that ought to be clear enough. If my friend could find one passage that says that the company began on the day of Pentecost, then there would be an offset to what I have just presented, but only an offset. It would make the Bible contradict itself.

And I also mentioned the fact that the name of the church has much to do in deciding this issue. What ought the church to be called? Call it what it is, certainly. My friend acknowledges that he cannot describe the New Testament church by giving scripture references in such a manner as will make people think that that church is the one he belongs to. He can not give a description from the Bible that will make anybody think that the church described in the Bible is the one he belongs to, for he must name it; he has to make the picture and then has to put a name under it, or folks never would know what it meant. I maintain that the description of the church of our Lord Jesus Christ is so unmistakable that anybody can see what it is after you read the description found in the word of God. My friend jumped the track and said, "Now I have got something on Mr. Bogard and he ought to know better." He knows enough about me to know that he can not catch me in a trap like that. He wrote on the blackboard—you see what he wrote. "Church of Christ." Now the proposition reads "The Church of Christ." I will give him ten dollars to find that passage in the Bible that says "The Church of Christ." I will go him one better; I will give him twenty dollars. But he comes down here and writes "Churches of Christ salute you." Yes sir, Churches of Christ means the congregations belonging to Christ. That is all.

My friend found some grammar this afternoon. He knows that names are not in the possessive case, but in the nominative case, if he knows anything, and this is the possessive case—"Churches of Christ." Names are in the nominative case; any seventh grade grammarian knows that to be true. For instance, there was a gentleman who was talking about his dogs. (Mr. Johnson was his name—a very fine fellow and happened to belong to the church my friend represents, so called Church of Christ—that is the nearest I will come to calling it the Church of Christ—does not belong to Christ at all; I will not put it in the possessive case even.) He was bragging on his fine dogs. He had three fine dogs. They were Johnson's dogs, Johnson's dogs. That is the possessive case. What are their names? Trip and Spot and Trailer were their names. The churches of Christ. Give me the name please. Every Baptist church you ever saw that was scripturally organized was a church of Jesus Christ, and belonged to Christ. And the way our letters read is: "The Missionary Baptist Church of Christ at Damascus, Arkansas." When we send letters, elect messengers, or write our minutes that is the way it is written. Every church that belongs to Christ is a church of Christ. But that's not their name. Now come on—the name. You harp on the name, "the Church of Christ." I will give you ten dollars for the first passage and add ten dollars for the next passage that has that expression. It is not in the Bible; it is in your proposition, but it is not in the Bible. Just bear that in mind now. We started out making pretty good progress.

My friend says, "Where did the Lord say, 'the Baptist Church'?" If the Lord had said the Baptist Church it would not have been correct. The church is a local congregation of baptized believers. There is no such thing as *"the Church"—that imaginable something constituting all the saved.* There is no such thing in the Bible. You can't find what is called the *universal church* in the Bible to save your life. It is not there, and if the Lord had said "the Baptist Church" *in the sense you use "the Church of Christ,"* the Lord would not have been correct *for it is not taught in the Bible;* hence the Lord did not say it. *He described the church, so that in any language, anybody could see what it is.* I showed you what it was by the Bible today, and we are going further into that tonight. And then, tomorrow and tomorrow night, believe me, business will pick up, for I am going to close in on the gentleman. The way to do these debates is to go along, take it easy, get the matters before the people, get the real issues before the people, then close down with the word of God.

My friend tried to say something about total hereditary depravity; he tried to get off some grammar on it. There *is not anything in the proposition about total depravity.* You said the grammar of it, according to the way I said it, makes the babies just as bad as the devil. I defined what I meant by total depravity: the *total man* is depraved, *not* the *degree* of the depravity. But *each and every part of the man* is depraved. Of what does a man consist? A body, mind, soul, or spirit, or whatever you want to call it. Well, the body is depraved; the mind is depraved; the spirit is depraved; the *total man* is depraved. And I shall not allow my friend to put words in my mouth and then answer what *he* says. He must answer what *I* say or give it up that he can not. I said the body is depraved. Let him deny it. The spirit is depraved. Let him deny it. The mind is depraved. Let him deny it. All that is meant by the term *"flesh"* is depraved. And I went through the scriptures and gave a Bible definition of the *"flesh."* The flesh has a mind, therefore is not just meat, muscles and bones and hair, and fingernails. The flesh has desires or lusts; the flesh has works and all of that. Then I quoted the scripture where it says, "the body of his flesh," and he comes back and says that makes Jesus Christ totally depraved. If my friend does not know enough to know that Jesus Christ took the place of the worst sinner on earth, then he does not know anything about the Bible. Jesus did no sin; He was without sin. But *He that knew no sin "became sin" for us.* He assumed our place and came in the "flesh" and took absolutely all that went with it, yet did not commit any overt act of sin. I think my friend gets that; I want to get it before you good and clearly. I want him to take another stagger at it. The more he staggers at it, and the more you think about the real statement that I made, then the clearer the subject will come to you.

Now we come to the next. I will take it up just as near as I can, as I do not want to leave anything out my friend said. That would not be fair. On the "house," in Mark 13 Jesus said He "left His house and gave His servants authority and a work to do, and commanded them to watch for they know not when the master of the house shall return." My friend says that does not necessarily mean the church. What does it mean? The devil's church, the devil's house, the farmer's union, the Masonic lodge? What does it mean? *He left His house.* Whose house? The Lord's house. He could not leave the house unless He had it. But some of you, directly when this session is over, will leave this house. Could you leave it if you were not here? Of all the nonsense. Talk about leaving a house and no house there. And Jesus said it was His house. He left *"his house,"* and *"gave his servants authority"* and a work to do, and commanded them to watch, for ye know not when the master of the devil's house comes back? Know not when the master of the farmer's union comes back? Know not when the master of the Masonic lodge comes back? No! It was His own house He left. This the Apostle Paul said was the "house of God which is the church of God, the pillar and the ground of the truth." So He left His house when He left the world. He did not come back after that to establish it on the day of Pentecost. My friend establishes his Pentecost theory when he gets to it, by citing scriptures that do not say Pentecost, citing some more scriptures that say Pentecost but do not say church, and citing more scriptures that do not say Pentecost or church either. But when *I* cite scripture I give you the exact chapter and verse in the exact wording: The Lord "left his house." When did that house begin? The company began from the baptism of John. (Acts 1:21-22) That company went with Him all the way through His ministry until the time He was taken up.

This afternoon I said (I am just trying to rehearse to get the matter before you, clearly—that is the big part of a debate—to get the matter clearly before the people) that John the Baptist was the first Baptist. He was a Baptist without baptism. You say, how can a man be a Baptist without baptism? How could Adam be a man without a mother? When God got ready to create the human race He created a man without a mother, but all the men since that time have had mothers. When God got ready to create the Missionary Baptist Church, He created the first Missionary Baptist without baptism. My friend perverted that and added the word, church. The first Missionary Baptist Church. I positively deny saying it. The records will not show it. And if I did say it, I told a lie. You can not make a lie out of it and answer your own falsehood. *If I did say it, I lied.* In the first Baptist Church every member was baptized, the last one of them, but the first Baptist, John, was not baptized; but after that all the others were baptized. I said that very plainly; the records will show it. And if by slip of the tongue, which I know did not happen, I did say it, if I did that—(voice from the audience: "Bro. Bogard, may I say something? You did say it. We played the record back and you said it twice.") All right. Then I will stand corrected. It is not so. The first Baptist was John the Baptist and he was a Baptist without baptism. But the first church, I named the members, they were all disciples of John the Baptist and had all been baptized. Thank you for that correction. I stand corrected and always will do it. If a slip of the tongue or something like that is to be corrected I am glad to have done it before it goes too far.

Very well, now I come to some advanced arguments. The Missionary Baptists teach that repentance comes before faith in Christ. Everywhere you find repentance and faith mentioned together, repentance comes first. No better authority is among the so called church of Christ than C. R. Nichol. And C. R. Nichol said in a recent issue of the Firm Foundation, "Surely they do not know what faith in God means. They do believe the facts about God, and the facts of the story of Christ, and the revelations in the Bible to be true and are deceived into thinking that the belief of such facts is faith in God. One may believe the facts about God and about Christ and not believe Christ." That is my position exactly. You first believe about God, believe about Christ, believe the facts related in the Bible about Christ, and then *trust* Christ for salvation. You can not do that until you repent unless you can be saved without repentance, which is nonsense, for he that "believeth on the Son of God hath everlasting life."

I come now to the next advanced argument and give my friend something to do because it is my business to put up something for him to do, hence being in the lead. The church undoubtedly existed during the personal ministry of Christ, as I have just proved by the scriptures, because Jesus was *king before Pentecost,* John 18: 37. Second, the *kingdom suffered* before Pentecost, Matt. 11:22. Men *pressed into the kingdom* before Pentecost, Luke 16:16. Some *hindered others from entering* the kingdom before Pentecost, Matt. 23:13. There was an *ordained ministry* before Pentecost, Mark 3:13-14. They were *authorized to baptize* before Pentecost, *John 4:2.* They had the *Lord's supper* before Pentecost, Luke 22:19. They had a *rule of discipline* before Pentecost, Matt. 18:15-17. They had the *gospel* before Pentecost, Matt. 24:14. *And Jesus said there was no doubt about the kingdom being in existence before Pentecost.* Luke 11:20. "If I by the finger of God cast out devils, *no doubt* the kingdom of God is come upon you." The Lord says there is *no doubt* about it. My friend says there is. Who are you going to believe? Peter said there was a company before Pentecost that followed the Lord all the time during His ministry, Acts 1:21-22. And then again, *"all power"* was conferred on the church before Pentecost, Matt. 28:18-20. *Jesus had the bride* before Pentecost, John 3:28-29. And John 13:2-4 says *all things had been given unto Christ before* Pentecost. What more is necessary to show that He had His organization, His kingdom, His church, *before Pentecost?*

Then I call your attention to another line of argument. We teach that salvation is obtained at the point of faith. Acts 16:30-31. "What must I do to be saved?" And the answer came back, "Believe on the Lord Jesus Christ and thou shalt be saved," an answer that my friend and his people never give without a lot of explanation.

Then again, we teach the Spirit of God was at work among men in salvation before Pentecost, and during the personal ministry of our Lord. The Spirit's work began, as far as that is concerned, back in the Old Testament. Mark 12:36 says "David himself said by the Holy Ghost." And Luke 1:41 says "Elizabeth was filled with the Holy Ghost." Luke 1:67 says "Zacharias was filled with the

Holy Ghost." *All that was before Pentecost.* Luke 1:15, speaking of the birth of John the Baptist, says he was to be "filled with the Holy Ghost from his mother's womb." Then Luke 2:25-26 says "Simeon had the Holy Ghost upon him." And in Matt. 3:16, Jesus, when He was baptized, went up straightway out of the water and, lo, the heavens were opened unto Him and He saw the "Spirit of God descending like a dove and lighting upon Him." Matt. 12:28 says "But if I cast out devils by the Spirit of God, then the kingdom of God is come upon you." John 4:23 says the hour cometh and now is when the true worshipers shall worship God the Father "in spirit and in truth." John 20:22, "He breathed upon them and said unto them receive ye the Holy Ghost." We see the Holy Spirit at work in the world during the personal ministry of Christ and Christ casting out devils by the Holy Spirit. What is meant, then, when He said the Spirit had not been given, is that He *had not been given as the administrator.* Christ was His own administrator while he lived on earth, and the Holy Spirit became administrator after Christ left the earth. But the Holy Spirit Himself was at work among the people doing His office work during the personal ministry of Christ.

Then I come to another, and that is concerning the kind of work that the church did. Churches had their own officers and elected them. Acts 1:15-26; Acts 6:1-6, where they elected deacons and one to succeed Judas. The church sent out their own missionaries, Acts 11:21-22 and Acts 13:1-6. The churches administered their own discipline, I Cor. 5:1-5; II Cor. 2:6; and II Thess. 3:6. Churches received their own members: Rom. 14:1, "Him that is weak in the faith receive ye but not to doubtful disputations." And the churches had a right to require evidence of conversion before they received a man into their fellowship. In Acts 9:26-28 we find where Saul came to Jerusalem and "assayed to join himself to the disciples" and at first they would not. But when Barnabas took him and showed how he was saved along the way, then he came in and out among them. This shows that the churches have a right to determine their own fellowship and that is all that is meant by voting people into the church or voting people out of the church.

Now here is another conclusion. My friend acknowledged that the church that received the commission was a missionary church. That was received before Pentecost. Jesus sent His church out to preach, "go ye therefore and teach all nations, baptizing them in the name of the Father, and of the Son, and the Holy Ghost, teaching them to observe all things whatsoever I have commanded you." So it began as a missionary church. John the Baptist was a Missionary Baptist preacher. I proved it to you. And then Jesus sent out His disciples two by two to preach. Those were missionaries. Then at the last He gave the final commission to go to all the world, and that is a missionary church, sent to do missionary work and to baptize —therefore, making it a Missionary Baptist Church. And that is a line of argument my friend must meet or he is bound to go down in confusion and frustration.

Here I put the matter before you, lay the things down as lawyers do in court. Here I am proving what he must disprove. And he must show that names are in the possessive case. They are not the possessive, but in the nominative case always, never in the possessive. Every school boy knows that to be true. It does not take a scholar to see that. I trust that we shall get along fine and have a glorious time in this debate for your good and for God's glory. Thank you.

First Day

PORTER'S THIRD NEGATIVE

Gentlemen Moderators, Mr. Bogard, Ladies and Gentlemen:

I am still following the trail of my opponent, endeavoring to show you the misapplication of Scriptures that he has made. His contention is not true that the church that he represents, "known as the Missionary Baptist Church, is Scriptural in origin, doctrine, name and practice." I believe it reads "practice and name." He spent a part of his time repeating the things that were said this afternoon. I shall go over those things briefly and then take up his arguments which he advanced before he sat down.

He called attention to the fact that he did say this afternoon, and repeated tonight, that "the church began *from* the baptism of John," introducing Acts 1:21, in connection with the selection of one to take the place of Judas Iscariot, as proof of that idea. Of course, there was nothing said about a "church." He just found where somebody "accompanied" him and decided that that meant a "church." You know, he said a little while ago that when Porter endeavors to establish his Pentecost theory, he will find some Scriptures that say nothing about Pentecost; and then he will find some Scriptures that say nothing about the church; and then he will find some Scriptures that say nothing about either: and then decide that the church was established on Pentecost. But he said, "When *I* give you the Scriptures, *I* give you exactly what they say." Well, Mr. Bogard, it happens to be the Scripture that you gave *doesn't say one single word about the church.* Not a word! It simply speaks about certain men who "accompanied" him "from the baptism of John." But not one single word is said about a "church." So he found a Scripture that *said nothing about a church;* and then he said, "Here is where the church began. Here are the first members of it." Not a word said about it! "Here it is. And I give you what the Scriptures say," declares Mr. Bogard. Well, you decide for yourself about that.

Then, too, I'm just wondering why he has not straightened up that little contradiction that he found himself in.

You know, he insisted this afternoon that the church "began *from* the baptism of John, and not *with* the baptism of John." I called attention to that in my closing speech this afternoon, but just before I finished my time was called. So it is a good idea to mention it again here. I picked up this little Baptist Waybook and turned to page 29, I believe it was, and there Mr. Bogard introduced the very same passage of Scripture concerning the very same company. And he said it "began *with* the baptism of John." Now, one time Bogard said it "began *from* the baptism of John, and *not with* the baptism of John at all." In his little book he said it "began *with* the baptism of John." Now, which time, Mr. Bogard, is the truth of the matter? Which must we believe? I wonder if that was just a *slip of the tongue* that you put in the book—or just what happened to cause you to put it that way, and why you haven't corrected it during all these years. You published that a long time ago. It's still in there that it "began *with* the baptism of John." But today he says it is "not *with* the baptism of John but *from* the baptism of John." If he has made a correction of it, it is in a recent issue, and we would be glad to see his correction. Turning to one of the late issues of it, we'll be glad to see if he has corrected it in this issue. All right, now, he says, "If Porter could find one passage that says the company began at Pentecost, why, he would be tickled to death about it" or words to that effect. I have an idea that Mr. Bogard would be very tickled if he could find in Acts 1:21 where it says "the church" accompanied from the baptism of John. But it just so happens that it doesn't say anything about "church."

Now, he came back to the name of the church and said that "I said this afternoon that you should call it what it is." Incidentally, that reminds me that he failed to answer my questions that I gave him this afternoon. I gave him a number of questions to answer, and he failed to say one single, solitary word about them. Perhaps, he will in his next speech; and so I'll pass him a few other questions concerning this matter.

Now, number 16, and I'm numbering from where I quit in the preceding questions.

16. Since you say that the New Testament Church is the Missionary Baptist Church, and should be called what it is, did Jesus and the apostles do what they should do and call it what it is?
17. Since you say the unsaved man can do nothing that is not a sin, is it sinful for him to repent and pray to God?
18. Which man becomes a member of the Baptist Church—the inner man or the outer man?
19. Is it possible for a child of God to get drunk and commit murder?
20. If he should die while drunk and in the act of murder, will he go to heaven?
21. Is it good for a child of God to get drunk?
22. Is it possible for the spirit of a child of God to commit sin?
23. Why are not the children of regenerated people born righteous? (Mr. Porter hands questions to Mr. Bogard)

I shall be glad for Mr. Bogard to answer those questions. He said awhile ago that it wasn't fair not to pay attention to what I said. And I am going to agree with him. So I think he ought to say something about those matters.

Back, then, to my notes and to what he had to say about them. I impress, again, on you this fact that Mr. Bogard says, regarding the name of the church, that "you should call it what it is." He says it is the Missionary Baptist Church; therefore, you should call it that. I have been pleading with him so far during this discussion to tell me whether the apostles and Jesus did what they should? They failed to call it the "Missionary Baptist Church." My friend has admitted that he can't find it anywhere in all the Book of God—that the name "Missionary Baptist Church" is not found in the Bible. Mr. Bogard agreed that that was so this afternoon. Well, that being true, then the church in the days of the apostles was either *not the Missionary Baptist Church* or they *didn't call it what it was.* So we are still insisting that he tell us whether they called it what it was. Then he said, "Porter can't describe the church to which he belongs and make it look like the New Testament Church without naming it," and he must not name it. Well, Mr. Bogard made a great deal to depend on the name to start with. He said in the very outset of his first speech that "the man who fails to prove the church is Scriptural in name fails in this debate." And Mr. Bogard, until this good hour, has miserably failed. In fact, he has agreed that the name *is not in the Bible,* and that the only man in the Bible who was ever called "Baptist" was not a member of the Missionary Baptist Church, and that all of those who were members of the church were never called Baptists. Well, that's a strange thing, isn't it—that the Book of God would call a man Baptist who was never a member of the Baptist Church, while all of those who were members of it were never called by that term. I wonder how Mr. Bogard can account for that. Oh, he said, "You can't catch Bogard in a trap." No, "you can't catch Bogard in a trap." Well, you'll see how these traps go before we get through. Just watch for yourself.

Then he came to the blackboard, and he said, "Now, this thing is not going to work. Porter thought he could put this over, but he can't. Porter's proposition says '*the* Church of Christ'," and so he wrote the little word "the" up there.

CHART NO. 1

Church of Christ	**Baptist Church**
Churches of Christ	**Baptist Churches**
— Rom. 16:16	————————

Well, I didn't endeavor to write down the full statement regarding all the matters. I didn't even put it over here. (pointing to "Baptist Church.") I put "Church of Christ" and "Churches of Christ"—"Baptist Church" and "Baptist Churches." I wasn't trying to put the whole expression—but just enough to get the thought before you. But I gave Romans 16:16 as the passage in which Paul said, "The churches of Christ salute you." I am going to put the little word "the" there. "The churches of Christ salute you."

(Writes "the" before "Churches of Christ.") Now, the little word "the" is there. Paul put it in Romans 16:16. All right, then, Mr. Bogard, if a number of churches in different localities were called "*the* churches of Christ," would not one of them in one locality be called "*the* church of Christ" in that locality? Now, tell us about it. If "the churches of Christ" refers to a number of them in different localities, then would not "the church of Christ" refer to one in one locality? So that takes care of your word "the." And besides, over here, Mr. Bogard, (pointing to board) I said you find "Baptist Church" or "Baptist Churches" either, and I'll take both of them. Will you find "Baptist Church" in the singular number? I'll have enough sense to know that if one of them is a "Baptist Church," then a number of them will be "Baptist Churches," and I'll take both of them. Or even find "Baptist Churches" in the plural number in the Bible, and I'll have sense enough to know that if a number of them were "Baptist Churches," then one of them would be "Baptist Church." I didn't try to make it hard for him. I didn't put "the" out here, (pointing to board) although he has it in his proposition—"the Baptist Church." So we will just add that up there. (Writes "the" before "Baptist Church") He offered me $10.00 to find "the Church of Christ." Well, here is the "churches of Christ" in the plural number. And if "the churches of Christ" is the plural number, for a number of churches, would not one of them be *"the Church of Christ?"* What would be the singular of that? Mr. Bogard, can there be a plural without a singular? And if the plural is "the churches of Christ," wouldn't the singular be "the church of Christ?" You have over here (pointing to board) "Baptist Church" and "Baptist Churches." Your proposition says "*the* Baptist Church." All right, I challenge you, and I'll give you twice the amount of money you offered me, to find either "Baptist Church," "the Baptist Church," "Baptist Churches" or "the Baptist Churches" anywhere in all of God's Book, and I'll pay you off and start home tonight. Now, *you try it.* That thing is not as easily kicked off as you think it is.

Now, then, we come to something else that's rich. I've

been waiting for this. I was afraid he wasn't going to get to it. I am going to erase this for the time being. But, incidentally, you saw that mark I had here? (Pointing to right of board) Over here (pointing to left side of board) Romans 16:16. It says "the churches of Christ." Over here (pointing to right side of board) I drew a line for Bogard to place his reference that mentioned either "Baptist Church" or "Baptist Churches," in the singular or in the plural. The line is still vacant, but when he gets ready to write it on, I'll put it back, so he will have it there to place it on. But for the time being I'm going to erase that in order to get something else before you here. (Mr. Porter erases the board) Now, I want you to notice this. Mr. Bogard says that "names are always in the nominative case." "The churches of Christ," he said, "is in the possessive case. But names are always in the nominative case. Every 7th grade grammar student knows that." Mr. Bogard, what 7th grade grammar did you study? (Mr. Bogard speaks, "Harvey's.") Mr. Porter continues—Harvey's. All right, will you tell us what Harvey says "case" is? *What is case?* I'll give you a minute of my time to answer. What is *case?* If you'll look into Harvey, you'll see that Harvey says that "case" has to do with nouns and pronouns, showing their relation, in the sentence, to other words. "Nouns and pronouns." What else is dealt with in *case?* "Nouns and pronouns." What is a *noun?* Mr. Bogard, did Harvey say that "a noun is the name of anything?" All right; all grammars say that "a *noun* is the name of anything." Well, what is a *pronoun?* Well, all grammars say that "a *pronoun* is a word used for a noun" or "instead of a noun." All right, get that then. *Nouns are names,* or "a *noun* is the *name* of anything," or "the *name* of anything is a *noun.*" And since "a *pronoun* is the word used for a *noun,*" then it is a word used for a *name.* And *case deals only with nouns and pronouns.* How many "cases" are there, Mr. Bogard? Harvey gives about four, doesn't he? Most grammars give only three. Most grammars give just three—nominative, possessive and objective. To that Harvey, I believe, adds the "nominative absolute" or "absolute," which is the case of address, as you would address a man, or call him by name, or something of that nature. The three cases generally considered are the nominative, the possessive and the objective. Now, then, Mr. Bogard says "names are *always* in the nominative case." The grammars say that "a *noun* is the *name* of anything." Therefore, nouns are *always* in the nominative case. You better look into that grammar again, Mr. Bogard. "Names are *always* in the nominative case." But a name is a noun —a noun is a name. A pronoun is a word used for a noun; therefore, "nouns and pronouns are always in the nominative case." Then what is in the objective case, Mr. Bogard? And what does the possessive case deal with? Can't be a noun, because a noun is a name, and you say a name is always in the nominative case. It can't be a pronoun, because a *pronoun* stands for a *noun*, and a *noun* is a *name;* therefore, "a pronoun is always in the nominative case." So you can't have a pronoun or a noun in any case except the nominative, according to Bogard. What, then, is there to be used in the objective case and the possessive case? Why, I suppose the possessive case can be used for a conjunction. The possessive case deals with conjunctions and the objective case deals with prepositions or something of that kind. It can't be a noun—it can't be a pronoun, because those are names, and Mr. Bogard says "names are *always* in the nominative case." Want to take it back? Well, we are not through with you yet. We're going to show you. I am going to use a little illustration here that I know everybody can see. Now, take the word "John." Well, that is the *name* of a man—the forerunner of Christ. There's been a lot said about him here. I think Mr. Bogard will be favorable toward this man; so we'll put him up there. (Mr. Porter writes on board: "John reproved Herod.") What's "John?" That is a name. What *case* is it in? It's in the nominative case. Why? Because it is the subject of a sentence. Nominative case deals with words used as the subject of a sentence or an attribute complement, or predicate nominative, as some grammars call it. All right; so that is the nominative case. "John"—that word cannot be used, according to Mr. Bogard, in any other case except the nominative. *That is the only use of it.* Well, then, Mr. Bogard, try your hand on this. (Mr. Porter writes: "Herod beheaded John.") Will you tell me, Mr. Bogard, Is "John" still a name? Is "John" a name in that sentence? "Herod beheaded John." Is there a 7th grade student in this house tonight who doesn't know that "John" is in the objective case in that sentence—the object of the verb "beheaded?" It's in the objective case, and not the nominative case at all. All right; (pointing to first sentence) here it is in the nominative case—the subject of the sentence. And here (pointing to second sentence) it is in the objective case—the object of the verb. Thus, we have the name "John" used in two cases. But Mr. Bogard says that names are always in the nominative case. And we are not through yet. I'm going to give you some more. (Writes on board: "John's head was brought on a platter.") All right; "John's head was brought on a platter." What's "John?" Is that still a name? Yes. Still the very same fellow and the name of the very same fellow we were talking about all the while. But in this sentence it is *not* in the nominative case —it's *not* in the objective case—it is *in the possessive case,* because it is used as a possessive modifier. Thus, we find that names are in *all* cases. A name can be used in the nominative case; it can be used in the objective case; it can be used in the possessive case. Mr. Bogard, go back and study your 7th grade grammar. Don't ever make a blunder like that again. Why, you've made that blunder all over this country, and over the radio. And Baptist preachers everywhere have thought it was a big load, and they've been shooting it everywhere, all over the country, thinking there's something to it. Why, absolutely, it violates every principle of English grammar pertaining to the matter. You better look it up, Mr. Bogard. Yet Bogard never gets trapped. Well, you see if he gets out of that trap—you see if he gets out of that trap. Well, I have plenty of time. I'm not through. But I'm about to run out of crayon though. We're going to try this one. (Writes on the board: "The churches of Christ salute you.") That's Romans 16:16. "The churches of Christ salute you." Mr. Bogard says this is in the possessive case. I deny it. And, furthermore, I aim to disprove it. There is no "possessive case" in this sentence. The word "churches" is a *noun.* A noun is the name of something. The word "churches" here is the subject of the sentence, and being the subject of the sentence, the word "churches" is in the *nominative* case—not the possessive case at all. The word "Christ" is also a noun. In this case it is the object of the preposition—the principal word of a prepositional phrase—and is in the *objective* case. "Churches" is in the nominative case; "Christ" is in the objective case; and the case construction of that sentence is not possessive at all. There is your grammar. Try it again, Mr. Bogard; you have a long way to go now.

Then he came to the "so-called Church of Christ" and referred to Mr. Johnson, who is a member of the "so-called Church of Christ," and he had three dogs. "Johnson's dogs —in the possessive case." Well, "dogs" *is not* in the possessive case. "Johnson's" is in the possessive case there—Johnson's dogs. "Johnson's" is in the possessive case but not the "dogs." He said, "Their names were Trip, Spot and Trailer." Those were their names, but " 'Johnson's dogs' is in the possessive case." Or, if you want to turn it around, you could say "the dogs of Johnson." Well, if he turns it around and says "the dogs of Johnson," he doesn't have any *possessive case* at all. He has both nominative and objective if he turns it around like that. So their names are Trip, Spot and Trailer. Well, if he hadn't told you what their names were, could you have ever told by looking at them? Mr. Bogard, if Mr. Johnson had not told you the names of his dogs, would you have ever known that their names were Trip, Spot and Trailer? If you had never heard their names and had never seen any writing from Mr. Johnson, or somebody who had authority to say, would you have known that their names were Trip, Spot and Trailer? Then, since Jesus Christ nor the apostles nor any writer of the New Testament ever called the church the Missionary Baptist Church, how do you know that is its name? *Not a word said about it. How do you know?* How did you find it out?

He said, "If the Lord had said 'the Baptist Church,' it would not have been correct." Well, you said it in the proposition that you are affirming. So I guess you're incorrect. Your proposition says "the Baptist Church," or "resolved that the church known as 'the Baptist Church' is Scriptural in origin, doctrine, practice and name." And, now, he says "the Baptist Church" is incorrect. If Jesus had said that, he would have been wrong about it. Bogard said it in his proposition; so he's wrong about it, according to his own admission. "The Baptist Church."

Then he came to total depravity. He said, "Why, there's nothing in the proposition about total depravity." Why, yes, there is. Why, yes, there is, Mr. Bogard. Your proposition says "Scriptural in origin, *doctrine,* practice and name," and that is one of your doctrines. So it is in the proposition. Certainly so. But he said, "I'm simply contending that the *total man* is depraved and Porter put words in my mouth." No, I didn't. I asked the question: Is the baby, or do you teach that the baby is totally depraved? You said, "Yes." I didn't put that in your mouth. You said it yourself. "The baby is totally depraved." I put those sentences on the board.

CHART NO. 2

The total baby is depraved
The baby is totally depraved

And I showed—"the total baby is depraved"—that the word "total" is an adjective. A definitive adjective—it modifies baby, telling *how much of the baby* is depraved. But I didn't say, "Do you believe *the total baby* is depraved?" I said, "Do you believe that the baby is *totally depraved?*" And he said, "Yes." Well, in that sentence—"the baby is totally depraved"—"totally" is an adverb of degree. It does not modify "baby"—it modifies "depraved"—tells *how depraved* the baby is. That is just as mean as the devil, and he can't get out of it. I'm sorry if you don't want to take it. That's what you said, and you are going to stay with it till you repudiate it.

Then he came to the Christ—about the body of his flesh. And he said, "Yes, I referred to Christ as having the body of his flesh." But, he said, "If you don't know enough to know that Jesus took the place of the worst sinner on earth, why, you don't know anything about the Bible." Yes, but that isn't the point. He became a sin offering for the world. I understand that. But here is the point—you make your argument on the word "flesh"—that "the flesh" meant "depraved nature." And you gave a passage that referred to Jesus Christ as having "the body of the flesh," and that's "depraved nature." Mr. Bogard, when Jesus became a sin offering for men, did he have a depraved nature? That's what I want to know. That is the argument that you made. I want to know: *Did Jesus have a depraved nature?*

Then to Mark 13—"He left his house." Bogard said he can't leave the house if there isn't a house. No. I referred to that this afternoon, showing that he left the material of which the house was constructed—that it was a house in preparation—not a house completed. That certainly was dealt with.

And he came back to John the Baptist—"John the Baptist without baptism"—and the charge that I made that he said that "when God created the first Missionary Baptist Church, He created one without baptism." He said he didn't say it. And he talked around about it quite a lot. And, finally, he said, "If I said it, I lied." And then, finally he stood corrected on it. Well, he said it. *He said it.* I don't know—I didn't think he intended to say it; but I waited, and he said it the second time. He made the statement two times in that connection—"Now, when God created the first Missionary Baptist Church, he created one without baptism." He *did* say it. And I'm glad that he stands corrected, since he agrees that it is wrong if he said it. And he did say it. I know that he said it. We'll just let him stand corrected, then, and pass on.

Then to some other arguments. And he didn't give very much on these. He just went through them in a running fashion. I'll deal with them like he introduced them, and when he gets ready to elaborate upon them, I'm ready for the fight. "Repentence before faith." He said, "We believe in repentance before faith," and C. R. Nichol he gave as one of the outstanding teachers—read a passage from him in the Firm Foundation. But I noticed carefully the reading, and he did not read a single thing where C. R. Nichol said repentance before faith. Maybe it's in there somewhere. I haven't read the article, but it's *not in that part* that Mr. Bogard read. If it's in there, why, let him read it—it's not in the part he read. He didn't say "repentance before faith." So he didn't agree with Bogard at all.

Then he came to some proof that he gave for the church being established. Jesus the King—John 18:37. He didn't quote the passages. He didn't make any argument at all. He just made a simple little statement and then introduced the passage, in Jehovah Witness style, to prove almost anything, whether it had any connection or not. The kingdom suffered violence—Matt. 11:22. Pressed into—Luke 16:16. Was hindered—Matt. 23:13. Ordained ministry—Mark 3:13-14. Authority to baptize—John 4:2. The Lord's supper—Luke 22:17. The rule of discipline—Matt. 18:15-17. No doubt about it—Luke 11:20. And, incidentally, while I'm passing that, you know he said this morning, when I gave a passage regarding his going into a far country to receive a kingdom, "We are not discussing the kingdom question." I told you before this debate was over he *would be* discussing it. And here he gave a passage—Luke11:20: "No doubt the kingdom of God is come upon you." He says we are not discussing the kingdom question, but now he gives a passage to prove that it was established before Christ died. Then the company—Acts 1:21. Had all power—Matt. 28:19. He had the bride—John 3:28-29. Do you mean, Mr. Bogard, he was married? Do you mean that Christ had the bride back there in the sense that they were married? Please tell us about that in your next speech. Don't forget it. It is fresh on your mind now and don't let it slip your mind when you get up here. And he received all things given, or all things were given into his hands. All of these statements refer to the preparatory state of the kingdom and not to an established, completed form. And since Bogard said no more about it than that, then that is my reply, until he sees fit to take these up and introduce them as arguments and base his arguments upon them. And then we'll see what he has to say. Then I'll deal with them. Until then I'll deal with them in the same running fashion because he can't pull a trick like that either.

All right, next he gave Acts 16:31. Salvation by faith.

Acts 16:31: "Believe on the Lord Jesus Christ and thou shalt be saved." And he said Porter wouldn't tell his people that at all. Well, we oftentimes do. That is not the only passage we have in the Book of God about being saved. Others will come up for discussion after a bit.

The Spirit of God that worked before Pentecost. He gave Mark 12:36. David spoke by the Holy Spirit. Luke 1:67—Zacharias. Luke 1:15—John filled with the Spirit. Luke 2:25—Simeon. Matt. 3:16—baptism of Jesus. Matt. 12:28—casting out the devils by the Spirit. John 4:23—worship in Spirit and in truth. And John 20:22—"receive the Holy Spirit." All these he introduced to prove the identity of the Baptist Church. What have they to do with the Baptist Church? Not a single word is said in any of those passages about the Missionary Baptist Church or any other kind of Baptist Church. Not a one. And so it doesn't prove anything along that line. Let him make his argument upon these passages, and we'll deal with them.

Then he came to the kind of work the church did. He said it had its own officers—Acts 1:21; Acts 6. Sent out missionaries—Acts 13. Had its own discipline—2 Thessalonians 3:6. Received its members—Romans 14:1. And required evidence of salvation—Acts 9:26-28. Some of these were discussed this afternoon; so I want to take this one that wasn't—Acts 9:26-28. He said Saul tried to join the church over there. This is where Saul came to Jerusalem. And he "assayed to join himself to the disciples." Mr. Bogard said he tried to join the Baptist Church in Jerusalem, and so they had to vote on him to see whether he'd be a member or not. Well, Mr. Bogard, before Saul came to Jerusalem he had been preaching a number of years. He was baptized back there a long time before he came to Jerusalem. Will you tell me what church he belonged to during that time? While Paul was out preaching in Arabia, and elsewhere, what church was he a member of? He didn't join the Baptist Church till he went to Jerusalem, says Mr. Bogard. Then what church did he belong to during those years that he preached out there? And if he baptized people, what church did that make them members of? Well, we want to know something about that.

You know, he said we would get the foundation laid and then we would tighten the cords. Well, I'm ready to tighten some cords. So they received the commission before Pentecost. Matt. 28:19. The Great Commission was received before Pentecost. Well, Mr. Bogard, I asked you this afternoon: Did they begin operation under that commission before Pentecost? Luke 24:46-49 gives us the same commission. According to Luke's record, he said: "Thus it behooved Christ to suffer and to arise from the dead the third day: and that repentance and remission of sins should be preached in his name among all nations, beginning at Jerusalem." And then we are told that he told them to tarry in the city of Jerusalem "until ye be endued with power from on high." They did not begin operation under that commission as soon as they received it but waited in Jerusalem until they were endued with power from on high. When did the power come, Mr. Bogard? On Pentecost? Yes, the power came on Pentecost, and that is when they began operation under that commission—not before Pentecost, but at Pentecost. So his little quibble on that is set aside. He's left hanging in mid-air.

Well, that covers the things that he said during this time, except one or two things that I might drop back to, if I have a little time now. Regarding these matters—Acts 1:21—they had their own officers. Yes, and he mentioned this afternoon (do you remember), that they had no such thing as *ruling elders.* No ruling elders. "The Baptist Church," he said, "has no *ruling elders.*" I turned to 1 Timothy 5:17, in which Paul, writing to Timothy, a young gospel preacher, said, "Let *the elders that rule well* be counted worthy of double honor." So Paul and Timothy did not belong to the same church that Mr. Bogard belongs to. The church that they belonged to *had ruling elders.* The church that Mr. Bogard belongs to *has no ruling elders.* He says its not fair not to pay attention to what you say. Well, he hasn't said anything about that. So come back Mr. Bogard, and tell us about that—whether or not there were ruling elders in the church to which the apostle Paul and Timothy belonged. "Let the elders that *rule well* be counted worthy of double honor." That isn't the only passage either.

A number of others will be introduced if he thinks it necessary, but I believe that's enough to stop him. I don't think he'll ever do anything with it—I just *know that he won't.* It's in the Book of God and cuts Mr. Bogard and the Missionary Baptist Church, according to his own description of it, completely out of the New Testament. It never was in it to begin with. There is no such thing in all of God's Book as the Missionary Baptist Church, or the Baptist Church, or Missionary Baptist Churches, or any other kind of Baptist Churches. They're just not there. Mr. Bogard knows they are not there. But in Romans 16:16, which I gave a while ago, and had upon the board, said, "The churches of Christ salute you." My opponent will be glad to give not only that $10—that $20—but ten times ten and twenty if he could just read a passage somewhere in God's Book that said, "The Baptist Churches salute you." Oh, *if he could just find that,* it would be wonderful. But it isn't there. Mr. Bogard knows it isn't there, and he'll never find it. We're waiting for him to look for it. We're going to keep on his heels until he does something about it.

First Day

BOGARD'S FOURTH AFFIRMATIVE

Gentleman Moderators, Ladies and Gentlemen:

While it is fresh on your minds, I want to call your attention to what my friend said about ruling elders. Elders that rule well have double honor. The word rule there comes from a word in the original that means lead, ruling in the sense of leadership. If that is not true then that flatly contradicts what Jesus said. And my friend has not deemed it necessary to say anything about that. In Matt. 20:25.26 Jesus said, "The princes among the Gentiles exercise dominion over them, and they that are great have authority upon them, but it shall not be so among you." Nobody is to be an authority over God's people except Jesus Christ. My friend has not said a word about that, but he comes back with another scripture to try to offset the word of God and pervert the meaning. If these elders are to rule in the sense of controlling, *having authority* like the elders of the so-called Church of Christ do, then it flatly contradicts Jesus when He said, "The princes among the Gentiles exercise dominion over them, and they that are great have authority upon them. But it shall not be so among you." But my friend Porter says *it shall be so among us;* we are going to do it anyhow, no matter what the Lord said about it. The Lord said *it shall not be so among you.* My friend says *it shall be.* We are going to have it that way anyhow, no matter what the Lord said. "Elders that rule well." Yes sir, but the word "rule" is in the sense of *leadership.* Elders that *lead well.* If that is not the meaning then you have scripture flatly contradicting scripture. Certainly my friend can see that.

About the passages that they use, my friend and his people, to prove the Pentecost theory, I said that they quote scripture that says nothing about Pentecost to prove it. Then they quote scripture that says nothing about the church prove it. Then they quote scripture that says nothing about church or Pentecost either to prove it.

He comes back and says the scriptures that I used said nothing about the church at all. I wonder. Acts 1:21

says one must be chosen to succeed Judas "who has *companied* with us all the time that our Lord Jesus went in and out among us beginning from the baptism of John." The word "company" means church. If it does not mean that, what does it mean? You find a word that *means church* in any of your passages used for Pentecost, then you will have something coming your way. What is a church? A church is a *company* of baptized believers called to serve the Lord. I quoted that the "company" had been with the Lord Jesus all the time. Then he said the scripture that I quoted did not say church. Listen here in the thirteenth chapter of Mark. Jesus said He left His "house" and told His "house" to watch for you know not when the master of the "house" comes back and *Paul says that was the church,* "the house of God, the pillar and the ground of truth." That is enough on that.

Acts 10:41 says "to Him give all the prophets witness that through His name whosoever believed in Him should obtain remission of sins." How many prophets were there? We had that up this afternoon about Cornelius' household being saved. How many prophets were there? Somebody said there were twenty-two of them. Very well, suppose the twenty-two prophets, Isaiah, Ezekiel, Daniel, and all the rest should walk in here and stand up before my friend and say that I witness that whoever believes in Jesus Christ obtains remission of sins, *all twenty-two of them.* Would my friend believe what they said? Well, the Bible said they did do just that. "To Him give *all the prophets* witness."

Salvation is at the point of faith. And remember I quoted that scripture, Acts 16:31, "Believe on the Lord Jesus Christ and thou shalt be saved," and I said my friend never gives that answer to anybody who asks the way of salvation. He *NEVER* does, unless he stops to explain that believe means more than the dictionary says it means. He made no reply to that.

My friend asked me the question, would everything be sin that a sinner does before he is saved? Well, I Cor. 10:30, 31 says "whether we eat or drink or whatsoever we do, do all for the glory of God." If a man eats and does not do it for the glory of God he is violating that scripture. And what is sin? Transgression of the law, New Testament law. And if a man drinks, takes a drink of water, and does not do it for the glory of God it is a sin. Why? Because he violated the scripture which says do all things for the glory of God. Again we read, I gave it to him this afternoon and he paid no attention to it, that *that which is not of faith is sin.* Well, when a man does not exercise faith isn't that sin, no matter what he does? If he feeds the hungry, pays his debts, tells the truth, and lives a sober life, *does it without faith,* the sin element comes in when he fails to do what the Bible says do. Do it all for the glory of God. If he were to pray, it would be a sin. Certainly it would. You asked me that. It would be a sin to pray unless he is doing it for the glory of God. Well sir, my friend says what about a man repenting? Would that be a sin? Yes sir, unless he did it for the glory of God. Whenever an unsaved man comes to God by prayer and repentance he is doing that for the glory of God that his soul may be saved. But if he comes there praying and going through a form called repentance and *not doing it for the glory of God,* the very act would be sin. Preaching the Gospel would be a sin. To preach would be sin unless you did it for the glory of God.

That cuts out every bit of the goodness of a man who is not saved. It takes away all merit, makes the best effort of your life, makes the best thing you ever did, have the sin element in it no matter how good you may try to be, no matter how you may try to live. It is a sin against God if you leave God out and do not do it for the glory of God. I will just put that down now for you to think about. There will be more about it tomorrow and more about it next day and more about it the next day. At first you may not fully comprehend these things, but as we go along you will comprehend them more fully.

Porter went to the board and put a whole lot of his grammar on there. He said you could not have a plural without a singular. Well, well, well. The *houses* of Damascus. Where is the singular? The *house* of Damascus, including all the little houses? The *men of Arkansas.*

That is plural. Where is your singular? The *man* of Arkansas including all the little men? The *trees* of the forest. Where is your singular? The *tree* of the forest including all the little trees? The *churches of Christ.* (Laughter.) The singular, all the little churches composing *the one big church, "The Church of Christ"?*

I offered ten dollars for the scripture which said *"the church of Christ."* He has not produced it yet. I have the money in my pocket. Do you want it? You can not find the scripture. You harp on the name, *"The Church of Christ."* They know all about the plural and the singular. Well, well.

He wants to know what case is John over there. It is nominative, of course. And that is the objective, of course. But names are never in the possessive case. John's head. Head is the thing you are talking about. He had all that confusion for no purpose on earth but to get you confused. Every school boy in the world knows very well that the naming case is the nominative case. It is a name case. That is what we call it nominative for; it is a name case. Certainly, when you put it in the possessive it is not a name. You are talking about ownership then, like the churches of Christ. Now listen, I am going to challenge you. I am going to ask two or three of the brethren to write this down. "I affirm," listen now, I am quoting Porter; he says, "I affirm that the Churches of Christ in the original Greek is not in the possessive case." Put that down and I will leave it to any college you have on earth. They will say you are wrong. It is up to you now. And we will publish it in the paper. I will leave it with any college you have—the Freed-Hardeman College, the Harding College here at Searcy, any other college. We will not have a Baptist College in it. There is no such thing as Baptist grammar, and Methodist grammar, Campbellite grammar. (Laughter.) No, just grammar. Will you accept the challenge? If they will not say that is in the possessive case I will quit. There it is. Now then, try to make out like that is not the possessive. Churches of Christ. Every one of his brethren that ever went to school knows he is wrong. It is just for the few that do not know, it is for them I am trying to make this correction. His own brethren know it. Now leave it to Harding College right over here at Searcy. We can get the word by tomorrow. Is that in the possessive case or not? It is up to you. Do not stand here and try to bulldoze these folks and make them think something that is not so. You can not pull that kind of thing over me successfully. I know what I am talking about. Very well.

That plural and singular is a joke. You can not have a plural without a singular. There is *no such thing* as the church in the *broad sense of taking in all of God's people.* It is not in the Bible. A church is always a local congregation. And I explained this morning that I used the expression "Missionary Baptist Church" in the sense of an *institution like the family.* He paid no attention to that. No particular family—like the *family* is the corner stone of civilization—no particular family but *as an institution,* in the institutional sense. I explained myself. He wants to *put his meaning* into what I say and *answer his own meaning.* Well, a man that could not answer his own tomfoolery could not do anything. He can not answer what I really say.

There is no such thing as "The Church of Christ" in name or in fact *including all of God's people.* Granting, sir, that you are right in your doctrines and practices in the local assembly there is still no such thing as "The Church of Christ" *in the sense of all of God's people being in it.* It is not in the scriptures. Only in the institutional sense can he use it. I say *"the family".* I don't mean any particular family, but the family as an institution. *"The eagle."* No particular eagle, but the eagle as a species. *The lion.* No particular lion, but any lion, the lion as a species. In the institutional sense only can we say *the church.* Very well.

He asked me today, "Is the baby depraved?" I said yes sir. Then he comes right back and says that makes the baby as mean as the devil. Who said so? Porter. *I did not. I am supposed to tell you what Baptists believe, not Porter.* Let him tell what Baptists believe and he can *answer his own perversions.* Let him misrepresent what Baptists believe and he can *answer his own misrepresentations*. But he can not answer me.

I defined what I meant by total, that the whole person was depraved—mind depraved, body depraved, soul depraved, *total man depraved*. Did he pay any attention to it? He put his own perversion on it, said that meant just as mean as the devil. Of course, if I had said the baby is mean as the devil, if I had said any man is as mean as the devil, he could whip me all over this hill here with it, and there would have been no use for me to start in a debate. I know that is not so for the Bible says "evil men and seducers shall wax worse and worse, deceiving and being deceived." I believe the *devil himself can get worse*. I bebelieve he can keep on sinking in depravity, but the *total devil* is depraved. The *total man* is depraved. The *total baby* is born with a disposition to sin just like a duck is hatched a swimmer. It is not hatched swimming. It is not hatched in the water, but hatched with a nature that will make it swim as soon as it gets to the water. A bird is a natural flyer. He is not hatched flying, but he is hatched with the nature to make him fly. A baby is *born a sinner* in the sense that he has a sinful disposition and will sin the first chance he gets, *and they all do*. Name one that ever got by without it, except Jesus Christ.

Now, my friend comes back about the expression, "body of His flesh," referring to Christ's body, the body of His flesh. He said that makes Christ totally depraved. *Christ took on the totally depraved nature*, yet without actually committing sin, so says the Bible. He had the nature. If He did not have it, there is no merit in His refusing to sin. If He could not have sinned there is no merit in His refusing to sin. *He did not sin!* And therefore, where the first Adam fell, He stood, having no sin. He was *"made flesh."* What does the "flesh" mean? Flesh means *what we are by nature*, what we are by natural birth.

Now some questions my friend answered. I am going to show you what he failed to get to in just a minute. "Since you say that the New Testament Church is the Missionary Baptist Church, and it should be called what it is, did Jesus and the apostles do that? Did they call it what it is?" They gave a description that *could not be mistaken.* And, by the way, the word *Baptist means immerser.* In those days came John the immerser, in those days came John the dipper, dipping in the wilderness. In the English language it is *dipping* and in the Latin language it is *immersing.* In the Greek language it is *baptizing* and in the German language it is *tauser.* And in the Spanish language it is *bautiste.* It depends on what language you are using, but it *means the same thing.* You are looking for names in *English* when the Bible gives a *description of facts,* so that any body in *any language* can see what it is you're talking about without having to write under it, "This is a cat," so to speak, to explain what the picture is. If I made a picture so imperfect that I would have to write under it what the name is, I would give it up and quit. The Bible describes the church of our Lord, describes it so that it can not be misunderstood. And when you have a description of it, everybody who hears the description, reads what it says, will say that is just what we call Baptists now. That is what the people here in Damascus call Baptists. But when Porter describes what he thinks is the true church of Christ you can not find it in the Bible at all. If you get a description of a Bible church nobody would guess at the church of which he is a member. Very well.

He asks, "Since you say an unsaved man can do nothing that is not sin, is it sinful for him to repent and pray to God?" If he repents and prays to God without a view to the salvation of his soul, which is for the glory of God, it would be sin. It would be like Catholic confession before a priest.

Again he asks, "Which man becomes a member of the Baptist Church, the inner man or the outer man?" Both, the inner man and the outer man. The inner man is saved. The outer man is adopted to be saved in the resurrection. I am not stopping to make arguments on this. I am answering his questions. Tomorrow we will go right on further along the same line. I want to get the matter before you so you can see what we are talking about.

He asks, "Is it possible for a child of God to get drunk and commit murder?" Yes sir, David committed murder and he was a child of God, but he did not lose the Holy Spirit, either, for he said in his penitent prayer, "Take not Thy Spirit from me." And Noah got drunk. He was a child of God, but he did not go to hell. He did not fall from grace. I quoted you the scripture this morning, but you would not notice. Psalms 37:23,24 says the steps of a good man are ordered by the Lord and he delighteth in his way, and though he fall, (like David did and like Noah) he shall not be cast down. You say he can be cast down utterly. God's book says he can not. God will pick him up. Very well.

Then, is it good for a child of God to get drunk? No sir. It was not good for Noah to get drunk, but Noah's drunkenness was overruled for his good. It was not good for David to kill a man but *God overruled it for his good.* It is not good for a man to commit sin at all, but God overrules it for his good. Here is a scripture you failed to answer and looked like you did not want to try to answer, Romans 8:28. We know that "all things work together for good to them who love God, to them who are called according to His purpose." If you say there is *anything,* no matter what it is, that may be done *not for the Christian's good,* then, Sir, you flatly contradict God's word. *What he does may be wrong but God will overrule the wrong.* Did not Peter curse and swear and deny the Lord? He certainly did. Did he go to hell for it? No sir. "The steps of a good man are ordered by the Lord and he delighteth in his way, and though he fall he shall not be utterly cast down." And the wicked thing that Peter did was overruled for his good, for he found out after all he was not better than his brethren, not stronger than his brethren as he thought he was. And that fall (the Lord did not let him stay down) taught him that he was not stronger and not better than his brethren.

Well, is it possible for the spirit of a child of God to commit sin? I John 2:9 says that "he that is born of God does not commit sin for His seed remaineth in him and he cannot sin for he is born of God." That scripture will answer for that.

Then again, why are not children of regenerated people righteous? Because salvation is not inherited; the kingdom of God is not inherited. It is an *imparted* gift, an engrafted thing. Receive with meekness the engrafted word and the seed out of a grafted peach tree *will not come up what the graft was.* You take the seed out of a fine Arkansas Black Apple and plant it and it won't come up an Arkansas Black Apple or a Winesap. It will come up a scrub peach, or scrub apple. And so the children of Christian parents do not inherit their own salvation. They get it by *direct gift from God* like their parents did. That answers all his questions.

He has referred to Saul coming up to Jerusalem and that he "assayed to join himself to the disciples." He asked, "What was Saul before that?" He was baptized, a member of the Baptist Church. What about his baptizing anybody before that? I never heard of his baptizing any before that. But when he came up to Jerusalem and "assayed to join himself to the disciples," JOIN, join, they would not have him at first (ninth chapter of Acts) and Barnabas had to come and vouch for him. Then they took him in. Each church decides its own fellowship. We do not have it forced on us by the preacher or elders.

Now, I want to show you what my friend has not done. I gave him plenty of scriptures for him to take up and answer. If the Holy Spirit was not in the world until the day of Pentecost, then what about these scriptures that I gave? Elizabeth was filled with the Holy Ghost. John the Baptist was filled with the Holy Ghost. And Zacharias was full of the Holy Ghost. All that was before Pentecost. You remember their doctrine, this doctrine of the so-called "The Church of Christ", that the Holy Spirit did not do anything until Pentecost. That is what I am getting at. And you have got to learn that, and after you get that in your mind real good you will see how far he failed to reply to what I put up to him.

Again, I called his attention to the churches sending out their own missionaries, transacting their own business, administering their own discipline, receiving their own members. I gave him the scripture and he just referred to it without making any sort of an effort to get out of it.

Well, as long as that is true I am perfectly willing to let it go at that. I am happy to know that he can not answer it, does not try to answer it.

Now, I have another series of arguments that I want to bring in just now and let him do all he wants to. Tomorrow we will take up these items, item by item, and discuss them pro and con. I will make one further advancement now. Let him get it on his books so that he can think what he is going to do tomorrow, and tonight, for that matter. We teach, Missionary Baptist Churches teach, the doctrine of restricted or close communion. My friend and his church teaches anybody can come take the Lord's supper that wants to. Porter says anybody can come. He makes fun of the Baptists for restricting the Lord's supper. Let me give you the scripture on it now.

The Lord's supper is restricted as to place. It must be in church capacity. 1 Cor. 11:18.

It is restricted as to motive. The social idea is forbidden. I Cor. 11:21,22. "Have ye not houses to eat and to drink in," to sow sociability and friendship?

It is restricted as to purpose, closed against everybody else. It is to discern the Lord's body, I Cor. 11:29, and therefore we do not invite anybody to take the supper, and we teach them not to take it unless they know how to discern the Lord's body.

It is restricted to those who are baptized. Matt. 28:18-20. "Teaching them to observe all things whatsoever I have commanded you and lo, I am with you always even unto the end of the world." And then also, "Teaching them to observe all things whatsoever I have commanded you." That is the Lord's supper among other things, close communion. I want that to go in. I want to see what he says in reply. If he gets up and says they teach the same thing, then keep your mouths shut hereafter about Baptists' close communion. If he says they do not teach the same thing, let him reply to what I am saying.

It is restricted as to church members. Acts 2:41,42. I gave him that today. He made no reply to it. "Then they that gladly received his word were baptized and the same day there were added unto them about three thousand souls.

And they continued steadfastly in the apostles doctrine and in fellowship and in breaking of bread and in prayers." Now, my friend Porter and his brethren will preach everybody else into hell because they are not dipped in the water by one of their preachers, then turn right around and say, "Now you hell cats come up here and take the Lord's supper with us." That is exactly what they say in substance. That is inconsistency. Why not teach the truth on it, be fair with the people, tell them they have no right to the Lord's supper unless they comply with the conditions laid down in the Bible?

It is restricted to those who live orderly lives. II Thess. 3:6 says "withdraw from every brother that walketh disorderly." Withdraw from every *"brother,"* that walketh disorderly, disorderly brother. Then again, it is restricted to those who live correct lives. I Cor. 5:11. Those in the sin of adultry, fornication, and the like of that, they are not allowed to eat the Lord's supper.

Then it is restricted to those who are *judged by the church* and found worthy. I Cor. 5:12,13 says very plainly, "Do not ye judge them that are within?" Every church judges the qualifications of its own members. My friend says just let them examine themselves, so let them eat. It does not say that anywhere in the Bible or anything like it. You pervert the scripture there. I will get to that in a minute if my time does not run out before I get to it.

It is restricted to those that have the same faith. Hebrews 13:8-10 says they are not allowed to eat if they serve the tabernacle.

Then it is restricted as to the elements used, bread and wine. Matt. 26:26; Luke 22:19,20.

It is restricted as to a united church, united congregation. I Cor. 11:16-20. Paul said, "I hear there be divisions among you and I partly believe it. When you come together therefore in one place this is not to eat the Lord's supper." You must have a united congregation.

And on top of *all* that, *in addititon to all that,* each individual must examine himself before he can eat. I Cor. 11:28. There is a church of baptized church members who had complied with *all* the conditions. Even then, after *all* that, each one of the members must examine himself on top of all that. That is not the only thing you have to do. My friend says let a man examine himself. Certainly, after he has passed the qualifications required by the Bible, required by the church. But there is no self-examination until after all that. The *church must judge him* to be worthy. I Cor. 5:12-13. And *then after all that* the church might misunderstand; the church might not know what is in his heart. The church might not know what is in his life. So he must examine himself. That is a thirteen stake and rider fence built around the Lord's table and it would take a mighty bad mule or ox to jump over that fence. I hope you will not *try to do it.* I hope you will not try to deny the word of God on that subject. Do not teach what the Bible flatly contradicts and do not hold to that which the Bible does not substantiate.

I have tried my best in a hurried way to get the general ideas before you. No extensive argument has been made, and tomorrow we will go on with the argument.

Time called.

First Day

PORTER'S FOURTH NEGATIVE

Gentlemen Moderators, Mr. Bogard, Ladies and Gentlemen:

Just thirty minutes more and the session for this time of the debate will be over. I wish, during that time, to pay my respects to the things that have been said by my honorable opponent during the preceding thirty minutes.

The first thing to which he called your attention was with respect to the "ruling elders." As he had said this morning, "The Baptist Church has no such thing as ruling elders." I gave 1 Timothy 5:17 in which Paul told Timothy to count the elders that *rule well* worthy of double honor. Well, he came back tonight and said the word "ruling" there was ruling in the sense of "leadership." Well, that's still a sense of *ruling*, isn't it, Mr. Bogard? And if they are *ruling only in that sense*, they are still ruling elders. That is the thing you said that the Baptist Church does not have. But in Matthew 20:25-26 he referred to the statement that Jesus made about the princes among the Gentiles exercising dominion over them. He said, "It shall not be so among you." Well, I'm sure that my brethren have never claimed to have any such authority as Jesus referred to in that case. We have no elders to exercise such dominion over the people in the church today. In the church which I represent, if somebody undertakes to do that, then the elders in that case are *not ruling well*. We do not advocate that idea at all. "Mr. Porter says *there shall be*—yes, *there shall be*, regardles of what the Lord says." No, Porter doesn't say any such thing, and his brethren don't say any such thing. We do not contend for any such authority for the elders as Jesus referred to in Matthew 20:25-26, when he said, "It shall not be so among you." But that does not eliminate the word "ruling" in the sense that it is used on these other occasions; and in that sense of the term there were ruling elders. And there are today in the church that measures up to the church of the New Testament.

He came back to Mark 13 about the Master leaving his house and said very little about it. That's been discussed already. I have shown that he referred to the house in preparation, or the material, of which the house would be composed, when he left this earth to go into a far country to receive a kingdom and to return.

Then to his new arguments. Acts 10:43: "Whosoever believeth in him shall receive remission of his sins," and all the prophets gave witness to this. He said there were about twenty-two prophets of them, and they said, "Whosoever believeth should receive remission of sins." Well, I believe that. It all depends upon what is meant by the term "believe." There are some believers who are obedient believers, and there are some believers who are disobedient believers. Every promise of salvation made in the Book of God to believers contemplates *obedient believers* and not *disobedient believers.* And so it is in this case. The believer who is obedient is the one who receives the remission of sins —the obedient believer, and not the disobedient one. And I challenge Mr. Bogard to deny that there is such distinction in the Book of God.

Then to Acts 16:31 in which Paul told the Philippian jailer to "believe on the Lord Jesus Christ and thou shalt be saved." My friend said he was simply showing to him the way of salvation. Yes, but if he tried to do it, it would be a sin, for the simple fact that Mr. Bogard says that the unsaved man can do no good whatsoever—that everything he does is a sin. So, if he undertakes to comply with the statement there made by the apostle Paul, he would be guilty of sin in doing that. He restricted that, then, by 1 Corinthians 10:31, in which Paul said, "Whatever you do,"—"Whether you eat or drink, or whatsoever you do, do all to the glory of God." Mr. Bogard, was Paul talking to alien sinners or Christians in that case? You've applied that to *alien sinners,* when Paul was speaking there to *Christians,* and not to *alien sinners.* So you have the wrong passage to sustain your idea.

He also said, "He didn't pay any attention to Romans 14:23"—that whatsoever is not of faith is sin. "Whatsoever is not of faith is sin." Well, then, whatsoever he does *before he is saved* is sin, because my opponent says *the very moment* that he has faith he is saved. Anything he does before he is saved, therefore, is *without faith* and, consequently, is a sin—and he *can't do anything to the glory of God.* Mr. Bogard said that it's all sin—it's all without faith —because, if it's *with faith,* he is already saved. *Saved at faith*—or at the point of faith—as Mr. Bogard said a while ago. So he can't do anthing before he is saved and do it by faith—he does it without faith. So the restriction he tried to make by saying that this just refers to those things he doesn't do for the glory of God is of no value for he *can't do anything for the glory of God,* Mr. Bogard, according to your position. He can't do anything for the glory of God, because (he gave the passage this morning in Romans 8) "they that are in the flesh cannot please God." And he said everything he does is displeasing to God. That being true, then, the sinner *cannot do anything to* God's glory. You say that everything is wrong—everything is a sin—and that includes repentance and prayer, that you say comes before faith. At least, the repentance comes before faith, and prayer comes before the salvation. So they both have to come before faith, because, if he has faith, he is saved, according to Bogard. "Yes," he says, "if a sinner prays, it is sin, if he doesn't pray to the glory of God." Why Mr. Bogard, don't you remember this afternoon you said that he that is "in the flesh cannot please God?" He *can't do one thing* that is *pleasing to God;* so he *can't do one thing* to the *glory* of God. Everything must be done otherwise. When he prays, he can't pray to the glory of God—the old depraved nature is there. He is totally depraved—depraved in body, mind and soul so completely that not one single thing can he do that pleases God. That was Mr. Bogard's argument this afternoon. Now, he backs up from it and says, "Yes, the sinner might do a great many things for the glory of God and still he wouldn't be saved." Then it's not all bad, is it, Mr. Bogard? Everything the alien sinner does is not bad, because you say he *can do some things to God's glory,* and it's not all sin. So you backed up on that.

Of the plural without the singular, he said, "Yes sir, there can be a plural without a singular." In other words, he gave the "houses of Damascus." There could be houses in Damascus and not be a house in Damascus. If you have a house somewhere that is singular. Mr. Bogard said,

"When you speak of the *houses* of Damascus, there is no singular in it." Can't even comprehend the singular—can't include the singular—plural without singular—"the houses of Damascus." Well, let's suppose I walk out here to the far corner of Damascus—wherever it is—and say, "This is the house of Damascus in this corner." This is "the house" in this location. There's your singular, even with the term "the." So with "the trees of the forest" and all these other illustrations he gave. You *can't have the plural without the singular.* When you have "churches of Christ," there must be "church of Christ" somewhere, and if you have "*the* churches of Christ," there must be "*the* church of Christ" somewhere. You can't get away from it. He said, "I'm still offering him the $10 for the expression *The Church of Christ.*" Well, Mr. Bogard, I'm offering it back to you, with $100 in addition, to find "*the Baptist Church*" or "*the Baptist Churches,*" either plural or singular. Have you tried to get it? No, no, he hasn't tried. He's not going to try. He knows it isn't there. And I've shown that "the churches of Christ" means a number of them, and that one of them would be "the church of Christ" in a certain locality. We'll get more on that presently.

Then he came to the nominative case and made quite a palaver about my grammar on the board. He went on to say that every school boy knows that names are always in the nominative case and not in the possessive case. Well, I'd like to see the school boy who doesn't know more than that. I certainly would—those in the 7th grade grammar who don't know more than that. Mr. Bogard has said that "names are always in the nominative case." I asked Mr. Bogard, What is case? Case is that modification of a noun or pronoun that shows its relation in the sentence to other words. Case pertains *only to nouns and pronouns.* But grammars also say that a *noun* is the *name* of anything. And a *pronoun* is a word used *for a noun.* So if *names* are always in the nominative case, then *nouns* are always in the nominative case and *pronouns* are always in the nomintive case. What's in the other cases, then? Did you tell us? No! Not a word! Did not tell us a word about what's in other cases? If nouns are always in the nominative case, because nouns are names, then what's used in the other cases?

CHART NO. 3

John reproved Herod
Herod beheaded John
John's head was brought on a platter
The churches of Christ salute you

Here (pointing to board) we have "John reproved Herod." All right, "John" is the subject of the sentence. That's the name of a man and, consequently, is in the nominative case, because the subject of a sentence or an attribute complement (or predicate nominative, as some grammars call it is in the nominative case. Here (pointing to the second sentence) we have "Herod beheaded John." Is this still a name, Mr. Bogard? I want you to tell us. *Speak up.* Bat an eye. Shake a head or something. Is this still a name? "John?" "Herod beheaded John." Is that a name, Mr. Bogard? *I dare you to answer it.* Will you answer it? Shake or nod. *Say something about it.* Is "John" still a name? Mr. Bogard, is that in the nominative case or the objective case? Huh? Don't you want to back out a little on that? Won't you take a back track just a little and say that names are sometimes in the objective case? Here's a name just as much so as it is here. In this sentence (pointing to first) it is in the *nominative case.* And in this sentence (pointing to second) it is in the *objective case.* Mr. Bogard says that every school boy in the 7th grade grammar knows that it is "*always* in the nominative case." Then what's this over here? (pointing to "John" in second sentence) It's either not a name or this is the nominative case. Well, if you have school teachers somewhere teaching like that, then you'd better have them examined—there is something wrong with them. Absolutely, friends, here (pointing to second sentence) we have "John," the name, in the objective case. All right, "John's head was brought on a platter." He said, "Oh, here's the noun." (pointing to "head") Yes, this is the subject of the sentence. Certainly, this is the subject of the sentence, but that's not the *only noun* in there. And here (pointing to "John's") is also a noun used as a modifier--

a possessive modifier—of a noun. And it's still the name we have up here in these, and *it's in the possessive case.* "John's head." Here (pointing to first sentence) "John" is in the nominative case. Here (pointing to second) it's in the objective case. Here (pointing to third) it's in the possessive case. So names are *not always* in the nominative case. If they are, then what's in the objective and what's in the possessive? Predicates? Conjunctions? Prepositions? Or what? Mr. Bogard. *You're going to tell us.* I'm going to put it in writing tomorrow, and I'm going to have you tell us what's in those cases. You can't get by with a thing like that. That's not going over. He said, "All the people, except just a few, know that Porter is wrong on that, and I'm just talking to those who don't know." The fact is *they all know* you're wrong on it, Mr. Bogard. The fact is anybody who has studied grammar just a very little bit *knows that you're wrong.* And if you want to, go home tonight, *please go home and get your text book,* because I don't care whose grammar it is. He said, "There's no difference in Baptist grammar and Campbellite grammar." And this, that and the other. All right, I don't care whose grammar you get. *Get any grammar on the face of the earth today* and look up on the word "case." See how many cases there are, and whether names are always in the nominative case; and if so, find out what's in the other cases. Investigate for yourself. You don't have to take my word for it. *Mr. Bogard is wrong.* And *he knows he is wrong.* And he can't get out of it. He has to stay hitched. He said this over here, "Herod," is in the objective case (pointing to first sentence). Mr. Bogard said that. Well, all right, "Herod" is the object of the verb "reproved." And if "Herod" is in the objective case here, then what's "Herod?" "Herod" is a name, isn't it? I haven't used that name to show the case, but "Herod" is a name. And it's in the objective case in that sentence. Mr. Bogard said it's in the objective case. All right, then, it's *not the nominative*—is it? So you've admitted that you're wrong about it. Furthermore, here is "John" that occupies the same place in this sentence that "Herod" does in that one. "John reproved Herod." "John is the subject; "reproved" is the verb; and

"Herod," the object complement. "Herod beheaded John." "Herod" is the subject; "beheaded" is the verb, and "John" is the object complement. And since this is the objective case up here with "Herod" (first sentence) then down here with "John" (second sentence) it is the objective case. And you can't get out of it, Mr. Bogard; you're in a trap, and in a trap you're going to stay—with all of your boasting and blowing about it.

"Oh," he says, "I'll tell you what I'll do. 'The churches of Christ salute you.' I'll tell you what I'll do. Let's put it up to these colleges around here and see if, in the original Greek, this isn't the possessive case." Elder Bogard didn't even know there is no "possessive" case in Greek. (Laughter) Mr. Bogard, tell me the cases in Greek, will you? (Bogard speaks: "Genitive man. Good Lord!") Genitive? "Genitive"—it is not "possessive" then. "Genitive" is not "possessive." Genitive case—that denotes the idea of possession *some times*. Doesn't it? And we have "possession" here—possession regarding "Christ" and not "churches." But it's not "possessive" case construction. Certainly, there is the possessive idea—possessive thought—but not the possessive case. "Churches" is the subject—"churches of Christ salute you." "Churches" is the subject. Is that possessive or nominative, Mr. Bogard? *Come on!* Is this possessive or nominative? "Churches?" The only possession indicated is in this expression here (pointing to "of Christ") and that pertains to Christ, but it's in the objective case. But it pertains to Christ. Here (pointing to "churches") we have a nominative—right in the passage where you say there is no nominative. You'll have to try it over, Mr. Bogard.

He says there is no such thing as "the church" in the broad sense—that the word church is always used in the sense of the local congregation—always refers to one congregation when it is used in the singular number. I believe that's what he meant by it. When used in the singular number, it is always a local congregation—just one congregation—the church. Well, we're going to see about that. I'm turning to Acts, the 9th chapter and verse 31, reading from the American Revised Version. We're going to see something here that Mr. Bogard says isn't true. Now this is following the persecution of Saul and following his conversion. And then it goes on to say, "So *the church* throughout *all Judea and Galilee and Samaria* had peace, being edified; and, walking in the fear of the Lord and in the comfort of the Holy Spirit, was multiplied." Now, that speaks of *the church*. Where? *"The church* throughout all Judea and Galilee and Samaria." And that's not one local congregation—that's the term "church" used in the singular number, denoting a number of them. Mr. Bogard is wrong as usual.

Well, "the baby is depraved." He said, "Let Bogard tell you what Baptists believe"—that Porter is not going to be allowed to tell. "Let Bogard tell you what Baptists believe." Well, Bogard says that Baptists believe that "the baby is totally depraved." He answered that question. That's what I asked him. And he answered it. "Yes." Then "babies are totally depraved." And I showed that *"totally"* is an adverb of degree, modifying "depraved," telling *how depraved* the baby is. What did he say about that? He got up and said that "he talked about grammar," but he never made any effort to set it aside. Let *him* try *his hand* on it. "Evil men shall wax worse and worse." I believe that. Certainly, I believe that. That's another thing that shows he is wrong when he claims they are "totally depraved." If they are *totally depraved,* they *can't wax worse and worse,* because there is no such thing as totally, more totally, and most totally. The adverb "totally" is not an adverb that admits of comparison. You cannot have totally, more totally, and most totally. If you have "totally," that is just as bad as it can be. That's the supreme degree of depravity—*totally depraved.* So, they couldn't get worse and worse. Just as mean as the devil, and they couldn't be any worse than that—nor any better—according to his idea.

All right, concerning Christ, he said, "Yes, Christ had a totally depraved nature, but he did not sin." Well, Mr. Bogard argued this afternoon if a man *has the nature,* he can't do anything but sin. "They that are in the flesh *cannot* please God" was his argument based on Romans 8. "A man with a *totally depraved nature,"* he said, *"cannot do anything that isn't sin.* If he loves his wife, it's sin. If he tells the truth, it's a sin. If he stays sober, it's a sin. If he pays his just debts, it's a sin." Mr. Bogard said that this afternoon, because "they that are in the flesh cannot please God." They that have the *totally depraved nature* cannot please God. That was his argument. Now, he comes along and says that Jesus Christ was *totally depraved,* but he didn't sin. Well, how did he keep from it? If he was totally depraved, he *couldn't* do *anything* that was *good,* according to your idea. According to his own argument, he couldn't do anything that was good—anything that wasn't sin. Therefore, everything that Jesus did was sin. And the Bible is wrong when it said he had no sin—if Mr. Bogard is right. The argument still stands.

Then he came to the questions. Incidentally, did you notice that he skipped those that I gave him this afternoon? He answered the ones that I gave him tonight, but the ones that I gave him this afternoon—he hasn't to this hour said one single, solitary word about them. He'll answer them, I suppose. He hasn't given them back to me. I'm going to read them again and see if he will answer them next time.

"Number 8. In conversion which man becomes a child of God—the inner man or the outer man?" "Number 9. Is faith without works living or dead?" "Number 10. Are the souls of infants pure at birth?" "Number 11. Is there any honor for a child of God that is greater than to be a part of the bride of Christ?" "Number 12. When did your people first take the name 'Baptist Church' or 'Baptist Churches'?" "Number 13. Is there any history written before the 17th century that speaks of the 'Baptist Church'?" "Number 14. Does it not take more to get into the Baptist Church than it does to get into heaven?" "Number 15. Can you find the expression 'Baptist Churches' in the Bible?" Those questions were given him this afternoon in my closing speech. He had all that time between the sessions to look them over, but he has made two speeches and has not even referred to them. What's the matter, Mr. Bogard? *Please pay your respects to those.*

Incidentally, I have two more for you. Number 24. Which man do you turn out of the Baptist Church—the inner man or the outer man? Number 25. Can a person with an impure soul enter heaven? Just two of them there.

Now, to these he undertook to answer a while ago. "Number 16. Since you say that the New Testament Church is the Missionary Baptist Church, and should be called what it is, did Jesus and the apostles do what they should do and call it what it is?" He said, "They gave a description of it so everybody could know." Well, they *didn't call it what it is?* Did they? You didn't answer the question. You side-stepped it. You side-stepped it. You said, "It should be called what it is." Now, they didn't call it that. You said, "It is the Missionary Baptist Church." But they didn't call it that. But you said, "It *should be called* what it is." Then Jesus and the apostles did not call it what it is. They *did not do what they should do*—or it wasn't the Missionary Baptist Church in the New Testament. Now, you come back and face that. You haven't touched it. "Number 17. Since you say the unsaved man can do nothing that is not sin, is it a sin for him to repent and pray to God?" He says, "If it's not to the glory of God." And I have dealt with that already. "18. Which man becomes a member of the Baptist Church—the inner man or the outer an?" He says, "Both." "Number 19. Is it possible for a child of God to get drunk and commit murder?" He said, "Yes." And "David committed murder and Noah got drunk." But he said, "They didn't go to hell." Well, did they die drunk? Did Noah die while he was drunk? And did David die in the act of murder? The next question said, "If he should die while drunk and in the act of murder, will he go to heaven?" You skipped that completely. Why did you skip it? Come back and tell us. If a child of God should die while he is drunk and in the act of murder, will he go to heaven or hell? *Come on, now, and tell us about it.* We'll have some more on that tomorrow, I'm sure. "Number 21. Is it good for a child of God to get drunk?" He says, "No." "22. Is it possible for the spirit of a child of God to commit sin?" He gave 1 John 3:9 and declared that it is not possible. "Number 23. Why are not the children of regenerated people born righteous?" He said, "Salvation is not inherited, but it is a result of being engrafted." That is, the word is engrafted like you graft an Arkansas Black Apple into some other kind—perhaps a Crab Apple, or something of that kind. "And when you plant the seed of the Arkansas Black," he said, "you won't get an Arkansas Black— you'll get a scrub." I suppose, then, that the children of regenerated people are "scrubs." Is that the idea? Is that what Mr. Bogard wants? Now, let me show you something more about it. We're out of crayon—or almost so—maybe I can write with my finger nails. Notice, now, here is the "graft." Over here is the "stump."

CHART NO. 4

Graft — Stump

Mr. Bogard's argument is that this "graft" is put into this "stump" or stock. (Someone hands Mr. Porter some crayon.) Thank you. You take the graft out of an Arkansas Black Apple or a Ben Davis Apple and put it into the Crab Apple stump. It *doesn't change the old stump,* but this graft grows and produces Arkansas Black, or Ben Davis, Apples, as the case may be. Then you take the seed from them and plant it, and it goes back to the *old stump,* you see. And so it is with a man that has been regenerated. The offspring—the children—go back to the old stump and they are depraved. So the *old stump remains depraved,* you see. That is the point. Now, then, Mr. Bogard, what I want to know is: What is the stump? What is represented by the stump? You said, "The graft is the word of God." "Receive with meekness the engrafted word." But that word has to be "engrafted into the stump by the power of the Holy Spirit in addition to the word." I want to know what the "stump" is? Is the stump the heart—the soul of man? *What is the stump?* Whatever it is, it is *not changed,* because the stump or the old stock that you grafted the Ben Davis Apple into doesn't change. It's *the same old stump.* Then, if it is the heart of man, and the word is grafted into the man's heart, *the man's heart is not changed.* It remains the same old stump—the same old depraved heart—that he had before. I just challenge you to say that it isn't the heart. If you do, then I'll show that you have said on other occasions that the stump is the heart, or the soul, of man, and the word is grafted into that heart. But it doesn't change the old stump. It's only the graft that grows, and *the old stump remains the same.* So the old heart of man is unchanged and remains the same old depraved, wicked heart—totally depraved as it was before the graft. And what have you done? Changed man? Not in the least. He is still the same old fellow he has always been. The only thing that grows is the word of God, and the man remains the same old sinner that he's always been. No change whatsoever is accomplished in him. That is his argument on the graft. I thank him very much for it.

He said, "He didn't refer to Psalms 37. Paid no attention to it. Didn't even notice it." But do you remember I called his attention this afternoon to verse 27 that said "Depart from evil and *do good* and *dwell forevermore?*" So it's conditional. Bogard says I didn't mention it, but the record will show that I did and made that argument on it.

Romans 8:28: "All things work together for good." There'll be more about that tomorrow. But he said regarding this that there are certain things that are not for man's good—that is, it is not good to get drunk, but it works out for his good. So if you get drunk, why, God will work it out for your good. It won't harm you in the least. We'll have more about that later on.

Then to Saul and the Baptist Church. He said, "Yes, and he was in the Baptist Church before that and came to Jerusalem and tried to join another." I suppose one of them was Missionary, and the other was something else.

"Porter says that the Holy Spirit didn't do anything till Pentecost—that they all preach that the Holy Spirit didn't do anything till Pentecost." Well, I never heard one of my brethren preach that in all my life. I'm sure I have never preached it.

All right; sending out the missionaries and the other ideas he gave. He said, "Porter just referred to these arguments." Well, you just referred to them when you gave them. You just made a statement and introduced a passage —didn't even quote the passage—merely referred to it, and then expected me to take up each passage and spend about five minutes on it—when you merely referred to them in passing. Come on and deal with them, and I'll be right behind you.

Then to closed communion. "It is restricted," he said. "Porter and his people make fun of Baptists because we have closed communion." No, that is not the idea. The fact is you say that all these other fellows are saved and are going right on into glory. They are good enough to reach heaven but not good enough to eat at the table with you. That is the point. I believe that communion is restricted. I believe it is restricted to God's people. I don't believe anybody who isn't a child of God has a right to eat the Lord's supper. My brethren have always taught that. But you say all these other fellows *are the Lord's people* and are already saved, and they are good enough to go on into heaven, but "they can't eat the supper with us." That is the point. That is where the trouble is with Baptist doctrine. And so I believe that there are restrictions about the Lord's supper. I certainly believe that it is in the church—as you say. And I believe that it is restricted as to motive—that it shouldn't be for a social purpose. 1 Corinthians 11:33. I believe that it's purpose is restricted. I believe it is for those who are baptized. I believe it is for church members only—and all those things. We've always taught those things. But the trouble with Mr. Bogard and his people is that he claims that all these others are going to heaven—yes, they have a right to go up there and partake of the blessings of eternity around the great white throne of God, but they can't meet around a Baptist table in the Missionary Baptist Church and eat the Lord's supper. That's the point. That's what's wrong with it. Well, that covers it. He said he had a thirteen rail fence around the Lord's table to fence out all the rest of the Christians everywhere that are good enough to go to heaven but not good enough to eat the Lord's supper in the Baptist church.

Now, then, friends, I want you to keep in mind these things, because tomorrow we are going to be right along the same line—Mr. Bogard still in the affirmative, endeavoring to prove that the Missionary Baptist Church, or the church known as the Missionary Baptist Church, is Scriptural in origin, doctrine, practice and name. He's already given up one of those, because he said he can't find either "Baptist Church' or "Baptist Churches"—can't find "the Baptist Church" or "the Baptist Churches." And he can't find "Missionary Baptist Church" or "Missionary Baptist Churches" in the Bible. Such is no where to be found in all of God's Book. When he gets ready to find it, I'll erase this (pointing to board) and put back what I had there and let him write down the reference that mentions one of them—*either the plural or the singular.* I don't care whether he thinks the plural includes the singular or not. Let him find either of them—"Baptist Churches" or "Baptist Church"—and I'll take both of them. I'll have enough sense, friends, to know that if he can find the Bible speaking about a "Baptist Church," that a number of them would be "Baptist Churches." I'll have enough sense to know, if he can find "Baptist Churches" in the Bible, that one of them would be a "Baptist Church." Friends, Bogard doesn't know that when you read about "churches of Christ" in the Bible, one of them is the "church of Christ." He doesn't know that. He thinks that it doesn't include that at all—that you can have the plural, but you can't have the singular. Well, that is Mr. Bogard's misfortune and not mine. I'm just sure that the Book of God is true. I'm sure that these great principles revealed therein will stand in spite of all the assaults made by Baptist preachers. Mr. Bogard has made more than any other Baptist preacher that ever lived, but *they still stand.* They will still be standing when he's passed on, for the simple fact is that he cannot overthrow these principles of divine truth. There is no such thing in the Bible as the Baptist Church—*it's never mentioned there.* And, furthermore, my friends, it's not mentioned in history prior to the 17th century. Cannot find "Baptist Church." *It's not there.* The world knew nothing about a Baptist Church till the 17th century. Mr. Bogard cannot find it prior to that time. It's not in the Book of God. It's not in profane history for about 1600 years after the Lord left the earth. Yet, he wants you to believe that the Baptist Church is the church of the New Testament—that it's Scriptural in origin, doctrine, practice and name. But not one single word is ever uttered about it in all the Book of God. It *just isn't there*. And it cannot be found. How much time do I have? Mr. Blue speaks: "Got four minutes."

All right, then, I'll go back and see some of these things that I might elaborate on just a little more during the four minutes. I don't care to introduce negative arguments, because that will come up when I take the affirmative. Oh, yes, I mustn't overlook this about John the Immerser and the picture of his death. He said at the very outset of this discussion, in the first few minutes of his first speech, that the name is important. In fact, he attached so much importance to it that he said that the man who fails to prove that the church is Scriptural in name fails in this debate. Then he comes along in this speech and says that Porter is depending on the name and not on the description. Well, you made the name the—(Time called). (This was not four minutes—the information was incorrect.)

Second Day

BOGARD'S FIFTH AFFIRMATIVE

Gentlemen Moderators, Mr. Porter, Ladies and Gentlemen:

We made wonderful progress yesterday, and things will begin to clear up with some who perhaps did not fully understand. There were so many things brought in, so many things said and such short explanations, but today things will be clarified more and more as we go along. Then for the next two days those things that you have heard which were perhaps new to you will not remain mystified as they may be in some of your minds.

My friend complained that I had not answered his questions. There are twenty five of them. I have all the questions right before me. And they are written as catch questions—not a fair way to debate. Real first class debaters have all quit that stuff long ago. I am surprised at my friend continuing that course. His purpose is to divert attention from the main issue and raise questions and quibbles. But I am answering every one of them one at a time, giving you the scripture for them. I will number them as I go along and I am quite sure they will all be answered satisfactorily.

First, is the name "Missionary Baptist Church" mentioned in the Bible? No. Neither is the name "The Church of Christ" mentioned in the Bible.

Second, can a thing be scriptural in name if not named in the scripture? Yes. Immersion is scriptural, but you can not find the word immersion in the New Testament.

Third, was John the Baptist a member of the church of the Lord? No. But God used this Baptist to prepare the material for His church.

Fourth, was any man who was a member of the church of the Lord ever called Baptist in the New Testament? Neither was any other called Adam after the first man Adam, but they are all of the Adamic race. All have the same nature and are the same kind.

Fifth, do you believe that infants are totally depraved? Yes, in the sense of the *entire infant*—body, soul, or spirit, and mind, all it takes to constitute a human being, is depraved.

Sixth, do you baptize the inner man or the outer man? This is another catch question. I baptize both. I do not separate them. God will do that in His own time at death.

Seventh, is a sinner saved by living faith or a dead faith? By living faith, certainly. That which produces life always produces works. But the *faith Porter is baptized on is a dead faith* that must go to work before it is alive. It only puts him to work, according to his own argument.

Eighth, again this question: In conversion in which a man becomes a child of God, is it the inner man or outer man? Both. The soul is saved now by the new birth, the body by adoption. Rom. 8:23. "We groan within ourselves waiting for the adoption to wit the redemption of our bodies."

Ninth, is faith without works living or dead? It is dead. And therefore the faith you were baptized on was dead for it didn't have any life until after it worked, you being judge.

Tenth, are the souls of infants pure in birth? No. They are not. Eph. 2:3. "We are all by nature the children of wrath." And the Greek word is "phusis" and Thayer says it is that which we get by natural birth.

Eleventh, is there any honor to the child of God greater than to be a part of the bride of Christ? None whatever. But some Christians do not avail themselves of that honor by joining the church of Jesus Christ. Rev. 22:17 says "the bride says come; let him that heareth say come." There are two classes: the bride, and those who hear.

Twelfth, when did your people first take the name Baptist Church or Baptist Churches? We never took that name at all. The Lord started it that way and it continued from the time of John the Baptist until now.

Thirteenth, is there any history written before the seventeenth century that speaks of a Baptist Church? Benedict's, page 343 and 344 says that the "old or Baptist church divided in the year 595 A.D." It was old enough to divide in the year 595. There is your history.

Fourteenth, does it take more to get into the Baptist Church than to get into heaven? Yes sir. It takes more to get married than it does to get to heaven, too. You had to court your girl and do a lot of extra work in order to get married. And yet marriage is honorable and scriptural.

Fifteenth, can you find the expression "Baptist Church" in the Bible? No. And you can not find the name "The Church of Christ" in the Bible. If it is an offset for me it is an offset for you.

Sixteenth, since you say the New Testament church is the Missionary Baptist Church and should be called what it is, did Jesus and the apostles do what they should do and call it what it is? Jesus and the apostles described the church so nobody could misunderstand what it meant. *To call it a name would not make it so.* To call a buzzard an eagle would not make a buzzard an eagle, would it? It would not take the stink off. Sure it would not.

Seventeenth, since you say the unsaved man can do nothing that is not a sin, is it a sin for him to repent and pray to God? It would be unless he did it for the glory of God. The salvation of his soul is for the glory of God, and when he moves in that direction God honors him.

Eighteenth, which man becomes a member of the Baptist Church, the inner man or the outer man? Both do—the soul by the new birth and the body by adoption.

Nineteenth, is it possible for a child of God to get drunk and commit murder? Certainly. David committed murder and Noah got drunk, and they were children of God.

Twentieth, if he should die while drunk or in the act of murder, where would he go, to heaven or hell? Well he would go to hell. But then that would flatly contradict the word of God. I John 3:3 says "every man that hath this hope in him purifieth himself even as he is pure." Two things would happen. *The man would go to hell and God would be a liar.* God said "*every man* who hath this hope in him purifieth himself even as he is pure," and you presume that he would not do that, but go on so far in sin as to be lost in hell.

Twenty-first, is it good for a child of God to get drunk? No. But if he does get drunk, God overrules it for his good, for Psalms 37:23,24 says "the steps of a good man are ordered by the Lord and he delighteth in his way and though he fall he shall not be utterly cast down, for the Lord upholdeth him with His hand." All right, is it good for a child of God to drink? No. Certainly not. But God overrules the evil for good or else Romans 8:28 is a falsehood, for it says "all things work together for good to them that love God, to them who are the called according to His purpose."

Twenty-second, is it possible for the spirit of the child of God to commit sin? No. I John 2:9 says plainly "that which is born of God doth not commit sin." The spirit is born of God.

Twenty-third question, why are not the children of regenerated people born righteous? Answer: I Cor. 15:50 says that "flesh and blood doth not inherit the kingdom of God." You can not inherit salvation from your parents. It is a direct gift from God.

Now the twenty-fourth question: Which man do you turn out of the Baptist Church, the inner man or the outer man? Both. They are both in.

Twenty-fifth, can a person with an impure soul enter heaven? No. I know the catch in that is that a baby with an impure soul will therefore have to go to hell. But they will not catch me on that catch. I Tim. 4:10 says that He is the Saviour of all men," and the word "men" comes from the Greek word *"anthropos"* meaning all mankind, "especially of them that believe." And so the Lord is the Saviour of babies. He does it by His blood. In the fifth chapter and ninth verse of Revelation, "that thou hast saved us by thy blood out of every nation, kindred and tongue," and they were singing that song. I asked you a question yesterday: Are babies allowed to sing in heaven? If so, *they sing that they are washed by the blood of Jesus Christ.*

Now we made some wonderful progress yesterday. I want to get the matter before you, what we have actually learned in yesterday's debate. We learned that the Lord had a company beginning from the baptism of John. My friend quibbled over that by turning to my Way Book, page 19, or page 29 of the book that he has, page 30 in the latest edition, where it says "began with the baptism of John." Some more quibbling. What is the difference? *It goes back to John just the same.* And when I quoted the scripture "beginning from the baptism of John," I emphasized the fact that it said beginning *from* the baptism of John. But it does not matter whether it begins *from* or *with,* it goes right back to John the Baptist. The Bible says that he was sent to baptize, sent to preach; therefore he was a Missionary Baptist preacher.

Well, we learned another thing, that the church or company of baptized believers began from the baptism, or with the baptism (I do not care which you call it; you can use the same expression). The scripture says from the baptism of John. If I slipped in the book and said with the baptism of John that slip does not change the facts at all. You go right back to the baptism of John. And that is the one the Lord sent to prepare a people for the Lord.

Then we find that this company went with Jesus all the time He went in and out among us "beginning from the baptism of John." He left that company, Mark 13, and left the servants *with authority and a work to do,* and commanded them to watch "for you know not when the master of the house comes back." I made the point that you can not leave this house unless you are at this house. You can not leave a house if there is no house there to leave. But Jesus did leave His house. And what is the house? I Tim. 3:15 says "the house of God, which is the church of God, the pillar and the ground of the truth." And He will return to that house by and by. These things my friend denies. He denies that Jesus Christ will ever reign on this earth again, ever put His foot on the earth again. The Bible says He is coming back for His chuch by and by. He quoted Luke 19 where it says that the "Son of man is as a man who went into a far country to receive for himself a kingdom." That refers to the millenial reign of Christ on earth. And Rev. 11:15 says that the "kindoms of this world become the kingdom of our Lord who is Christ." And that is what the Lord will receive when the kingdoms of the world are all turned over to Him and they become His kingdom at the end.

Then we learned that Cornelius and his household were saved before they were baptized. How do I know? Acts 10:43-44 says "to him give all the prophets witness that whosoever believeth in Him shall obtain the remission of sins, and while Peter yet spake these words the Holy Ghost fell on all them that heard the word." And then Peter commanded them to be baptized. Who? Those who had received the Holy Ghost. They received the Holy Ghost. John 14:17 says "Him the world cannot receive." So there were some who had the Holy Ghost and were baptized after they received the Holy Ghost, and therefore were saved before they were baptized. That is clear as can be, but my friend got up and said that they were saved without hearing any preaching at all. If he did not I am not on this platform. He quoted what Peter said in the Revised Version, "As I began to speak", before he spoke at all. All right, if he could take it that way, they *were saved before baptism.* But if he did, if they were saved before baptism, there was another thing that happened. He turned to the eleventh chapter of Acts and fourteenth verse where the Bible plainly says that he would hear words by which he and his household should be saved. And you turned around and said they were saved without hearing any of the words at all—before he spoke the word, just started. So Cornelius was saved, undoubtedly, before he was baptized, and if you say he was saved without hearing the word at all then you flatly contradict what the Bible says on the subject, that he should hear words whereby he and his household should be saved.

Now we come along to James 1:21. How are people saved if they are depraved? James 1:21 says "receive with meekness the engrafted word which is able to save your souls." No graft ever put itself into a tree. We know that. So that means the direct work of the Holy Spirit in the conversion of a soul, unless that graft can put itself in, which is absurd. Then there must be a work of the Holy Spirit in connection with salvation, or else they could not be saved. But he said, "Hold on, here. That did not change the nature of the man." No, but it subdued the nature of the man and gave him two natures. The Bible plainly speaks of that. You can turn right here to Romans, if you please, in the seventh chapter beginning at the fifteenth verse and I will read about those two natures. My friend does not seem to think a man has two natures. *Before a man is saved he only has one nature.* That is a sinful nature. When he is saved he has the *graft of divine truth put in* and that gives him *two natures.* And here is where we read about it in the seventh chapter of Romans.

"For that which I do I allow not; for what I would, that do I not but what I hate, that do I. If then I do that which I would not, I consent unto he law that it is good. Now then it is no more I that do it, but sin that dwelleth in me. For I know that in me (that is, in my flesh,)"—that is the natural man as I proved on yesterday,—"dwelleth no good thing: for to will is present with me; but how to perform that which is good I find not. For the good that I would, I do not: but the evil which I would not, that I do. Now if I do that I would not, it is no more I that do it, but sin that dwelleth in me. I find then a law, that, when I would do good, evil is present with me. For I delight in the law of God after the inward man: But I see another law in my members, warring against the law of my mind, and bringing me into captivity to the law of sin which is in my members. O wretched man that I am! Who shall deliver me from the body of this death? I thank God through Jesus Christ our Lord."

So there are the two natures, the *natural man* and a *new nature* engrafted in him. That new nature subdues the old and they both grow together. My friend said, "Why, didn't it change the old nature?" Certainly not. It added to it. And the *new nature* is just like a graft put into a crab-apple tree. After that the graft will bring forth winesaps or whatever kind the graft nature is and that tree becomes a good tree, a fruit bearing tree, because of the graft. What is the graft? "Receive with meekness the engrafted word which is able to save your souls." So when a man is saved he has *two natures* thereafter—one serving God, the other serving the devil—*one warring against the other.* Now if my friend never had that warfare in him it is because he never had the graft put in. If he never had that conflict in him, it is because he never has been saved. If you have been saved you have the new nature imparted, and *the new birth means simply the impartation of that new nature that holds in subjection the old nature until, in the resurrection, the old nature itself will be born again.*

Then we come to another thing that is very interesting. My friend gave up on the close communion question, completely gave up. I built a thirteen rail fence around the Lord's table. I gave you those passages of scripture that restricted it in thirteen different ways. Then he got up and said, "I do not object to that. I believe in restricted communion. Sure I do. I said I think the Lord's supper should be restricted." All right then, don't be forever harping on the Baptists for saying that we practice close communion. That is all that we do, restrict it according to the scripture. Read what the scripture says on the subject. You say that these men are all going to hell if they are not dipped by one of your preachers. Then you turn right around and say, "Come right on up and take the Lord's supper with us. Glad to have you." Now you take it back and say, "I believe in restricted communion." All right. "Only," he says, "I object to this feature of Baptist doctrine on that subject. Baptists acknowledge that other people are saved and then refuse them the Lord's supper."

All right. That is exactly what the Bible says do. II Thes. 3:6 says withdraw from every *horse thief?* No. Withdraw from every drunkard? No. Withdraw from eve every *liar? No.* Withdraw from every *murderer?* No. But *"withdraw from every brother,"* B-R-O-T-H-E-R, brother, that walketh disorderly. So when we find a brother walking disorderly and not living according to scriptural order, though he may be saved and a "brother," we restrict the

Lord's supper so he cannot come to it until he lives an orderly life.

And then, again, he failed to notice that I brought out clearly, that the church is to judge who shall be in fellowship and who shall partake of the Lord's Supper. I Cor. 5:7-13 said, "Do not ye judge them that are within?" "Do not ye," talking to the church at Corinth, "judge them that are within?" Every church and every organization in the *world must be the judge of its own membership,* and declare who shall be in fellowship. That is bound to be . And that is what Paul said the church at Corinth was to do.

Now we come to the ruling elders. We learned something that is very, very interesting. I quoted the scripture showing that my friend and his people were unscriptural in their ruling elders. He comes and reads over there in Timothy where "the elders that rule well should have double honor," but he made no reply to my reply in which I said plainly, and gave the scripture to prove it, that these who ruled did it by influence, did it *by leadership* and *not by authority.* The elders in my friend's church, the one that meets right here inside of this building that we are holding this debate in, transact the business for the rest of the members. They decide who shall be the preacher that shall preach for them, who shall hold their protracted meetings, and they also try those who are supposed to be in disorder. The church does not exclude members with my friend and his people. The elders do it. When they go to build a new house the elders decide. If they put a new roof on the house the elders decide. They are in *authority.* And that is strictly unscriptural. Why? Because Matt. 20:25,26 says that "the princes among the Gentiles exercise dominion over them and they that are great have authority upon them. But it shall not be so among you." He said all the eldership they had was just influential elders who led, just leaders, was all. Do you mean to tell me that your elders do not discipline the members? Do you mean to tell me that your elders do not exclude or withdraw from fellowship? You know you do and everybody else knows you do, who knows anything about you. You mean to tell me that when you put a new roof on the house your elders do not decide? You mean to tell me that your elders do not decide every matter of business, and if they consult any of the other members it is merely a matter of consultation and not a matter of right on the part of the membership? I have shown you plainly from God's word that they are wrong on that, as they are wrong on everything.

Now one very interesting thing on yesterday. My friend said, and I am going to have that reduced to writing tomorrow when he gets in the lead, that there is *no such thing as the possessive case in Greek,* and he said that this was not in the possessive case, "the Churches of Christ." All right, now John's head was borne to Herod, that is not in the possessive either. *No such thing as possessive case in Greek, says my friend.* There is *no way to tell ownership in the Greek language,* no way to show possession in the Greek language. This simply says the churches belong to Christ. But what were their names? You can not find "The Church of Christ" in the Bible. It is not there. But he says now if we have churches of Christ, there is bound to be a singular. Is that so? Then "the trees of the forest" is bound to have a singular—*the tree* of the forest. See the point ? A big tree that includes all the smaller trees. Wouldn't that be a whopper? That is what my friend said. The house of Damascus—therefore there is *one big house including all the little houses. Mark you,* his contention is "The Church of Christ" means all of God's people, including all of the smaller congregations. Do not switch off and say if you see a house over here on the corner that is the house at that corner. That is not what we are talking about. You are talking about all of God's people as all in one great big aggregate called "The Church of Christ." It is not in the Bible. It is all in your imagination. You can not find it there. And I offered him ten dollars if he could find it. I surely did. He has not found it yet.

If he will write the passage on the board where it says "The Church of Christ," I will get out of the debate, sign a written statement that I am defeated and go home and never hold another debate while I live. Isn't that fair? I am going to put that in black and white tomorrow. I will agree to quit the debate, acknowledge my defeat, let the world know that I, Ben M. Bogard, (after having held 237 debates and this makes my 238th) am defeated, I am whipped, I am knocked out. I will publish it to the world. If you will publish it in your paper I will publish it in the Searchlight, if you will find where it says "The Church of Christ" anywhere in the lids of the Bible. You contend that you are speaking where the Bible speaks and keeping silent where the Bible is silent; now is a fine time for you to show up. It is simply not there. If he wants words, why, he can have all the words he wants to. Give me the scripture and I will be glad to resign my position, walk out in defeat, in shame, hang my head in shame, say I am whipped once, I am out completely, when he finds The Church of Christ—those exact words in the Bible. That is what he contends for. He says I must find the words "Missionary Baptist Church" in so many words. You can not find the name of your church in so many words, to save your life.

The point is, *the Bible describes the Missionary Baptist Church*; it describes it so you can not miss it if you know what a description means. But he goes *by names*. So if you would call a buzzard an eagle that would make it an eagle. Does calling your church "The Church of Christ" make it that? If so, you can call a horse thief an honest man and that would make him an honest man. If you would call a polecat a skunk it would be correct, but call him a pig and it would not be correct. It would not take the stink off the polecat to call it a pig. So calling your organization "The Church of Christ" does not make it so. My friend seems to think that by his calling this "The Church of Christ," folks will be silly enough to fall in and say, "Why, yes." We can not find it in the Bible, can not find a word about it in the Bible, for it is not there.

Now that complements about everything my friend said and we are ready now to hear what else he has to say in the next thirty minutes. Then my last speech will be had tonight, and we will go on with this debate happy as can be. And I will not start anything else, for I have one eighth of a minute left and therefore I will not continue with any further argument.

Thank you.

Second Day

PORTER'S FIFTH NEGATIVE

Gentlemen Moderators, Mr. Bogard, Ladies and Gentlemen:

It gives me pleasure to appear before you again for the negative of the proposition which my opponent has been affirming—although he did not state to you what the proposition is. Many of you are here for the first time, and you are left dangling in mid-air, wondering what it is all about. The proposition which Mr. Bogard is affirming is that "the church known as the Missionary Baptist Church is Scriptural in origin, doctrine, practice and name." That is the thing he has been trying to prove for four hours yesterday and during his speech this afternoon. I repeat the proposition for those who are here for the first time, so that you may understand just what we're discussing and just what Mr. Bogard is trying to prove.

While it is fresh on your minds I want to take care of his buzzard and skunk. As you know, at the very outset yesterday afternoon, Mr. Bogard attached great importance to the name. Now he is trying to turn the thing loose. One of the very first statements my opponent made in the first few minutes of his first speech was, "Whoever fails to prove the church with which he is identified is Scriptural in name, fails in this debate. I want to emphasize the last part of that proposition—Scriptural in name. Whoever fails to prove that fails in this debate."

Now, Mr. Bogard has failed, and he doesn't attach much importance to the name any more. But he said that calling a buzzard an eagle wouldn't make it so—it wouldn't take the stink out of the buzzard. And calling a skunk a pig wouldn't take the stink out of the skunk. Well, I am sure that's right. But if some men were walking down through the zoo somewhere looking for an eagle, they wouldn't expect to find that eagle in a cage behind the label that said "buzzard." Would you? And if you were walking down through a zoo, looking for a pig, you wouldn't expect to find that pig behind a label that said "skunk." And so if you are looking for a New Testament church, you don't expect to find it behind the label "Baptist Church," because that is not in the Bible. Thank you, Mr. Bogard, for giving us that illustration.

Then to this other part—in connection with that—and I shall go back to the first. He said, "I offered Porter $10 for the passage that said, *The Church of Christ.*" You who were here yesterday remember that I wrote on the board—I have erased it for the purpose of illustrating some other matters—four expressions. Over here I wrote—"Church of Christ," and "Churches of Christ" below it; and beneath "Churches of Christ" I wrote the reference, Romans 16:16, that says, "The churches of Christ salute you." Over on this side I wrote "Baptist Church" and then down below, "Baptist Churches." Beneath that I drew a line.

CHART NO. 1

Church of Christ	**Baptist Church**
Churches of Christ	**Baptist Churches**
— Rom. 16:16	—————

I asked Mr. Bogard to put on that line the passage of Scripture that mentioned either the "Baptist Church" or "Baptist Churches." If you could find "Baptist Church," in the singular number, I would have enough sense to know that if one of them is called the "Baptist Church," a number of them would be called "Baptist Churches"; and I would be willing to take it all. Moreover, if you could find "Baptist Churches," in the plural number, I would still have sense enough to know that if a number of them were "Baptist Churches," one of them would be "Baptist Church." If he would find either the singular or the plural, I would quit the debate and go home and pay him $100 instead. If you'd just find either of them in God's Word—I gave the reference that contained "churches of Christ"—"The churches of Christ salute you;" and I am still insisting that Mr. Bogard tell us if a number of them are "churches of Christ," what would one of them be? You can't have "churches of Christ" without having "church of Christ"—you couldn't have a plural without having the singular. He said, "Oh, yes, you can. The houses of Damascus—you can have houses of Damascus and never have a singular house; and you can't have the singular if you have the plural." What about "the house of Damascus at 15 Vine Street?"—I don't know whether there is a Vine Street here or not—I'm just illustrating. The house of Damascus at 15 Vine Street. Is that singular, Mr. Bogard? All right; we have "churches of Christ." Suppose that covers all the country round about. Then how about "the church" that Paul was writing to, if we just consider one of them? *The church* in Rome, *the church in Ephesus,* the churches in various other places, such as *the church* at Corinth? You take all these together and put them together and call them "churches of Christ." One of them would be "church of Christ," Mr. Bogard. Put it down and tell us about it. Mr. Bogard knows that "the churches of Christ," in the plural number, is in God's word; and if his mind is not strong enough to make the deduction that there must be a singular involved in that plural, I'm just sorry for him, that's all.

Now, then, back to the questions. He said, "My opponent asked me a whole lot of questions—twenty-five of them. He complained about my not answering them." Well, he answered most of them yesterday—I didn't expect him to go back and answer them all again. There were just a few of them that he skipped, and those were the ones that I was complaining about. They were the ones that I was insisting that he answer—not the ones he had already answered—but the ones he had skipped, that he hadn't said *anything* about. Oh, but he says that "first-class debaters quit that long ago." Mr. Bogard, how long is "long ago?" Just how long is "long ago?" I hold in my hand a little book—you've heard of it, haven't you, Mr. Bogard? Hardeman-Bogard Debate? This was held over here in Little Rock, about 1938, I believe it was. And here in one speech, Mr. Bogard asked Brother Hardeman twenty distinct questions. *In one speech!* That was only ten years ago. Was that long ago? "All first-class debaters quit that long ago," Mr. Bogard. Well, here's another debate. This is the Smith-Bogard Debate. This was held in Dallas, Texas, in 1942, which was only six years ago, Mr. Bogard asked Smith those very same questions in one speech—twenty of them. And I gave *him* twenty-five in four speeches and he says that "good debaters quit that long ago." Mr. Bogard.

only six years ago and only ten years ago, asked twenty questions in one speech. Mr. Bogard hasn't been a first-class debater except here in the last six years. All those other years he wasn't, because he asked questions. The fact is it got him into trouble and now he wants to turn it loose.

Now I have a few more questions I want to ask—if the *course* is not beneath a first-class debater.

26. Inasmuch as you claim the church should wear the name "Baptist," would the bride be wearing the name of the bridegroom or of a friend of the bridegroom?
27. If a number of congregations were called "the churches of Christ" in the Bible, what would one of them be called?
28. Is it possible for a child of God to lie and call his brother a fool?
29. In the expression, "the churches of Christ salute you," are not the words "churches" and "Christ" nouns?
30. As nouns are the names of anything, and if this expression is in the possessive case, would we not have nouns or names in the possessive case?
31. Inasmuch as all names are nouns, and you say that names are always in the nominative case, then what parts of speech are dealt with in the possessive case and the objective case?
32. As you say Christ had his bride before Pentecost, do you mean that the wedding of Christ and the church had occurred?

(Mr. Porter hands questions to Mr. Bogard)

I'm not going to take time just now to go over all of these questions which he answered, because we dealt with a number of them yesterday, but the ones that he skipped I want to get to—the ones I talked about awhile ago.

"8. In conversion which man becomes a child of God—the inner man or the outer man?" He said, "Both. His soul is saved now, and the body will be redeemed on the day of the resurrection." Then the body is not saved now. Is that it, Mr. Bogard? Therefore, you have an unsaved child of God. Or, at least, half of the child of God is unsaved. His spirit is saved; his body is unsaved. His spirit is saved now; his body won't be saved until the resurrection. And he went on to say that one of them serves God, and the other one serves the devil. All right; keep that in mind.

"9. Is faith without works living or dead?" He said it is "dead." But awhile ago he answered another question which I asked him—"Is the sinner saved by a living faith or by a dead faith?" He says, "Living faith." That's what he said awhile ago. All right, then, the sinner is saved by a living faith, and Mr. Bogard says that faith without works is dead. Therefore, Mr. Bogard says that the sinner's faith must have works in order to save. Thus he convicts himself by saying the sinner must be saved by works. For, he said, if you are saved by faith without works, you are saved by a dead faith—for "faith without works," he says, "is dead." But the sinner cannot be saved by a dead faith, Mr. Bogard said—it must be a living faith. All right, then, he cannot be saved by faith without works. Thank you, Mr. Bogard. I thought you wouldn't get into a trap like that.

"10. Are the souls of infants pure at birth?" He said, "No." Then later on to another question, Number 25, "Can a person with an impure soul enter heaven?"—he said, "No." Look at this again. Now, the souls of infants are not pure at birth. Impure souls cannot enter heaven. Infants, therefore, if they should die in the same condition in which they are at birth, would go to hell, according to Mr. Bogard's statement. They can't go to heaven. That's infant damnation as sure as you are born. "Oh," but Mr. Bogard says, "We can take care of all of that." How? 1 Timothy 4:10. We are told that Christ is "the Savior of all men"—all men—"especially of those that believe." Therefore, Jesus is the Savior of babies. Just *when,* now, does he save babies? They are not saved at birth—they are born with impure souls. Their souls are impure when they are born; and you say that impure souls cannot go to heaven; so if the child should die right soon after he is born, then he would go somewhere else. How long after it is born, Mr. Bogard, before Christ saves him? Will you tell us about that? *When does Christ save babies? When does he save babies?* As soon as they are born? Four hours later? Ten days later? Or when? When they are born their souls are impure, my opponent says; and he says impure souls cannot go to heaven. Therefore, if infants die as soon as they are born, they are bound for hell, according to Bogard. Swallow it if you want to; my appetite doesn't run that way.

12. (I'm skipping Number 11.) "12. When did your people first take the name 'Baptist Church' or 'Baptist Churches'?" He said, "They never took it. The Lord started it, and it has been going ever since. The Lord named it the Baptist Church." How do you know what the Lord did except what's in the Bible? How do you know what the Lord did except what is recorded here? You admitted both yesterday and today that you cannot find the name "Baptist Church" or "Baptist Churches" in the Bible. Then *the Lord didn't do it,* and you have admitted he didn't. Then you turn around and say that the Baptists didn't take it—that the Lord gave it to them way back there in the days of John —and they have had it ever since. Where do you find it? He hasn't done it; and he can't do it. He's merely putting up a camouflage along that line that's not going to get by.

I want to read to you from some of these Baptist people about this matter. First, I read to you from the testimony of Vedder. In the Short History of Baptists Mr. Vedder says, "The word Baptists, as *the descriptive name of a body of Christians was first used* in English literature, as far as is now known, *in the year 1644.*" That's page 3 of his history. Also he says, "For the fact that *the name Baptist comes into use at this time* and in this way, but one satisfactory explanation has been proposed: it was at this time that English churches first held, practiced, and avowed those principles ever since associated with that name." - p. 3.

Mr. Lofton says, "It may be asked: *When and where did the Baptists take their name?* For centuries they were called Anabaptists, Antipedobaptists, and usually designated, in different countries and periods, by the name of some great leader, or body, holding Baptist principles or peculiarities; but *it was not until the 17th century,* in England, when after centuries of struggle and blood, 'the woman in the wilderness' came finally and fully into the open and *took the general denominational name* of Baptists as we now have it." Lofton-Smith Debate, p. 10. Again, from the same author: "The word 'Baptist' grew out of the usage which began with immersion when Anabaptists were called baptized people, baptized churches, and hence, finally, 'Baptists,' 'Baptist Churches,' and so on. The Baptists had always protested against the name of baptist which implied re-baptism and which Baptists denied upon the ground that those baptized by them from other sects had never really been baptized at all; but *it was not until after 1641* that they could the more effectively get rid of the odious name of Anabaptist by adopting immersion which 'nullified every other form of baptism' and which gave them the claim of being the only people who baptized at all—and hence, the only baptized people, par excellence, Baptists." English Baptist Reformation, p. 244. That's what Baptist historians and Baptist scholars say about when Baptists took their name.

Well, we have another question here: "Is there any history written before the 17th century that speaks of the 'Baptist Church'?" He said, "Yes, Benedict, page 344." Mr. Bogard, will you tell me when Benedict's History was written? When did Mr. Benedict write his history? Seventeenth century? The question says: "Is there any history *written before the 17th century* that speaks of the 'Baptist Church'?" Mr. Bogard says, "Yes, Benedict, page 344. He wrote about Baptist Churches in A.D. 595." Yes, my friends, but Mr. Benedict *did not write before the 17th century*—he wrote *in the 19th century, 200 years this side.* Then he went to Benedict to prove that there were Baptist Churches back *before the 17th century,* when Benedict wrote 200 years this side of that century. That's not what I asked you, Mr. Bogard. I asked you for a history, *written before the 17th century,* that speaks of the Baptist Church. I'd just as soon take Bogard's word for it as to take Mr. Benedict, because he was writing away down this side of that time. I asked you "back of that time." Why did you dodge? Why didn't you just come up and say you can't find it, or produce it, whichever you want to do? If you have it, we'd like to see it. Well, since he gave Mr. Benedict, I suppose he's relying upon him; so we'll let Mr. Benedict speak again. On page 304 of Mr. Benedict's History, we have this statement: "The first regularly organized Baptist Church of which we now possess any account, is dated from 1607, and was formed in London by a Mr. Smith, who had been a clergyman in the Church of England." History of the Baptists, page 304. All right; that's the first one Mr. Benedict could find.

Not only that, but we have others. Mr. Lofton has something to say about it. In his history, The English Baptist Reformation, he said, "It is here devoutly wished that the Baptist denomination, *founded by our Anglo-Saxon fathers* in tears and blood, may rise to wider fields of usefulness and progress and grander achievements." Page 8. Again, "Dr. Angus goes on to give the usual historical citations regarding the Anabaptists of England as far back as 1538, 'for a hundred years,' he says, 'before we hear of Baptist Churches;' but *he fixed the dates 1611 to 14 as the earliest at which any authentic history of Baptist Churches, as such, begins." That's on page 36.* Then, again, "John Smyth founded a church upon the Baptist model, believer's baptism and a regenerated church membership; and, organically speaking, *this was the 'beginning' of the present denomination of Baptists,* though begun with an unscriptural form of baptism." P. 254. Now, Mr. Vedder says, in his history, *"The history of Baptist Churches cannot be carried, by a scientific method, farther back than the year 1611,* when the first Anabaptist Church, consisting wholly of Englishmen, was founded in Amsterdam, by John Smyth, the Se-baptist. *This was not, strictly speaking, a Baptist Church,* but it was *the direct progenitor* of churches in England that a few years later became Baptist, and *therefore the history begins there."* P. 4. Now, then, if Mr. Bogard can find the history beginning back of that, let him give us the proof.

Then to the matter of "from" and "with." He said, "Porter, just quibbled about this—that I said began *from* the baptism of John—when he comes up and reads from my Waybook that says *with.*" "Well," he says, "there is no difference." Why did you emphasize the fact, then, that it wasn't *"with* the baptism of John" when you made the argument? You said it "began *from* the baptism of John—not *with* the baptism of John." I read to you from your Waybook where it said *"with* the baptism of John." So now you say it is all the same. Why, then, did *you make the distinction?* Tell us, Mr. Bogard. He said, "If I did slip in the book, it is still *from."* Well, there is no "if I did" about it. *You did,* and you might as well say you did.

Now, I want to get to the other matter regarding "case." We had a discussion about the case, and Mr. Bogard made the statement, as those of you who were here yesterday know, that "all names are in the nominative case." What was the purpose of that statement? Well, it had to do with the expression in Romans 16:16, "The churches of Christ salute you." He said, "Churches of Christ is in the possessive case, and, therefore, it cannot be a name, because all names are in the nominative case." I showed Mr. Bogard up on that matter.

CHART NO. 3

John reproved Herod
Herod beheaded John
John's head was brought on a platter
The churches of Christ salute you

I took the name *John.* "John reproved Herod." John is a name. In that case "John" is in the nominative case because it is the subject of a sentence. Mr. Bogard says, "names are always in the nominative case." All right, I reversed it and said, "Herod beheaded John." We still have the same name "John," but this time "John" is in the objective case because it is the object of the verb "beheaded." That is not the nominative case there, (pointing to sentence) is it, Mr. Bogard? No nominative case there. In this (points to second sentence) "Herod" is the nominative case, and "John" becomes objective case—the object of a verb. Then I said, "John's head was brought on a platter." Here we have the same name "John" transferred into possessive form—therefore, the possessive case. The same name "John" is one time in the nominative case, one time in the objective case, and one time in the possessive case; and Mr. Bogard is perfectly wrong when he says that "names are always in the nominative case." I showed that nouns are names, a noun is the name of anything, and that case is used only with nouns and pronouns; so if names are always in the nominative case, what are the other cases used for—adjectives, verbs, prepositions or conjunctions? Just what, Mr. Bogard? Please tell us.

Then last night he said, "Churches of Christ is the possessive case." I said, "It is not." *It is not in the possessive case.* "Of Christ" denotes ownership, but the *case construction* is not possessive. I never said that there is not a possessive idea there, but *the case construction is not possessive.* You are wrong, Mr. Bogard, when you say it is possessive case. "Churches" is the subject of the sentence; (pointing to board) therefore, in the *nominative case.* "Of Christ" is a prepositional phrase, modifying "churches," and "Christ" is the principal word of the phrase, the object of a preposition; therefore, in the *objective case.* "Churches" is nominative case and "Christ" is objective; and, therefore, *it is not in the possessive case. The case construction is not possessive.*

I said the Greek has no "possessive" case. Mr. Bogard thought he had something—thought he would make something out of it—but I was trying to get him to "call things what they are." I didn't say there is no case in Greek that indicated possession. He came along and said, "Why, he says there is no way to show possession in Greek." I didn't say that. I was just trying to get him to "call things what they are." You know he said you ought to call things what they are; and he said, "The church is a Missionary Baptist Church, and we ought to call it what it is." I have been trying to get him to tell us if Jesus and the apostles did what they ought to and called it what it was, since they never called it the Baptist Church. So I am calling things what they are. In the English we have "possessive" case that denotes possession. In the Greek we have the "genitive" case that *sometimes* denotes possession. *It doesn't always denote possession but sometimes it does.* But it is "genitive" case, Mr. Bogard. And in this sentence we have "churches of Christ," and my opponent says that *this is possessive case.* What? Churches? If that is the *subject* of the sentence, what is it? So let's call things what they are. Certainly, there is a case in the Greek that denotes possession, and "genitive" *sometimes* does, but it *doesn't always; and, even then,* it is not a strict parallel to the "possessive" in English. If Mr. Bogard thinks it is, we'll put some sentences on the board and let him see whether it is or not.

Now to the engrafted word. "Receive with meekness the engrafted word which is able to save your souls." He said, "Now, here is the engrafted word. The word is the graft. The old man is the stump. And just like you take the graft of the Ben Davis apple and put it into the Crab apple stump, so the graft, the word of God, is put into the sinner." I tried to get Mr. Bogard to tell me whether that graft was in the heart of the sinner, or where, but he hasn't yet.. *What is the stump, Mr. Bogard, into which the graft is put?* You came along and agreed that there is no change in the stock or the stump; it is the same old thing. If the graft is put into the heart of a sinner, the heart isn't changed. Mr. Bogard says there is no change in a man; he is just like he was; there is just a *new nature* put in there—the word of God. The word of God is the graft. What is saved? The word? The man is the same old stump—never has been changed—just as depraved in his body, mind and soul as ever; and, consequently, there is no chance for him to be saved, according to Mr. Bogard. We would like to have him say more about that.

He came to the two natures in Romans 7. He referred to these as the two natures that a man receives. And remember that the graft is not the man. And when the graft is put in, if that is a different nature, it is the word of God that grows and produces fruit, and not the man. So the man has the same old nature left. The word of God is put in man, and it grows, but the man doesn't. The man remains just as sinful as he ever was before.

Now, there are a few things I want to get to, and I haven't much more time. How much do I have? Mr. Blue:

"Three minutes." Porter: "Two minutes?" Mr. Blue: "Three minutes." Porter: "Three? All right."

On Cornelius the Spirit fell. He said, "Porter said he was saved without hearing any preaching." Porter didn't say anything that resembled that or anything that is a forty-second cousin to it. I said, "According to Mr. Bogard, Cornelius was saved before he received the Spirit, because he said the world cannot receive it, and *he did receive* it." He said, "He was saved before he received it." And I said, "*If that is so,* then he was saved before he believed, because Peter said, '*As I began to speak* the Holy Spirit fell'." Mr. Bogard says they were saved *before the Spirit fell.* So they were saved, according to Bogard, *before Peter began to speak.* If he was saved before Peter began to speak, he was saved without faith. I said that was the conclusion of your argument. I didn't say any such thing. I know more about the Bible than to take a position like that. I am just showing what your doctrine is in the matter—what is the conclusion of your argument. You're the man—not Porter.

Then there was closed communion. He says, "Porter gave up." We've always preached that certain people are eligible for communion and only those who are God's children have a right to partake of it. We have never preached anything else. I've never heard my brethren preach anything else. Well, he said, "Well, don't harp on the Baptists." But you Baptists say, "You fellows are all children of God, and you are on your way to heaven. You are good enough to go to heaven and be with us around the throne of God, but you can't be around the Lord's table with us." That's the point.

The ruling elders. He said I didn't refer to them in Mt. 20:25, 26. Yes, I did, and showed you that we didn't advocate any such dominion in the church by the elders as Jesus speaks of in Mt. 20. My opponent claims to have the Scriptural form of eldership, but in Acts 14:23 we read that there were ordained "*elders in every church.*" My opponent has *one elder* in a *number of churches.* So it looks like it isn't quite so Scriptural.

In Mark 13, which has been stressed a number of times already, my opponent speaks again about Christ's leaving the house and the house being the church of the living God. I have shown before that if reference is made here to the church, it was the material which constructs the house, the material out of which the house was to be built; and, in that sense, *he left the house.* I thank you.

Second Day

BOGARD'S SIXTH AFFIRMATIVE

Gentlemen Moderators, Ladies, and Gentlemen:

I am delighted to see my friend make such a miserable failure in his effort to answer what I put before him. If I have ever seen a man so completely addled I do not remember it. He brushes around and beats the brush and makes a noise, but I notice what he says and I will not do like he did, slop over it, try to make people forget what has been said. But I will answer item by item without any sort of failure.

He asked me for a history written before the seventeenth century that called the name Baptist. Catch question. I wanted that to come out good and plenty before I said anything further about it. I quoted from Benedict, page 344, where it said the church was old in the year 595. It said, "Old or Baptist Church." He asked if Benedict was written before the seventeenth century, showing that it is purely a catch question. "Will you name any history on the church at all that is written before the seventeenth century?" That is your question, purely a catch question. I presented a history that gives the account of the Baptists. They were old enough to split in the year 595, called "the old or Baptist Church," Benedict's History, page 344. On page 343 are the names of the members of the Baptist association with thirteen preachers in it. You find a college and Dynawt, the president of that college, on page 343 of Benedict's History, back there in the year 595. You want me to find something back yonder written before the seventeenth century. No matter when it was written, if it is history it is history. I am not running an ancient library. I am giving you history, authentic history, giving you the chapter, the page, and the verse and all about it. Meet facts instead of quibbling around. Show me another history that says something different. I gave you a history. You won't answer it. Then, "Now give me another one, one that was written way back yonder a hundred years before that time." Well, suppose you put it back five hundred years before that time. That would be just as well. I gave you a history that gives the account of the Baptists back there, a whole association of them, and gave you the names and the dates and all that, and you say, "Give me another one." Well, what is the difference? You would not take that if I were to give it to you. If you will not take the one I gave you, what is the use in giving you one earlier than that? If I were to give you one back before the seventeenth century, you would say, "Find one in the twelfth century." If I were to give you one in the twelfth century you would say, "Well, find one back in the fifth or sixth century." Such quibbling as that and call it debating! I would be ashamed. Honest, before God I would be ashamed to face an audience with that kind of quibbling.

You cannot find a history on earth that names a church like you are a member of *even one hundred years ago.* Just name one that has the name, "The Church of Christ," like you have it, with your doctrines and practice back of Alexander Campbell and I will give you ten dollars. No wonder he doesn't like history. He has nothing on his side.

Well, he brought up Benedict, page 304, where it says that "the first regularly organized Baptist Church of which we have any account was in 1607, established by John Smith." He did not have the honesty or the manhood to read the heading of it. It says, "English Baptists," first *English Baptists.* The first one in Arkansas is a whole lot later than that. The first one in America was later than that. "English Baptists" is what he is talking about. Suppose I were to go over here and tell you to write over here to Morewood in Arkansas to the first regular organized Baptist Church in Arkansas and he would have the gall to get up here and say that Bogard said the first Baptist Church in the world was organized over here near Morewood, Arkansas. Remember Benedict was talking about "English Baptists"; the first regularly organized Baptist Church in England was in 1607. That is what Benedict says there. That shows how he is trying to darken counsel by quibbling. I would not do that way if I were you. Honestly, I would not. I would walk right up and face the issue and not try to make people forget it by asking all kinds of silly questions and making all kinds of quibbles.

Now coming to the grammar cases again. We are going to have a good case of this before we get through. (Laughter) We have two full days, two full days before us, understand. And I thought he would come around. Why he says, "I never meant to say there was not any possessive case or means of showing possession in the Greek." You did say that there was no possessive case in Greek. That is exactly what you said, and several took notes on it. And I agreed to leave it to Harding College. Why, he says it is the genitive. Well, all right, the word is the same thing and some English grammars put it genitive also. Why quibble over that thing? In order to confuse some people who may not know and he can get by better with that quibbling than he can by coming right out like a man and meeting the issue.

He says this is not in the possessive case. All right, "Christ's churches." Would that be possessive? "Churches of Christ" is the same thing, showing that the churches belonged to Christ. But what is the name of the church that belongs to Christ? Why, when you name a thing you put it in the nominative case. When you note possession, of course, you use a word that shows possession. Names are in all cases, but the *naming is in the nominative case.* If you do not know that you need to go up here to the school house and get a grammar. The naming of a thing is done in the nominative case. When you do that you use the nominative. John already had the name and you want to express possession, John's head, showing that the head belonged to John. Well Christ is a name here and the church is what belongs to Him, the churches of Christ. Christ's churches. Everybody can see that. My friend sees it. His only point is to try to raise confusion and get you muddled and confused. He ought to meet the issue.

Coming to the word "graft." He talks of the old stump. My friend does not know much about grafting. He thinks you graft in a stump. (Laughter) I never heard of orchard men grafting in a stump. They put the graft in the tree. What is the stump? No stump about it. What is the graft put in? The graft is put in the man. "Receive with meekness the engrafted word which is able to save your souls."

Why, he says that leaves the old nature there. Certainly it does. And I read about both in the seventh chapter of Romans. He made no reply to it. Paul said I, of the inner man, I serve the Lord; I, of the outer man, I do not serve the Lord. There is warfare between the two. He says ,"Why, Mr. Bogard, that will leave the old stump there, the old man unchanged." Exactly so. That old man will stay there till he dies and be raised from the dead a regenerated body, for "we groan within ourselves waiting the adoption, to wit, the redemption of our bodies." Rom. 8:23. On that you have been as silent as death. Our bodies are not redeemed but our souls are redeemed and the two natures hitch up when you become a child of God. When you are born again the graft of the word goes in and that produces another nature, *becomes a part of the man.* Ever after then he will have two natures. He had the old nature to start with and now the engrafted word gives him a spiritual nature that causes him to bring forth spiritual fruit. The point, though, he dodges. A graft never puts itself in. Why do you not say something about that? A graft never puts itself in. If a graft ever gets in, some outside power must put it in. All right, why do you not say something about that? What puts the graft in? There comes the work of the Holy Spirit that you deny. You do not believe there is any Holy Spirit work; that is the trouble with you. I gave him half a dozen passages of scriptures yesterday showing how people had the Holy Ghost, that they spoke by the Holy Ghost and all that before Pentecost and he has been as silent as death on the subject.

Now, lest I forget it, come to Cornelius again. He goes square back on what he said. I brought the point out in Acts 10 where Cornelius was saved before he was baptized. And in the 43rd verse it said "to Him give all the prophets witness," to that fact that you are saved when you believe. Porter quibbled around and asked, "Is your faith a live faith or a dead faith?" I said a live faith. Certainly a faith that is alive *saves a man's soul and then puts him to work.* According to your doctrine, he has got to do some work before he is alive. In other words, a dead horse comes to life when you hitch him up to a plow and go to plowing.

Your faith is not alive before you are baptized. You were baptized on a dead faith and everybody knows that. If your faith was alive before you were baptized then the live faith caused you to be baptized and put you to work after saving the soul. The point to it is that Cornelius got the Holy Spirit before he was baptized. John 14:17 says "Him the world cannot receive." If Cornelius received the Holy Ghost before he ceased to be a child of the devil then Jesus Christ told a falsehood when He said, "Him the world cannot receive." Cornelius was not of the world when he received the Holy Spirit. He was a child of God. And then Peter said, "Can any man forbid water that these should not be baptized which have received the Holy Ghost as well as we?" Peter said they had received the Holy Ghost, and therefore he baptized them. You would not baptize a man like that. You say that he does not get the Holy Ghost until after he is baptized. In fact, you *do not believe he gets the Holy Ghost at all.* That is one of your doctrines. You do not believe in the Holy Spirit at all, except that you have it here in the word. Personal work of the Holy Spirit, you deny, every step of the way.

Now what put that graft in? The man received the graft. The old nature remained and the graft gives him a new nature, so ever after he has *TWO* natures instead of one. And they war one against the other, so says Paul in Romans 7. You deny that. Then, when I brought out the fact that if what you said were true, that when he first began to talk, before he preached any, that they received the Holy Ghost, then they were saved without words when the Bible plainly says they were to hear words by which he and his household should be saved. *He quibbles now,* "No I did not say that; I said if Bogard's argument is true." Bogard's argument or anybody else's argument, *Cornelius had the Holy Ghost before he was baptized.* And there are not enough Philadelphia lawyers in the world to explain that away. He had the Holy Ghost before he was baptized. And Jesus said nobody could have the Holy Ghost except a child of God, therefore Cornelius was a child of God before he was baptized. That is one of the things I will haunt you with till the very last, Friday night. There is plenty more, but that is one thing that is going to be with you to the very last. These folks have got to remember.

Coming now to close communion. Well, well, well! Without answering what I said, he said, "You Baptists say a man is saved and can go home to heaven, but it not worthy to take the Lord's supper." That is exactly what the Bible says. 2 Thess. 2:6 says withdraw from every *horse thief?* No. Withdraw from every *liar?* No. Every *drunkard?* No. "Withdraw from every *brother* that walketh disorderly." There is your brother, a child of God in disorder. And when we find Christian people we recognize as saved but in disorder, we obey the scriptures and withdraw fellowship from them and refuse to fellowship them until they get back in order again. He said nothing in reply to that. Just quibbled over it. You are bound to remember that.

Remember we are going along slowly, taking it as we come to it. What did he say about the church being the judge? Did not I give him the scripture? 1 Cor. 5 said, "Do not ye judge them that are within?" The church judges its own fellowship, judges its own members. He made no reply; the record will show. So, then he has given up on the question of the Lord's supper, close communion. I built a thirteen rail fence around it, stake and rider fence. Everybody knows and the record will show that he let it go up to this present time.

About ruling elders, oh, he dies hard. He switched it off on the plurality of elders now, instead of meeting what I said. I said the ruling elder must be one who ruled by influence and leadership unless it contradicts what Jesus said in Matt. 20:25, 26 where Jesus said "the princes among the Gentiles exercise authority upon them. They that are great have authority over them, but it shall not be so among you." Jesus forbade any such elders as you have. Your elders control the church. Your elders rule the church in the *sense of authority*. You elders decide what shall be done and what shall not be done. Your elders decide who shall preach for you and who shall not preach for you. Your elders decide who will put a new roof on the house. *Authority*. Jesus said it shall not be so among you. One of the worst things about my friend's church is that they have these so-called ruling elders in the sense of authority. I have a right to rule you; you have a right to rule me, if we can do it by teaching and by influence. But no man must be an authority over God's people for Jesus said it shall not be so among you.

You know how they get their elders? The evangelist comes along, like Mr. Porter at this church house here. I read your paper. I keep up with all your papers, practically all. The evangelist comes and he *appoints elders in the congregation right here at Damascus.* The church does not appoint your own elders; the *evangelist does it.* Then that evangelist will appoint the elders and they will be in charge of what? They will control the church. The church does not even elect its own elders. Talk about having a scriptural church government!

Now, I come to some other things before I go any further. I have some other matter I want to put in. We have two more days of this particular feature about the name, "The Church of Christ." He says, "What would that church over there on the corner be?" That is not what you mean when you say "The Church of Christ." You mean *all of God's people, all* of the saved, all that have been born again. That is what you mean by "The Church of Christ." He asks, "What about the church over there on the corner?" That would be *a* church of Christ, if it is Christ's church at all. That still would not be a name. It would denote ownership. There is no such thing, get it now, as a *great big aggregation of God's people called "The Church"* of any kind, the Church of Christ, or anything else. It does not exist—pure guess work. You are not speaking where the Bible speaks when you do that.

The houses of Damascus. Where is *the house of Damascus?* He says, "Why one over here on the corner would be *the house.*" Why, any ten year old boy knows better than that. Where is *the house* that includes all the little houses of Damascus? There is none. The men of Arkansas. Where is *the man of Arkansas* that includes all the other men in Arkansas? He does not exist. The trees of the forest. Where is the *great big tree* that includes all the smaller trees? That is what you mean when you say *"The Church of Christ*" and you know it. You are not referring to a local congregation saying "The Church of Christ." You mean the aggregate and you can not find it in the lids of the Bible. It is simply not there.

Porter said I answered most of his questions yesterday. I am satisfied I did. And I, for good measure, answered them all over again today. I am an accommodating man. Ask some more and I will answer them. He said I asked Mr. Hardeman and Mr. Smith a lot of questions. I certainly did, questions that Hardeman did not try to answer in public. If you read his answers there in public I will give you a nickel. You had the book in your hand. (Laughter) I put them out of business on the question business. I thought they all had sense enough to quit it long ago. I thought you had learned that by this time.

Now, he comes back and perverts again. I am taking my time because I want you to see it. If a baby is born with an impure soul and that baby dies, won't that baby go to hell? There is baby-damnation, boo, hoo. Get the women to weeping about their little babies dying and going to hell. That is your fabrication, not my affirmation. I showed you how babies were saved. Babies in heaven will be singing, "Thou hast saved us by thy blood out of every nation, kindred and tongue," or else you will not allow the babies to sing when they get to heaven. Then I quoted what is said in Timothy where it said He was the "Savior of all mankind, especially to them that believe." There is a blanket salvation for babies and idiots. It covers that case. The blood of Christ covers the baby's salvation and the idiot's salvation without faith. But all who attain the age where they can exercise faith must believe, for He is a special Savior of them that believe. Why do you not notice that instead of trying to get up sentiment here about babies being in hell?

He could not debate, his brethren could not debate to save their lives, without perverting what Baptists believe and then answering their own perversions. You can get up and state that Baptists say so and so and then answer what you say about that, but you can not answer what the Baptists say about themselves. Pay you to try to do that.

Since he brought up history, to history we shall go. The Baptist Church is the only church that can trace its history back to Jesus Christ from Arkansas, now, clear on back to Christ. In the second century, right back to A.D. 150, in Justin Martyr's Apologies there he says, "I will declare to you also what manner we, being made new by Christ, have dedicated ourselves to God . . . They who are persuaded that do believe that those things which are taught are true, and do promise to live according to them, are directed first to pray and ask God, with fasting, the forgiveness of their former sins, and also pray and fast with them. Then we bring them to a place where there is water, and they are baptized." That is the way they did it in A.D. 150. Is that your kind of folks? Pray for salvation? Then after they got it go be baptized? That is the way they did in 150 A.D. Well, now the Bible closed in A.D. 97 and sixty years after that they were doing that way at that time.

The third century. Baxter's Saints Rest, Chapter 8: "Tertullian, Origen and Cyprian, who lived in the second and third centuries, do affirm that in primitive times none were baptized but such as engaged themselves to obey Him." This refers to the Lord, personal obedience to the Lord. Then again, Tertullian's words, page 204: "The person is led down into the water, and with a few words said, is dipped." That was taken in the third century.

In the fourth century Jerome, who lived in the fourth century said, "The Lord commanded His apostles that they should first instruct and teach all nations, and afterwards baptized them that were instructed in the mysteries of the faith; for it cannot be that the body should receive the ordinance of baptism before the soul has received the true faith." (Jerome's comment on Matt. 28:19, 20) Is that your kind of folks? They were not back there, but Baptists were back there.

The fifth century. Chrysostom, who lived in the fifth century, said, "The time of grace, or when a man obtained grace, or conversion, was the only fit time for baptism." That is on century five, page 368. That cuts you out and cuts out infant baptism entirely.

The sixth century, Benedict's History, page 343 (you brought up Benedict first), "From the coming of Austin (A.D. 595) the church in this island (Wales) was divided into two parts, the old and the new. The old or Baptist Church maintained their original principles. But the new church adopted infant baptism, and the result of the multiplying superstitions of Rome." That is in the Benedict's History you quoted. And in the year 595 the church was old enough to split.

The seventh century. Page 344 of Benedict's History gives the names of thirteen Baptist preachers, the name of a college, and tells of a Baptist Association at the beginning of the seventh century. Here it is exactly now, and I want the record to get it. It gave the names of Faganus, Damicanus, Alban, Aaron, Julius, Gildas, Dyfrig, Dynawt, Tailo, Padarn, Pawlin, Daniel, Dewi or David, as noted Baptist ministers in the time of Austin's visit, and that Dynawt was president of the college at Bangor at that time, and was chief speaker in a conference or association of Welch ministers or messengers, who met the famous reformer and had a debate with him on baptism. (This same account may be read in Davis' History of Welch Baptists, pages 8-21.) Now that is the history you quoted from a while ago trying to make out the Baptists started in England in 1700.

Very well, in the eighth century Bede's Eccesliastical History, page 220, says, "Men are first to be instructed in the knowledge of the truth, then to be baptized as Christ taught; because that without faith it is impossible to please God." First saved, live faith, and then baptized. Then in Waddington's History, page 554, it says, "It was asserted that baptism was useless and of no efficacy to salvation." Was that your kind of folks back there at that time? Well, that is what we had back there.

The ninth century. Rebana, chapter four, says, "The catechism which is the doctrine of faith must go before baptism; to the extent that he who is baptized may first learn the mysteries of faith, and the Lord Jesus anointed the eyes of him that was born blind, with clay made of spittle, before He sent him to the waters of Siloam, to signify that he who is to be baptized must first see." Porter says they are as blind as bats till after they are baptized. They don't get the Spirit until after they are baptized. That is not your kind of folks back there. It is the kind we have back there.

Then Robinson's History, page 220, says, "Three things are visible in baptism—the body, the water, and the administrator; and three things are invisible—the soul and the Spirit of God, which are all joined by the word of God." Is that the kind of folks you have back there? *You haven't any back there.* You can not go more than a hundred years behind where you are now. You are a new sect started up by man, a man made organization claiming to be "The Church of Christ." You can not find it in history. You cannot find it in the Bible. It is not there.

Again, in the tenth century. Smaragdo, page 187, and who lived in the tenth century, said, "Men are to be taught in the faith, then after to be baptized therein; for it is not enough that the body be baptized, but that the soul, by faith, first receive the truth." Is that your kind? Did you have any back there at that time?

The eleventh century. Dutch Martyrs, chapter 11 says, "Peter Bruise, a learned author in Toulouse, France, and his numerous followers, were zealous asserters and practicers of baptism after faith and repentance." Twisk, Chronicles, page 423, says, "In this century, the Waldenses and Albigenses loudly asserted and extensively practiced believer's baptism." In this century the Waldenses and the Albigenses had among them those that are what Baptists are now.

The twelfth century. Alburtus Magnus, who lived in the twelfth century, said, page 413, "The law of baptism is not proper but to the illuminated and called, who can draw virtue from the death of Christ."

Thus we have traced Baptists down to modern times.

Time called.

Second Day

PORTER'S SIXTH NEGATIVE

Respected Opponent, Ladies and Gentlemen:

I am before you now for the closing speech of this session. It will just be thirty minutes long. I want to take up the things which my friend has just said; and I'll show you who is quibbling and who isn't quibbling. Incidentally, my opponent said something about the questions asked, and he said, "I asked Hardeman those questions." He said, "I put them all out of business with the questions." Well, it seems you didn't get them all out, Mr. Bogard. It seems you didn't get them all out, because the questions are still bothering you. Well, "I'm good natured, and I answered most of them yesterday—Porter said I did." Such as the answers were. I mean he made a stab at it. Maybe these questions will get you into more trouble as you go along. Why didn't you answer the ones I asked you today? I gave him a list, and he has them on his desk now, but not a single, solitary word did he say about them. And he said if I would ask some more, he'd answer them. Why don't you answer the ones asked? What are you putting it off for? There was a question: "Is it possible for a child of God to get drunk and commit murder." He said, "Yes." Then I said, "If he should die while he is drunk, will he go to heaven or hell?" He said, "He will go to hell." Now, one of two things is true. Either it's possible for a child of God to go to hell or he couldn't die while he is drunk—one or the other. My opponent said, "It is possible for a child of God to get drunk and to commit murder, but if he dies while he is drunk, he'll go to hell." "But," he says, "a child of God can't go to hell." Then, that being so, according to Mr. Bogard, a *child of God cannot die while drunk.* Will you take that position, Mr. Bogard? Can't a child of God die while he is drunk? *Come on now.* You want some more questions? There is one of them—grapple with it. Put it down on your paper there. You'll forget it if you don't. That forgettery of yours works wonderfully. Put it down! *Tell me something about it.* "Is it possible for a child of God to die while drunk and in the act of murder?" Mr.

Bogard says if he dies while drunk and in the act of murder, he'll go to hell. He says it's possible for him to get drunk and commit murder, all right, and if he dies in that condition, he'll go to hell. Then either it's possible for a child of God to go to hell—and you give up your contention about the impossibility of apostasy—or you're going to have to say that it's impossible for a child of God to die while he's drunk. Come on, Mr. Bogard, *put it down* and *tell us about it tonight.* If you don't, I'll put it in writing for you. You haven't bluffed me away from the questions yet. *Come on and tell us.*

I'm going to show you, my friends, what Baptist doctrine is just here—before I go on with this speech. According to Baptist doctrine—you've heard it during this debate already—an unsaved man, before he is regenerated, cannot do anything that's good. Every thing that he does is sin. Mr. Bogard says that if he tells the truth, it's a sin. Even plowing in the field is a sin, he says. If he pays his debts, it's a sin; if he loves his wife, it's a sin—anything he does before his conversion is a sin. Now, I want you to take a look at Baptist doctrine. Before conversion, the sinner, if he tells the truth, commits a sin—he'll die and go to hell; but after conversion he may tell a lie all of his life and die with a lie on his lips and go to heaven. And before conversion, the sinner, if he pays his debts, commits sin—he'll die and go to hell; but after he's converted he can beat every man in the country out of everything he owes, die and go to heaven. Before conversion, according to Baptist doctrine, a man can stay sober, refrain from drinking intoxicating liquors—it's a sin for him to do it—he'll die and go to hell; but after conversion a man can get drunk and stay drunk all his life and, if possible at all, die drunk and still go to heaven. And before conversion, a man, if he loves his own wife, sins—he'll die and go to hell. After conversion he can love every other man's wife and die and go to heaven. That's Baptist doctrine. *Ben M. Bogard will not deny it.* That's just a little sample of it. I have in my hands here a little tract, a pamphlet, written by Sam Morris, who at that time was pastor of the First Baptist Church, Stamford, Texas. The title of this is: "Do A Christian's Sins Damn His Soul?"

On page 1 Mr. Morris says: "We take the position that a Christian's sins do not damn his soul. The way a Christian lives, what he says, his character, his conduct, or his attitude toward other people have nothing whatever to do with the salvation of his soul . . . All the prayers a man may pray, all the Bibles he may read, all the churches he may belong to, all the services he may attend, all the sermons he may practice, all the debts he may pay, all the ordinances he may observe, all the laws he may keep, all the benevolent acts he may perform, will not make his soul one whit safer; and all the sins he may commit from idolatry to murder will not make his soul in any more danger." That's Baptist doctrine. Mr. Bogard, do you endorse what Sam Morris says? That's a question. You want to answer some questions—answer that one. *Do you endorse what Sam Morris says?* Did Sam Morris teach Baptist doctrine in that pamphlet? "All the sins that he may commit, from idolatry to murder, will not make his soul in one bit more danger." Is that Baptist doctrine? Do you endorse it, Mr. Bogard? Yes, I think folks are going to see things as this discussion goes on. I'm here to help them see. Bogard said he never saw a man so "addled," and how I "slopped" over him! Well, it looks like he got some of the slop on him. He's certainly covered up with it—whatever it is. (Laughing) He's certainly covered up with whatever it is, and he never can redeem himself from it. He's fallen—hopelessly gone. Then he said, "Porter came with a history, and he wanted a history written before the 17th century." And he said that was a "catch question." "I gave him Benedict, and Benedict said that Baptists were old in 595." Yes, but when did Benedict write? I said, "Give me a history written before the 17th century." You said, "Benedict." You either, my friend, intended to mislead these people and make them think Benedict wrote before the 17th century, or what did you intend to do? That's what I asked for. Why didn't you say, "I can't find a history written before then"—just shell down the corn and be honest about it? Why did you say "Benedict" when you knew I asked for one *written before the 17th century?* Why did you select one written in the 19th century and say this is it? Then come back and say,

"Oh, that was a catch question?" Yes, Bogard got caught. "Oh," he says, "name any history written before the 17th century." Do you say there's not any, Mr. Bogard? Be careful now! Do you say there's not any history written before the 17th century—concerning churches? If there is not any history written before the 17th century concerning churches, as you intimated, then, since you admit that you can't find it in the Bible, and there was no history written before the 17th century concerning churches at all, then it couldn't be in the first sixteen centuries. So Mr. Bogard admits he can't find "Baptist Church." He can't find it during the first sixteen centuries, for, he says, there's no history written then about churches. Then the only time he can find it is at the beginning of the 17th century—and what I said stands. "But" he says, "you can't find any history anywhere that speaks about your church—the church you are a member of." I gave him Romans 16:16, the greatest history in the world—a divine history—and that said, "The churches of Christ salute you." Let him find "the Baptist Churches salute you," and we'll admit we're on the same ground—we're in the same predicament. But until you find either the singular or the plural of "Baptist Churches" in the Bible, the cases are *not parallel.* And this audience can see it, whether Mr. Bogard can or not. I'm sure he can—he's feeling it too. "Oh," he says, "it doesn't make any difference when it's written." Well, that's funny. "It doesn't make any difference when it was written, just so it's history." Well, I read to you some of these histories which said the first Baptist Church was founded in the 17th century. And that the name "Baptist" was first taken by the Baptist people about 1644. That was history, wasn't it? You said it didn't matter when it was written— so will you take that? Was that authentic history? But he came back to Benedict, and he said, "Now, Porter made a mistake on this, and he was not honest enough to tell you this was English Baptists. He was talking about English Baptists." Certainly so. I knew that all the time. Mr. Bogard, did you not know that the first Baptists of which we have any record in the world were ENGLISH BAPTISTS? That's the point. (Laughter) They were not your kind, of course, but *the first were English Baptists.* You can't find any kind before that. *Certainly, they were English Baptists.* You can't find *any back of them*—that's the point I'm getting at. Well, he said, "If I should say the first Baptist Church in Arkansas was at Moorehead, Arkansas, would Porter think I meant that was the first Baptist Church in the world? Well, if I never heard of one before that time, or at any other place—if I had never read in any literature about one anywhere else, or had any information about one anywhere else but that, I would have to make that decision, I guess. But if there were some somewhere else, and before that one was established over there, then I'd point out the place and the time and the record that shows it and show that Mr. Bogard was wrong about it. And so that's the thing for him to do. If there were Baptist Churches before the 17th century in England, then the thing for him to do is bring up the proof of it and produce the record of it. And then we will see that Mr. Benedict was wrong. He said, though, that Porter implied that this was the first one. No, Porter didn't. If there was any implication, it was Benedict that implied it, Mr. Bogard—not Porter. That wasn't Porter's statement—that statement was made in the very history you quoted from—the very one that you gave to prove Baptist Churches back before the 17th century. I quoted from it. And he said, "The first regularly organized Baptist Church of which we possess any account, dated from 1607." Porter didn't imply anything. I just read you what your history said—the very one that you introduced —that's all.

Then he said we're going to have a good "case" of this before it's over. I think Bogard has one already. He talked about this possessive case and "Churches of Christ" and "Christ's Churches." He said, "Well, what's the difference —Churches of Christ and Christ's Churches? Well there's a difference in *case construction,* Mr. Bogard. Absolutely. If you don't know enough about seventh grade grammar to know that, then I'll teach you a little lesson right here. "Christ's Churches" and "Churches of Christ." Let's do a little digramming—it will take a little time, but I want you to get this. All right, "Churches—salute you." "Churches of Christ salute you." (Pauses during the diagramming on the black board) Now then, we'll get the same thing down on this other. "Churches salute you." "Christ's Churches salute you."

CHART NO. 5

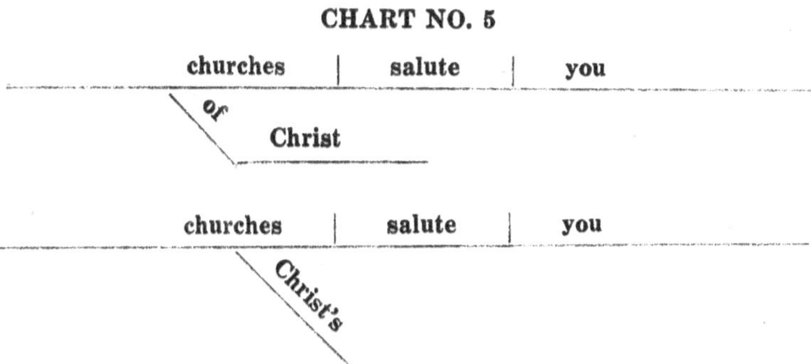

Now, then, is there a seventh grade grammar student in this house that doesn't know there's a difference in case construction? "Churches salute you." What's the subject? "Churches." What case is that in, Mr. Bogard? Nominative or possessive? "Churches salute you." "Churches" is the subject of the sentence; therefore, it is in the *nominative case.* "Churches of Christ"—"of Christ" is a prepositional phrase, modifying "churches." "Of" is a preposition. "Christ" is the principal word in the prepositional phrase, and your seventh grade grammar tells you that the principal word of a prepositional phrase is in the *objective case.* Will you let me have your book? Turn to "case" and let me read it. "The principal word of a prepositional phrase is in the *objective case.*" All right, then, "churches" is the *nominative* case, and "of Christ" is the *objective* case. All right, let's see if the case construction is the same. "Christ's Churches salute you." "Churches." Well, by the way, that's still *nominative* case. "Christ's" in this sentence is not a prepositional phrase, nor a part of a prepositional phrase, but a possessive modifier, given the office of an adjective; and, therefore, is in the *possessive* case. All right, the word "Christ's" in this sentence is in the *possessive* case—"Churches" is in the *nominative* case. In this sentence (pointing to first sentence) "Christ" is in the objective case and "churches" in the nominative case. Mr. Bogard, didn't you know that? Have you studied grammar all of these eighty years, or nearly, and don't know enough about grammar to know that "Christ" is in the objective case and this down here(pointing to "Christ's") is in the possessive case; and it's a *different case construction?* Didn't you know enough to know that? If you didn't, I'm ashamed of you.

Now, then, my opponent did a lot of boasting about this, and he said, "Why, this is all in the possessive case." Why, he said, "Take this to the college over here, to Harding —Harding College—over at Searcy and ask them about it. All of this is possessive case." Well, it happened we did that very thing. I have a telegram from Harding College that came today, Mr. Bogard, regarding this passage— "Churches of Christ salute you." You said, "I'll take what they say." "We don't have to have any Campbellite Greek," he says, "or Baptist Greek, or anything. We'll just take what Harding College says." You remember his saying that yesterday. All right—here is the telegram, coming from W. L. Burke, the professor of Greek in Harding College at Searcy, and he says, "All the churches in the nominative case plural. Of Christ in genitive case singular. Both together make complete subject of the verb." So it's a nominative construction, and not possessive construction as Mr. Bogard has been contending. (Laughter) There it is. All right, Mr. Bogard, now will you agree with me and Harding College that "churches" is in the nominative case? If so, let's shake hands. (Bogard speaks: "I'll agree with this telegram, but I won't shake hands with you.") (Laughter)

He agrees with the telegram. All right, the telegram says that "churches" is in the *nominative* case, doesn't it? Look at it, Mr. Bogard. (Holds telegram down) Does it say, "Churches in the *nominative* case?" Does it say that? Or did I misread it? Did I pervert it, Mr. Bogard? Or does it say that?

(Bogard speaks: "Yes, sir, you perverted it.")

I perverted it? (Laughter) All right; you read it to the audience—you read it to the audience. (Porter hands telegram to Bogard)

Bogard speaks: "I'll read it tonight." (Laughter)

Yes, sir, it hurts him. "Churches" is the nominative case and "Christ" is in the genitive case.

(Bogard speaks: "Amen.")

Amen; but the whole construction *is not possessive;* and I told you all the time that "Christ" is in the *genitive* case in the Greek and in the *objective* case in the English. Therefore, the genitive case in the Greek corresponds, in this passage, to the objective case in the English and not to the possessive case. Now, don't you keep that—I want it back.

Bogard speaks: "I'll use it tonight."

All right; I want you to use it. Now, then, my friends, here we are. "Churches of Christ salute you." "Churches" in the nominative case, and Mr. Bogard doesn't need to say that it doesn't say it. "Of Christ"—"Christ," the genitive —the very thing I've said all the time, and the genitive corresponding to the English objective. Is this the objective case in English, Mr. Bogard? Tell us about it. You want to answer some questions. You said, "I'll answer all of them." *Tell me—put it down—don't forget it*—Is "Christ" in the objective case in the English? Mr. Bogard sees it, and the rest of you do too.

Then he came along and said, "Why, we can use names in all of the cases." Will you stay with that and shake hands with me on that, Mr. Bogard? "We can use names in all of the cases?" Do you agree with that statement you made? Or do you want to take it back?

Bogard speaks: "Neither one."

Neither one? (Laughter) Well, he's on the fence now. (Laughter) He doesn't know where he belongs. (Laughter) He won't agree with it and he won't take it back. (Laughter) Absolutely, my friends, talk about a man being "addled." (Laughter) My opponent said, and the record will bear me out in it—and if he disputes it we'll play the record back and show him up as we did yesterday—that you can use "names in all the cases." And the record will also bear me out that yesterday Mr. Bogard said, in the very first speech he made concerning this matter, that "names are always in the nominative case." Will you dispute that you said that, Mr. Bogard? Am I perverting it? Better not say I am or we'll play the record. All right; Mr. Bogard said "names are *always* in the *nominative case,*" but he gives it up today and comes back and says "you can use names in *all the cases.*" Well, then, they are not always in the nominative case, are they? And Porter is right, and Bogard is wrong. He doesn't know now where he wants to land.

But he said, "The *naming* of things is in the nominative case." The naming of things. Well, that isn't what you said. You said, "All names are in the nominative case." That means they are always in the nominative case. Do you want to change it—want to revise it before it goes to print? He would like to revise some of those that are already in print. I wonder if he wants to revise this one before it goes to print. Yes, he has a "case" on his hands he's not able to take care of.

Then about the graft in the stump. Oh, he said, "Porter had the graft over here in the stump." He said, "I didn't say stump—I said tree." Well, I don't care. He said grafting was never done in the stump. But I'm sure he is wrong about that too. But we'll just let it be "tree" then. Over here the graft . . . (Pauses—writes "graft" on board) Over here the tree, Mr. Bogard. (Writes "tree" on board)

CHART NO. 6

Graft — Tree

What is the tree? And what is the graft? You've told what the graft is—you say the "graft" is the word of God. I have been trying to get you to tell me what the "stump" is and you wouldn't do it. And so you say it's the "tree" and not the "stump." So now what's the "tree?" What's that graft put into? The heart? The soul? Or what? If the graft is put into the heart or the soul, it doesn't change the heart or the soul, because Mr. Bogard says it doesn't change the stock into which it goes. It remains the same—the same old unchanged nature. So the heart has the word placed into it by the direct operation of the Holy Spirit. But it doesn't change the heart. It's the same old thing that was there before. Well, he said, "But who ever heard of a graft getting in by itself." Who ever heard of a graft wanting to get in, Mr. Bogard? You tried to literalize an illustration there.

Who ever heard of a graft wanting to get in? But you've heard of people wanting to be saved, haven't you? Yes, you've heard of people wanting to be saved, but did you ever hear of a graft wanting to get into a tree? You're trying to attribute to a literal graft, or a literal tree, the matter of intelligence.

Romans 8:23—the body is redeemed. Yes, *redeemed from death* but *not redeemed from sin.*

Again we note Cornelius. "Went back on what I said." No, I didn't. I still stand on what I said. Bogard said, "Cornelius was saved *before* he received the Spirit." But Peter said, "He received the Spirit *as I began to speak.*" If Bogard told the truth, and if Peter told the truth, then he was saved *before Peter began to speak.* Why? Because Peter said that the Holy Spirit fell *"as I began to speak."* Bogard says Cornelius was saved *before he received the Spirit.* Let this mark represent the time when the Spirit fell (Drew perpendicular line on board)—when Peter spoke —"As I began to speak." Bogard says he was saved over here (pointing before the line) *before* he received the Spirit. All right; if the *coming* of the Spirit and the *beginning* of Peter's speaking took place *at the same time,* then the salvation took place *before,* Mr. Bogard. So, according to Bogard, he was *saved before he heard Peter speak*; and, therefore, saved without faith. It still stands, Mr. Bogard. You're still in it and you can't get out.

Then to closed communion. I want to get to that. You said, according to 2 Thessalonians 3:6, we should withdraw fellowship from those who walk disorderly—"every brother." It didn't say "every thief" and "every liar"—or "every drunkard," but from "every *brother* that walketh disorderly." "We should withdraw fellowship," he says, "until they get back in order again." Can you withdraw fellowship from someone you never did have any fellowship with? When were the Methodists ever in fellowship with you? How are you going to *withdraw* fellowship from them? They've never been in fellowship with you. Ah, this refers to people *in the church,* Mr. Bogard—not people who are *out of the church.* Then in connection with that, 1 Corinthians 5:12, 13, about the church "judging them that are within." It says we have the right to *"judge them that are within."* Yes, but are Methodists within, or are they without? Paul is writing to the Church at Corinth. Were there Methodists in that church? You say that was a Missionary Baptist Church. Did it have some Methodists in it? Some Presbyterians in it? And did they judge them that were within? Why, you're judging some that are without—you have the wrong passage. Because you say the Methodists and Presbyterians are *without*— they're on the *outside of your church.* But this deals with persons *within the church,* Mr. Bogard. You'll have to hunt for some other Scriptures.

Regarding the ruling elders and Matthew 20, he claims that I referred not to that, but I showed that the dominion that Jesus referred to was such that could not be exercised in the church, and I believe that as strongly as he does. And in 1 Peter 5, verses 2 and 3, Peter showed the same thing—that they shouldn't be "lords over God's heritage but examples to the flock." We believe that same thing. Oh, he says, "Your elders rule the whole thing—they decide who'll preach and every thing." No, that's just a misrepresentation. Somebody might fail to rule well—somebody might some time get aside from the truth, but just because somebody does that, that doesn't mean that that is endorsed by us as a people—not at all. Mr. Bogard, who *ruled for the Baptists* when you came to this debate? Tell us! Who *ruled for the Baptists?* You brought up Damascus. You talked about "the Church of Christ at Damascus did so and so." *Who ruled for the Baptists in Damascus* when you came to the debate? Now *you answer that question.* You want a question.

You said that no aggregate group is called "the church" anywhere in the Book. Well, I read from Acts 9:31 last night, and he hasn't paid a bit of attention to it—just as silent as he can be about it. I'm going to read it again. That "the church," in the singular number, never refers to an aggregate group larger than a local congregation—that's his contention. We want to read it again. "So *the church throughout all Judea and Galilee and Samaria* had peace, being edified; and walking in the fear of the Lord and in the comfort of the Holy Spirit, was multiplied." Now, then, the Revised Translation says *"The church in all Judea—throughout all Judea and Galilee and Samaria."* Was that *one local congregation?* If not, then that is "the church," in the singular number, embracing a number of congregations, Mr. Bogard. Come back and try your hand on it. You haven't touched it— *you haven't even referred to it.* Get up here and do a lot of bragging and blowing and bluffing and boasting and talking about what you can do, and what you've done, and things of that kind, and just pass this by. Talk about somebody "quibbling." Why, you don't get close enough to some of those things even to quibble about them. *So come on—do something about it.* We want you to handle it. We want you to grapple with it. The audience has a right to know something about this. So you come and tell them about it.

What about "the baby?" All right, "the baby." You said, "Now the baby is saved." Yes, he said, "I've showed you *how* the baby is saved." Yes, Mr. Bogard, except you didn't give any Scripture for it that said anything about babies. But we'll just grant that you did show us *how* babies are saved. Just grant you that babies were lost to start with—I don't believe a word of it—but we'll just grant you that it is so. Did you show us *when* babies are saved? That's what I asked you. Now, you said babies are born with an impure soul, and an impure soul can't go to heaven. *When are babies saved?* The minute they are born? Two hours after they're born? Six days after they're born? Or when? "Oh," he says, "I answered all his questions." You see how he answered that. Just sits there as silent as a tomb—as still as a statue—and makes no effort to even take a note on it. *When are babies saved?* But we're going to read another passage, if I have time, from Mr. Bogard's Way-Book. This concerns the "fall of man." He says, "Man was created holy, and under the law of God. By voluntary choice he fell from his holy state and brought all mankind under the curse of sin." (That's the babies too, you know.) "Not by choice are his descendants sinners, but by nature, being void of holiness, inclined to evil, and therefore, under just condemnation without defense or excuse." That's

Baptist doctrine—that's Bogard's doctrine. That's found on page 78 of this edition of the Baptist Way-Book.

Then to this history. How much time do I have?

Mr. Blue: "About a minute and a half."

Mr. Porter continues: Then to some history here, beginning with the first century and on down. He quoted from Justin Martyr—and the quotation *didn't say one word* about "Baptists" or "Baptist Churches." The third century he quoted from Baxter—and Baxter *didn't say one word* in that about either "Baptists" or "Baptist Churches." He quoted the fourth century from Jerome. *Not a word* was said in the quotation about either "Baptists" or "Baptist Churches." In the fifth century he quoted from Chrysostom—but *not a word* was said about "Baptists" or "Baptist Churches." In the sixth century he quoted from Benedict—and that's the first place he found "Baptist Church"—and that was written in the 17th century to prove what was in the sixth century, or in the 19th century, rather, to prove what was in the sixth century. He came to the seventh century and made another quotation from Benedict to prove his succession, and he found "Baptist Churches" there, but it was from a man's writing who was living in the 19th century and not in the seventh century at all. Then the eighth century he quoted from Bede—and *not a word* said in the quotation given about either "Baptists" or "Baptist Churches." I noted all of them as he read them. Also from Waddington. And Waddington's statement mentioned neither "Baptists" nor "Baptist Churches." In the ninth century he quoted from Rebana—and Rebana said neither "Baptists" nor "Baptist Churches." And the 10th century from Smaragdo—and he mentions neither "Baptists" nor "Baptist Churches." In the 11th century, the Dutch Martyrs—and they say *nothing* about a "Baptist Church." And in the 12th century he quoted from Magnus—and *not a thing* was said about "Baptists" or "Baptist Churches" in that quotation. That's as far as he got. When he gets to those other centuries I'll show the same thing about them. He went back there to prove the existence of the "Baptist Church." Why, I thought you said there wasn't any history back in those days about churches.

Now, you went back there to get some history to show there were Baptist Churches back there—but not a single quotation mentioned "Baptist Church" or "Baptist Churches," or even "Baptists"—except the ones you gave from Benedict who wrote in the 19th century; and I would just as soon take Bogard. Thank you.

Second Day

BOGARD'S SEVENTH AFFIRMATIVE

Gentlemen Moderators, Ladies and Gentlemen:

In just two hours this first feature of our debate will be at an end. Tomorrow we will take up the other side of the proposition. I shall endeavor the best I can to answer everything my friend said and give a rehearsal of what we have had so as to make it fresh on your minds and rivet the thoughts on your minds.

He asked if it were possible for a child of God to die while drunk or in the act of murder. Those questions were all catch questions put out for the purpose of confusing. I answered him at least twice on this. What was my answer? That if a man should go into wickedness and die in wickedness, fall into sin, remain in sin, not be rescued by the almighty God according to promise, it would flatly contradict God's word. 1 John 3:3 that he has not noticed up till now, said, *"Every man that hath this hope in him purifieth himself."* If every man does that who has this hope in him then none will fall so as to be utterly cast down. If that comes to pass then God's word has failed. *It makes God a liar.* Then Romans 8:28 says, "We know that all things work together for good to them that love God." If a man can go so far in sin (die in sin), as to go to hell then that certainly would not be for his good. And hence God's word would be a lie again for it said all things work together for good to them that love God.

Another question he put to me is this, where he read from Sam Morris' book. I have not seen Sam Morris' book. I do not know whether I endorse what he said or not, for I do not know the qualifications he put around that statement that seemed to be so heretical. But here is what I think Sam Morris meant. He meant that all sin was laid on Christ. In Isa. 53 it says that "on Him was laid the iniquity of us all," and that includes every kind of sin. I do not know whether I endorse Morris or not. I have not seen his book. The first time I ever saw it was when he held it up here. But I do say this, that no matter what sin a man commits, the blood of Christ is quite sufficient to cover it. Otherwise, the Lord's word has utterly failed.

Then he comes to history and wants to have a history that was written before the seventeenth century. What is the difference when the history was written? Historians gather their facts from the records—sometimes *court records,* sometimes the *accounts of the persecution of good people* and all that sort of thing. And from these fragments they gather together what we call history. No matter when the history was written it is as true one time as another unless it contradicts the facts.

So I read from Benedict's history where the Baptists were "old" in the year 595, so old that a Baptist church divided at that time. He said give me one written before the seventeenth century that says that. If I would give him one written before the seventeenth century he would want to go back to the twelfth century or some other time for another history. Please reply to what I gave you and not ask for more until you do reply.

Then he read from Benedict's History, page 304, where Benedict said the first church of which we have any knowledge, the first Baptist Church, was in 1644 and founded by John Smith. I called his attention to the fact that that was English Baptists he was talking about—headed with great big headlines, *"English Baptists"*—the first English Baptist Church, 1644. But he said that means all churches everywhere. Well then, Benedict flatly contradicts himself for he said on page 343 plainly, that the church was old in the year 595. That is enough on that.

Then we come to his diagram on the board about that grammar. Oh, we have had some wonderful times about the grammar. If I had been my friend, I would have been ashamed to have presented this telegram from the teacher of Greek, W. L. Burke, in Harding College—the very thing I knew I would get if I called for it. Now what does it say in "the churches of Christ salute you"? What does that sentence mean? What is the grammar of it? Says Mr. Burke, *"All the churches in the nominative case, plural."* All right, names—church names, are in nominative like I said. All names are in the nominative. *"Of Christ" is in genitive case, singular.* What is genitive? Possessive. Possessive case, singular. All right, *"Christ," genitive singular, possessive case,* genitive case, "Christ's churches salute you." The *churches that belong to Christ* salute you. That is exactly what I have been saying all the time. *Christ is in the genitive singular.* Genitive means possessive. What does He possess? He possesses the churches. The church is His property. There you are, and they both together make the complete subject of the verb. What is the subject of the verb? "The churches of Christ," Christ's churches, the *churches that belong to Christ.* That is the subject. What is the verb? "Salute". Salute you. The Lord's congregations, Christ's churches, salute you. No where does it say "The Church of Christ" salutes you. But Christ is genitive singular and genitive means possessive case. What does He possess? The churches. And Christ's churches, (the names not given), the congregations of Christ, *the congregations that belong to Christ, salute you.* "The churches of Christ" is *not the name,* but the churches are owned by Christ. It means that, or it means nothing. *That is why I was willing to leave it with Harding College.* I have it right here in my hand. He sent for it and saved me the trouble. Genitive means possessive. If it does not mean that what does it mean? Possessive case, genitive case—well, what Christ owns. "Christ" is genitive singular, possessive singular. What does Christ own? He owns the churches. Christ's churches, the Lord's churches. That is *not giving the name.* It is the property of the Lord. So that fixes it. Here is your telegram. Take it back and make the most of it. It fell right into my hands just exactly like I wanted it to do, to jointly request Harding College to tell us what it means. And they told it. Christ owns the churches.

Now Johnson's dogs bark. (Laughter) Whose dogs? Johnson's dogs. What do they do? They bark. They bark at you. Johnson's dogs bark at you. Is "Johnson's dogs" the name of the dogs? Certainly not. It denotes ownership. The dogs belong to Johnson.

Now my friend thinks he has found one place where the term church includes all the people in a given territory and reads from the ninth chapter of Acts about the churches—"the church in Judea, in Galilee, and Samaria." There was only one congregation at that time. Read the eighth chapter, if you please, where they—the Jerusalem church—were scattered abroad. And they that were scattered abroad went everywhere preaching the word, and that church was the only church there was, the only congregation there was. It was scattered all over Galilee, Samaria, and Judea. There was only one congregation—just like, for instance, if some terrible thing should happen to this congregation and scatter us all over the county. It would still be only one local congregation with its membership scattered temporarily. So he got nothing from that.

Now I come to his questions. I always answer everything my friend puts up. And the reason I did not answer them this afternoon was that I wanted to have time to get the scriptures and make intelligent answers. Now here is the first one of the last batch of questions.

"Inasmuch as you claim the church should wear the name of Baptist, would the bride be wearing the name of the bridegroom or of the friend of the bridegroom?" But listen, the church is not yet married to Christ. In Rev. 19 it says the marriage of the lamb has come. That is prophecy. A bride is a lady about to be married or who has just been married. And the church is the bride of Christ in the sense of one who is engaged. Read, if you please, II Cor. 11:3 where Paul says, "I have espoused you," talking to the church, "espoused you to one husband that I may present you as a chaste virgin to Christ." The church is now in its virgin state, not yet married. The marriage will take place in the nineteenth chapter of Revelation, yet future. And besides that, if the church is to wear the name of the bridegroom, it would not be Christian or Christ's at all, because Matt. 1:21 says, "Thou shalt call His name Jesus," not Christ. Christ is His title. And so if you are going to be *called by the name,* let it be *Jesusites* or *Jesuits* or something like that, certainly not Christian. You would not call a woman after her husband's title —Lawyer Smith and Mrs. Lawyer? No. Mrs. Smith. Certainly not Mrs. Lawyer. Mrs. Christ? Certainly not. Very well, next one.

"If a number of congregations are called the churches of Christ in the Bible, what would one of them be called?" It would be called *a* church. That is what one of them would be called. Certainly, not *the* church. If there is a number of them you would not call any one of them *the* church. And then even if you did, it only denotes that the church belongs to Christ, Christ's churches or Christ's church.

"Is it possible for a child of God to lie and call his brother a fool?" Yes. And he is in danger of hell fire when he does, but he is protected from that danger by the blood of the Lord Jesus Christ. My friend does not seem to have any idea of the protection furnished by the Lord Jesus.

The next question is, "In the expression 'Churches of Christ salute you' are not the words churches and Christ nouns?" Certainly. And "the churches" is in the nominative and Christ is in the genitive. Christ owns the churches. Certainly that answers that, as Prof. Burke of Harding College says.

Then the next question is the thirtieth question. "As nouns are names of anything, and if the expression is in the possessive case, would we not have nouns as names in the possessive case?" Certainly, we have noun as names in the possessive case and all cases. But when you name a thing you do it with the nominative case. When you denote possession you do it with the genitive or possessive case. And "Christ's" is in the genitive there; it denotes possession. He possesses His churches and Christ's churches salute you. Inasmuch as all nouns are not in the nominative, *but all the naming is in the nominative.* You can not name a thing in the possessive. You name it in the nominative. You denote possession in the possessive case. Now that is sufficient on that.

One more. "If you say Christ had His bride before Pentecost do you mean that the wedding of Christ and His church had occurred?" It has not occurred yet. I have already answered that. In Rev. 19 it says, "Let us rejoice and be glad for the marriage of the lamb is come," way over yonder in the future. That answers the question my friend asked, and complemented all that he said.

Now listen, when I ran a line of Baptist Church succession from the time of Christ clear up to the last century, what did my friend say? He said, "Why, it didn't say Baptist Church anywhere up along the line." I read to you over and over again where it described what they did in the first century, second century, third century, fourth century, and fifth, sixth, seventh, eighth and ninth century what they did, describing what they did. And some said "Bapists" and others described it so that it could not mean anybody else. And I turned to him and asked him if he had anybody back there like that that he could find descriptions of and he made no reply.

Then, coming to the Lord's supper we will come to a fine conclusion. The Lord's supper is restricted, restricted to church members, orderly church members. That is what Baptists mean by close communion. So that thing is settled forever in this community to all those who have listened. Do not ever talk to Baptists with close communion. Your man, your representative, has said he believed in that very same thing only he thinks that when a person is a child of God, no matter who he is, he ought to take the Lord's supper. But the trouble with him is that he thinks *nobody is a child of God unless he has been dipped by one of his preachers.* And that makes him have double and twisted close communion. My friend Porter will not get up here and say anybody is a Christian, anybody is saved, he will not get up here and say anybody is on the road to heaven, unless he has been dipped in the water by him or some other preacher like him. See the point? That reduces the thing down. He does not believe in communing with anybody or having the Lord's supper with anybody except members of his church, of his own order. Why, that is the closest kind of close communion. He not only refuses to take the Lord's supper with them, but sends them to hell by his preaching. Now that is settled. We have that thing all fixed good and plenty, and thank the Lord for it.

Now I come a little further along the line of history. I did not quite get through today in tracing the line of Baptist churches from Christ down to the present. I will go further with it right now. I am going to give the testimony of unquestioned historians who were supposed to know what they were talking about.

I will give Alexander Campbell, the founder and establisher of the church of which my friend is a member. You say, "Well, that is not proved." Well, you wait and see if that is not proved when we get through two days of following him. (Laughter). You wait and see if it is not proved. But I will give Alexander Campbell anyhow. If you deny that he is the founder of your church, you are bound to acknowledge that he was a great man and a scholar. And here is what he says in Campbell on Baptism, page 409. He said, "From the Apostolic age to the present time the sentiments of Baptists and their practice of baptism have had a continued chain of advocates, and public monuments of their existence in every century can be produced." Then again he said, Campbell on Baptism, page 409, "The Baptist denomination in all ages and in all countries has been as a body the constant asserters of the rights of man and the liberty of conscience." Now if you say Mr. Campbell was a liar, you call your daddy a liar. (Laughter). You call the founder of your church a liar. If you say he told the truth then I have fastened it on you that the Baptists have come all the way from Christ down to the present time. No use to get excited over this thing. Take it easy. And the further we go the happier we will all get. (Laughter).

Now here is a Methodist historian, John Clark Ridpath. Who is he? Well, he is the teacher of history in the Methodist University in Indiana, Dupaw University, and here is what he says on page 59 of Church Perpetuity: "I shall not readily admit that there was a Baptist church as far back as A.D. 100, though without doubt there were Baptists then as all Christians were then Baptists." Who said that? John Clark Ridpath. Who was he? He was teacher of history in Dupaw University. He wrote Ridpath's History of the World. It is the biggest history we have of that sort. So we got it from Alexander Campbell, the founder of my friend's church, and from John Clark Ridpath, the great Methodist historian.

Then here comes what Benjamin Franklin said in Living Pulpit, page 348. "If popery was born too late or is too young to be the true church, what shall be said of those communions born in the past three centuries? They are all too young, by largely more than a thousand years. No church that has come into existence since the death of the apostles can be the church of the living God." I am going to prove tomorrow and next day—I make the assertion now without proof, but let you know what is coming—that the church of which my friend is a member was founded by Alexander Campbell in 1827 and so, according to Benjamin Franklin, any church that was started up since the time of Christ can not be the one that Christ established. Very well.

Reading in Jones history, page 353, we find, "As for the Waldenses, I may be permitted to call them the very seed of the church since they are those that have been upheld, as is absolutely manifest, by the wonderful providence, so that neither those endless storms and tempests by which the whole Christian world has been shaken for many succeeding ages and the western part at length so miserably oppressed by the Bishop of Rome, falsely so-called, nor those horrible persecutions which have been expressly raised against them were able to so far as to prevail as to make them bend or yield in voluntary subjection to the Roman tyranny and idolatry." That is talking about the people that were called Waldenses and *among them* were our Baptist people as everybody acknowledges.

And then I come to Beza, a Presbyterian and a successor of John Calvin. And now such testimony ought to have some weight with people who believe anything in history at all. My friend has been quoting history and I am matching his history.

Oliver Cromwell, speaking of the Waldenses, said, "Next to the help of God it seems to devolve upon you to provide that the most ancient work of pure religion may not be destroyed by this remnant of the ancient professors." That is Jones' History, page 330. And Oliver Cromwell, who was the dictator of England, called the Waldenses the most ancient stock of pure religion. Here is what he says in the preface of the French Bible, the first French Bible that was ever printed. They say that they have "always had a full enjoyment of heavenly truth contained in the Holy Scriptures ever since they were enriched with the names of the Apostles themselves, having in manuscript preserved the entire Bible in their native tongue from generation to generation."

Thus we have it from historian after historian that the Baptists have come all the way down from Christ to the present time. What more do you want? What more is necessary? I traced the line today and have a little book here that you can buy, if you wish it, and read for yourself in full with all the historical references. And my friend merely said, "Why, he did not find the word Baptist, he did not find Baptists." You have his bare word against the record of the historians.

Now what have we found? We have found this, that the church began with material prepared by John the Baptist. Who was John the Baptist? He was one sent from God. That made him missionary, for missionary means one who has been sent on a mission. John 1:33 says, "He that sent me to baptize." Very well, he was sent to baptize. That made him a Baptist, for one who has been sent to baptize, authorized to baptize, is a Baptist. Therefore, he was a Missionary Baptist.

He prepared the material that the church was organized with by Jesus Christ and I read, plainly, in Acts 1:21, where one must be chosen to succeed Judas, "who has companied with us all the time that our Lord Jesus went in and out among us, beginning from the baptism of John." There is a company of baptized believers associated with the Lord all the time. Beginning when? Beginning from the Baptism of John. How long? Clear on down till Christ was taken up from among them. Then that company received the commission. In Matthew, the last chapter, it says, "Go ye therefore and teach all nations, baptizing them in the name of the Father, and of the Son, and of the Holy Ghost, teaching them to observe all things whatsoever

I have commanded you and lo, I am with you alway, even to the end of the world." So that church that began right at the close of John the Baptist's ministry with nothing but John's baptism, organized by the Lord Jesus Christ Himself, and stayed with Him all the time during His personal ministry till He was taken up from us, received the commission to go teach all nations. Since He sent His church to go teach all nations that makes it a missionary church. He sent His church to preach and baptize. That makes it a Missionary Baptist Church. And so it started Baptist. The first one was Baptist and continued Baptist all the way through His personal ministry, and remained Baptist to the end, and now is Baptist because, "Lo, I am with you alway, even to the end of the world."

When Jesus left the world, what did He do? Mark 13 said "He left his house and gave his servants authority and a work to do and commanded them to watch for ye know not when the master of the house will return." So He left His house. Can you leave this house if there is no house here? I have called you to witness: You could not leave this house if there is no house here. We are inside these four walls. Could you leave it if it were not here? Christ Himself could not do that. He left His house. He could not leave a thing He did not have.

Well, what is His house? I Tim. 3:15 says "the house of God which is the church of God, the pillar and the ground of the truth." He promised to come back to that house. He said. "Watch, for in such an hour as ye think not, the son of man will return." He is coming back to this earth again, a thing which my friend denies and his people deny. They deny that Christ will reign on earth with His saints. And that promise was made to nobody in the world but Baptists, as I have just proved to you beyond all question if you are reasonable.

Now this is all going on record and everybody can read it in book form later on, I am quite sure. I do not think there will be any slip in having it printed in book form. And in that way we will be better educated in the service of the Lord.

Now that church that our Lord established, beginning from the baptism of John, taught the doctrine of salvation by grace. Eph. 2:8-10. "For by grace are you saved, through faith, and that not of yourselves; it is the gift of God."

Time called.

Second Day

PORTER'S SEVENTH NEGATIVE

Gentlemen Moderators, Mr. Bogard, Ladies and Gentlemen:

I shall be glad to take up the things which my opponent has just said and show you again that he is at sea without a rudder. He came to the questions which I gave and gave his answers to them; so I want to notice something about those questions. But before I do so, I want to call attention also to two questions which he answered this afternoon.

One question was: "Which man do you take into the Baptist Church—the inner man or the outer man?" Mr. Bogard said, "Both." Both the inner man and the outer man. That was question, I believe, number 18, in the list. Then in question number 24, I said, "Which man do you turn out of the Baptist Church—the inner man or the outer man?" He said, "Both." All right, both the inner man and the outer man are taken into the Baptist Church, and both the inner man and the outer man are turned out—when a man is turned out. But question number 22 I asked him, "Is is possible for the spirit of a child of God to sin?" He said, "No." And now, Is the spirit the inner man? He said that the inner man serves the Lord, and the body, or the outer man, serves the devil. Do you remember? That was his words this afternoon—the inner man serves the Lord; the outer man serves the devil. He takes both of them into the Baptist Church—both the servant of the Lord and the servant of the devil. Then, when he turns them out, he turns both of them out.. Now, Mr. Bogard, what I'm wanting to know is: Since you say the inner man cannot sin after conversion why turn *him* out? Mr. Bogard said in one of his debates that his soul is just as pure as God Almighty himself. So after conversion Mr. Bogard says that the spirit, or the inner man, of a child of God *cannot sin.* Now, Mr. Bogard, I want to know why you turn *that man* out? *The inner man cannot sin.* All the sin committed after conversion, according to Mr. Bogard and Baptist Doctrine, is committed by the outer man. He goes right on serving the devil until the resurrection or until he dies—and the inner man cannot possibly sin. Mr. Bogard says the soul, or the inner man, after conversion is just as pure as God himself—there is no possibility of his sinning. Then, Mr. Bogard, I want you to tell me—Why do you turn the *inner man* out? He hasn't done anything; he hasn't committed any sin; he hasn't done anything that is wrong; he can't possibly do anything that is wrong. Why do you turn him out? Do you turn him out for what the outer man did? All the sins are committed by the old body, the outer man. The spirit is not responsible for it. Why do you kick him out? So we asked him that question. He said to ask him any questions—he would be glad to answer them. *Let him answer that.* Why turn the inner man out of the Baptist Church since the inner man cannot possibly sin?

Then to the other question which I asked him. "If a sinner should die while he is drunk, will he go to heaven or hell?" He said, "He would go to hell." He said these are catch questions and are intended to confuse. Yes, and they seem to have Mr. Bogard pretty badly confused. A child of God *can* get drunk—he *can* get drunk and commit murder—Mr. Bogard said; but if he dies drunk, he will go to hell. Then he says a *child of God cannot go to hell.* So he cannot die drunk—that's the point. Mr. Bogard came on to say if he remains in sin, then it contradicts God's word. Well, that isn't so—that is merely Bogard's assertion. We'll deal with that presently. In other words, it sums up to simply this: God will not let a man die while he is drunk—because if he dies drunk, he'll go to hell—and Mr. Bogard says that a child of God *can't* go to hell, but he *can* get drunk. So God will not let him die while he is drunk. You know there's a big threat of World War III coming up just now, isn't there? And people are very fearful of the atomic bomb. You know how to be safe from that thing? Get drunk and stay drunk—if you are a child of God. Even the atomic bomb cannot kill you—because, if it does, it makes God's word contradict itself. (Laughter) The word of God contradicts if an atomic bomb can kill a child of God while he is drunk. So if you want to be sure that you will not be killed in the next war that will be fought by the atomic bomb—if you are a child of God—just get drunk and stay drunk, and you'll be safe. You will not need any bomb shelters at all. I would like to see him fix that up.

Now, then, to 1st John 3:3—we're going to deal with that. This is what he says that makes it contradict God's word. "Every man that hath this hope in him purifieth himself, even as he is pure." Mr. Bogard, this says "Every man *purifieth himself.*" Now, that is putting it back on the *man.* You say that God takes care of all of that. But this says, "Every man purifieth himself." And then, Mr. Bogard, I want to know *which man he purifies?* Now, to which does he refer—the *inner man* or the *outer man?* He doesn't purify the *outer man,* does he? Because you say *he* goes right on serving the devil—is not redeemed till the resurrection. So he *doesn't* purify the *outer man.* Well, does he purify the *inner man?* You say, "No, God took care of that at his conversion." Fixed him so that he never could sin anymore; and he doesn't need to purify that. So the man that hath that hope in him *is already purified in his soul* and never can become impure; and so he can't do that himself. Neither can he purify his body—the outer man—because that remains a servant of the devil until the resurecction—goes right on sinning. So, according to Bogard, that thing *can't work either way.* The man can't purify his soul. He can't purify his body.

Now, that gets back to this. You know, we've got him off the stump and up a tree, and he's still up the tree—right where this graft grows. (Laughter) The graft is the word of God put into the tree. I've been trying ever since Mr. Bogard introduced this argument to get him to tell me what the tree is—with respect to the man. Is it his heart? His soul? Or what is it? Mr. Bogard, *whatever it is,* you said it didn't change the tree. It doesn't change the old stump—that remains the same. And if that tree is the heart— if that tree is the soul—then the graft, he word of God, being put into it by the Holy Spirit, doesn't change the heart, or the soul, of man. Why don't you answer that? You say it's not fair to miss anything. But I've just been pressing that, and pressing that, and pressing that, almost in every speech, and you haven't said *one single, solitary word* about it. What's the matter with you, Mr. Bogard? *Are you afraid of it?* Come up and try your hand on it.

Then, regarding Sam Morris, he said, "I don't know whether I endorse what Sam Morris said in these seemingly radical statements." Well, they're no more radical than you've been making all the time. Why, you've been declaring all the time that a man can't possibly sin so as to be lost. Why, you went right on just following that and said that all the sin is laid on Christ; and if a man sins, the blood of Christ covers it all. Well, that is just exactly the same principle that Sam Morris introduced. That whatever you do will in *no way endanger your soul.* Any sin you may commit, from idolatry to murder, will not endanger your soul in the least. I didn't ask you if you endorsed what Sam Morris meant. I don't know what he meant. I suppose he meant what he said. Maybe he didn't. Maybe Baptist preachers never mean what they say—I don't know. But I just suppose he meant what he said. I merely asked Mr. Bogard if he endorsed what Sam Morris *said.* I'm not asking you to endorse what he *meant.* If he didn't mean what he said, I don't know what he meant; but I want to know if you endorse what he said—that all the sins that a man may commit—that a child of God may commit—from idolatry to murder will not make his soul in one bit more danger. Do you endorse that, Mr. Bogard?

Then he came to the history and said, "What difference does it make when it's written? They got it from the records." Well, Mr. Benedict said on page 304, and that's the history introduced, that "the first regularly organized Baptist Church of which we have *any account—*" I suppose "account" means "record," doesn't it? "The first regularly organized Baptist Church of which we have *any account* (or record) dates from 1607." So that's his own history that he introduced. But "it means English Baptists." Yes, I admitted that he referred to English Baptists, but the English Baptists were *the first Baptists on earth.* That's the thought. So let him find some Baptists back of them that were not English Baptists, back in some history before that. Well, while we're on that we're going to have some more to say about Benedict. He quoted from page 343 of Benedict to prove that there were Baptists back in 595. So we want to look at that just a moment and see something about it. Mr. Benedict, when you refer to "Baptists" in history, what do you mean? When you use that term "Baptist" in history, do you mean, Mr. Benedict, what Mr. Bogard makes you mean—that it is a regularly organized Baptist Church like the one at Damascus or over at Little Rock? Is that what you mean? Let Mr. Benedict tell us what he means. I think he is qualified to do it. In Mr. Benedict's History of All Religions, page 198, he said, "The peculiar sentiments of this denomination having spread so much *among people of all opinions*, to affirm that a man is a Baptist, *proves nothing more than that he rejects infant baptism, and holds to believer's baptism by immersion; he may be a Calvanist or Arminian, a Trinitarian or Unitarian, a Universalist or Swedenborgian, for some of all these classes come under the broad distinction of Baptists.*" That's what Mr. Benedict says he means—when he speaks about "Baptists" in those ages back there; that's what he says Baptist historians mean.

All right, then, to the Harding College telegram. He said, "I'd be ashamed to introduce this." I don't see why. He agreed exactly with the very contention I made all the time and made Bogard admit that he'd been wrong all the time, because, the telegram says, "All the churches in the nominative case." Bogard said, "Yes, that's just like I said it was— 'all names in the nominative case'—just like I said." Why, you went back on that this afternoon. You said it yesterday, but you took it back today. Now, you've come back and said it again. "That is just like I said—all names in the nominative case." But that isn't what Mr. Burke said, the professor of Greek up at Harding College. He didn't say "all names are in the nominative case;" but he said the expression, "all the churches" is "in the nominative case." He was quoting from the Revised Version. The Revised Version says, "All the churches of Christ salute you." He was just giving the quotation from that Scripture. "All the churches in the nominative case." He didn't say, "All names in the nominative case," but "all the churches"—that is, that expression in Romans 16:16 is "in the nominative case, plural." "Of Christ in the genitive case singular." And "Both together make complete subject of the verb." That's exactly the contention I made. I said all the time that "churches" is in the *nominative case*. "Of Christ" is a prepositional phrase, modifying it. "Christ," being the principal word in the prepositional phrase in the English language, is in the *objective case*—the object of the preposition. Have you ever said anything about that, Mr. Bogard? *Have you ever said one single word about that?* Tell me, Mr. Bogard, in the English expression, is "Christ" in the *objective case* in that sentence? I just "double-dog dare" you to answer it. Will you do it? All right. In the Greek Grammar it is in the *genitive case*, and I said that "Christ" is in the *genitive* and in the *objective* in the English—but "churches" is in the *nominative*. And my opponent said the expression, "churches of Christ," is in the possesive case. He comes along now and says, "I agree with W. L. Burke up there that 'churches' is in the nominative case." Well, then, you are wrong—you've been wrong all the time. That's what I've been contending for, and I'm not ashamed of it, because it's exactly what I have contended for. Well, he said more about that. No where do you find "the church of Christ salutes you." Mr. Bogard, I found in Romans 16:16, "The churches of Christ salute you." Now, then, I tell you—Can you find anywhere that it says "the Baptist Church salutes you" or "the Baptist Churches salute you?" Either of them—I don't care which you find—just find the singular or the plural, and I'll be satisfied to take them both. He won't even make an attempt to find either of them because he knows he can't find them. Well, but more about it. He said, "Johnson's dogs bark." " Johnson's dogs bark." He said, "That's not the name." Yesterday he said the names were Spot, Trip and Trailer. And I asked how he found out their names were Spot, Trip and Trailer. (Laughter) How did he learn that? If Mr. Johnson hadn't told him that those were the names of his dogs, could he have told by looking at them that they were? If Johnson had merely given the description of those dogs, could he have told what their names were? What about that any way? Their names were Spot, Trip and Trailer, but if there had been no record and no information given about what their names were, Mr. Bogard would have never known. And so he says that the name "Baptist church" is not found anywhere in the Bible. Then, how do you know it's the name of the church of the New Testament since there's nothing said about it?

Then "the church is not married" is his answer to one of the other questions. Now, about the church wearing the name of the bridegroom. He said, "The church is *not* married." He gave 2nd Cor. 11:3—"I have espoused you to one husband." So the church is now only engaged to Christ—the wedding will take place when he comes again. The church is not married to Christ, and, therefore, has no right to wear His name. Of course, during the period of engagement she has a perfect right to wear the name of a friend of Christ. (Laughter) John the Baptist said on one occasion, "I'm not the bridegroom—I'm a friend of the bridegroom." And so during the period of engagement the church, the bride, that's about to be married, has a right to wear the name of a friend of the bridegroom and not the name of the bridegroom. Mr. Bogard, if the woman who became your wife, during your period engagement, had insisted on wearing the name of your friend, I wonder if the ceremony would ever have taken place. (Laughter) That's mighty bad, but I'm not through. I'm not through yet, Mr. Bogard. I hold in my hands the Hardeman-Bogard debate. I want to turn to it and note some statements here made. On page 167 of the Hardeman-Bogard debate, Mr. Bogard made an argument based on Isaiah 54 concerning the widowhood of the church, endeavoring to show that the church became a widow when Jesus died. He said, "At no time has this picture been fulfilled except the time that Jesus died on the cross, left his church in confusion, and crushed. They thought everything was ruined, but when he rose from the dead, like a widow happy when her husband comes back, they were refreshed and had a lively hope renewed within them." Then on page 186, 187, "And I wonder if Jesus Christ didn't actually die, and leave the church in gloom and despair, and then when he rose from the dead, and came back and the husband was restored, I wonder if they didn't say there was begotten within them a lively hope by the resurrection of the dead." That's what Mr. Bogard said ten years ago—that the church became a widow when Jesus died. It has been 1900 years since Jesus died. Mr. Bogard now says that the church is not married to Christ and will not be until he comes again. Now, Mr. Bogard, I want to know—How can a woman become a widow 1900 years before the ceremony takes place? (Laughter) Here it is—in black and white. This is your debate. You said it, didn't you, Mr. Bogard? You said it, didn't you? Mr. Bogard said it and made an argument upon the widowhood of the church—trying to prove the church in existence before Jesus died, because she became a widow when he died. Therefore, she became a widow 1900 years, maybe ten thousand years, before the ceremony will be said. I want to know how a woman could become a widow hundreds of years before the ceremony is said, Mr. Bogard? That's another one he'd like to revise. (Laughter)

But now, then, regarding the history, he referred to his line of succession. I want to show you what he has said about history. He's been advertising the Bogard-McPherson debate during this debate, and here is what he says. Mrs. McPherson endeavored to prove miracles by means of history. Mr. Bogard says on page 56: "You can prove any absurdity by appealing to history. I went into this debate believing that we were to take the Bible as our rule and not history." (Well, that's the way I went into this one, Mr. Bogard. I went into this debate believing that we were to take the Bible as our rule and not history.) "For that matter, you can get many to testify right now that they have been healed." And on page 57, the next page, "The Bible is our rule and if they testify contrary to the Bible, their testimony is false no matter what history you read it in nor who says it." It is *our rule* in *this debate,* and if you find history that testifies contrary to the Bible, Mr. Bogard says that testimony is false, no matter what history you read it in—nor who says it. So, if you can find some Baptist history saying that there were Baptists back yonder in the days of Christ, why, that's contrary to the Bible—because the Bible says nothing about it. And so the history is wrong; I don't care whose history it is. Mr. Bogard says that's so. Do you want to revise that one too, Mr Bogard? That's another thing.

He said, "Now if you want to wear the name of Jesus, you can't call yourselves 'Christians,' you've got to call yourselves 'Jesuits,' because his name was Jesus." He supposed there's a woman—her husband is a lawyer. She says, "I'm going to call myself Mrs. Lawyer." The name is Smith, and she is not going to wear the name "Smith" but is going to call herself Mrs. Lawyer—wearing the title. And "Jesus" is the *name* and "Christ," the *title*. Well, Jesus had a friend whose name was "John"—the Book says his name was John—just as definitely as it says the other's name was Jesus. And he was also called the "Baptist," and that was his title, just as much as "Christ" was the title of Jesus. So, according to his illustration, Mrs. Smith might come in and say, "Mr. Smith, I'm not going to wear your name—I'm going to wear your title. No, I'm *not* going to wear your title either, but you have a friend whose name is John and his occupation or his title is carpenter. I'll not even wear *his name* but I'll wear *his title* and so call myself Mrs. Carpenter. That's what Mr. Bogard says. The church *will not wear the name* of Jesus—she is not married to him. The church will *not wear the title of* Jesus. The church won't even wear the *name* of John, the friend of Jesus, because then you'd have to call *them* "Johnites." So they just take *his title* and call them Baptists. They just wear *the title* of a *friend* of Christ—not even *his* name. Thank you, Mr. Bogard; try again.

Bogard said, "Campbell is the founder of the Campbellite Church." And he quoted from Baptism, on page 409, that the "sentiments of Baptists" and their "practice" had advocates "in every century" and also "the Baptist denomination in all ages." And he said, "If you dispute what he said, then your daddy is a liar." Well, how about your stepdaddy, John Smith? I don't suppose you could call him a direct daddy, because he was an English Baptist, you see, and established the first Baptist Church that we know anything about. The first one of any kind. And Bogard can't find one of any kind back of that. (Laughter) So I just told you it must be his step-daddy, or maybe it was his granddaddy, or something of that kind. (Laughter) But, Mr. Bogard, why were you not honest enough to tell what Mr. Campbell meant when he made those statements about there being "Baptist sentiments in all ages"? Why did you just give that and try to put it off on this audience that Alexander Campbell meant that there were Baptist churches like the one in Damascus, and like the one in Little Rock that you're a member of, and like these others around over this country? Why didn't you show that Campbell had no such idea in mind? Why did you just give a little statement like that and claim that that is what Campbell meant? Why didn't you read enough to show what Campbell meant? Here's another quotation from Campbell. This quotation is made from Ford's Repository. It was published in the Tennessee Baptist of December 22, 1883. It was republished in the Orthodox Baptist Searchlight of August 25, 1943. Mr. Bogard published it and commented on it. And here is what Alexander Campbell says about it: "The grand peculiarity from which the Baptists have their name is found in the Scriptures as a part of Christianity and is simply this: *To require faith and repentance, as previous to baptism,* and *to immerse the subject* professing faith and repentance in water, in the name of the Father, Son, and Holy Spirit. This is the peculiarity from which Baptists have their name. *All that believe and practice in this way are Baptists;* and *all that do not are not Baptists.* I now proceed to show that the Baptists have existed in every century from the Christian era to the present day." Campbell, what did you mean when you said there were "Baptists in every century"? *People who practice believer's baptism by immersion. Anybody* who practiced that, Campbell said, was a Baptist. And those who did not practice that were not Baptists. Mr. Bogard, you published that in your own paper. *You knew about it.* Why did you skip it? Why did you try to leave the impression on this audience that Alexander Campbell meant that there were organized Baptist Churches, like you represent, in all ages? He had no such idea in mind. He meant exactly what Mr. Benedict meant and what other Baptist historians mean when they refer to "Baptists" in history—

simply *somebody who believes in baptism by immersion and in baptism of believers* instead of infant baptism. That's what he meant; that's what Campbell said he meant. And Bogard knew that he said it, because he commented on part of this passage in his own Orthodox Baptist Searchlight not long ago. And yet he comes up here and skips the whole thing and tries to make you believe that Campbell endorsed his idea of Baptist succession. *There's not a word of truth in it.* The same goes for Ridpath and Franklin. Ridpath said, "All Christians were then Baptists." Well, he had the same idea in mind. And Jones and Oliver Cromwell referred to the "Waldenses"—went back and referred to the Waldenses as being "the most ancient stock of pure religion." Well, I didn't know I called for "Waldenses." I called for "Baptists." I know you can find Waldenses mentioned back in those days, but we want to know something about Baptists. That's the question.

But those ancient sects would not be fellowshipped in any Baptist Church today. We have evidence of that from the history which my opponent has introduced, and I'm sure that it will stand just that way. Armitage, one of the main historians on which he depends, said, "Dr. Abel Stevens says: 'Obscure communities, as the Cathari of the Novatians, the Paulicians, the Albigenses, and the Waldenses, maintained the ancient faith in comparative purity from the beginning of the fourth century down to the Reformation.' *These and other sects held one or more distinctive Baptist principles, but none of them were thorough Baptists, through and through.*" Now, that's what one of his histories says. And Lofton says, "And so we are accustomed to speak of far more unbaptistic sects before them—such as the Montanists, Novatians, Donatists, Paulicians, and the like, *who would not now be fellowshipped,* ecclesiastically speaking, *in any regular Baptist Church in America.*"—English Baptist Reformation, Page 76. Ah, so that's true regarding Baptists! Then this quotation from Franklin simply said that no church that came into existence since the apostles could be the church Jesus built, but he didn't say a word about Baptists. So that's a misconstruction of the statement made by Franklin.

That gets all of those, and if I have skipped anything, now I'll get back to it. I may have just a little time. Yes, I believe—how much time do I have? Mr. Blue: About two and one-half minutes.

Mr. Porter continues: Well, all right, during those two and one-half minutes I'm going to show you what Baptist histories say about the matter. My opponent has tried to trace the history of the Baptist churches through all the ages back, and he gave you that little pamphlet, and read from that little pamphlet, and said to read it for yourself. Well, if you bought it, read it; and if you find the name of Baptist or Baptist Church mentioned in those quotations he gives in that little pamphlet, except those he quotes from men who lived since the 17th century, you come and show it to me. And show it to Bogard too, because he'd like to find it. All right, then, regarding church succession, Mr. Vedder says, "By some who have failed to grasp this principle, there has been a *distressful effort to show a succession of Baptist churches from the apostolic age until now.*" Vedder, Pages 7, 8. Armitage says, "Robert Robinson has well said: *'Uninterrupted succession is a specious lure, a snare set by sophistry,* into which all parties have fallen'." History of the Baptists, Page 2. He also says, "The very attempt *to trace an unbroken line* of persons duly baptized upon their personal trust in Christ, or of ministers ordained by lineal decent from the apostles, *or of churches organized upon these principles,* and adhering to the New Testament in all things, *is in itself an attempt to erect a bulwark of error.*" And that's one of the very Baptist historians he quotes from to trace Baptist succession. Mr. Armitage says it can't be done . . . the very attempt to do it is "an attempt to erect a bulwark of error." (That's on page 2.) Then, again, on page 9, "But *the pretense that any one communion* now on earth *can trace its way down from the apostles,* in one line of fidelity and purity of New Testament teachings, *is to contradict all reliable history.*" And, then Mr. Lofton, "Crosby, with *all the English Baptist writers* I have read, *repudiates the doctrine of visible succession, in any form, among Baptists.*" *Lofton's History,* Page 77. On page 113 he speaks of "the *unprovable* and *impossible doctrine of visible Baptist Church Succession.*" And on and on it goes. Mr. Benedict, the one he's been using tonight, says, "I *shall not attempt to trace a continuous line of churches,* as we can for a few centuries past in Europe and America. This is *a kind of succession to which we have never laid claim;* and, of course, *we make no effort to prove it.*" History of Baptist Denomination, Page 51. Mr. Bogard, that's Benedict, the very man you've introduced to prove Baptist Churches in all ages. And Mr. Benedict says it can't be done—in the very history you've quoted from. Why do you ignore all these facts and then get up here and try to prove to this congregation that Mr. Benedict endeavors to prove Baptist Churches in all ages, when *he says it can't be done?* I thank you.

Second Day

BOGARD'S EIGHTH AFFIRMATIVE

Gentlemen Moderators, Ladies and Gentlemen:

I am coming now to my last speech on this proposition and I am very happy over the situation. I shall notice what my friend said and pass on to review so that all will have in their minds the things that we have been debating all day today and all day yesterday.

He says, "Why turn a man out of the church when his soul is perfect, does not commit sin?" Mark you, he has never answered what I said on that. I John 2:9 says "that which is born of God does not commit sin." Somehow he forgot that. Why turn a man out of the church, then, if his soul does not sin? The Bible says turn that incestuous man out for the destruction of the flesh. That is why, to bring his flesh into subjection, keep that subdued. That is the answer to that.

He says suppose he dies in wilful sin, gets drunk, stays drunk. Why, he said an atomic bomb could not kill him. And they laughed about it like that was funny. The Bible plainly says in 1 John 3:3, "Every man that hath this hope in him purifieth himself, even as he is pure." Is that true, or is that false? Well, my friend came back and said, "He purifies himself"—no matter whether he does it or the angels of heaven do it or God does it. It says every man that hath this hope in him purifieth himself, even as he is pure. And he guesses that if he turns out to be a reprobate and dies that way, what will become of him? He will be lost in hell, he says. All right, then every man has not purified himself. And if every man has not purified himself that hath this hope in him, then the Bible told a positive falsehood. *You can not prove your doctrine of falling from grace except by giving the Bible the lie.* It says "every man" that hath this hope in him, *not nearly all,* not all those except those that turn out bad and go to the dogs or the devil, but "*every man* that hath this hope in him purifies himself, even as he is pure." So that shows nobody will get drunk and stay drunk in order to show God that God can not kill him. Just such nonsense as that is quibbling, purely quibbling, flatly contradicting God's word.

Then Romans 8:28. We come back to it. We know that *nearly all* things work together for them that love God? No. We know that *nine hundred ninety-nine things out of one thousand* work for good? No. All *except one thing* work for good to them that love God? No. But it says "*all things* work together for good to them that love God, to them who have been called according to his purpose." Now, if something works so as to cause me (I love God) to fall from grace, lose my salvation and die and go to hell, that is a flat contradiction of the statement that all things work together for good to them that love God. You cannot make your suppositions to answer for God's word. God's word says plainly that all things work together for good to them that love God. And if you fall from grace that will not be to your good. If you go to the dogs and the devil that will not be for your good. The thought is simply this, that God has charge of us and that He will take care of us and will present us faultless before the presence of His glory in His own time.

Romans 6 answers you. "Shall we continue in sin that grace may abound? God forbid." You say, "Why, just get drunk and stay drunk. Just lie drunk all the time. And while you are drunk the atomic bomb could not kill you." Shall we continue in sin that grace may abound? God forbid. The Bible says of those who take a position like that, that their "*damnation is just.*" That applies to you. That is what you said you would do if you could get by with it. You said you would just get drunk and stay drunk and lie drunk all the time to keep God from killing you. Well, friend, the Bible answers you on that by saying, "Shall we continue in sin that grace may abound? God forbid."

Then he said, "What about that blood covering the sins, Sam Morris' argument, what about that?" I John 1:7,8 said "the blood of Jesus Christ his Son cleanses us from all sin." My friend said if you do real bad the blood will not cleanse you from all sin. So Isaiah 53 is wrong when it says "on him was laid the iniquity of us all." What about that blood covering anyway? Let me read over here, if you please, in Romans the fourth chapter and the very thing he has for us is given here. "But to him that worketh not" (fourth chapter and fifth verse on down) "but to him that worketh not but believeth on him that justifieth the ungodly, his faith is counted for righteousness even as David describeth the blessings of the man on whom God imputed righteousness without works saying, blessed are they whose iniquities are forgiven and whose sins are covered. Blessed is the man to whom the Lord will not impute sin." The blood of Christ covers all sin, I do not care how bad you may make it. It says the blood of Jesus Christ His Son cleanses us from all sins. And "blessed is the man whose iniquities are forgiven, whose sins are covered." If the blood of Christ does not cover all sin then there is no use for us to try if it only covers just some small sins, some of the ordinary sins like little white lies and things like that, does not cover lying, stealing, and murder and things like that. The blood of Christ *cleanses us from all sins and blessed is the man whose sins are forgiven and* whose iniquities are covered. That is what the Bible says and I am taking God's word for what it says. And my friend can take it or leave it, just as he pleases.

Now we come to the graft again. He said he had me up a tree and the folks laughed. Well, well! I asked him, "Could a graft put itself in?" He never answered. A graft must have some outside power to put it in. Who ever heard of a graft puttting itself into a tree by itself? That shows that here must be a power outside of itself. What is the graft? The Word of God. The Word of God, therefore, is engrafted by the Holy Spirit and then that overcomes the old man and keeps him subdued, as I read in the seventh chapter of Romans where it says we have the two natures after we are saved. We only had one nature up until the time we were saved. And when the graft went in, that *imparted a new nature,* a spiritual nature. That made us bring forth spiritual fruit. And the one wars against the other, the inner man against the outer man. I read that to him. What has he said in reply? Sure enough, what has he said? Up until you are saved you only have *one nature.*

When you have the graft of the word put in and you are saved, then you have *two natures* and there they are at war. And by and by the old nature will be destroyed. When? In the resurrection. Romans 8:23. But up to this time he has never said a word about it. "We groan within ourselves waiting for the adoption, to wit the redemption of our bodies." The soul is saved in the new birth. That soul is made perfect by the blood of Jesus Christ. And the body will be saved in the resurrection for "we groan within ourselves waiting for the adoption, to wit the redemption of our bodies."

Now comes my friend and asks, "What about the woman that is called by the name of the bridegroom's friend?" Baptist is not the name of John. His name was John. His title was Baptist because he was sent to baptize. And so we do not call ourselves by John's name, but as John was called the Baptist (God called him Baptist) because God *sent us to baptize.* It is exactly the same thing. If God *did sent us to baptize.* It is exactly the same thing. If God *did* not make any mistake when John was sent to baptize and called him a Baptist because of that, we make no mistake, for those whom God sends to baptize are Baptists. If God sent John to baptize and called him a Baptist because he was authorized to baptize, then when He sent the church to baptize there is no mistake in that in calling it the Baptist Church, the baptizing church. I think everybody can see that. And I see no reason why anybody should doubt it.

He comes back to Benedict. He says Benedict meant by Baptist, those who believe in believer's baptism. Certainly. And he traces a line of Baptist believers who baptized upon believer's baptism all the way back to Jesus Christ. That book he quotes from does that very thing. So that is enough on that. Benedict certainly did mean those who practice believer's baptism. You baptize an unbeliever. Why? Because your faith is dead until it acts. It acts in baptism, so you say we are the only ones who have a live faith before baptism. And those who baptize in order to make your faith alive had a dead faith until it acted, like hitching up a dead horse and working him so the horse may come to life by the work.

As I called to your attention today, my friend dies hard on "the churches of Christ salute you." "The churches of Christ" is not the name any more than "the dogs of Johnson" is the name of the dogs. How did you know the names of those dogs if somebody did not tell you? I would not. And how are you going to know the names of those churches unless God tells you? And God never did say that they were named "The Churches of Christ." It was not a name but a possession. The dogs of Johnson bark at you. What are their names? Well, no matter what their names are, that expression means that the dogs belong to Johnson. The churches of Christ salute you means the churches that belong to Christ. That telegram he got says very plainly that *"Christ" is genitive singular.* Genitive, we agree, means possessive case. Well, what did Christ posses? He possessed churches. Christ possessed churches. And Christ's churches, the churches that Christ owns, the churches that belong to Christ, salute you. The dogs that belong to Johnson bark at you. That is not the names of the dogs. "Johnson's dogs" is not the names, and churches of Christ is not the names of the churches. And I come back again and ask you to find one single, solitary place in all the lids of the Bible where the church is called, "The Church of Christ." It is simply not there, simply not there.

Now, on the point of the church not being married to Christ. I read you the scripture on it. Where is it? Revelation 19, "The marriage of the lamb is come." Then what did I mean when I spoke of the widowhood of the church, the virgin widowhood where the espoused husband died and left that virgin a widow, the worst sort of widowhood? Why, it is found very plainly in God's word that the church is not yet married to Christ, but espoused as a chaste virgin to Christ. That is found in 2 Cor. 11:3. Paul said, "I espoused you to one husband so that I may present you as a chaste virgin to Christ." The church is in the virgin state. Now, if a virgin is about ready to be married to a man and that man lies down in death, she is a virgin widow. Undoubtedly, for she is pledged to him in her life and waiting for him and now he dies and leaves her in that widowhood.

There is no question about that in my mind and no question in anybody else's that wants to know God's truth about it.

Very well, now the next is that you can prove anything, any absurdity, by history. You have to understand the background of that statement I made in the McPherson-Bogard Debate. Mrs. McPherson went to prove divine healing by looking back in history to find where John Wesley and others professed to heal. I said you can find any absurdity in history, for that matter, and that is true. But authentic history is one thing and that bogus history is another thing. Certainly, you can find all kinds of irregularities back there if you are going to quote that in order to prove our doctrine up to the present time. But they must be square with the word of God. But I came and proved the Baptist doctrine and practice by the word of God; I proved that Christ had a church, a company, all the time He went in and out among us until that same day He was taken up from us. Then I proved that it began from the baptism of John. Then I proved that He left His house and told His servants to watch for He was coming back again. I proved that Paul said that that was the church of God, the pillar and the ground of the truth. Then I have it *proved by the Bible. And then I back it up with history such* as Alexander Campbell and these others and you have the thing established. If I could contradict the history by the Bible, certainly the history would have to go down. But if the end of the world." The Bible demands history. Then I be that way, then it is settled. Why? Because Ephesians 3:21 says "unto Him be glory in the church by Christ Jesus throughout all ages." The Bible says there must be a history. They must have a continuance and Jesus said in the great commission, "Go ye therefore, and teach all nations baptizing them, and lo, I am with you always, even unto the end of the world." The Bible demands history. Then I gave the history to back up what the Bible said. What more do you want? But leaving the Bible out and going into history to find all kinds of wild stuff that men have believed and palm that off on us as our doctrine and practice—of course, I will not have it. I can find any kind of absurdity by going back to history that way. But when the

Bible demands that this church that the Lord established, this church that I read to you in the Book about, this church that was started back yonder beginning from the baptism of John, when I read that and then it demands that the history continue, then go to history and prove and back it up. You have it double and twisted, got it from the word of God and the Bible is substantiated by the historians.

Now Mr. Ridpath said, "I would not readily admit that there were Baptists as far back as A.D. 100." Why would not he readily admit? Because he is a Methodist, greatest Methodist historian on earth. "I would not readily admit" that but, "without doubt there were Baptists then for all Christians were then Baptists." Who said that? John Clark Ridpath. And Porter said, "Why, Mr. Campbell just meant when he said the Baptist denomination those who practice believer's baptism." Well, suppose he did. Then there have been people who have practiced believer's baptism, according to Campbell, all the way back to Jesus Christ. You cannot trace your church back like that. (Laughter.) You cannot go back just a fraction over a hundred years to save your life. And I will give you a premium if you will find any church like the one that meets within these walls back of the days of Alexander Campbell. You cannot find it to save your life. You are going to see him try tomorrow and watch how he fails. If you undertake to prove you have a succession of your churches like the one that meets within these walls, back of Alexander Campbell, then just show me one, just one congregation (I do not ask you for two; I ask you for *just one.* I do not ask you for two or three; I ask you for just one, *just one,*) and when you do, then I will confess I am wrong. I am surprised at my friend making such wild statements. Very well.

Now, he comes and says the Waldenses were such that we would not fellowship them and said that he could find things *among them* that none of us would fellowship. Well, let me see here. Mosheim says they were "subdivided into various sects which differed from each other in points of no small moment. The most pernicious faction of all those that composed the multitude was that which pretended that the new and perfect church already mentioned was under the direction of divine impulse and were armed against all opposition, by the power of the working of miracles, etc. It is this detestable faction which began the fanatical work in the year 1521 under the guidance of Munger and Stockton, Stark and other leaders. And the serious complexions excited the unhappy tumult and commotion in Saxony and other adjacent territory."

Now I read from Grayfield, page 89. Grayfield's letters show that all the atrocities were not in agreement with Munger and in reference to baptism they did not believe in the use of the sword. And Munger aims at the social and political chiefly.

Now my friend said that there were folks among them that we would not fellowship. Of course, there were. It is like the word Protestant now. Among those who are called Protestants there are people that I would not fellowship. But among those who are called Protestants are true Baptists. That made no answer when he said there were people among those Waldenses that we would not fellowship. Of course not, and there are people among Protestants that I would not fellowship either, but among those *the world calls* Protestants there are true Baptists. Waldenses was a general term like our word Protestant.

Now take Fisher's History. He was a Presbyterian historian and I read from pages 424 and 425. "The church, speaking of these Waldenses, they insisted must be composed of exclusively the regenerated. And they insisted it is not a matter to be regulated or managed by the civil rulers under the name of Waldenses including different types of doctrine and Christian life. It is a gross injustice to impute to all of them the destructive fanaticism with which a few are chargeable. This fanatical class was first heard of under Thomas Munger." My friend says there were people in those Waldenses that we would not endorse, we would not fellowship. Of course, but Fisher says it is a gross injustice to do just what you have just now done. You charge all of them with what you have found some of them guilty of. Among the Waldenses were those just like

Baptists. Among the Waldenses were some just like those commonly called Campbellites. Among the Waldenses there were those like the Mormons who believed in a plurality of marriages. Among the Waldenses were other fanatical sects, but among them were folks just like among Protestants, so-called Protestants, *we find Baptists* today.

Now take the new American Encyclopedia and it says it is certain that the disturbances in the city of Munger were begun by a Pedo-Baptist, a minister of Lutheran persuasion. There were folks in there like the Lutherans and all that.

Now then, there is Phillip Shaff. Who is he? He is a Lutheran historian. "The excesses of a misguided faction have been charged upon the whole body. They were made responsible for the Peasant's War and the Munster Travail, although the great majority of them were quiet and orderly and peaceful citizens and would rather suffer persecution than to do any violence."

Now, we have your answer completely. You said the Waldenses were not Baptists. Why, not all of them, any more than future historians will say that among Protestants there were people called Baptists. And now somebody gets up and says, "Why, you do not endorse all those Protestants?" Certainly, I do not. But among the people the world calls Protestants are people we know to be Baptists in good and regular order. So, among those Waldenses were people who are what we now know as Baptists. And historian Fisher says you have done a gross injustice in trying to impute to all of them what you found a small faction among them guilty of.

So we have plainly before us the church our Lord established beginning from the Baptism of John, using only John's baptism. It came all the way through His personal ministry and when He was taken up, He left His church, promised to come back to His church and told His disciples to watch, for at such an hour when you think not the Son of man comes. So the church was there during the personal ministry of Christ with a promise that he would perpetuate it to the end of time, for unto Him be glory in the church by Christ Jesus throughout all ages. And when He comes back here, He is going to find the Missionary Baptist Church that He commissioned to go teach all nations baptizing them in the name of the Father, and of the Son, and of the Holy Ghost, when He comes back to reign on earth. That, my friend says, will never be. I have thrown that at him four times now. I want him to say whether he believes Christ will ever set foot on this earth again to reign with His saints on earth or not. The Bible says He will. And we will be right here to meet Him, right here to greet Him, and even so come, Lord Jesus, come quickly. That is the hope of the world and that is one of the great doctrines held by the Missionary Baptist Church.

God knows I have no disposition to want to put something over on you that is not true. I have given you the word of God. I have given you the truth. I have quoted the scripture, quoted history, and he has been unable to contradict any of it successfully. Now, tomorrow when he gets in the lead, I will show that every single doctrine and practice he holds is contrary to the Bible. I will show his church started with man and not with the Lord. And I will show that he does not even expect the Lord to come back to His church. I will show all of that. And when we get through all can decide for themselves. Read the book and read it prayerfully and God will bless you in it.

Thank you.

Second Day

PORTER'S EIGHTH NEGATIVE

Mr. Bogard, Ladies and Gentlemen:

My opponent is a very promising young fellow. He went to length to promise you just what he was going to do tomorrow when I get into the lead. Well, it's time he is doing something—I can say that. So we wait to see him fulfill his promise.

And the charge he made about whether Jesus Christ is coming back—he said I deliberately refused to notice it. I overlooked it in my notes. I certainly believe that Jesus Christ is coming again. He is coming back as the Book teaches he is coming back—coming back in the same manner he went away. But I do not believe he is coming back to reign on the earth for 1000 years, and *Ben Bogard can't read it in all of God's Book.* That's enough for that.

Now, then, I want to call attention to two or three more of these questions that he answered a while ago that I didn't notice. No. 27 said, "If a number of congregations were called 'the churches of Christ' in the Bible, what would one of them be called?" He said, "A church." "A church." Why, it looks to me like it wouldn't be just "a church"—it would be "a church of Christ," wouldn't it? Why did you leave off the rest of it? If a number of them were called "the churches," then one would be called "a church," of course, or "the church" in some particular community. When you have "the churches of Christ," the singular of that, Mr. Bogard, *is not "a church."* It would have to be more than that to be singular of "churches of Christ." You'd have to have "the church of Christ" to have the singular—not just "church." You can't get by with a thing like that.

No. 28. "Is it possible for a child of God to lie and call his brother a fool?" He said, "Yes, and if he does, he is in danger of hell fire." Jesus said in Matt. 5 that "whosoever shall call his brother a fool shall be in danger of hell fire." And Mr. Bogard says that if a child of God does that—and he *can* do it—that he is in danger of hell fire. And yet, he said the blood protects him and he can't possibly be lost. Well, where is the *danger* then? Is there danger of the blood's failing? The blood of Christ covers all of his sins—he can't possibly be lost—and yet in spite of the blood of Christ, he is in danger of hell fire. Now, if that isn't something. Why, if the blood of Jesus Christ covers every sin that he commits so that he cannot possibly be lost, there is *no danger* of hell at all to him, Mr. Bogard. You're just in the "middle of a fix" and can't get out of it.

"No. 29. In the expression, 'The churches of Christ salute you,' are not the words 'churches' and 'Christ' nouns?" He said, "Yes, 'churches' in the nominative case and 'Christ' in the genitive. "Christ" is a noun? All right, let's see the next. "No. 30. As nouns are names of anything, and if this expression is in the possessive case, would we not have nouns or names in the possessive case?" He said, "Certainly, in all cases." Yes, sir, Mr. Bogard says we have "nouns or names in all cases." But he said yesterday that "names are always in the nominative case—never a name in the possessive case." "Names are always in the nominative." This he said yesterday. But now he says the "naming is in the nominative case." The *name* isn't, but the *naming* is. All right, try this, Mr. Bogard. They called him John. Or put it the other way. *They named him John.* Is that the *naming* of him? What's "John?" What case is "John" in? "John" is the objective complement, and is in the objective case, Mr. Bogard; and there is the very *naming* of a man in the objective case. But you say it's always in the nominative case. Why, the further you go, the worse you get into it. You'd better let things alone; let them stay as well as they are.

I asked a question about turning the man out of the church. Mr. Bogard says, "Mr. Porter asks, Why turn a man out of the church?" He said, "Why I gave you a Bible answer on that. The Bible says turn the incestuous man out for the destruction of the flesh." But you didn't answer the question I asked you, Mr. Bogard. I didn't say, "Why turn the man out?" You side-stepped it; and you dodged it; and you twisted around from it; and you didn't *even get near it*. You turned around and answered something I didn't ask, but you *evaded the thing I did ask*. I didn't ask, "Why turn a man out of the church?" I said, "Why turn the *inner man* out of the church?" You said the inner man can't sin; it isn't possible for the inner man to sin; he can never do anything that's wrong. I didn't say, "Why turn the man out?" I said, "Why turn the *inner man* out?" Why didn't you answer it? Why did you dodge it like that? You think you can get by with it? You ought to begin to learn a few things by now. "Oh," he says, "the Bible says turn the incestuous man out." Well, is the *inner man* the *incestuous man?* Or is that the *outer man?* Now, if the *inner man* is the *incestuous man* that was turned out, why, then, you have the *inner man* sinning—if incest is sin. And thus you go back on your idea that the inner man cannot possibly sin. If the *inner* man is not the *incestuous man,* then you evaded the question, because I said, "Why turn the *inner man* out?" I didn't say, "Why turn the *incestuous man* out?" The *inner man,* the man that doesn't commit incest, the man that is not guilty of any sin, according to you—*why turn him out?* He hasn't done anything that's wrong; he's committed no sin—why kick *him* out? Why not just kick the *outer man out* and leave the *inner man in?* He hasn't done anything wrong. Do you turn him out for what the old *outer man,* the servant of the devil, did? Well, he can answer that tomorrow if he wants to. He's such a promising fellow—maybe he will take up that and deal with it.

Oh, but he said, "I gave you I John 2:9 about he that 'is born of God does not commit sin for his seed remaineth in him: and he cannot sin, because he is born of God'." He has given that several times, but he gave the wrong reference every time. It's not 1st John 2:9—it's 1st John 3:9. And besides you didn't make any argument on it. You merely referred to it, and you didn't make any effort to prove that what you said about it is true. Now, you make your argument on it, and we'll see about that thing. But you haven't made any yet.

And then about the man dying drunk. He said, "Porter said, According to that, a man could get drunk and just stay drunk and even the atomic bomb couldn't kill him." And he said, "You folks laughed like it was funny." Yes, but Bogard *didn't* laugh like it was funny. In fact, it wasn't funny to Mr. Bogard, but it was serious to him—it got him into trouble. Now, he said that a man, a child of God, can get drunk—it's possible to get drunk—and he said if he died while he was drunk, he'll go to hell. But it's not possible to go to hell. If you can put two and two together, then the conclusion must be *it's not possible to die while he's drunk.* So get drunk and stay drunk, and the atomic bomb can't bother you. Mr. Bogard said that Porter said, "Why, I'd get drunk and stay drunk." Now, Porter didn't say any such thing—the record will show that Porter made no such statement as that. I said, "According to Mr. Bogard, if you want to shun the atomic bomb, just get drunk and stay drunk." I didn't say I would do it. I don't believe your doctrine in the first place. I'm sure that I could die while I'm drunk, but Mr. Bogard said he can't die while he's drunk, or that he *can* get drunk but he *can't* go to hell. But if he does die while he is drunk, he will go to hell—which means, of course, that he can't die while he is drunk. That's the only thing you can get from it. But he said, "He will not stay drunk. A child of God may get drunk, but he'll not stay drunk." Well, can he get drunk? Can he die while he is drunk? He will have to stay drunk a while. If a man gets drunk at all, he'll stay drunk for a while. Suppose he stays drunk just thirty minutes. If a railroad locomotive runs over him during that thirty minutes, will it kill him? He won't stay drunk? Well, maybe he won't stay drunk forever; Mr. Bogard says he won't. But certainly, he'll stay drunk a while, because if he gets drunk, he'll have to stay drunk for a while. If he stays drunk just thirty minutes, is it possible for that man to die during that thirty minutes? If it is possible for the man to be killed during the thirty minutes that he is drunk, he will go to hell, because Mr. Bogard said that if he dies drunk, he'll go to hell. Otherwise, you couldn't kill him during that thirty minutes with an atomic bomb or anything else, according to Bogard's argument. Well, that's the reason it wasn't funny to him.

1st John 3:3 again—the man purifieth himself. "He that hath this hope in him purifieth himself." Bogard said, "I don't care whether he purifies himself, or whether the angels purify him, or whether God purifies him, or who does it." Well, the Book says—the passage says—*he* does it. The passage says *he does it.* Well, he says, "Not nearly all of them, but all of them—all of them—purifieth themselves." Well, suppose we just say that not a single one of them does otherwise. Now, Mr. Bogard, I want you to answer my question I asked you: "What does he purify—the *inner man* or the *outer man?* The old outer man remains the servant of the devil till the resurrection. The inner man serves God; the inner man does not sin; he cannot sin. The outer man sins. Now, then, since the outer man *is not purified until the resurrection,* then this man that has the hope in himself *doesn't purify the outer man,* does he? According to Bogard's doctrine, he *can't purify the outer man,* because the outer man remains impure until the resurrection when he is redeemed. All right, he doesn't purify that. Then, does he purify the *inner man?* No, Mr. Bogard says God took care of all of that when he was converted. And so, according to Mr. Bogard's position, *the man does not purify himself at all.* Not *any man* does it. Not nearly all—not *even one* does it, according to Bogard, for he can't purify the inner man, because God did that and took care of it. That was when he was saved. He never can do anything about that. So no man—*not even one man*— Mr. Bogard, according to you, can purify himself— *not one.* You didn't touch it at top, edge, side or bottom. The audience knows it now.

Romans 8:28—"All things work together for good to them that love the Lord." My opponent reasons that that means all the sins he may commit will work out for his good. It means no such thing. The passage refers, of course, to surrounding circumstances that follow the man who serves God—who loves God and keeps his commandments. Those circumstances around him will work out for his good, but it doesn't say *his sins* will work out for his good. If so, then if some man—some married man who is a child of God—would elope with some girl, would this be for his good? If it means his sins, that's the result of it — that would be for the good of the man, if he elopes with some girl. That's Baptist doctrine. But Romans 6, he says, answers you. "Shall we continue in sin, that grace may abound?" No, that doesn't answer me. I agree with Paul on that. We shouldn't continue in sin, but Paul wasn't teaching what you're teaching. So that doesn't answer it at all, for the simple fact that Paul is not teaching that the sins of a man will work out for his good.

The blood of Jesus Christ — 1st John 1:7, which he gave—cleanses us from *all* sin. Bogard said, "Not nearly all of them—it cleanses us from *all* sin." Well, why didn't you read the rest of it? Why did you stop so soon? Why didn't you go and read the 9th verse right in connection with it. "If we confess our sins, He is faithful and just to forgive us our sins, and to cleanse us from all unrighteousness." Why didn't you read the rest of it? Why did you quit so soon? The blood of Jesus Christ won't cleanse a man of his sin if he doesn't confess his sin—the very passage says, "If we confess our sins." You say it will cleanse him whether he confesses them or not. So you have the wrong passage.

In Romans 4—"Blessed is the man to whom the Lord will not impute sin." And Mr. Bogard said that our sins are charged on Jesus Christ, and when we sin, that Jesus Christ is held responsible for them. And we're not held accountable at all—they are not charged against us. That's the meaning of the passage, he claims. Did you ever ask God to forgive you, Mr. Bogard? When you sin, do you ask God to forgive you? If you do, why? If God hasn't held it against you—if God doesn't charge it against you—why do you ask forgiveness? And, incidentally, does this refer to the *inner man* or the *outer man?* Just which one do you ask God to forgive and cleanse? The outer man? Well, you say he won't do that till the resurrection. Do you ask God to forgive and cleanse the inner man? Well, you say, he's already done that, and he *never can* become unclean. So there's just no ground for it at all.

Then to the woman and the name. He said John's name—yes, the name is John. "John" was the *name.* And he said "Baptist" is the title. Well, a while ago you said if we wore the name of Christ, we would have to be called Jesuits and not Christians—that Christians couldn't be a *name* because it is a *title.* If "Christian" couldn't be a *name* because it's a *title,* then "Baptist" couldn't be a *name* because that's a *title* too; Mr. Bogard says so. Yes, sir, he said, "John is his *name*—Baptist is his title." So "Baptist" can't be a name, for it's a title. He said "Christian" couldn't be a name of Christ, because it's a title. But here's Mr. Bogard's paper, the Orthodox Baptist Searchlight, Dec. 27, 1944. And he says that "John the Baptist was so called by God Himself. The personal name of John the Baptist was simply 'John.' That was what his father called him. His *religious name was Baptist* for that was what God called him." So Mr. Bogard said God called him a *name*. and the word "Baptist" was his *name*—that God called him that for his *religious name*. Not his *title*—but his *name*. Now he says that "Baptist" is *not a name*—it's *the title*. He met himself coming back, you see.

I come again to "Johnson's dogs." (Laughter) He would never know, of course, what the names of Johnson's dogs were unless he was told. Well, he would never know what the name of the church of the New Testament was unless he was told. But he knows it's Baptist—yet he never was told that in the Book of God. Mr. Bogard, why would you rather take a name for the church that the Book says nothing about—why would you rather call the church by some designation that the Book says nothing about—than to call it by something by which it was designated in the New Testament? The churches in the New Testament were called "churches of Christ." You wouldn't want that—you wouldn't have that—but you'll take a name that is not there and wear it instead. Why do you prefer a name that isn't there to the terms that are there? I believe in accepting the terms that are there—and if you will find "Baptist Church" in there, I'll tack that on before the rising of another sun. But even in "Johnson's dogs" we have a noun. The word "dogs" is a noun, and a noun is the name of anything. Even the word "dog" itself is *the name* of the four-legged animals. The dogs of Johnson, Mr. Bogard, because *nouns* are *names*. Well, we might try another.

I'll let that pass, though, for the time being, and come to this one. "The church of Christ." He says there is no such thing as "*the* church of Christ." You just can't find it—no such thing as "*the* church of Christ." Well, I'm going to read again from Mr. Bogard in this same Orthodox Baptist Searchlight, Dec. 27, 1944. Mr. Bogard said, "Therefore, it was in fact a Missionary Baptist Church. It belongs to Christ and is therefore the Lord's Church, *the church of Christ.*" (Laughter) Thank you, Mr. Bogard.

Another thing that I have learned is that a woman can become a widow before she is married. (Laughter) I remember one time in Paul's writing that he was speaking "to the widows and the unmarried." But he had the thing all mixed up, because a lot of those unmarried were widows too. (Laughter) "The widows and the unmarried" — the distinction is made in the Book of God between the widows and the unmarried. But Mr. Bogard says some of the unmarried are widows. They never have been married and never had a ceremony said, and yet they are widows—"virgin widows." Will you read me something in the Bible, or somewhere, about virgin widows, Mr. Bogard? "Virgin widows"—widows who were never married—who never had a ceremony said. Maybe they'll have a chance — it's Leap Year now. (Laughter)

Regarding what I read in the McPherson-Bogard debate—"you can prove anything—any absurdity—by history," he said, "You need to know the background for it—that Mrs. McPherson was trying to prove by history the continuation of miracles from the apostolic age." That's the same background we have now. Mr. Bogard is trying to prove the continuation of the Baptist Church, for he can't find anything in the Bible about it—it has no Bible background. He said you "can prove any absurdity by history." Regardless of whose history you go to, you say it's wrong if it's contrary to the Bible. There is nothing in the Bible about the "Baptist Church" or "Baptist Churches" or anything of that nature.

Well, "suppose Campbell did mean—or suppose Campbell did refer to—those who had practiced believers baptism by immersion through the centuries." He said, "Your church can't trace it back like that." Why, *that's what we believe,* Mr. Bogard. I can trace back just like you do. I can find principles for which the people stand, with which I'm identified, through all those centuries just like you can. We believe in believer's baptism. We believe that people must believe before they are baptized, and that's what Campbell said he meant by "Baptists." We believe that baptism is by immersion, and that's what Campbell said he meant by "Baptists in all those ages." Therefore, if you find *those principles in all ages,* you find principles *for which we contend in all ages.* I can trace it just like you trace it—with just as much success, Mr. Bogard. He said, "I don't ask for two—I just ask for one such church back of Campbell's day." Well, I'll give you more than one. Romans 16:16 said, "The churches of Christ salute you." We'll have more about that before I get through. But, Mr. Bogard, I called upon you for one—not two—not a half dozen—not a hundred—just one—just one "Missionary Baptist Church," or any kind of Baptist Church, *in all history,* prior to the 17th Century, and *anywhere in all of the Book of God. Just one.*

Concerning the Waldenses he said, "Yes, these Waldenses were divided into various sects." And he gave a number of histories that referred to the *Munster riot* and things of that kind. And he said that Porter said there were *folks among them* that "we wouldn't fellowship." No, that isn't what I said, and that isn't what the history said that I read. *It didn't say that.* I'm going to read it again to see if that's what I said; we'll see if that's what the history said. He went on to prove by those historical records, or quotations that he made, that it's a "gross injustice" to charge all of them with what some of them did. Well, I'm not doing that. I made no effort to do that. He spoke about certain evils of the Munster riot and things of that kind. I wasn't talking about that; in fact, the history I quoted from wasn't talking about that. Let's read it again: "Dr. Abel Stevens says 'Obscure communities, as the Cathari of the Novatians, the Paulicians, the Albigenses, and the Waldenses, maintained the ancient faith in comparative purity from the beginning of the fourth century down to the reformation.' These and other sects held one or more distinctive Baptist principles, *but none of them*"—. He didn't say "some among them";—he said "*none* of them." Who? Why, these Novatians, and these Paulicians, and these Albigenses, and these Waldenses. These fellows that stirred up trouble back there and caused all kind of evil to come about? Was that it? No, that's not what he said. That wasn't the quotation I gave. But what Waldenses? and what Novatians? and what Paulicians? and what Albigenses? Those who committed those gross evils? Was that it? No, he referred *not to them* but to those who "maintained the ancient faith in comparative purity from the beginning of the fourth century to the Reformation." Those were the ones he was talking about, Mr. Bogard—*not some among them*. But *those who maintained* the *greatest purity* during that period. They are the ones the historian spoke of that I quoted from—Mr. Armitage—one that you rely upon to prove your Baptist succession. And he says it can't be done, and you didn't even pay attention to what I read from him a while ago. Well, what about "these that maintained the ancient faith in comparative purity from the beginning of the fourth century on down to the Reformation?" What about them? Mr. Armitage says "these"—*these*—not *some of those* wicked fellows *among these*. But he said *these* who *maintained that comparative purity of faith*—"these and other sects held one or more distinctive Baptist principles, but *none of them*," Mr. Bogard. Mr. Armitage says, "*None of them*" — *none of them*—not *some among them*, but "*none of them* were *thorough Baptists through and through*." That's what he said. Again you dodge, and you knew you were dodging; and the audience knows it now. And they're going to keep finding it out when you keep dodging, and you just keep on that way and you're going to get into more trouble as the debate goes on. And, then, I quoted from Mr. Lofton also, page 76, of the English Baptist Reformation. He says, "And so we are accustomed to speak of far more unbaptistic sects before them—such as Montanists, Novatians, Donatists, Paulicians and the like, *who would not now be fellowshipped, ecclesiastically speaking, in any regular Baptist Church in America*." My friend twisted around from it, and he didn't touch it at all. He didn't come to what I said. He simply perverted the things he's been talking about and replied to something that *the history didn't say*. It still stands, Mr. Bogard; you're still in trouble.

That covers the speech that he just made, and I want to get back now to just a little. I have a few minutes left, I think. And we want to see some things. Now, I want to come back to the board.

CHART NO. 5

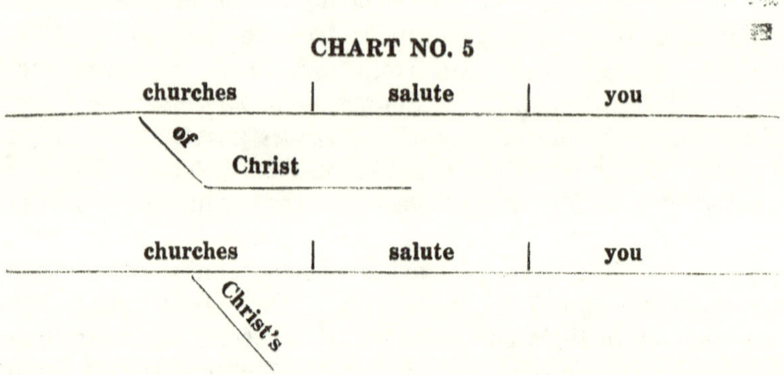

You notice he hasn't done anything with this yet. He admitted that "church" is in the *nominative* case—that "Christ" is the *genitive* case in the Greek, but he *never has told me* whether it is the *objective case in the English*. I've begged him—I've almost begged him with tears in my eyes—to tell me whether "Christ" in this expression is in the objective case in English, but he never has said one single word about it. *Why?* Are you afraid of it, Mr. Bogard? The audience will not forget that.

Remember, too, that first I had him treed on a stump. Now, I've got him stumped up a tree. (Laughter)

CHART NO. 6

Graft — Tree

And he comes to this matter of the graft—he comes to it, in fact, in about every speech. "I'm talking about the engrafted word." And he says, "What is the graft?" "The word," he said. Well, I know you said that. But I have been begging you, Mr. Bogard, to tell me what the tree is. And that's the thing you've never touched—that's the thing you've never said anything about. What's the tree? The word is *the graft*. What's *the tree?* I have asked him, "Is that the heart of man? Is that the soul of man?" Mr Bogard, what have you said about it? (Pause) Just as much as you would have left if you'd rub the rim off a circle. Nothing! *What is the tree* into which the graft is put, Mr. Bogard? Is it the heart? Is it the soul? *What is it?* Whatever it is—you say the tree isn't changed. And if Mr. Bogard doesn't answer that question, I'm going to read from his debates and show what he says it is. Now, it's up to him to answer that tomorrow, and if he doesn't, I'm going to read from his published debates and show that Mr. Bogard says that that tree is the soul or the heart of man. Mr. Bogard says the tree isn't changed. So the soul is not changed; the inner man isn't changed. And if it's the soul or the heart of man, the graft, or the word of God, is put into his heart. But it doesn't change the tree; it doesn't change the stock; it doesn't change the heart. The old heart, the soul of man, remains the same depraved heart—the same depraved soul—that he had when he was born. And the man isn't *changed at all*. He said, "The old outer man is not changed." But this is the *inner man*, you know. The old outer man isn't changed, because the outer man remains a servant of the devil until the resurrection when he is redeemed from death and he has all of his sins there. The *outer man*, then, *is not changed*. Well, is the inner man? The inner man is the heart, the soul. Mr. Bogard says it is in his published debates. The heart—the soul—is the tree into which the graft is put. All right, the tree, Mr. Bogard says, isn't changed. So *the soul is not changed*. The outer man isn't changed in conversion, according to Mr. Bogard; and the inner man isn't changed in conversion. Neither of them is chaged in conversion. I wonder what's accomplished, then, by conversion? Conversion means a change, but there's no change taking place, according to Mr. Bogard, because neither the outer man nor the inner man is changed. The heart is the tree; the soul is the tree; the inner man is the tree—and that remains the same. Mr. Bogard has agreed that it's so. He says the outer man continues in sin, a servant of the devil, till the resurrection. So neither man is changed in conversion. Just what is conversion anyway? Now, we'll erase that since we've got him stumped up the tree, and he cannot get down, and treed on the stump; he's still there somewhere.

We're going to pass on now to something else. I have perhaps three or four minutes?

Brother Blue answers: "A little over two."

Mr. Porter continues: Little over two? I think that will be time enough. Yesterday I wrote on this side (pointing to black board) "Church of Christ." I wrote on this side—"Baptist Church." On this side I wrote "Churches of Christ." And on this side I wrote "Baptist Churches." Here I put Romans 16:16. Here I put a dash.

CHART NO. 1

Church of Christ	**Baptist Church**
Churches of Christ	**Baptist Churches**
— Rom. 16:16	————————

And in Romans 16:16 we have the expression, "The churches of Christ salute you." My opponent won't take "church of Christ," because that's singular. "Church of Christ"—he wants the singular in the Bible. Over here I said, "Mr. Bogard, put on this line (pointing to line on the board) a reference that mentions either "Baptist Church," in the singular, or "Baptist Churches," in the plural, and I'll take both of them." Until this day the line has remained blank. He never endeavored to put it there. There is no "Baptist Church" in the Bible — there are no "Baptist Churches" in the Bible. Mr. Bogard has admitted it. He has also failed to write the reference that mentions the matter, and so it stands that Mr. Bogard has failed to prove that the "Baptist Church" is Scriptural in name, because it isn't named in the Scriptures. And in the first speech of this debate, he said, "The man who fails to prove that the church is Scriptural in name fails in this debate." Mr. Bogard has gone down, according to his own contention. If he'll find "Baptist Church," I have sense enough to know that a number of them would be "Baptist Churches." If he'll find "Baptist Churches" in the plural, I'll have enough sense to know that one of them is a "Baptist Church." And if he'll find "Baptist Church," I'll have sense enough to know there are "Baptist Churches," and I'll take both of them. *Find either of them*, Mr. Bogard, and *I'll accept them both* as Scriptural designations of the Church. I don't demand that you *find both*—just one—just find either one of them. Find one and I'll take the other. You don't have to find any particular one. I won't say you must find "Baptist Church" —just find "Baptist Churches" and I'll accept that. I won't say you have to find "Baptist Churches"—find "Baptist Church" and I'll accept the other too. Find one of them—either of them—and I'll accept both of them. Mr. Bogard *cannot do it*. I thank you.

Third Day

PORTER'S FIRST AFFIRMATIVE

Gentlemen Moderators, Respected Opponent, Ladies and Gentlemen:

For the next 30 minutes I shall affirm the proposition that Brother Blue has just read in your hearing. That proposition, I think, is plain, simple, easily understood and certainly needs but very little defining. By "origin," of course, I mean "beginning;" and by "doctrine," that which it "teaches;" "practice," that which it "practices" in religion; and "name" that by which it is called. In all these respects the church known as the Church of Christ is Scriptural. That's the issue between us now for these two closing days of the debate.

I want to begin where Mr. Bogard began on his, taking the last first. I am not saying so much about it, because we have discussed that pretty thoroughly already, on both sides of the question, as far as that goes. Do you remember that Mr. Bogard said in the beginning of his affirmation, day before yesterday, that the name of the church is important? And he emphasized it to the extent that he said whoever fails to prove that it is Scriptural *in name* fails in the debate. So I'm turning to just a few things about that here. And I still have on the blackboard the diagram, which I have had there a number of times before, to which I again call your attention.

CHART NO. 1

Church of Christ	Baptist Church
Churches of Christ	Baptist Churches
— Rom. 16:16	————

Over here (pointing to left) I have written the expression "Church of Christ." And over here on the right hand side of it, "Baptist Church." On this side, "Churches of Christ," and over on the right side parallel with it, "Baptist Churches." I placed beneath this (pointing to "Churches of Christ") Romans 16:16 as the passage and left a mark over on this side for Mr. Bogard to fill in his passage. In Romans 16:16 the apostle Paul said, "The churches of

Christ salute you." I have insisted that there cannot be a plural without a singular; and if a number of them were "churches of Christ," one of them would be "church of Christ." Consequently, by that simple law of deduction, by subtracting a certain number from a larger number, you have one left. Therefore, from that point of view, certainly that must be a Scriptural designation. Mr. Bogard has been unable to do anything with that during the course of this discussion, and, of course, will remain unable as this discussion continues. So note the fact that Paul said, "The churches of Christ salute you." We've been told, of course, all along that that denotes "ownership." No one has ever denied that "ownership" was affirmed in that. But would it not be much better to take a designation that affirms ownership, by which the church was called in the Scriptures, than to take one that is not even mentioned there in connection with the church, that may designate something else—or doesn't even designate ownership—as the case may be. Yes, we have used the term—we have used the designation—that is found in the New Testament. My opponent has one that is *not found there*. Now, the term by which his people are called, or the expression which they use, is no where found in all of God's Book, as my opponent admitted. We are using a Scriptural designation then—let it denote ownership or what not. It is still a Scriptural designation. One found in the Bible certainly is Scriptural, and because of that we stand upon it. Incidentally, as the discussion continues, if Mr. Bogard happens to find the passage somewhere in God's Book that mentions "Baptist Church" or "Baptist Churches," he still has the right to put his reference up here on the line that I have left blank for that purpose.

It was insisted by Mr. Bogard, remember, that "the church" is nowhere used — that is, the expression, "the church," is nowhere used in God's Book to designate more than one local congregation. I called attention to the fact found in Acts, the 9th chapter and verse 31. Reading from the Revised Version the record says, "The church throughout all Judea and Samaria and Galilee had rest." Here we find the section of the country covered is designated as "throughout all Judea, Samaria and Galilee." Consequently, here is used the term, "the church," referring to a number of congregations throughout that country. Mr. Bogard has insisted that that cannot be true—that that was only one congregation—the one at Jerusalem that had been scattered. He says that it was still the one congregation referred to, mentioned in the 8th chapter of Acts, as the place where the scattering took place, when havoc was wrought against the church in that day. Well, it so happens that this incident—this record—mentioned in Acts 9:31 is mentioned just after Paul returned to Jerusalem and tried to join the Baptist Church, according to Mr. Bogard. So after he came back to Jerusalem the record says "the church" throughout all that country had rest. How long was it before he came back to Jerusalem? The church was scattered abroad before the conversion of Saul of Tarsus. Under the work of persecution, such as he carried on, the church was scattered, and Paul himself declared in Acts, 26th chapter and verse 11, that he had persecuted this way, and even went unto strange cities. That was *before his conversion.* There were saints of the Lord in strange cities *even in those days.* After his conversion we are told that he preached straightway in the synagogues of Damascus. Then after many days he went to Jerusalem, but it doesn't tell how many. But over in Galatians, first chapter and verses 16 to 18, Paul declared it was three years. He first preached in Damascus, then went to Arabia and returned to Damascus, and after a period of three years he went to Jerusalem. So there had been three years' time since his conversion before Paul went to Jerusalem. During all of that three years preaching had been done by him throughout various sections of the country, and, in the meantime, we find other work was carried on. In fact, even *before his conversion* we have recorded things of that nature. Philip went down to Samaria and preached Christ to them, in Acts the 8th chapter, and a number were baptized down there. They were not "Jerusalem" people either—they were people of Samaria. Hence we have a number of congregations scattered over that country. But the Book says, "*The church* throughout all Judea, Galilee and Samaria had rest." Therefore, the term, "the church" as used there referred to *more than one congregation,* and Mr. Bogard is wrong.

Next I call attention to "origin." This refers, of course, to the time of "beginning." And I am insisting that the New Testament church began *after the Lord's resurrection.* In 2nd Samuel, the 7th chapter and verse 12, we have this statement made which says: "And when thy days be fulfilled, and thou shalt sleep with thy fathers, I will set up thy seed after thee, which shall proceed out of thy bowels, and I will establish his kingdom." Here is the promise of the establishment of the Lord's kingdom after David's death. In connection therewith the prophet said that "I will set up thy seed after thee." But what is meant by "setting up thy seed after thee?" Well, we turn to Psalms 132, verse 11, and we read there that God had sworn in truth to David that "of the fruit of thy body will I set upon thy throne." Then to "set up thy seed after thee" means "set thy seed upon the throne—upon thy throne." Whenever, then, the seed is set upon the throne the kingdom is established. When the kingdom is established he is on the throne of David. But when did or when would that occur? Turning to the second chapter of the Acts of the Apostles, we read from the lips of the apostle Peter, verses 29 to 31: "Men and brethren, let me freely speak unto you of the patriarch David, that he is both dead and buried, and his sepulchre is with us unto this day. Therefore being a prophet, and knowing that God had sworn with an oath to him, that of the fruit of his loins, according to the flesh, he would raise up Christ to sit on his throne; He seeing this before spake of the resurrection of Christ, that his soul was not left in hell, neither his flesh did see corruption." Thus, we learn that Jesus Christ was the seed of David referred to—to whom he swore to give the throne of David—and that he was to be placed upon that throne. Peter says he was raised from the dead to fulfill that. So the establishment of his kingdom—the placing on the throne—was to occur *after the Lord's resurrection.*

In the second place, we learn also that it was to occur *after his ascension to heaven.* In Luke 19, verse 12, we are told of a parable that Jesus uttered about a certain man going "into a far country to receive for himself a kingdom, and to return." The far country is heaven. The nobleman is our Lord Jesus Christ. The return, of course, refers to his second coming. So he "went into a far country to receive for himself a kingdom, and to return." The kingdom was to be received *after he went into a far country*—after he went to heaven—and *before he came back.* In Daniel the 7th chapter, verses 13 and 14, we have also a statement pertaining to the same act. Daniel says: "I saw in the night visions, and, behold, one like the Son of man came with the clouds of heaven, and came to the Ancient of days, and they brought him near before him. And there was given him dominion, and glory, and a kingdom." Hence we find the Lord went with the clouds of heaven to the Ancient of days—whoever the Ancient of days is. If you will read the Scripture in connection therewith, you'll find the Ancient of days is God. Jesus, therefore, went in the clouds of heaven to God to receive for himself a kingdom, and there he was given glory, dominion and a kingdom. And these he received after his ascension—when he went in the clouds to the Father above. Thus we learn it was to occur *after his ascension.* His ascension took place, of course, according to Acts 1:11, in the clouds of heaven when he went back to God.

Then, in the third place, we learn that it was accomplished *on the first Pentecost after Christ arose.* In Mark the 9th chapter and verse 1 we have the statement made by Jesus Christ himself: "That there be some of them that stand here, which shall not taste of death, till they have seen the kingdom of God come with power." Now, note the fact that Jesus says some standing there would live to see the kingdom of God come with power. Yes, note the fact that he said it would *come with power.* Then, if the kingdom was to come with power, that means they would come at the same time. The kingdom would "come with power." If we can find when the power came, then we'll know when the kingdom came, because the kingdom was to *come with power.* Turning to Acts the first chapter and verse 8 we find that Jesus said to his apostles: "Ye shall receive power, after that the Holy Ghost is come upon you." So the *kingdom* was to come *with power,* and the *power* was to come *with the Holy Ghost.* If we can find when the Holy Ghost came, we will know when the power came, and therefore when the kingdom came, because they were all to come together. Next I turn to Acts, the second chapter, and begin reading with verse 1, and the record says, "And when the day of Pentecost was fully come, they were all with one accord in one place. And suddenly there came a sound from heaven as of a rushing mighty wind, and it filled all the house where they were sitting. And there appeared unto them cloven tongues like as of fire, and it sat upon each of them. And they were all filled with the Holy Ghost, and began to speak with other tongues, as the Spirit gave them utterance." All right, the Holy Ghost came when? "When the day of Pentecost was fully come." But the power was to come *with the Holy Ghost.* Therefore, the power came "when the day of Pentecost was fully come." Yet the kingdom was to *come with power.* Hence, the kingdom came "when the day of Pentecost was fully come." And thus we have the fulfillment of those promises when the kingdom came on the day of Pentecost. This marks the beginning of the church or the kingdom of Jesus Christ in the established form in the world.

Passing on from the point concerning the "origin," I come next to consider something regarding "doctrine" — that is, some of the things that we teach—some things that are taught by the people known as the Church of Christ today. These things, I insist, are also taught in the Scriptures, and therefore the church is Scriptural in doctrine.

The doctrine now to which your attention is called—for which we contend and which we believe to be taught in the Scriptures—is the fact that salvation for all responsible beings *in this age of the world* is in the New Testament church. I want to call your attention to that. We have a number of things along that line to consider, and I want my opponent to grapple with them and show that these applications are wrong.

In I Timothy 3:15—the Scripture which my opponent has used on several occasions—Paul spoke of "the house of God, which," he says, "is the church of the living God."

Well, certainly, we'll both agree that in that passage Paul referred to the church—the church of God, the house of the living God. All right, then, we turn to 1st Peter 4, verses 17 and 18, and hear the apostle Peter saying, "The time is come that judgment must begin at the house of God." Here Peter speaks of the same thing, and I think Mr. Bogard will agree with me that he refers in that case to the church. "The time is come that judgment must begin at the house of God: and if it first begin at us, what shall the end be of them that obey not the gospel of God? And if the righteous scarcely be saved, where shall the ungodly and the sinner appear?" Now, I have a contrast drawn on the board here, to which I invite your attention, with a line drawn between them.

CHART NO. 7

The house of God	**Them that obey not**
Us	**The ungodly**
The Righteous	**The sinner**

Note the fact that Peter says "the time is come that judgment must begin at the house of God," which Mr. Bogard and I will agree refers to the church. All right—"the time is come that judgment must begin at the church: and if it begin at *us*." Thus we find Peter using the pronoun "us" as equivalent to "the house of God." It's going to begin at the *house of God*: "and if it first begin at *us*." So "us" is used referring to the same people as "the house of God." If it first begin at us, what shall the end be of *them that obey not the gospel* of God?" This is contrasted with *us* and *the house of God*. "And if the righteous scarcely be saved, where shall the ungodly and the sinner appear?" In other words, on this hand (pointing to left of board) Peter refers to "the house of God" which he also says is "us" and likewise "the righteous." Likewise on this side (pointing to right) he refers to "them that obey not the gospel" as "the ungodly" and "the sinner." *The house of God*, therefore, includes *us*. *The house of God* includes *the righteous*. And those in contrast with *the house of God* are *them that obey not the gospel*—them that obey not God. If men can be saved out of the house of God, away from this part of the number to which

Peter referred, then they can be saved without obeying the gospel, for *the house of God* includes *us*—it includes *the righteous.* And those who are not among *the righteous,* among *us,* in *the house of God,* are among *them that obey not the gospel.* They are *the ungodly,* and they are *the sinners.* We have, therefore, a contrast drawn between the house of God—the church of God—on one hand, and on the other hand, them that obey not, the ungodly, and the sinner. And if those "that obey not the gospel of God" will be lost—if those who are "ungodly" will be lost—then they will be lost who are not of "the house of God" and who are not in the church of God. I intend for that thing to stand when this discussion is over.

My second argument upon this point is that *Jesus is the Savior of the church.* In Ephesians, the 5th chapter and verse 23, the apostle Paul said, "For the husband is the head of the wife, even as Christ is the head of the church: and he is the saviour of the body." I want you to note that expression, my friends. Paul said that Jesus is "the saviour of the body." Well, what does he mean by "body" in that case? I think Mr. Bogard will agree with me that he refers to the church. In Ephesians, the first chapter and verses 20-23, he referred to the same thing. He spoke about the power of God, "which he wrought in Christ, when he raised him from the dead, and set him at his own right hand in heavenly places, far above all principality, and power, and might, and dominion, and every name that is named, not only in this world, but also in that which is to come: and hath put all things under his feet, and gave him to be the head over all things to the church, which is his body." Now, Paul declares the church is his body. And then in Col. 1:18 Paul says, "He is the head of the body, the church." One passage says *the church is the body*; the other passage says *the body is the church.* But Paul says in Ephesians 5:23 that Christ is "the savior of the body." Therefore, he is the Savior of the church; and if he is the Savior of the church, or the Savior of the body, then he is not the Savior of men who are out of the body. If he saves every man before he enters the church, he cannot be said to be the Savior *of the church.* He would be the Savior of men before they enter the body but not the Savior of the body at all. But the Book says "he is the saviour of the body," and, therefore, he is the Savior of the church. That means he saves those who are in the body—those in the church—and not those who are out of the church, because, if so, then he ceases to be the Savior *of the body.* He would be the Savior of men *before they become any part of the body.* And no man *in the body* is saved by the Savior, but every man is saved before he becomes a part of the body, according to Mr. Bogard. That, too, will not be damaged.

I shall come then to the third argument. I note the fact that *the church comprises the saved.* In the second chapter of Acts, verse 47, we are told that "the Lord added to the church daily such as should be saved." Note the fact now—the Lord added to the church daily such as should be saved." Now, that either means they were saved before they were added to the body or the church or they were saved *when* they were added to the church. "The Lord added to the church daily such as should be saved." Now, I'm submitting to you the fact that if anybody in Jerusalem was saved before he was added to the church, he was saved *when he should not have been,* for it says, "the Lord added to the church daily *such as should be saved.*" All right, then, that shows the *church comprises the saved.* And they are saved when they are added to the body, and not before, for the simple fact is if they were saved before they were added to the body, then Jesus ceases to be the Savior of the body, as was shown in the preceding argument.

Next we come to *the cost of the church.* This is argument number 4 in this particular line. *The cost of the church.* We note that the church was purchased with the blood of Jesus Christ. In Acts, the 20th chapter and verse 28, Paul said, when he gave his farewell address to the elders of the church at Ephesus: "Take heed therefore unto yourselves, and to all the flock, over the which the Holy Ghost hath made you overseers, to feed the church of God, which he has purchased with his own blood." Here we have "the church of God which he purchased with his own blood," or as the Revised Version reads, "the church of the Lord." Yes, the church of the Lord which he purchased with his own blood. And, incidentally, I might ask Mr. Bogard to which local congregation does that refer? Yes, to which local congregation does this refer in these passages that *the Lord purchased with his own blood?* Then in Ephesians 5, verse 25, we have this statement made: "Husbands, love your wives, even as Christ also loved the church, and gave himself for it." The Lord loved the church. The Lord gave himself for it. The Lord purchased the church with his own blood. And since the Lord purchased the church with his own blood, then that church is a blood-purchased institution, of course, and any benefit to be derived from the purchase must be derived from that which was purchased with the blood. All right, note this fact—the benefit of the blood must be derived from that for which the price was paid. If you bought a stick of candy and paid a nickel for it, if you ever get any value out of that nickel, you must get it out of that thing for which you spent it. You'd get it out of the stick of candy. And Jesus Christ shed his blood for the church. Jesus purchased the church with his blood. Therefore, if you get the benefit of the blood of Jesus Christ, you must get it from the institution for which the price was paid—the thing that was bought with the blood. And since the church is the thing that was bought with the blood, if you get the benefit of the blood of Christ, you must get it from the church. Consequently, it's in the church that you reap the benefit of Christ's blood and, therefore, become saved.

In the 5th place I note *the fact* that *we are redeemed by the blood.* 1st Peter 1:18-19. The statement is made that we are not redeemed with corruptible things, as silver and gold, from our vain conversation, "but with the precious blood of Jesus Christ, as a lamb without blemish and without spot." Note the statement that we are not redeemed with corruptible things—not by silver and gold—but by the precious blood of Jesus Christ. Redeemed by his blood. But in connection with that note this—that the very act that puts a man into the blood is the act that puts him into the church. *The same act that brings a man into the blood of Jesus Christ brings him into the church.* In Romans, the 6th chapter, verses 3 and 4, the apostle Paul said,

"Know ye not, that so many of us as were baptized into Jesus Christ were baptized into his death?" The act of baptism puts us into the death of Jesus, where his blood was shed, and where, therefore, we reach his blood. That very same act is the act that puts men into the church, for we read in 1st Cor. 12:13: "For by one Spirit are we all baptized into one body." Certainly, we'll agree that the body is the church. So by one Spirit are we all baptized into one church. Then baptism is the final act that puts a man into the death of Christ, where he reaches the blood. But the act that puts him into the blood is the act that puts him into the church. If a man, therefore, can be saved without getting into the church, he can be saved without reaching the blood, for the very same act brings him in contact with both of them. Since a man cannot be saved without reaching the blood of Jesus Christ, he cannot be saved without reaching the church of our Lord Jesus Christ. Consequently, salvation is in the church and not out of it.

Number 6. *In this age of the world* we find those who are saved or those *who have their names written in heaven.* In Rev. 21, verse 27, the statement is made regarding that celestial city that "there shall in no wise enter into it anything that defileth, neither whatsoever worketh abomination, or maketh a lie: but they which are written in the Lamb's book of life." Only those who have their names written in heaven, then, will be allowed to enter that celestial city. In Rev. 20:15 we are told: "Whosoever was not found written in the book of life was cast into the lake of fire." So those who have their names written in heaven will be among the redeemed, but those who have not their names written will be cast into the lake of fire or hell. But, in this age of the world, who are they which have their names written in heaven? I turn to Heb. 12 and verse 23, and there the apostle says, "To the general assembly and church of the firstborn, which are written in heaven." All right, it's the church of the firstborn who have their names written in heaven in this age of time. And those who have their names written in heaven are those that are going to be saved in that day. Those who have not their names written in heaven are the ones that are going to be lost. Consequently, my friends, only those who are in the church *in this age* have the promise of salvation, according to the statement there made. Let Mr. Bogard show that somebody besides those who are in the church have their names written in heaven in this age of time. Let him show that it is not the church that is written in heaven, or all who do not have their names written there may go to heaven anyway. Or at least make some effort along that line to set aside these facts.

Number 7. I find that *men are reconciled in the church.* Ephesians 2:16. Paul talks about the Jew and the Gentile and declares "that he might reconcile both unto God in one body by the cross, having slain the enmity thereby." Note that he says that both Jew and Gentile are *reconciled* to God *in one body.* And the body means the church as I have already shown. Then Jew and Gentile are *reconciled* to God *in one church.* We have found that the church means the body in Ephesians 1:23 and Col. 1:18 which I gave awhile ago. Yes, here is the church—the body of Christ—and men are *reconciled,* both Jews and Gentiles, *in the body.* That means in the church. I'm telling you, my friends, that today if men can be saved out of the New Testament church, they can be saved without being reconciled to God. Yes, *they can be saved without being reconciled to God,* because it's in the body, Paul said, that both Jew and Gentile are reconciled to God. But the body is the church. So it's *in the church* that both Jew and Gentile are reconciled to God.

Number 8. I note now that *the church is the house of God.* In first Timothy 3:15, of which Mr. Bogard has already made use, and which we'll agree refers to the church, Paul speaks of "the house of God," which he says "is the church of the living God." All right, here is the house of God, the church of the living God. *The house of God is the church. The church is the house of God.* But I learn from 1st Peter, the 2nd chapter and 5th verse, that it's only in the house that men offer to God acceptable sacrifice or acceptable service, for in 1st Peter 2:5 Peter said, "Ye also, as lively stones, are built up a spiritual house." I do not believe that Mr. Bogard will deny that spiritual house is the church. "Ye also, as lively stones, are built up a spiritual house, an holy priesthood, to offer up spiritual sacrifices, acceptable to God by Jesus Christ"—to offer to God acceptable service by Jesus Christ. All right, then, the acceptable service or acceptable sacrifices offered to God—the sacrifice offered to God which will be pleasing to him and accepted by Him—are offered where? *In the spiritual house.* He built up a spiritual house to offer up these spiritual sacrifices acceptable to God and to Jesus Christ. The man, therefore, who is out of the house cannot offer to God spiritual sacrifices that will be acceptable unto him. And if a man cannot offer to God spiritual sacrifices which will be acceptable to God except in the house, then he cannot do so except in the church. Certainly, a man of that kind cannot be saved. Surely God would be pleased with a man who is saved. But this says that "acceptable sacrifices" are offered to him "in the spiritual house"—not on the outside. Then Paul in 2nd Timothy, chapter 2, verses 20 and 21, referred to the same man. He said, "In a great house there are not only vessels of gold and silver, but also of wood and of earth, and some to honor, and some to dishonor. If a man therefore purge himself from these, he shall be a vessel unto honor, sanctified, and meet for the master's use, and prepared unto every good work." Well, the great house, of course, referred to the church. That is the application Paul is making of this matter. And so in the great house, or in the church, there are vessels of gold and silver, and some to honor and some to dishonor. But he said, "If a man therefore purge himself from these, he shall be a vessel of honor, sanctified, and meet for the master's use, and prepared unto every good work." A man *who is not a vessel in the Lord's house* then is *not sanctified,* is not *meet for the master's use,* and is *not prepared unto every good work.* Certainly, a man who is saved is sanctified and fit for the Master's use. But since he is not sanctified and fit for the Master's use except in the house, then certainly he is not saved on the outside of the house and out of the church.

Then number 9. *The church is the family of God.* In Ephesians 2:19 we learn that the church is referred to as "the household of God." It refers to men as belonging to the household of God. In verse 16 of the same chapter it is called one body. In verse 21 Paul calls it the building. In verse 20 he speaks of the fact that it is built on Christ. And those very same ones who are referred to as the one body.

(Time called.)

Third Day

BOGARD'S FIRST NEGATIVE

Gentlemen Moderators, Ladies and Gentlemen:

When you have heard my friend deliver his address you have heard the best that can be given from his viewpoint. I have inquired concerning my friend Porter over and over again, and his own brethren regard him as having just about the best ability as a debater that any of them have. So you have heard the best, and when I answer that you will know the very best has been answered.

My friend was not satisfied with the discussion of the name for the last two days. We had that more than any other one thing. So he goes back and starts in where he left off on the name. I am rather glad he did, for that gives me an opportunity that I would not have had. He says you cannot have a plural without a singular. Now I do not want to be disrespectful; I do not want to say things that sound harsh, but that is too silly to talk about. The trees of the forest—therefore there must be a *great big tree that includes all the little trees of the forest.* So you cannot have a plural without a singular. The men of Arkansas—you cannot have a plural without a singular, so there must be *one great big man that includes all the little men in Arkansas.* The houses of Damascus—that is plural; there has to be a singular, so there is bound to be *one great big house that includes all the little houses in Damascus.* Now anybody knows that is not so who has any sense at all. My friend has got good sense, therefore he knows better than that. The churches of Christ, he finds, therefore there must be a great big church including all the little churches, or congregations. That is the argument.

Since he went through two whole days arguing all the time in favor of the very thing he brought up again this afternoon, it gives me a chance to bring out something that I did not have time to bring out unless he had done as he has done just a little while ago. He asked what the church is to be called in Damascus, for instance, just one local congregation. Would not that be *"The Church of Christ?"* In making the argument in favor of the name Missionary

Baptist, showing it to be scriptural, I showed the idea was scriptural. Now he said, "I would like to know what a local congregation would be called, if it is not the church, in that particular locality."

I am going to challenge my friend now to do something, and he must do it or acknowledge he cannot find the name of his church anywhere in the Bible. "The Church of Christ", that expression, is not in the Bible. Now write down the passage of scripture where it says "The Church of Christ". Why that is what you mean when you say the general body, including all the saved. When I made the argument that a thing ought to be called what it is, he said, "Where do you find where the Missionary Baptist Church is named anywhere in the Bible?" I come right back now, and say, "Where do you find the Church of Christ mentioned in the Bible?" It is not there. That is an offset, so he has got to *find the idea* if he finds anything at all. That is what I found. I found the *Missionary Baptist Church idea.* Somebody will say, "Then why was it not named in the Bible?" Why was not the Church of Jesus Christ named in the Bible? It is not there. The name you harp on, the name you talk about most, the name that you depend on, is not in the Bible.

Now we come to the local congregation. That amuses me. He ought to know. He says if the *local congregation* is not the church in that particular place, "The *Church of Christ*" in that particular place, why isn't it? And now listen. I call your attention to the very same chapter where he finds the churches of Christ in Rom. 16:16. In the fourth verse it says "the churches of the Gentiles." Is "the churches of the Gentiles" the name? Churches of the Gentiles, is that the name? In the fourth verse it says the churches of the Gentiles. In the sixteenth verse it says the churches of Christ. What is meant? Why, of course, it means the churches that belong to Christ, and the churches that belong to the Gentiles. They were the Lord's churches in both cases.

Very well, now come over to Galatians, if you please. I read in Gal. 1:22, "and was unknown by face unto the churches of Judea which were in Christ." Is that the name of the churches, the churches of Judea? If it is not, then why do you say "the churches of Christ" is the name?

Now again, I will call your attention to what the Bible says. Turn right over here to the book of Revelation. My friend says would not that be "The Church of Christ," if it is located in Damascus, "The Church of Christ" at that particular place? Well, let us look and see now. He asks why does not the Lord call it Baptist Church, if it is? I am going to ask you, why does not the Lord call it The Church of Christ, or something like that, over here in the book of Revelation? Turn to the seven churches of Asia in the second chapter. It does not say the seven churches of Christ. It left the name off. I reckon the Lord did not think it was important or He would have put it in. Now, "let him that hath an ear hear what the Spirit saith" unto the churches of Christ. No, sir. The Lord did not think it necessary to name this group of churches. Then come on down, "To the angel of the church" of Christ "in Smyrna." No, sir. It says "to the angel of the church in Smyrna." My friend says it ought to be called the Church of Christ that is located in Damascus. Why did not the Lord call it that in Smyrna? Then we come on down to the twelfth verse, "the church in Pergamos." Did that say the Church of Christ in Pergamos? No. But if it ought to be called the Church of Christ in Damascus, why would not it be the church of Christ in Pergamos? Now come down still further. "And unto the church at Thyatira"—church, not The Church of Christ. The Lord did not think it necessary to call it the church of Christ. Why, then, do you insist on saying the church of Christ every time, when *not one single time in the Bible* can you find the name, "The Church of Christ," as applied to all of God's people? And not one single time can you find the name, "The Church of Christ", in any locality. It is not in a general sense nor in any locality. Look at all seven of the churches of Asia. The Philadelphia church was not addressed as the church of Christ. They insist on The Church of Christ always being put in.

That is not the name. It only denotes possession, ownership. The churches of Christ salute you. What is that?

The churches that belong to Christ salute you. That is not their name. The dogs of Johnson barked at you. (Laughter). Now what is funny about that? You can not laugh off the truth. I gave you a parallel sentence. If "the dogs of Johnson bark at you" is not their name, but only denotes ownership, then "the churches of Jesus Christ salute you" is not their name, but only denotes ownership. It does not require a scholar to see that. Wise cracks and laughing do not meet the argument. I lay this challenge down right now. Put on the blackboard the chapter and verse where it says the church of Christ referring to all of God's people. Put on the board where it says the church of Christ in any given locality in the Bible. You cannot find it to save your life. You cannot find the general name and you can not find the local name. If you are going to call that argument, just help yourself to it.

Passing now to my friend's speech on the origin of the church. He read in Luke 19:12 where Jesus said He was as a man going into a far country to receive for Himself a kingdom. Well, is He going to do that? Yes, sir. Rev. 11:15 says the kingdoms of this world are become the kingdom of our Lord Jesus Christ and He is not coming back here until that takes place. That refers to that.

He goes to the seventh chapter of Daniel to prove that the church began on the day of Pentecost. Well, I'll declare! Turn right here and read in the seventh chapter of Daniel, if you please, and see what there is to that. Begin reading at the seventh verse. And he put that up to prove that the church began on Pentecost. "After this I saw in the night visions, and behold a fourth beast, dreadful and terrible, and strong exceedingly; and it had great iron teeth: it devoured and brake in pieces, and stamped the residue with the feet of it: and it was diverse from all the beasts that were before it; and it had ten horns . . . I beheld till the thrones were cast down, and the Ancient of days did sit, whose garment was white as snow, and the hair of his head like the pure wool: his throne was like fiery flame, and his wheels as burning fire. A fiery stream issued and came forth from before him: thousand thousands ministered unto him, and ten thousand times ten thousand stood before him: the judgment was set, and the books were opened. I beheld them because of the voice . . ." That refers to the final windup if it refers to any thing at all. Were the books opened and judgment set and ten thousand times ten thousand standing there on the day of Pentecost? Why that is nonsense and my friend knows it. And you know it.

Very well, now we come to the next. He said the church began on the day of Pentecost and before he got through talking said they were added to the church on the day of Pentecost. How are you going to *add* to a thing that is *not already there?* If you want to add something to this building, the building is bound to be here before you can add to it. There were three thousand added on the day of Pentecost, and my friend says the church began on that day.

Now comes my friend and says there is no salvation out of the church, for only those are saved whose names are written in the Lamb's book of life. Then he read the scripture where the church of the firstborn had their names written. That is true, about the names being written. But listen, were there no names written before the church was organized? You mean Abraham, Isaac, and Jacob all died and went to hell or have not reached heaven yet? You mean all the apostles—Peter, James, John, Andrew and Bartholomew, and all of those were outside of Christ, not saved? You mean that they were all the children of the devil up to the day of Pentecost, nobody saved till Pentecost? Is that what you mean? Was nobody saved till the church was organized and the church was not organized until Pentecost? Therefore, Peter, James, and John—that Jesus Christ Himself said were clean ("Now are ye clean through the word which I have spoken unto you.") —all of them were lost. But hold on. What about their names being written in heaven? Well I believe I will just turn and read. I confess to you that I am surprised at my friend. When Christ sent out his disciples two by two, in Luke 10, they came back and reported, "Devils are subject unto us. Why, we had a wonderful time." Jesus said, "Rejoice not that devils were subject unto you, but *rather rejoice because your names are written in heaven.*" That was back before Pentecost. Porter said nobody's names were written in heaven before the church was organized, and he argues that the church was organized on the day of Pentecost. Now that is enough on that particular line.

I want to take up now his argument about the judgment beginning at the house of God. What of that? Does it say that the house of God started when the judgment began? Suppose judgment does begin at the house of God. And again read John 10:16 where Jesus said, "I am the good shepherd. I give my life for the sheep and other sheep have I that are not of this fold." What was the fold? It was the church of the Lord Jesus Christ, evidently so, and He had some outside.

Then he read again where the church was purchased by the blood of Christ. Certainly, the church was purchased by the blood of Christ. And what has that got to do with when the church started? What has that go to do about Pentecost? Eph. 5:25 says the church is like a wife. It mentions the husband and the wife. The husband; the wife; the church. He tries to say that because it says the church and the wife and the husband, it is bound to be a great big church including all the little churches. The very same verse that says *the church,* says also *the husband* of *the wife.* What kind of wife? *A great big wife including all the little wives?* Why that is nonsense to start with.

Then he read where by one Spirit we are baptized into one body. The Greek preposition there, e-n, "en", means exactly what our English preposition i-n, "in", means. *In one Spirit* we are all baptized into one body—in the Spirit first, baptized into the one body after we get into the Spirit. Well that complements the gentleman's speech, every argument he made.

Now, I am going to come to this argument for him. Suppose you prove that the church began on Pentecost, what good would that do you, when the church of which you are a member began eighteen hundred years after Pentecost? Suppose you prove that the church of the Lord began on the day of Pentecost? It would be the Missionary Baptist Church. There was not any other church back there at that time. The church of which you are a member began in 1827, under the leadership of Alexander Campbell. What good would it do you to prove the church began on the day of Pentecost when you can not back up and hitch on by eighteen-hundred years? What advantage would that give you?

Now, even your theory is wrong. I am going to come right here and show you by the word of God that your theory is wrong. My friend quoted scripture that had no Pentecost in it to prove Pentecost. He read scripture that had the church in it, but did not say Pentecost. Then he read scripture that did not say church or Pentecost either and tried to put them all together and make it say that it was the church starting on the day of Pentecost. Even if you should prove it, it would not do you any good. For the church of which you are a member does not reach back that far. But you are even wrong in the theory.

Now I will give you what the Bible says on the subject of the kingdom and church. Jesus was king before Pentecost, John 18:37. His *kingdom suffered* before Pentecost, Matt. 11:12. *Men pressed into the kingdom* before Pentecost, Luke 16:16. Some *hindered others from entering* the kingdom before Pentecost, Matt. 23:33. Could you hinder anybody from entering this house if the house were not here? Some did hinder people from entering. Then there was an *ordained ministry* before Pentecost, Mark 3:13-14. He ordained and sent out His preachers. Again, the *commission to preach* was given before Pentecost. He sent out His disciples to preach and they came back and reported that they had wonderful success, and Jesus said, "Do not rejoice over your success, because the devils were subject to you, but rather rejoice because your *names are written in heaven.*" So there are names written in heaven—saved before the church was organized, if my friend is right on the time when the church was organized. They were *authorized to baptize* before Pentecost, John 4:2. For it says Jesus made and baptized more disciples than John, though Jesus Himself baptized not, but His disciples. They had the *Lord's supper* before Pentecost, Luke 22:19, where Jesus instituted the supper and said observe it till I come again. They had a *rule of discipline* before Pentecost; Matt. 18:16-17 tells how to deal with your erring brother. They had *the gospel* before Pentecost, Matt. 24:14, and also in Mark 1:1 we read about the beginning of the gospel of Jesus Christ.

Jesus said there was *no doubt* about the kingdom being in existence before Pentecost, Luke 11:20. "But if I with the finger of God cast out devils, no doubt the kingdom of God is come upon you." Who said there was no doubt about the kingdom of God existing back there just as sure as He cast out devils? Jesus said it. Who said there *is doubt* about it? My friend Porter. Who are you going to believe? Jesus said there was *no doubt* about it. My friend says, "WHY I DO NOT BELIEVE IT AT ALL." Who are you going to believe—Porter or the Lord Jesus Christ? Then Acts 1:21 said a company accompanied Jesus all the time He went in and out among us beginning from the baptism of John. That company that our Lord had begun when? Beginning from the baptism of John, and staying with Him all the time that Jesus went in and out among us, "beginning from the Baptism of John unto that same day He was taken up from us." And to that company He gave the commission and promised to come back to that company again. And Luke 11:33 says the kingdom thus begun shall have no end. There is your kingdom of which there shall be no end.

Matt. 28:18-20 tells us that Jesus gave all power, Porter said the power came when the church did. All right then, sir, they got the power before Pentecost. Matt. 28:19-20 says, "All power is given unto me in heaven and earth. Go ye therefore and teach all nations, baptizing them in the name of the Father, and of the Son, and of the Holy Ghost: . . . and, lo, I am with you alway, even unto the end of the world." And so Jesus gave them authority and power. Porter said the church came when the power came. Why that was way yonder before Pentecost. Then the bride and the bridegroom existed before Pentecost. John 3:28-29. "He that hath bride is the bridegroom." And then John 13:3-4 says all things were given unto Jesus, all power. That was before Pentecost. Porter said the church and the power came at the same time. And Jesus, when He left the earth, Mark 13, said He left His house, and give His servants authority and a work to do and commanded them to watch, for in such an hour as ye expect not the Son of man comes. He *gave them authority and a work to do* when He left. You can not leave your house unless there is a house to leave. You can not leave this house unless there is a house here to leave. Jesus Christ with all power could not leave a thing that was not there. He said He left His house and gave His servants authority and a work to do and commanded them to watch, for ye know not when the master of the house comes.

Now my friend is wrong on the origin of the church, but if he were right on it, it would not do him any good. For the church of which he is a member began eighteen-hundred years after the time he says the church began. He tried to prove it and if he had succeeded in proving it, he would have only succeeded only in a theory. I want to know if a Mexican, a "greaser" Mexican, had the correct idea about when the United States government began, would that make him a citizen of the United States? Why you say, "No." Then if you have a correct idea about when the church began that will not make you a member of that church. It is only a matter of historical interest. And it would not hurt me a bit in the world. I could just acknowledge right here, and say, "Why sir, you are right. The church started on Pentecost." I could say I will give it up right now. It would not hurt me a bit in the world, for the Baptists are the only ones who can back up and hitch on to Pentecost. Absolutely. All the others began since Pentecost. What good would it do you to prove the church started on the day of Pentecost when your church started eighteen-hundred years after Pentecost? Now somebody says, "You have not proved that." Well, you wait. I have two days to prove it in. And I can not do everything in the first thirty minutes. I am showing you where he is. *What good would it do him?*

Now when you get up here, please put down somewhere some passage of scripture on the board that has called all of God's people "The Church of Christ." You can not find that expression in the lids of the Bible. Then I want you to find some local congregation that is called "The Church of Christ" in the Bible. You can not find it to save your life. You can not find the general name and you can not find the local name, the thing you harp on all the time. And suppose you did; suppose you did. Why it would not prove that you belonged to that particular organization. It would not prove that you belonged to that church that Christ owns and possesses. Certainly, you have got to go about that to prove it some other way.

Now somebody asks why did not the Lord call it by name? *The Lord did not name the church at all.* We got that clearly. "The churches of Christ" denotes ownership, possessive case, genitive. We proved it by the telegram from Harding college, your own man. Christ is genitive, singular. That is what your professor said. Genitive means possession. What did He possess? He possessed churches. The churches that Christ possessed salute you. The Lords' churches salute you. And so, find where that is the name. You can find where the Lord owned it, but you can not find where that is the name, not to save your life. And if you did find that was the name it would not do you any good, for the church to which you belong started eighteen-hundred years after all this, after the Bible was closed. Now what is the benefit, what is the use, of standing up here and arguing to prove a thing that will not do you any good after you get it proved? You did not prove it to start with, but if you did prove it, it would not do you any good at all. Why, it would do the Catholics more good than it would you, because they can go further back toward Pentecost than you can, to save your life. You have got to back up and hitch on to Pentecost. That is all there is about it, or else you can not prove anything beneficial to the church.

Now Alexander Campbell himself said in Religious Encyclopedia, page 465, that after the Baptists had, in the year 1827, declared nonfellowship for the brethren of the reformation, thus by constraint and not by choice, they *were obliged to form societies* out of those communities that stood upon the ground of adherence to apostolic doctrine. *Alexander Campbell says your church started when they were excluded from the Baptists.* Page 465 of Religious Encyclopedia. It was made up of a bunch of excluded Baptists in 1827 and then you claim to back up and hitch on to Pentecost. (Laughter). And you can not laugh it off. You can not laugh it off. And I am going to call attention to the fact that a laugh will not go down on these records, except a little jar. If you think you can meet the Bible by laughing at the word of God, why that is a very poor idea, I think. Why not meet the arguments? Why not face facts? What good will it do you to ridicule the truth? I have shown you where Campbell said Baptists turned them out before they started their organization. You can not prove that your church reaches back beyond Alexander Campbell. Give me the name of one congregation like the one that meets within these walls, that has every Sunday the Lord's Supper, that teaches salvation by baptism, that teaches falling from grace, and all these other things like you teach. Find just one back of Alexander Campbell, and I will acknowledge I am mistaken about one. But even then you could not find enough to go all the way back to Jesus Christ. And the Bible says "unto him be glory in the church by Christ Jesus throughout all ages," and you do not go through all ages. Therefore, you can not fit the descripion laid down in the word of God.

Thank you.

TIME CALLED

Third Day

PORTER'S SECOND AFFIRMATIVE

Gentlemen Moderators, Mr. Bogard, Ladies and Gentlemen:

You've seen a man fail again. I was really amused at Mr. Bogard. He took about one passage out of each argument I gave, and made a reference to it, and said, "I've answered everything he said." There were dozens of Scriptures, upon which I made definite arguments, that he didn't even refer to. He just took one here, skipped, and got one out of one passage, skipped a whole argument, and got one out of another argument, and then skipped along. He got three or four during the time and skipped others entirely. *Didn't even refer to a bunch of them that I made.* And then he said, "I answered all the gentleman said." He meant he answered all that he took down. Yes, he answered all, according to the notes he had. The fact is he doesn't make any notes. He'll sit there and look up here and just once in a while write down a word. He makes no notes at all to speak of. And therefore it helps him to forget. If he had them down there, they might remind him of the arguments, but he doesn't put them down so he can forget them. Well, that's one way to get by if you didn't have an opponent, but you have an opponent, and you're not going to get by on that.

I want to notice, while it is fresh on your minds, some of the last things that he said, and then I shall go back to the beginning. He said, "The Catholics can go further back than you can. You can't go back beyond 1827, back beyond Alexander Campbell." Well, suppose that is true; yes, just suppose that's true, why, you'd be in the same hole, Mr. Bogard. The Catholics can go further back than you can. (Laughter) Yes, because your own authority said, your own history said, that the first regularly organized Baptist Church, of which they had any account, dated from 1607. The Catholics go further back than that, Mr. Bogard. And Mr. Bogard said that wasn't *his kind*—that was English Baptists. So the first ones of his kind can't go back even that far. (Laughter) But what would it hurt if what he said were true? He would be in the same predicament. It wouldn't damage anything particularly. And, besides, suppose the church that I belong to did start with Alexander Campbell. Well, I would just as soon have one that started with Alexander Campbell—I had just as soon be a member of Alexander Campbell's—as to belong to one that started with John Smith. At least, Alexander Campbell did have *somebody to baptize him,* but John Smith *baptized himself*—the man that started the first Baptist Church. And I challenge Mr. Bogard to deny it. John Smith baptized himself when he started the Baptist Church. There would be some advantage, at least, in being a member of one that a man started who had somebody to haptize him than to have him baptize himself. So just granting that all that is so, why, he's in a worse condition for it.

Now, then, he read from Religious Encyclopedia to prove by Campbell that we had been excluded from the Baptist Church. Mr. Bogard, you can't prove that Alexander Campbell was ever a member of the Baptist Church if your life depended on it. If you can, let us have some proof. He gets up here and says that Alexander Campbell was excluded from the Baptist Church. Well, Alexander Campbell *was never a member of the Baptist Church.* Why, when Alexander Campbell was baptized by Mr. Luce, he came to him and requested baptism *contrary to Baptist usage,* and Mr. Luce baptized him that way. He had some hesitancy about it, but finally agreed to baptize him *precisely according to the* New Testament, but he said it was contrary to Baptist usage. *It still is.* He wasn't baptized according to Baptist requirements at all, and that didn't make him a member of the Baptist Church. Do you baptize anybody that way today, Mr. Bogard? Will you take a man into the Baptist Church today who was baptized like Alexander Campbell was? Put it down and tell us about it. *Will you accept a man for membership in the Baptist Church who was baptized like Alexander Campbell was baptized?* If it will not make a man a member of the Baptist Church today, it wouldn't make Alexander Campbell a member of the Baptist Church. Also, I call your attention to this — quoting from Reformatory Movements, page 169, which contains the quotation from Millennial Harbinger of 1848 — Mr.

Campbell said: "I had no idea"—get this—"I had no idea of uniting with the Baptists more than with the Moravians or with the mere Independents." Mr. Campbell was never a member of the Baptist Church. He said that he wasn't—he had no idea of ever becoming one. And then once more—page 344 in the Millennial Harbinger of 1848, he made this statement: "They all pressed us to *join their Redstone Association.* We laid the matter before the church in the fall of 1813. We discussed the propriety of the matter. After much discussion and earnest desire to be directed by the wisdom which cometh from above, we *finally concluded* to make an overture *to that effect,* and to write out a full view of our sentiments, wishes, and determination on the subject. We did in some eight or ten pages of large dimensions, exhibiting our remonstrance against all human creeds as bonds of communion or union amongst Christian churches, and expressing a willingness, *upon certain conditions, to cooperate or unite with that association,* provided always that we should be allowed to teach and preach whatever we learned from the Holy Scriptures, regardless of any creed or formula in Christendom."

And then again, from the same page, "They pressed me from every quarter to visit their churches, and, though not a member"—*though not a member*—"to preach for them. I often spoke to the Baptist congregations for sixty miles around." Well, Alexander Campbell, himself, said he *was never a member of the Baptist Church.* But you come up here and tell me that the Baptist Church kicked him out and he started a church of his own. There's not a word of truth in it. You can't prove, Mr. Bogard, that Alexander Campbell was ever a member of the Baptist Church. *I challenge you to do it.* He simply worked in connection with the Baptist Association, and that's all there was to it, but he was never a member of the Baptist Church. You should begin to know by this time that you can't get by with things like that.

Now, back to the beginning. He said, "I have inquired much about Mr. Porter, and I find, among his brethren, that he is regarded as perhaps one of the best in debating, and if I answer that, I have answered the best." Yes, and if you skip that, I guess you skip the best. (Laughter) If that's true, then Mr. Bogard, instead of answering the best, you skipped the best—because you skipped. I'm going to show this audience the passages that I referred to that you didn't even mention. And what did you do with this one? (pointing to the blackboard) A bare reference to it but he made no effort to meet the argument that I made whatsoever.

Mr. Bogard said: "Porter was not satisfied about the name. We discussed that on two other days, and he went back to it again." Well, my proposition says "name." That's the reason I went back to it. Certainly, I went back to it because it is in my proposition just like it's in yours. That's the very thing you would expect me to do. If I hadn't gone back to it, you would have said, "Why, Porter is afraid of the name, isn't he?" Well, Porter goes back to it, and Bogard says: "He's dissatisfied with it." Why, my proposition mentions name. That's why I went to it.

Then "the plural without a singular." Why, he said, "That's so silly—that it's just too silly to think about." Well, what he's talking about is even sillier. Yes, a plural without a singular. He said, "You can have a plural without a singular. The trees of the forest." Since you have "the trees of the forest," you can't pick out one tree—you can't find the singular anywhere in the forest. Is that silly or is that intelligent? And "the men of Arkansas." You have "the men of Arkansas" but you can't find an individual man anywhere in Arkansas." You can't find a singular anywhere. Is that silly or is that intelligent? "The houses of Damascus." And you can't have any singular there. I wonder how many this one is? Yes, the houses of Damascus. You can't find a singlar house—you can't find a house in the singular anywhere in Damascus. Is that silly or is that intelligent? That's pretty good, I call it, with a big question mark after it. Now, what's he trying to do? Why, he's trying to say that you've got to find one great big tree that contains all the little trees; and one big man that contains all the little men; and one great big house that contains all the little houses. Why don't you get a parallel, Mr. Bogard? Try your hand on *the Masonic Lodge*. That's an institution. You're dealing with institutions here. Try your hand on the Masonic Lodge. Let's see what they say about *the Masonic Lodge.* Does it refer to the institution as a whole? Doesn't that *include all their local organizations?* Try your hand on an institution. Come and get something that is parallel with it. You know you haven't got a parallel. This audience knows it now.

He said, "You can't find *the church of Christ* in a locality," and we'll get some more of that in just a minute—but he also said that I declared that it ought to be called what it is. And then he went on to say, "Where does it say *the church of Christ?* It ought to be called what it is." Well, it *wasn't called the Baptist Church.* So I guess it wasn't. Mr. Bogard right before this speech said (do you remember) that "the Lord did not name the church." "The Lord did not name the church." Why, Mr. Bogard, what on earth is the matter with you? I asked you a written question yesterday or the day before—day before, I believe I asked it—and you finally got to the answering of it yesterday. *When did your people first take the name Baptist Church?"* You said, "They didn't take it—*the Lord named them that.* And they've had it ever since." And then you came along today and said *the Lord did not name the church.* Just another one of Bogard's blunders. He just met himself coming back again. Yes, sir, "the Lord did not name the church." But yesterday he said the Lord named it back there in the days of John and we have had it ever since. It came right along with us. But today the Lord never named the church.

And then he said, "Suppose you could find the church was established on Pentecost. That wouldn't do you any good, because it would just prove the Baptist Church started there. The Baptists are the only ones who can back up and hitch on." Well, where are you going to hitch, Mr. Bogard? I left you a place here (pointing to board) to stick up your hitching post and you haven't put it there. (Laughter)

CHART NO. 1

Church of Christ	**Baptist Church**
Churches of Christ	**Baptist Churches**
— Rom. 16:16	————

I left a place here, Mr. Bogard, for you to erect your

hitching post—some place to hitch on in the New Testament. And you said, "If you can find it back there—if it was established back there on Pentecost—the Baptist Church is the only one that can back up and hitch on." You can't hitch on till you have a hitching post. You've got to have a coupling somewhere before you can hitch on. Where are you going to get it? You can't find it. It's not here (pointing to board). The place is still blank. Will you please erect one and show me how you are going to hitch on to it. The fact is the Baptist Church is one of those which *absolutely cannot hitch on.* For there is no mention in all of God's Book of the Baptist Church or Baptist Churches of any kind or nature, and there's no reference—there's no passage—in God's Book that will give him any place to hitch on, and he knows it. If he does know otherwise, let him erect his post here, and we'll see how he can hitch on to it.

"But you cannot find *the church of Christ.*" Well, I'm still insisting that the plural included the singular, and therefore the law of deduction is all you need. Let's try it. Get a little of the law of deduction here. Yes, sir, a man has fifteen apples. All right, he has fifteen apples. We're going to follow the law of deduction and we deduct fourteen apples. What does he have then? He has one apple. All right, try it on churches. Suppose there are fifteen churches of Christ. Suppose we deduct fourteen churches of Christ. We have one church of Christ. *Is that silly? Is that silly?* Let me show you how Mr. Bogard gets his by the law of deduction. There are fifteen churches of Christ. Deduct fourteen churches of Christ. Left—one Baptist Church. That would be like having fifteen apples. Deduct fourteen apples and have one *peach* left. Now, that is the difference. If you think our positions are parallel, I think you'll get by anyway. Now, I'm sure that Mr. Bogard has enough sense to know that that is so. If you deduct fourteen churches of Christ from fifteen churches of Christ, you have one church of Christ left. You don't have one Baptist Church, Mr. Bogard. If you deduct fourteen apples from fifteen apples, you have one apple left—not one peach. Oh, but over in Romans 16:4 he read about the churches of the Gentiles, and then about the churches of Judea in Gal. 1:22, and the seven churches of Asia—the church at Pergamos and the church at Thyatira and the church at Smyrna. He said it didn't say "the churches of Christ in Judea" and "the churches of Christ in Asia" and "the churches of Christ in Smyrna" and "the church of Christ in Pergamos" and "the church of Christ in Thyatira." No. Well, *here is what it did say:* It said, "the seven Baptist Churches of Asia." It said "the Baptist Churches of Judea" and "the Baptist Church at Smyrna" and "the Baptist Church at Pergamos and Thyatira." That's what it said—or did it? *No, it didn't say anything* about Baptist Church anywhere or Baptist Churches either. Of course, you don't have to use the expression "church of Christ" every time a reference is made to it. How many times does the Lord have to say a thing, Mr. Bogard, to make you believe it? I talked with a fellow one time about this, and he said, "Why, that's not in the Bible." I gave him this passage. And he said, "Well, it just says it one time." I said, "Well, how many times do you think it ought to say it before you'd believe it?" And he said, "I think it ought to say it at least three times." I believe that is the way with Mr. Bogard. He thinks that it ought to be said everyime that it's referred to in order to make him believe it. If the Lord says a thing one time, that is enough. He wouldn't have to say "churches of Christ" or "church of Christ" everytime he refers to it. We do not. We refer to the church in Damascus, the churches in Little Rock, the church in Monette, the churches in various localities round about, without saying "churches of Christ" every time we refer to them. Certainly, "churches of Christ" denotes ownership—in that passage they belong to Christ. *Certainly, they do.* Well, Mr. Bogard, isn't it better—isn't it more Scriptural—for a church to wear a designation that is found in the Bible, even though it does designate ownership, than to wear one that is not found in the Bible as you do—the Baptist Church? Now, who is going to be the more Scriptural? The one who wears that which designates ownership or the one who wears that which doesn't designate anything in the Bible—because it's never mentioned in the Bible?

Then back to the dogs of Johnson and their barking

again. (Laughter) He said you can't laugh that off. Yes, but I called attention to the fact last night that even in his illustration—"the dogs of Johnson"—that the word "dogs" is a *noun* and that it is the *name* of four legged animals that belong to Mr. Johnson. But he said yesterday, you know, when he introduced it—or day before yesterday, as the case may have been—that their names were Spot, Trip and Trailer. I said, "Mr. Bogard, how do you know that their names were Spot, Trip and Trailer? Could you have told by just a description of them?" He is claiming that if you get a description of the church, that you will know what the name of the church is. All right, then, let Mr. Johnson give you a description of the dogs, and you'll know what their names are. Is that silly—or intelligent? Furthermore, Mr. Bogard, while you're on that you might try your hand on this: Suppose you substitute for "dogs of Johnson" and say "sons of Johnson." I wonder if you'd have any name then? "Sons of Johnson." Would you know anything about what the names of the sons are? Would you know anything about a name when it says "sons of Johnson?" *Would that indicate a name anywhere?*

All right, then to his reply to my speech. He came to Luke 19:12 that the Lord received the kingdom. He said this is where Porter started. No, that is not even the argument that I started with, Mr. Bogard. That is the "Number 2" argument I gave. You skipped "Number 1" completely. I gave "No. 1" argument, showing that *it was to be after the resurrection of Christ.* And I gave 2nd Samuel 7:12 and Psalms 132:11 and Acts 2:29-31, but you did not even mention it. Didn't even act as if you thought it had ever been introduced. Not a word did you say about it. *You skipped it completely.* I showed that the Lord would be placed upon David's throne *after David was dead* and that he spoke of *the resurrection of Christ,* and that he *ascended* to heaven to *take his seat on that throne.* You did not *even refer* to it. Yet "I answered all that Porter said." "Answered all that he said." Then to Luke 19:12, and what do we have there? A man "went into a far country to receive for himself a kingdom, and to return." He said, "Yes, Rev. 11:15 shows that the kingdoms of the world become his kingdom—and that's after while sometime." Is that when the Lord comes back, or when is it, Mr. Bogard? When does the Lord receive those kingdoms there? When will the kingdoms of the world become his kingdom? Tell us something about that and show us that it has an application to that passage. And then to Daniel 7:13-14. Mr. Bogard said, "Why, Jesus came in the clouds of heaven to the Ancient of Days and was given glory, dominion and a kingdom, but this refers to the final wind up." And he went to verse 7 that tells about the thrones being cast down and judgment being set. Well, Mr. Bogard, did you ever read the first verse of that chapter where Daniel had VISIONS—VISIONS—not just one vision, but several visions are mentioned here. But you're trying to make the whole thing one vision. Daniel referred to visions in the plural number. Of course, *you* couldn't have a singular anyway. (Laughter) Well, then, Mr. Bogard, I want to know this. You say that refers to the second coming of Christ—when he'll come back in the clouds of heaven. The passage says I saw him "come *to the Ancient of days*." You will agree with me that the Ancient of days is God. When Jesus comes the second time is he coming *to God* or *from God?* Now, you tell me. This says he came *to God* and received the kingdom. You said it is the second coming. In the second coming, Mr. Bogard, he is coming *from God*—he is not coming *to God.* This says he came *to the Ancient of days*—he came *to God*—and there was given him glory, dominion and a kingdom.

Oh, but he said some were added on Pentecost—the Lord added on Pentecost. Well, he said it had to exist first. If somebody was added to it on Pentecost, it had to exist before Pentecost. Well, I'll declare, Mr. Bogard. What on earth is the matter with you? Suppose enough members come out here to build a house on this lot if there wasn't any house here. And they would get the thing completed by noon of that day. Enough men could build it by noon on one particular day. Could there be anything else added to it *that day?* Why, certainly, the church had to exist before others could be added to it, but it didn't take all day to be brought into existence. The Lord didn't take all day at it. After the

Lord brought it into existence—after it came—certainly they could add to it. But it came then.

Did you notice how he skipped Mark 9:1? Yes, Mark 9:1; Acts 1:8 and Acts 2:1-4. I showed that the kingdom would come *with power*. What did he say about it? *Nothing.* I showed from Acts 1 and 8 the power would come *with the Holy Ghost.* And I showed in Acts 2:1-4 that the Holy Ghost came "when the day of Pentecost was fully come." And he got up here and said that Porter introduces Scripture that said nothing about Pentecost, and then Scripture that said nothing about the church, and so on. Well, here are definite Scriptures — definitely located and connected — and they say that the kingdom would *come with power*, and the power would *come with the Holy Ghost*, and then they say *the Holy Ghost came on Pentecost.* When you put two and two together, that says the kingdom came on Pentecost, because that is when the power came. The kingdom came with power and the power came with the Holy Ghost. So the kingdom came on Pentecost, according to that. Well, he finally got around to the idea of power, and he said "No, they received power before then, according to Matt. 28:18—all power—that Jesus gave them all power." It doesn't say anything of the kind. Jesus said, "All power is given unto me." He didn't say, "I have given you all power."

I come to salvation in the church. You notice how he skipped those? I want to take them up again, and call your attention to them, just to show you how he skipped those arguments that I introduced. First, this house of God. 1st Peter 4:17-18.

CHART NO. 7

The house of God	**Them that obey not**
Us	**The ungodly**
The Righteous	**The sinner**

"For the time is come that judgment must begin at the
"For the time is come that judgment must begin at the
house of God: and if it first begin at us, what shall the end be of them that obey not the gospel of God? And if the righteous scarcely be saved, where shall the ungodly and the sinner appear?" What did Mr. Bogard say about that?

He said, "Well, suppose judgment does begin at the house of God. Does that mean the house of God began there?" No, I never said anything about that. You're talking about something that wasn't even used or based on the passage at all. The thing I made the argument about you didn't even mention. You didn't even act like you ever heard it. The fact is you havn't heard it before, I suppose. And that's the reason you couldn't say anything about it. Well, here it is. It doesn't say anything about when the house of God began. I wasn't trying to prove when the house of God began by this passage. I was proving that *salvation is in the house of God.* I wasn't trying to prove when the house of God began. It says, "The time is come that judgment must begin at *the house of God:* and if it first begin at *us.*" The "house of God" and "us" mean the same thing. That is what I was showing. And in contrast with that, "if it first begin at us, what will be the end of *them that obey not* the gospel?" Those *who obey not the gospel* are used in contrast with *the house of God* and *us.* "And if *the righteous scarcely* be saved, where shall *the ungodly* and *the sinner* appear?" On the one hand, we have house of God, us, and righteous—meaning the same people. In contrast with that, them that obey not the gospel, the ungodly, and the sinner. Therefore, those who are no part of *the house of God* are no part of *us* and no part of *the righteous,* but they are *them that obey not* the gospel; they are *the ungodly;* and they are *the sinners.* And if they can be saved out of the house of God, without being a part of us, without being a part of the righteous, then they can be saved while disobeying the gospel, while ungodly and in sin. That's the argument, Mr. Bogard, and you know, and this audience knows, that you haven't touched it. And you can't touch it.

Then he came to the second argument, after having skipped that one entirely. The second argument I made was Ephesians 5:25. "For the husband is head of the wife, even as Christ is head of the church: and he is the saviour of the body." What did he say about that? He said, "The wife—one big wife contains all the little wives." Why, I didn't introduce that along that line at all. That wasn't what the argument was, Mr. Bogard. You sidestepped it. The argument made was on the statement: "He is the saviour of the body." Why didn't you notice the argument? "He is the savior *of the body.*" I showed that he is the Savior of the body, but he doesn't save men out of the body, because if so, then they are saved *before they get into the body.* So in no sense of the term can he be *the Savior of the body,* unless they get lost again after they get into the body, and you say that they can't do that. (Laughter) Consequently, you haven't even touched that. Just made a little quibble about it, as you said — about something that didn't even have anything to do with the argument. You tried to divert the people's attention away from what I said, and what the argument was, and to make them think about something else. Please notice the argument. Take the passage—take the statement upon which the argument was based — and show us something about it. "He is the saviour of the body." Mr. Bogard, does that mean that he is the Savior of the church? And if it does, you tell me how he can be the Savior of the church if everybody is saved before he enters the church? I challenge you to do it. You will not have done it when this debate is come to a close.

Then to *the church comprises the saved.* Acts 2:47. He did not even refer to this one except that he said he added them on the day of Pentecost, and the church was already there. But that has no connection with this argument. That was on the origin, but this is on salvation in the church. "The Lord added to the church daily such as should be saved." I showed that they were either saved *before* they entered the church or they were saved *when* they entered the church. If they were saved before they were added to the church, then the Lord *isn't* the Savior of the body. But since he *is the Savior of the body,* then they were saved *when* they were added to the church. Therefore the church comprises all the saved.

Then *the cost of the church.* What did he say about that? *Nothing.* Skipped it completely. Acts 20:28. He purchased the church with his own blood. And Ephesians 5:25. "He loved the church and gave himself for it." I said that the benefit of that blood must be obtained out of that institution for which the price was paid. When you buy a stick of candy for a nickel, if you ever get any benefit out of that nickel, you will get it out of the stick of candy that you bought with it. Jesus shed his blood. How much of it? All of it. And purchased the church with his own blood. If you ever get any benefit from the blood of Christ, you'll get it out of the institution for which the price was paid. What did he say about it? *Not one single word.* Yet "I answered all that Mr. Porter said." Yes, sir, that is the way he answers.

My fifth argument was based upon the fact that *we are redeemed by his blood.* 1st Peter 1:19. "Forasmuch as ye know that ye were not redeemed with corruptible things, as silver and gold, but with the precious blood of Jesus." I showed that the same act that puts us into the church puts us into the blood. Romans 6:3—"baptized into his death." 1st Cor. 12:13—"baptized into the body." What did Mr. Bogard say about this? Only one passage he referred to, and that was 1st Cor. 12:13, and he said the little word "by" there—"by one Spirit are we all baptized into one body"—comes from the Greek word "en" and means "in." "*In* one Spirit are we all baptized into one body." Therefore, you must be *in the Spirit* and saved before you are baptized into the body. Well, let's try it again, right in the same chapter. Mr. Bogard, try verse 3. In verse 3 Paul said that no man can say that Jesus is the Lord except "by the Holy Ghost." And the word "by" there is from the very same Greek word as found in verse 13, which you said means *in the Holy Ghost.* Therefore, a man must be *in the Holy Ghost*—he must be saved—before he can even say that Jesus is Lord. That's the hole he is in.

Come now to these "written in heaven." He said, "Porter said that nobody had his name written in heaven before Pentecost." Porter never said a thing that's even a 42nd cousin to that. I said, "*In this age* those who have their names written in heaven is the church." I never said about other ages. Certainly, in other ages men had their names written in heaven. I'm talking about salvation *in this age*—not salvation in the Old Testament age or some other age—but about salvation *in this age.* And in this age the church has their names written there. Heb. 12:23. "Come to the church of the firstborn which are written in heaven." Mr. Bogard, I called upon you to show me somebody *in this age* that has his name written in heaven except the church. That's the point. Not back *before this age.* We're talking about *this age.* You're side-stepping. Come on and deal with what pertains to this age.

Then he ran in a lot of Scriptures about Christ being king, and the kingdom suffering violence, and they pressed into it, and hindered it, had an ordained ministry, and a commission and was ordered to baptize, and the Lord's Supper, and discipline, and gospel, and no doubt, and the company, and going into it, and all power, and the bride, and all things, and he left his house. All of these we have gone over and over for the past two days. He introduced every one of them two or three times. In the other proposition we have discussed them all.

But if a Mexican had a correct idea about when the United States Government began, would he be a citizen of it? No. I have never claimed that having the correct idea about when the church began makes you a member of it. You never heard any such argument made by anybody. Not at all. Not at all, Mr. Bogard. That is merely a quibble that you had to make because you couldn't meet the argument. You had to do something to put in your time, and so you just followed that plan.

I showed also in my 7th argument that *both Jew and Gentile were reconciled in the church.* Ephesians 2:16. Both reconciled "unto God in one body." And I showed that the body is the church. What did he say about it? *Not a word.* Did not even mention it. Yes, the church is the body. "Reconciled in the body."

I showed, No. 8, the church is the house of God.

(Time called.)

Third Day

BOGARD'S SECOND NEGATIVE

Gentlemen Moderators, Ladies and Gentlemen:

While it is fresh on your minds I will respond to what Mr. Porter said about being reconciled in the body. But he cannot find where it says you are reconciled *by being in the body*. Certainly, those who are in the body are reconciled to Christ but *not reconciled by being in the body*. He must show that.

My friend says I did not reply to what he says here on the board. I would like to know why. He took the position there that nobody was saved outside of the church and the church was not organized till Pentecost. I answered that by showing that they had their names written in heaven before Pentecost. Was not that salvation before the church was organized, he being judge? Luke 10:20. Rejoice not that the devils were subject unto you but rejoice "because your names are written in heaven." Then I read to him from the tenth chapter of John where it says, "Other sheep have I which are not of this fold." Mr. Porter presumes that you will forget all that—the way I answered about salvation being in the church and in the church only.

I also called attention to the fact that all the apostles were on the road to hell until Pentecost if that doctrine is true. Notwithstanding the fact that Jesus said, "Now are you clean through the word which I have spoken unto you", nobody was saved until the day of Pentecost. That is a theory. That is what he tried to prove. That is what I answered. He wants me to take up each and every item and kill time on that when I can knock it in the head with just the plain word of God. He took a long-winded argument and put two and two together and called that four and came to a conclusion. I thought you men were the ones who spoke when the Bible spoke and were silent when the Bible was silent. You did not have to put two and two together.

Now, I asked him to show one single place, just one single verse of scripture that used the expression "The Church of Christ" including all of the saved. Where is that verse? It is not on the board. Anybody that remembers it raise your hand and tell me where it is and I will turn and read it and get off of the platform and quit speaking right now. I asked him to show just one time, one chapter and one verse, where any local congregation was called the church of Christ and he has not done it yet. Yet they bank on the name "The Church" meaning *all of God's people* and "The Church" referring to the *local congregation,* but what has he done? He cannot find it. If anybody could find it he could. Now, where is it?

Well, he said the Baptists cannot back up and hitch on. Well, I wonder in my soul if that is so. I thought we could. I thought I did it yesterday and the day before. I will give you another testimony now. We read on page 796 in Religious Encyclopedia: "We have now seen that the Baptists who were originally called Anabaptists, re-baptizers, were the original Waldenses and who long in the history of the Church received the honor of that origin. On this account the Baptists may be considered as the only Christian community which has stood since the days of the Apostles and as a Christian society which has preserved pure the doctrine of the gospel through all ages." At the same time, those refute the erroneous notions of the Catholics that they are the most ancient. I backed up and hitched on. I put a hitching post right here. Baptists were the only one. He says, "Hitch on." I just hitched.

If you can find somebody that will say, some historian that will say, the church of which you are a member came down through the ages, then perhaps you will have some thing that will kind of half way offset what I have said, but I have hitched on. Beginning right here and running back through all the ages, if that does not hitch on, what does hitch on? Very well.

Now, he said I could not prove that Alexander Campbell ever was a member of the Baptist Church. But he was a member of the Baptist Association. If my friend is so green that he does not know that an association is made up of churches—you can not have an association without churches. Alexander Campbell was a member of the association but not a member of the church. What kind of a mess is that you have? He says he was a member of the association, but not a member of the church.

All right, I will call your attention to some other history right along that line. It will not do you any good if you prove the church began on the day of Pentecost and you cannot back up and hitch on to save your life. You cannot do it with Scripture. You cannot do it with history. Very well.

See Zeigler's History of Denominations which says, "The Christian or Campbellite Church was *founded* by Alexander Campbell of Virginia in the year 1827."

Charles B. Seeger in the Life of Campbell, page 25, (and Seeger was a member of the church that you are a member of—so-called Church of Christ) said, "Alexander Campbell soon became chiefly and prominently known as the recognized head of a *new religious movement,* the purpose of which was to restore primitive Christianity in all its simplicity and beauty. Out of this movement has grown a people who choose to call themselves Christians or Disciples, now numbering not less than five hundred thousand in the United States." Very well.

Richardson's Memoirs of Alexander Campbell (and Richardson was a son-in-law of Alexander Campbell, in the family, and a member of the so-called Church of Christ) on page 548, Volume II, said, "Dr. Campbell is among the most eminent citizens of the United States, distinguished for his great learning and ability, for his successful devotion to the education of youth, for his piety, and as the head and *founder* of one of the most important and respectable religious communities in the United States."

You cannot go back of Alexander Campbell to save your life. I asked you to show me just one congregation, just one, like the one that meets within the walls here, teaching the doctrine that you hold to—just one—back of Alexander Campbell. Now you wait till this debate is over and see whether he does it or not.

About the name, I am amused at the gentleman. Give me the chapter and verse where the expression "The Church of Christ" is used to designate all of God's people. Put it on the board. Write it on a slip of paper and hand it up here to me and I will read it now and save you the trouble. Give me the name and address in the Bible of one local congregation that was called "The Church of Christ" like "The Church of Christ" at Ephesus, or something like that. Come on, write it down on a piece of paper and hand it up here and I will read it and quit speaking, give up right now. You bank on the name—name—name. *You cannot find your name in the Bible to save your life.*

Where it says "the churches of Christ salute you", that is not the name. Why, he says, "Are the names of those dogs 'Johnson's Dogs'?" (Laughter) Why no. He says suppose you substitute "Sons of Johnson." I will. The sons of Johnson salute you. Does that mean the name of those boys, or does it mean the boys belong to Johnson? You know it is in the genitive or possessive case and not a name at all. Certainly, we believe the churches belong to the Lord Jesus Christ. Certainly, they did belong, but what was their names?

Now here is the point. We are getting to it. Jesus Christ and the Apostles all put together never gave any name to His churches. Do you know why? Suppose He has said that it is the Mormon Church (Latter Day Saints). Why, everybody would want to imitate that thing, adopt the name. Suppose He had said the name is "The Church of Christ." Here would come along a whole bunch of people like you and try to imitate and grab the name. Suppose the Lord had said the Missionary Baptist Church, named it. If the Lord had said that then here would come every false church in the world claiming that name and you could not tell a thing in the world about it. Instead of that the Lord described the church, gave a description of the doctrines and practices of the church, so that anybody can see what the church is. He left it *nameless* and said these nameless churches belong to the Lord.

Now, if you cannot meet the *description* then you are not scriptural. You cannot find a description of your church in the Bible. You cannot find the name of your church in the Bible. You say, "I can find the idea." That is exactly what I have done in finding the idea of the Missionary Baptist Church. I found Bible doctrine and practice and described it as plain as words could speak so anybody could see. If anybody comes along and says we are the church, then prove it by going to the Bible and getting the description, the Bible doctrine and practice describing the church.

My friend said, "The Bible ought to call it what it is. Bogard said that." And I say so yet. Well, the Bible never did say "The Church of Christ". It did not say it with reference to the whole, all of God's people. It did not say it with reference to any local congregation, not one time. Not one time. Well, he comes here with an addition of apples and all that. Fifteen apples—subtract fourteen and have one apple. That would be the apple including all the other fourteen? What you mean when you say "The Church of Christ"—you mean all the churches and all of God's people combined into one. That is what you mean and what you call it when you talk about "The Church of Christ." You cannot find that in *name* and you cannot find it in *fact* in the Bible. It is not there.

"Unto him be glory in the church," used *in the sense of an institution,* institutional sense. "The husband is the head of the wife even as Christ is the head of the church." If *the church* means a universal body including all of God's children then *the wife* means all the wives in one big wife. Would not she be a whopper? (Laughter). Why, he says it does not mean that when it says the wife, the husband of the wife. All right, then it does not mean that when it says that Christ is the head of the church.

The seven churches of Asia—I read every one of them. And my friend says that this church here ought to be called "The Church of Christ at Damascus." He says that is what it ought to be. Why did the Lord not think of that? He named the seven churches of Asia and did not say "Church of Christ" once. The churches of Judea in Gal. 1:22. He did not say the Churches of Christ in Judea. In the very same place, Romans 16:16, where you find *"the churches of Christ* salute you", in the fourth verse it says *"the churches of the Gentiles"*. And if churches of Christ means the name, then the churches of the Gentiles means the name. Why, anybody can see that.

You cannot find your name in fact or in idea. You cannot find a *description.* You cannot find the *word.* Then you are down and out. If you can find "The Church of Christ" in the Bible I will give it up and quit the debate. I will quit this very afternoon. I will ask one of the boys to take me back to Little Rock. You cannot find it. You talk about "The Church of Christ" being the name. It is not in the Bible. I will give you ten dollars. Write it down there, the chapter and verse, and hand it up to me and I will turn to the Bible here and read it, walk down before my speech is over and get out of this debate. You talk about the name. You cannot find it in the Bible to save your life, nor can you find a description of anything that looks like it in the Bible.

My friend asked, "How did you know the names of those dogs?" Johnson's dogs. I would not unless somebody told me. "Johnson's dogs" did not give the name and "churches of Christ" does not give the name either, and I will not know unless somebody tells me. Well, nobody told me the names of those churches. "Johnson's dogs" is not the name of the dogs but denotes ownership. "Churches of Christ" is not the names of the churches but denotes ownership. If anybody ever was completely routed on this thing my friend is and he knows it. Stand up here, grin and make folks laugh, wise crack, and all that kind of thing. That will not help you one bit in the world, will not help you one bit in the world. (Laughter).

He read from Daniel, (Hand me the Bible) Daniel the seventh chapter, and said Daniel had visions, but in the seventh chapter he did not have visions. There is only one there. And the vision you read from said the judgment was set and the books were opened and that a fiery stream should pour forth and ten thousand times ten thousand stood before Him and the books were opened and judgment was set. That was one vision. He referred to numerous other visions, to be sure, about the coming of the kingdom and a lot of things like that but this one vision says it refers to the wind up of things when the kingdoms of this world will become the kingdom of our Lord Jesus Christ.

But my friend said, "Hold on here. In this passage it said He went to the Ancient of days. Is not that God?" Yes, sir. Ancient of days there means God. And when Jesus ascended upon high after the resurrection He went to God and there He will receive for Himself a kingdom when the kingdoms of this world become "the kingdom of our Lord Jesus Christ", Rev. 11:15. That is a thing you do not believe at all. You do not believe Jesus Christ ever will reign on the earth. And I charge that one thing against you. You do not believe in the *personal reign of Christ* on this earth. You do not believe in the *Millennial reign* at all. Well, here it is as plain as words can speak it here in the Bible.

Now take the next. He says he will try to prove it by the Masonic Lodge. Well, you can prove it a whole lot better by the Masonic Lodge than you can prove it by the Bible. I know that every local lodge is a member of the Grand Lodge but you cannot prove that every local congregation is a member of a great big institution called "The Church of Christ" to save your life. Yes, you can prove it by the Masonic Lodge. I am a member of the Masonic Lodge. I am a member of the local lodge and all the lodges of Arkansas make up the Grand Lodge, but *you cannot show where the local churches, local congregations, make up a big church called "The Church of Christ"*, not to save your life. It is not in the Bible.

Now, he said he would just as soon have Alexander Campbell be the founder of his church as to have John Smith. So would I. So would I. But you know, and the record will show that you know, that John Smith never was the founder of the Baptist Church. John Smith, in 1644, established a *General Baptist Church in England.* I am a member of the Missionary Baptist Church, thank you, sir, and not of the General Baptist Church at all. We have General Baptists here in Arkansas. And the *first General Baptist Church*, page 304, Benedict's History, was founded by John Smith in 1644. Benedict said, however, the same Benedict that you quoted from, page 343, that in the year 595 the old or Baptist Church divided, nearly a thousand years back before the time you say the church started. That is the very same book you quoted from. Yes, I would just as soon have Alexander Campbell as to have Smith. But I do not have either, since Smith baptized himself and Campbell he says was baptized by a root of a tree by Luce or somebody. But Campbell says he is a member of the association.

Very well, I showed my friend was wrong on the very theory of the origin of the church and I gave you (I will count to be sure how many—one, two, three, four, five, six, seven, eight, nine, ten, on down—) *I used seventeen passages of scripture to prove the church existed before Pentecost.* He got up here and just referred to them, had no sort of idea of answering. He said we discussed that the other day. Yes sir, just like you discussed it this time. The record will show that you just looked at it and those scriptures are there. Yes, sir. If they are there then you are gone, world without end.

When Jesus left His house He could not leave a house that was not there. You cannot leave this house unless the house is here. Jesus Christ could not leave anything *unless it was there.* He left His house and gave His servants authority and gave them work to do. What does the word power mean? Authority. And so He gave the church authority or power. And you said the church and power came at the same time. Well, the Lord gave them power to go out and preach the gospel to the whole world and baptize. He left His house, gave them authority and a work to do, and said watch for at such an hour as you think not the Son of man comes.

And now I come to some more history. He cannot find his church in the Bible, cannot find a thing in the world about it. Find it there in name, either a general name or a local name. And if you will write it down on a slip of paper I will read the general name or the local name and quit the debate right now.

All right, now since you cannot find it in the Bible and *must go to history,* now here is the one hundredth anniversary of the Disciples of Christ, page 20, of the book entitled *"Centennial Celebration of the Disciples of Christ"*. The introduction says, "In a house of logs built by the association, in a farm house here, Thomas Campbell wrote the declaration and address. Such a publication was deemed highly expedient. The declaration and address was a statement of principles upon which we associate. This document has been fittingly called "The Great Charter of Our Movement'." He lived in a log cabin up there in Pennsylvania and *wrote a charter.* You celebrated your one hundredth anniversary just a little over two or three years ago. Talk about reaching back to Christ!

Now, according to your doctrine, Abraham, Isaac, Jacob, Peter, James, John and all the men of the past failed to get to heaven for nobody was saved till the day of Pentecost. I want that to go in good and plenty. *"Nobody was saved till the day of Pentecost."* Then, sir, if nobody was saved till the day of Pentecost—You say no? There is a fellow out there shaking his head. *That nobody was saved except in the church* is what you said, *and the church was not established till the day of Pentecost.* Then when Christ said, "Your names are written in heaven," He told what was not true. Our friends, the so-called Church of Christ, tell us that we cannot take Matthew, Mark, Luke and John as a rule of our faith and practice. Then they turn right around and quote John 3:5 to prove salvation by baptism, found in the book of John. Have you ever heard them in their preaching say unless a man is born of water and of the Spirit he cannot enter the kingdom? Have you ever heard them say that? Well, that is in John. Very well. They will not take Matthew, Mark, Luke and John as their rule of faith and practice. If you do then I will go back there and find numerous people saved, for Jesus said, "Thy sins are forgiven, go in peace." "Now are you clean by the words which I have spoken." "Your names are written in heaven." Very well.

Our friends deny heart felt salvation, make fun of it. They constantly refer to it as folks going by their feelings. Let me read.

Acts 3:19. "Repent ye therefore and be converted that your sins may be blotted out when the time of refreshing shall come from the presence of the Lord." You never felt that glorious refreshing. You deny it, make fun of it, ridicule it.

Romans 5:5. "Hope maketh not ashamed; because the love of God is shed abroad in our hearts by the Holy Ghost which is given unto us." Did you have the love of God in your heart before you were baptized and got in the church? If so, then you were born of God before you got in the church. His church salvation goes down.

I John 5:10 says, "He that believeth on the Son hath the witness in himself." Have you got any witness in you that you have been saved? If so, then you go back on your ridiculing those who believe in salvation by grace and have joy of salvation in connection.

Another thing, *you say nobody can love God until he is baptized.* Yes sir, you say it. Do not shake your head, old man down there. Somebody is trying to knock me off by shaking his head. If you can love God before you are baptized, I John 4:4 says, *"He that loveth is born of God and knoweth God."* If you cannot love God before you are baptized then here goes a man who is a hater of God, an enemy of God, an alien of God. He hates God as he wades out into the water; he hates God hip deep in the water; he hates God until his nose goes clear under the water; and he still hates God till you get him out of the water and presto! Change! That dip makes him love God. Now, if that is not so then you love God before you are baptized. And if you love God before you are baptized, "He that loveth is born of God and knoweth God for God is love." You either say you love God before you are baptized or you do not. If you say you do not, then you are a hater of God and a dip in the water by one of these preachers makes you love God. And if you do love God before you are baptized then you are born of God before you are baptized, flatly contradicting your doctrine every step of the way.

My friends, these so-called Church of Christ people, are wrong on everything. They are wrong on that ruling eldership. Why, he quotes where the elders rule well. Yes sir, but that means *rule by leadership and by influence.* Jesus said in Matt. 20:25-26, "The princes of the Gentiles exercise dominion over them and they that are great exercise authority upon them. But it shall not be so among you." Here comes along an evangelist and appoints elders over the congregation. They at once assume charge and have authority. Jesus said it shall not be so among you. Flatly contradicting what the Lord said at every step of the way!

Our time is up. I cannot go forward with any other argument now.

Third Day

PORTER'S THIRD AFFIRMATIVE

Gentlemen Moderators, Mr. Bogard, Ladies and Gentlemen:

We continue at this time the study of the proposition that was discussed this afternoon. "The church known as the Church of Christ is Scriptural in origin, doctrine, practice and name." We have, of course, as you see, what is known as the general church question. Not being limited to any specific subject, or any specified question, we are discussing any number of differences that might develop during the course of the investigation. Mr. Bogard followed the same plan on the first two days regarding the Baptist Church, and we have just reversed it now, and I am in the affirmative on this question and will be again tomorrow and until the debate comes to a close tomorrow night.

Before replying to the speech which my friend Bogard made this afternoon, I want to introduce just a few more affirmative arguments along the line that we had during the afternoon session. When these are made I shall return to the speech that was made in the closing part of the session and pay my respects to it. The point of doctrine which I endeavored to develop during the affirmative this afternoon is that "salvation for all responsible people in this age is in the New Testament church." I want you to remember that I said "in this age." Mr. Bogard hasn't let that dawn on him yet. Or else he purposely ignored it and tried to misrepresent the case and make you think that I said something that I didn't even think of. And that was a distinction that will be made during this thirty minutes. So remember that I said "in this age." Salvation for all responsible people in this age is in the New Testament church.

This afternoon I introduced a number of distinct arguments; in fact, eight of them were completed in my first speech. To a number of these my friend paid no attention whatsoever. He made reference to a very few of them in a very feeble way. When my time was called at the close of the first speech I was developing an argument upon the church as the family of God. I want to begin right there at this time. This was Argument No. 9. In Ephesians, the second chapter, and the nineteenth verse, Paul referred to the Ephesian brethren, those who were in the church at Ephesus, as being "the household of God." In verse 16 they are referred to as "one body." In verse 21 Paul called them the "building." In verse 20 he said they were built on Christ as the foundation. These same people who were referred to as the building built on Christ, and who were called the one body, are referred to in verse 19 as "the household of God." But what's the meaning of the term "household"? Just to illustrate that I turn to 1 Corinthians 1, and verse 16, in which Paul declared that he baptized the household of Stephanas. This indicates that he baptized the family of Stephanas. Likewise, in Matt. 10, verses 35 and 36, the Lord declared that "a man's foes shall be they of his own household." These and many other Scriptures that might be introduced show that the term "household" refers to "family." "The household of God" is "the family of God," and since the church is the household of God, then the church is the family of God. Therefore, the church of God is the family of God; and if men can be saved out of the church, they can be saved without being a part of God's family. Now, Mr. Bogard, don't come up here and say that Porter said that was true back in the days of Moses, or back in the days of Abraham, because we are talking about "this age," Mr. Bogard, since the church was established. Now, you come up and face the issue. Since the church is the household of God, or the family of God, those who are not in the church are not of God's household. And they are not of God's family. And, of course, if they are not in God's family, then they are not God's children; and therefore, they are not saved. The church of God, the household of God, the family of God, the children of God, but those on the outside do not constitute that household.

Argument No. 10. We find the church also is sometimes referred to as "the kingdom." In Matt. 16, verses 18 and 19, we have the statement made that uses the two terms interchangeably. Verse 18 refers to the building of the church—"Upon this rock I will build my church." Verse 19 says, "I will give unto thee the keys of the kingdom." And thus we have the terms "church" and "kingdom" used interchangeably in that passage. Furthermore, the Lord's table is said to be in his kingdom. Luke 22:30. The Lord said, "I appoint unto you a kingdom, as my Father hath appointed unto me; that ye may eat and drink at my table in my kingdom." But we learn from 1 Corinthians 11, verses 18-20, that the Lord's supper is in the church. All right, the Lord's table, the Lord's supper, is placed in the kingdom; and yet the Lord's supper is in the church. So in this case the terms "kingdom" and "church" refer to the same institution. But men cannot be saved out of the kingdom of the Lord. In Colossians, the first chapter and verse 13, Paul, writing to the Colossian brethren, the church at Colosse, declared they had been "delivered from the power of darkness" and "translated into the kingdom of God's dear Son." All right, then, all those "delivered out of darkness" have been "translated into the kingdom of Christ." Those who are not in the kingdom of Christ, or who have not been translated into the kingdom of Christ, are still in the power of darkness, and, consequently, unsaved. Thus again we see that salvation in this age is placed in the kingdom of God's dear Son—in the church of the Lord—and men cannot be saved out of it.

Argument No. 11. "In Christ" equals "in the body of Christ." I am going to show this by a number of Scriptures to which I call your attention just here. And in the first place, this is proven by the fact that the same act puts into both. In Gal. 3:27 Paul declared that men are "baptized into Christ." But in 1 Cor. 12:13 Paul said we are "baptized into one body." Thus the same act that puts men "into Christ" puts them "into the body of Christ." Paul declares the body is the church. "Baptized into Christ"—"baptized into the body of Christ." Since the same act puts into both of them, then I insist that "in Christ" means "in the body."

In the second place, this is proven by the fact that those who are said to be "in Christ" are also said to be "in the church." In 1 Cor. 1:2 Paul addressed "the church of God which is at Corinth, to them that are sanctified *in Christ Jesus.*" So the church at Corinth were said to be "in

Christ." In Galatians 1, verse 22, Paul speaks of "the churches of Judea which were *in Christ.*" Then we have the same principle revealed there. 1 Thes. 2:14 mentions the same fact regarding the churches of Judea. In Ephesians, the first chapter, verse 1, writing to the church at Ephesus, Paul addressed it to "the saints at Ephesus—the faithful *in Christ Jesus.*" So the church at Ephesus was said to be in Christ—those in the church were said to be in Christ. Likewise, Philippians, the first chapter, verse 1, Paul, writing to the church at Philippi, addressed it "to all the saints *in Christ Jesus* at Philippi, with the bishops and deacons." In Colossians 1, verse 2, addressing the church at Colosse, we find it addressed "to the saints and faithful brethren *in Christ* which are at Colosse." Now, likewise in 1 Thes. 1:1. Also 2 Thes. 1:1. The letters addressed to the church of Thessalonica were addressed to "the church of the Thessalonians which is *in the Lord Jesus Christ.*" Now, taking all of these statements together we find that those who were said to be "in Christ" were said to be "in the church," or "in the body." Those "in the body" were said to be "in the church" or "in Christ." Consequently, to be "in Christ" and to be "in the body" is the same thing, because those terms are used interchangeably in these very passages.

Then in the third place, reconciliation is said to be in both. In 2 Cor. 5:19 we have reconciliation referred to as being "in Christ," but in Eph. 2:16 as being "in the body" of Christ. The inheritance is said to be in both. Eph. 1:11 declares we have the inheritance in Christ. "In whom we have obtained an inheritance," said Paul. But Eph. 3:6 reveals that inheritance is in the body. Then the conclusion must be reached that the blessings which are "in Christ" are "in the church" or "in the body." That brings us down to this fact. There are a number of blessings which are said to be in Christ which, consequently, must be in the body of Christ, because we have found these two expressions used interchangeably. Those in the church are said to be in Christ—those in Christ are said to be in the church.

Then we find as a result of that that redemption is in Christ. Rom. 3:24 and Eph. 1:7. "Being justified freely by his grace through the redemption that is *in Christ Jesus,*" said Paul in the Roman passage. But men are still in iniquity, are still lost, till they are redeemed; but redemption is in Christ. "In Christ" is "in the body," and, therefore, redemption is in the body. But the body is the church. So redemption is in the church. In the next place, we find forgiveness is in Christ. Col. 1:14; Col. 2:11. As such forgiveness is in Christ, then that puts it in the body, because "in Christ" and "in the body" are expressions used interchangeably. The body means the church—so that's forgiveness in the church. Sanctification is also said to be in Christ. 1 Cor. 1:2. Certainly, men are not saved until they are sanctified. As sanctification is in Christ—and "in the body" and "in Christ" mean the same — then it is in the body — in the church, and not on the outside. The inheritance is in Christ, as I called to your attention awhile ago. Eph. 1:11. Also we are told that "all spiritual blessings are in Christ." Eph. 1:3. "Blessed be the God and Father of our Lord Jesus Christ, who hath blessed us with all spiritual blessings in heavenly places *in Christ.*" All right, "in Christ" means "in the body." The two expressions are shown to be interchangeable, and, consequently, all spiritual blessings are thus placed in the body. We are said to be new creatures in Christ. 2 Cor. 5:17. Also we are told that the promise of life is in Christ. 2 Tim. 1:1. Inasmuch as all of these blessings are in Christ, (and I have shown that the act that puts into Christ puts into the church, and the act that puts into the church puts into Christ; all those who were said to be in Christ were in the church, and all those who were said to be in the church were said to be in Christ; that the two expressions mean the same thing) and all of these blessings, therefore, that are said to be in Christ are also in the church. And, consequently, unless a man can be saved *without any spiritual blessing,* unless a man can be saved without salvation, without forgiveness, without reconciliation, without sanctification, without any of these blessings presented, then he cannot be saved *in this age* out of the church.

Then Argument No. 12. This is to be based upon the record concerning Saul's persecution. In the first place, we are told that Saul persecuted *disciples.* Acts, the ninth chapter and verse 1, reveals the fact that he was "breathing out threatenings and slaughter against *the disciples* of the Lord." Now, the word "disciple" sometimes means simply a learner. But in its broad sense it is used to mean children of God, or Christians. Just as in Acts 11:26 "the disciples were called Christians first in Antioch." And in John 8:31 Jesus said, "If ye continue in my word, then are ye my disciples indeed." Certainly, that's the kind of disciples that Saul persecuted, when he was "breathing out threatenings against the disciples of the Lord." But in the second place, we are told that he persecuted *saints.* In Acts, the ninth chapter and verse 13, is mentioned the fact about "how much evil he hath done to thy *saints* at Jerusalem." In Acts 26:10 Paul speaks about himself and declares, "Many of *the saints* did I shut up in prison." Now, Paul persecuted *the saints,* but certainly the saints means the children of God, those who are saved or sanctified. In the third place, we are told that he persecuted those of *"this way."* Acts 9, and verse 2 tells us he was going to Damascus "that if he found any of *this way,* he might bring them bound to Jerusalem." The Revised Version says of "the way." In Acts 22, and verse 4, Paul said, "And I persecuted *this way* unto the death." All right, of course, when he persecuted "this way," or "the way," he was persecuting those who were identified with "this way" or "the way." Jesus said in John 14:6 that "I am the way, the life and the truth." Therefore, he was persecuting those who belonged to Jesus, who belonged to "the way." But also in the fourth place, we learn that he persecuted *believers.* In Acts 22:19 we are told that he "imprisoned and beat *them that believed* on thee." All right, now, we put all of that together. Here he persecuted disciples; he persecuted saints; he persecuted those of "this way;" he persecuted believers. But, in the fifth place, we are told that he persecuted *the church.* Acts 8, verse 3, declares that "he made havoc of the church" by delivering into prison both men and women. In 1 Cor. 15:9 he declared himself that he "was the least of all the apostles," not meet to be called one, "because he persecuted *the church* of God." In Gal. 1:13 he referred also to the fact that he "persecuted *the church* of God, and wasted it." We note the facts here then: He persecuted the disciples; he persecuted saints; he persecuted those of "this way;" he persecuted believers; and in doing all of that he said he persecuted the church. Therefore, the disciples, the saints, the believers, those of this way, were identified with the church. And when Paul persecuted the church he persecuted those who were saved. He persecuted those who were the Lord's disciples; he persecuted the saints; he persecuted those who belonged to "this way," or those who were believers in Christ; and, consequently, I am insisting that when Paul persecuted the church, he persecuted the saved people. And those on the outside of the church were not embraced in this work of persecution which Paul carried on. I beg my opponent to pay his respects to these arguments. Don't skip them, Mr. Bogard, like you did those this afternoon.

Now, I go to the speech which my opponent made in the closing part of the session this afternoon. I gave him one argument this afternoon concerning the fact that *we are reconciled in one body,* that the body is the church; and since we are reconciled in one body, and the body is the church, if men can be saved out of the body, out of the church, in this age, they can be saved without reconciliation. Do you remember my friend's reply to that? He said, "Yes, I agree that we are reconciled *in the body,* but it doesn't say reconciled *by being in the body.*" Some twist, wasn't it? The man was drowned *in the river,* but he wasn't drowned *by being in the river.* Was drowned on the outside, I guess, and then got in the river. "Reconciled to God in one body." That is, reconciled unto God and then went into the body. Drowned in the river doesn't mean drowned while being in the river, but drowned on the outside and then thrown in. Is that silly? Or is that intelligent?

Well, yes, he said that Porter said that nobody was saved out of the church, and he went back to Abraham, or to Isaac and Jacob, and those Old Testament worthies, and declared that Porter says all of them went to hell because the church wasn't established until Pentecost. Mr. Bogard, I am constrained to believe that you knew you were making a base misrepresentation in that charge. Because you knew that I emphasized over and over that this proposition concerns "this age." Not how God may have saved men before he established the church. Not how Abraham was saved, or Isaac, or Jacob, or David, or any of the worthies of the Old Testament, or even during the personal ministry of Christ. The point that I made was that responsible beings of *this age* are saved in the church. And the audience knew that I said that; and Mr. Bogard knew that I said that. He wanted to get up here and camouflage and make you forget what I did say, and misrepresent it, and then answer his misrepresentation. Mr. Bogard, why don't you come up and face the issue and answer what I am saying? Meet the arguments that I am making, instead of misrepresenting and putting words into my mouth that I didn't say, and which you know that I didn't say. And you knew that I didn't say them when you made the charge. I am just sure that you did. I don't believe that you were asleep when I made those statements; and I don't believe that you lack sufficient intelligence to keep you from understanding what I said about it. All right, again.

He said in John 10:16 that Jesus said, "Other sheep I have which are not of this fold." And the fold meant the church. "Other sheep I have which are not of this church" then; and so he had sheep on the outside of the church. Well, if the term "fold" there means the church, you have ruined yourself, Mr. Bogard. Because in verse nine Jesus referred to himself as the door of this fold. And he says, "By me if any man enter in, he shall be saved." And the very passage you have introduced puts salvation in the church, if that's the church there. "If a man enter in by me into the fold," and that's the thing that is being discussed. "If a man enter in, he shall be saved." You say, "No, Lord, he is saved on the outside." Now, you better try that over.

Another thing I learned this afternoon is the fact we have two kinds of evidence. You know, upon the board here I have a number of things, and I have been begging my opponent to write over on this line the passage that will serve as his hitching post.

CHART NO. 1

Church of Christ	**Baptist Church**
Churches of Christ	**Baptist Churches**
— Rom. 16:16	________

He said that nobody can back up and hitch on to the New Testament church except Baptists. I declared there must be a hitching post somewhere in order to hitch on, and since he hasn't put the reference up there where he can hitch on, that I am still convinced that Baptists can't hitch on. So this argument he quoted from Religious Encyclopedia, about page 796. "So there is my hitching post. I put my hitching post up here—Religious Encyclopedia, page 796." (Writes on board) There is his reference. There is his hitching post. Well, over here is mine (pointing to Rom. 16:16). Rom. 16, verse 16. And over here is his, taken from Religious Encyclopedia. He said, "That's my hitching post." Well, if you want to hitch on to that, you have my permission, Mr. Bogard, because I don't like to hitch on that way. I would rather hitch on to some statement made in the Book of God.

And then again, regarding Campbell's being a member of the Baptist Church, he made the charge this afternoon, you remember, that Alexander Campbell was excluded from the Baptist Church. I said, "Mr. Bogard, you cannot prove that Alexander Campbell was ever a member of the Baptist Church." And I called upon him to prove it. Has he done it? No. Has he made any effort? No. I read from Mr. Campbell where Mr. Campbell said he "had no intention of becoming a member of the Baptist Church." He had no intention of uniting with the Baptists. And while he preached for them he said he was "not a member." A group of people associated with him, or identified with him, worked for a while in their Association. Bogard said that means they were members of the Baptist Church. No! If they were, Campbell didn't know it. If Campbell was a member of the Baptist Church, he never found it out, Mr. Bogard. Guess he must have got in accidentally someway. He never had discovered the fact for he himself said he was not a member of it and had no intention of being a member of it. I asked my friend this afternoon if he would take a man into the Baptist Church—accept him for membership in the Baptist Church—who was baptized like Alexander Campbell was. What has he said about it? He "observed the passover." Yes, he "observed the passover." He simply passed over it. That's all. He didn't say a word about it. Now, Mr. Bogard, please tell us in your next speech: Would you take a man into the Baptist Church—would you accept a man for membership in the Baptist Church today—who was baptized like Campbell was baptized by Elder Luce? Tell me! Will you do it? He requested Elder Luce to baptize him, dispensing with all of those formalities, that had been formerly used—the experience of grace, and things of that kind—and baptize him upon a simple confession of his faith in Jesus as the Son of God. Luce said that was "contrary to Baptist usage," but he would take the risk of censure any way, and went ahead and did it. Now, Mr. Bogard says, "That put Campbell into the Baptist Church." Now, to anybody in the Baptist Church—did you ever take anybody into the Baptist Church after that fashion? Will you accept a man for membership in the Baptist Church today who is baptized that way? Don't you forget it. Now, you tell us about it.

Then he came to some quotations—some history. I want to turn to them. I have the same little book that he is quoting from; so it is very easy to find it. He quoted from Charles V. Segar in "Life of Campbell." He said, "Alexander Campbell soon became chiefly and prominently known as the recognized head of a new religious movement." Well, that said a "movement." What kind of movement? He was the leader of what kind of movement? Well, the rest of the quotation says, "the purpose of which was to restore primitive Christianity in all its simplicity and beauty." Not to start another denomination like the Baptists did but simply to *restore primitive Christianity*—that was all. A movement back to the Bible—not a movement to start another human organization, Mr. Bogard. You misrepresented the quotation. And then he quoted from Richardson in Memoirs of Campbell, page 548, and he commented on this. He said, Mr. Richardson was the son-in-law of Alexander Campbell. He was right in the family and ought to know what he was talking about." And that Mr. Richardson said that "Dr. Campbell is among the most eminent citizens of the United States, distinguished for his great learning and ability, for his successful devotion to the education of youth, for his piety as the head and founder of one of the most important and respectable religious communities in the United States." So my friend, Mr. Bogard, declares that Campbell's son-in-law, being right in the family and knowing all about it, said that Mr. Campbell was the head and founder of a religious community—one of the leading in the United States. I hate to do this, Mr. Bogard. *I hate to do this.* But truth demands it. The quotation that Mr. Bogard gave here was not a quotation from W. P. Richardson at all, but a quotation from a letter of commendation written by Henry Clay. It was right there before you, Mr. Bogard. Why did you misrepresent it? Here it is. If you have his book, turn to it and look at it. Right here on page 4. You have this little book—many of you. Get it out of your pocket and look at it. Right on page 4, here is Mr. Bogard's comment: "In Richardson's Memoirs of Campbell, page 548, Vol. 2, is found a commendatory letter written by the great statesman, Henry Clay, in which he uses the following words:" And then the words that Mr. Bogard quoted and attributed to W. P. Richardson, the son-in-law of Alexander Campbell. Can you think he did it accidentally? With it right here in his own comments right before his eyes? Do you think he did it accidentally? Or do you think he was trying to becloud the issue?

Then he said, "The Bible never says 'the church of Christ'." We have discussed the name quite a lot. I am perfectly satisfied with it as far as that is concerned. But "it never says *the church of Christ.*" My opponent is willing to admit that that is a perfectly good designation. For I read to you last night from the December issue—December 27, 1944—of the Orthodox Baptist Searchlight, this statement from Mr. Bogard: (I'll get it in just a minute) "And therefore it was in fact a Missionary Baptist Church. It belongs to Christ and is therefore the Lord's church—*the church of Christ,* if you please." And Mr. Bogard took that—"the church of Christ, if you please" — as perfectly Scriptural. Now, he comes along and makes a lot of braggadocia and does a lot of blowing about the singular number not being found in the New Testament. Well, he accepted it. He will accept both of these expressions. This is in Rom.

16:16—"The churches of Christ." And he said that is a Scriptural expression. He also has endorsed this (pointing to "the Church of Christ") because he put it in his own paper. And now then, he hasn't anything to substantiate this over here (pointing to "Baptist Church" and "Baptist Churches" on the board)—not a thing. Nowhere in God's Book is there one thing said about "Baptist Church" or "Baptist Churches," but Mr. Bogard has said, you know, today that the Lord never named the church. Yesterday in answer to a question I asked him—"When did your people first take the name "Baptist Church?"—he said, "They did not take it—the Lord named them that in the days of John, and they have been that ever since." Yes, sir, he said the Lord named them, but today he says he didn't name them anything. Well, take either one you want—you can't take both of them.

Then to the big apple containing all the little apples, and the big wife containing all the little wives. I showed that my opponent was using an illustration that isn't parallel. He was trying to make a big wife containing all the little wives and a big tree containing all the little trees parallel with an institution, such as the church is. So I gave him a parallel example—the Masonic Lodge. That is an institution—make it parallel. Mr. Bogard came along and said, "I'll agree that there is a big Masonic Lodge containing all the little ones." All right, Mr. Bogard, if there can be a big Masonic Lodge containing all of the little ones, I suppose from the same standpoint then that there can be a big wife containing all the little wives, and a big tree containing all the little trees, even according to Bogard, because he admits there is a big lodge containing all the little ones.

Then to Daniel 7—I want to get that concerning the visions. He says there was only one vision there, but read verse 7 and it speaks of visions, and at the beginning of verse 13 he speaks of visions again. And it is shown to be a different vision that Daniel reveals. In this vision he went in the clouds of heaven to the Ancient of days and received a kingdom.

How about Mark 9:1? My opponent says that Mark 9:1

was fulfilled in Matt. 28:18. Mark 9:1 says the kingdom would "come with power." He said that power was given in Matt. 28:18—all power was given to them then. But in Luke 24:49 we have Luke recording the same commission, and Luke says that Jesus told them to tarry "in the city of Jerusalem until you are endued with power from on high." And so, they hadn't received that power yet, according to what Jesus said. He told them to wait at Jerusalem until they got it, and so they went there and waited for it, and they got it on Pentecost. And I have proved that Bogard is wrong.

Third Day

BOGARD'S THIRD NEGATIVE

Gentlemen Moderators, Ladies, and Gentlemen:

I did not expect to get my friend so completely addled as he shows himself to be tonight. I expected better of him. Now we will start in and take to pieces what he has said.

The last thing he mentioned, or right about the last thing, was the question of the name. I made the statement when we began this debate that if you cannot prove your name, your church name, to be scriptural then you are out. He came back and said that in order for it to be scriptural that you had to have it named in the scripture. I answered him by saying that immersion is scriptural but you cannot find the word immersion in the Bible. The point is that when we find the idea here we ought to call it what it is.

Now, he has been insisting on the name "The Church of Christ", meaning all of God's people. And then he thinks every local congregation should be called "The Church of Christ" in that particular place. I will renew the challenge that I made this afternoon and I will quit the debate right now, not even finish this speech, if he will write on a slip of paper and hand it up here to me the passage of scripture that says "The Church of Christ". I will quit right now, close the debate and acknowledge that I am defeated. Then again I said I will quit the debate if you will show where any local congregation in the New Testament was called "The Church of Christ", locally. Now write those two passages on a slip of paper and hand them up here to my moderator and I will read the passages and get down out of this pulpit and never speak again. It is not there. My friend knows it is not there. If he knew it was there he would close this debate and have a wonderful victory right off the bat. "The Church of Christ", that expression, is not in the Bible. The name is not there and the idea is not there.

Well, he quoted those scriptures about Christ being the head of the church as the husband is the head of the wife.

My answer was if the church there means all the little churches combined like the lodges in the Grand Lodge of Masons to make the church, then the wife has got to be composed of all the little wives, so would she not be a whopper? Christ is the head of the church as the husband is the head of the wife. If the church means *all the little churches,* little congregations, put together to make one great institution then the wife means *all the little wives* put together in one great big wife. Why he says that is absurd. Exactly; I know it is absurd. That is why I am putting it to you to show you how absurd your position is.

Now, I will repeat the announcement that if you will write on a piece of paper and hand it up here by Brother Christian, you do not have to get up, the passage where it says "The Church of Christ", I will read it, get down out of the pulpit and quit right now. I will acknowledge I am defeated. If you will write on a piece of paper where it says "The Church of Christ", any local congregation mentioned in the Bible, I will get down out of the pulpit and never preach again. I went through the Bible today and showed you plainly where every church mentioned left off the expression "The Church of Christ". The church of Colosse, church at Ephesus, church at Smyrna, church at Thyatira, and all those. Not one time does it say "The Church of Christ" at these places. You cannot find it in the general sense and you cannot find it in the local sense. And yet you harp around about the name of the church. That ought to be enough on that. I am quite sure it is. He has not handed up the slip of paper I notice.

Well, he said I put it in the Searchlight that the church of Christ was Christ's church. Certainly, but that is not the name. It is owned by the Lord. The horse of Johnson—the horse owned by Johnson—that is not the name of the horse. The horse might be named Maude or Jerry or something. What a strange kind of a mess you are getting yourself in here.

Now, he comes and makes an argument on church salvation. Now all of you listen. The trouble about so many good people is they do not really listen to what a man says. He says you have got to be saved in Christ. You are saved in the body of Christ. That makes the *body* of Christ and *Christ* the same. What is the body of Christ? The church. Then Christ is the church and the church is Christ. What is the church made up of? Of imperfect men like my friend, Porter, presuming he is in the church; of course he is not. But such imperfect men as he and this congregation, this church, this body, is Christ. If it is not then there is no sense in saying that to be in the church is to be in Christ *unless they are one and the same.* Now everybody here that believes that the church is Jesus Christ and to be in Jesus Christ is to be in the church, one and the same, I would just like to see you hold up your hand. I would like to look at you. See how ignorant you do look. The church here that meets inside these walls that he calls "The Church of Christ", that is Jesus Christ Himself, so he says. If that is not true then to be in this congregation, in this church, is not to be in Christ.

That answers absolutely everything the man said on church salvation. You want me to take up those particular passages one by one and give my time. But of course I know that to be in Christ is not to be in this congregation. To be saved you have got to be in Christ. But I deny his assumption that the church itself is Christ. Why, the church is not Christ and to be in Christ does not mean to be in the church. Very well.

He speaks of the household of faith. He said the house is the church. All right, sir, then where we find the house we have the church. Mark 13. Jesus left His house and gave His servants authority and a work to do and said watch for you know not when the master of the house returns. My friend said when you find the house you have found the church. I have found it over here in Mark, way before Pentecost. Jesus promised to come back to that church. Could He come back to Himself? He left something to come back to it. He left His house and gave His servants authority and a work to do and said watch for you know not when the master of the house comes back. There is your completed church or house.

How do I know it is a house? Why, Paul in I Timothy 3:15 says "The house of God which is the church of the living God, the pillar and the ground of the truth." He argues today that the house is the church and yesterday he said the house is not the church. Which time did you tell the truth? You got things badly mixed up someway, it seems to me.

Then he read from Matt. 16:18. "Upon this rock I will build my church and the gates of hell shall not prevail against it." He asked me to back up and hitch on. I backed up to the Apostolic age and gave you a statement of history that the Baptist is the only one that could go back to the Apostolic age. And he makes a wise-crack talking about a hitching post—a hitching post, like we had a kind of a rack out there to hitch a horse to. If that is the argument in your mind, why you are welcome to it. What I meant by backing up and hitching on, and anybody with any sense knows, was that we go back from now, church by church, to Jesus Christ. And I defied him to show that in his case, where his so-called "Church of Christ" goes back of Alexander Campbell, one step back of Alexander Campbell.

Now, all those scriptures that he reads about sanctification being in Christ and redemption being in Christ and the promise being in Christ and all of that—why, certainly we all believe that. I will not kill my time answering what we all believe. But I *deny that Christ is the church.* You can be in Christ without being in the church. If not, then listen, this congregation that meets here within these walls is Jesus Christ. That makes Jesus Christ a very imperfect being, in all due respect to these fine people who meet here.

He read about the Colossians being in Christ and then said, "Well, to be in Christ is to be in the body; to be in the body is to be in Christ." Who said so? I will give you ten dollars for a passage of scripture that says the body is Christ and Christ is the body. They chirp that off and some folks think that is in the Bible, but it is not there.

Then he came to Saul's persecution, how he persecuted the church. Yes sir, he certainly did. Does that mean *the church is Jesus Christ?* Salvation is in Christ, certainly. That does not mean that salvation is in the church unless the church is Christ and Christ is the church.

Now he comes and says, "Mr. Bogard, I affirm that nobody was saved in this age except those who are in the church." Is that so? When did this age begin? Turn right here to Hebrews, first chapter and the first verses. "God who at sundry times and in divers manners spake in times past unto the fathers by the prophets, hath in these last days spoken unto us by his Son." What is the "last days" when Christ was talking? So we are living now in the last age and my friend says that that is what he refers to.

Very well, now come over here. He says there is a difference in the salvation back yonder in olden times, in the Jewish dispensation for instance, and the present dispensation. Well, that is not the way that Paul talks about it. Turn right here, if you please, and read in the fourth chapter of Romans and we will see about that. He says Abraham was saved one way and we are saved a different way now. What does it say here?

"What shall we say then (fourth chapter of Romans) that Abraham our father, as pertaining to the flesh hath found? For if Abraham were justified by works, he hath whereof to glory; but not before God. For what saith the scriptures? Abraham believed God, and it was counted to him for righteousness. Now to him that worketh is the reward not reckoned of grace, but of debt. But to him that worketh not, but believeth on him that justifieth the ungodly, his faith is counted for righteousness. Even as David also describeth the blessedness of the man, unto whom God imputeth righteousness without works, saying, blessed are they whose iniquities are forgiven, and whose sins are covered. Blessed is the man to whom the Lord will not impute sin."

David and Abraham were saved like we are, by grace through faith in the Lord Jesus Christ. There never has been but one way of salvation. Nobody ever was saved by law. Law never was intended to save. Law was intended to condemn and point to the Saviour, a schoolmaster to lead us to Christ. That is what Paul said about it in Galatians. The law pointed to Christ, directed attention to Christ, and we are saved by Christ just like they were back there or else this scripture is absolutely false.

Very well, now pass on to the next one. By the way, that is all. That is all.

He wanted me to take up those scriptures where we were saved in Christ. Well, bless your soul, I will not fool away my time on that which was preached in that book before Alexander was born. You want me to take up that scripture about redemption being in Christ. We were preaching that before your church ever had any existence on the face of the earth. I am not going to answer them myself. All those scriptures are mine for they teach salvation in Jesus Christ. You want me to kill time? That is what you read them for, to get me to kill my time. I agree with the last one of them, but I *deny that Jesus Christ is the church*. That is what you have got to prove. *I deny that Jesus Christ is the body.*

Very well, coming to history my friend said, "Well now, does not Mr. Bogard know very well that I quoted the words of Henry Clay instead of the words of Richardson?" Yes, I know that very well, but Richardson, the son-in-law of Alexander Campbell, put it in the memoirs of Alexander Campbell, page twenty-five, with his endorsement and said he got a letter of commendation from Henry Clay that recommended him to the Kings and Queens of Europe, and Alexander Campbell used that recommendation. It said, "Alexander Campbell soon became chiefly and prominently known as the recognized head of a religious movement, the purpose of which was to restore primitive Christianity in all its simplicity and beauty. Out of this movement has grown a people that choose to call themselves Christians or Disciples, now numbering about five hundred thousand in the United States."

And then going right on down, Volume 2, page 548, Henry Clay said of Mr. Campbell that he put that letter in his pocket and carried it around in Europe. He was admitted before crowned heads with it. He said, "Dr. Campbell is among the most eminent citizens of the United States, distinguished for his great learning and ability, for his successful devotion to the education of youth, for his piety and as the head and founder of one of the most important and respectable religious communities in the United States." There it is—plain history. I read from Charles P. Seeger and my friend will not deny what it says.

Ziegler's History of Religious Denominations says, "The Christian or Campbellite Church was founded by Alexander Campbell of Virginia in the year 1827." Then Charles P. Seeger said, in The Life of Campbell, that he established this church to restore primitive Christianity.

Now, find one single solitary congregation like the one that meets in these walls where we are holding this debate like the one that you belong to, that existed before the time of Alexander Campbell—just one. Then I will acknowledge that you have one before Campbell and then you will be 1800 years this side of the Apostolic age. You tried to prove that the church began on the day of Pentecost. What good would that do you when you cannot reach Pentecost by *1800 years?* The church of which you are a member began with Alexander Campbell in 1827, or these historians tell a falsehood.

Oh, he says Mr. Campbell never belonged to the Baptist Church. Never did. But he belonged to the Baptist Association and anybody knows that associations are made up of churches. And now here is what Campbell said about it. "It was not until the year 1827 when the Baptists declared non-fellowship with the present reformation, thus by constraint and not by choice, they were compelled to organize societies of their own." Campbell says it was not until after they had been turned out, withdrawn fellowship from. Now, did Campbell tell the truth? He said they did not start this new movement until after the Baptists had withdrawn fellowship from them. That is plain as can be. It has gone down on record and you will not deny his saying it.

Would I take a man into the church now, baptized like Alexander Campbell was? No sir, I would not. But Alexander Campbell got into the Baptist Church on a false pretense and they kicked him out just as soon as they found it out. And he did not start his new movement until after he had been kicked out. If we find somebody that comes into the Baptist Church today on a false pretense, comes in contrary to the rules of the word of God, we will turn him out too, just like the Baptists turned Alexander Campbell out. Well now, you say they did not turn him out. They turned the whole church out. *Bethany Church stands to this day* right where your church began. It is standing there, a house to this day; the very house that it was organized in is standing to this day. Then talk about going back to Jesus Christ and the Apostolic age and all that kind of thing!

Now, I read today from some very authenic history that says that just a little over a few years ago they celebrated their one hundredth anniversary and in the International Centennial Celebration of the Disciples of Christ, a history I read from today, we read on page 47 in the beginning of the Restoration movement: "It is closely connected with the city of Pittsburg. Not only are Washington, Brush Run, and Bethany in the Pittsburg district, but in the city itself the path of the Pioneers continually leads us." In the Pittsburg district, there is where it started a little over one hundred years ago. On page twenty-seven of that book I am talking about it has the picture of that Bethany Church, the house that your church was organized in. Alexander Campbell organized it.

Now come on over and I will read again what Campbell said. I want this to go in good and plenty. Page 465 of Religious Encyclopedia tells where Campbell said over his own name, "After the Baptists had in the year 1827 *declared non-fellowship* for the brethren of the Reformation, thus by constraint and not by choice *they were compelled to organize a society of their own.*" Campbell says they were kicked out of the Baptist fellowship. They non-fellowshiped the whole business and then they were compelled to organize a society of their own.

What did my friend do about those seventeen passages of scripture that I read today showing what existed before Pentecost? I counted them right before you. I showed today, and I repeat:

They had the kingdom before Pentecost, Matt. 11:12, for the kingdom suffered.

They had a king before Pentecost. John 18:37 said He was king.

Men pressed into the kingdom before Pentecost, Luke 16:16.

Some hindered others from entering the kingdom before Pentecost, Matt. 23:13.

There was an ordained ministry before Pentecost, Mark 3:13-14, where Jesus ordained them and sent them out.

They were authorized to baptize before Pentecost, John 5:2.

They had the Lord's Supper before Pentecost, Luke 22:19.

They had a rule of discipline before Pentecost, Matt. 18:15-17.

They had the Gospel before Pentecost, Matt. 24:14, Mark 1:1.

Jesus said there was no doubt about their having the kingdom before Pentecost for in Luke 11:20 He says, "If I by the finger of God cast out devils, no doubt the kingdom is come upon you." Jesus said *there is no doubt about it.* My friend says he doubts it. He says he does not believe it is so. What Christ had no doubt about, you flatly deny. Jesus said, "If I by the finger of God cast out devils." Did He do that? Why, we all know He cast out devils by the power of God. He says, "If I by the finger of God cast out devils, *no doubt* the kingdom of God is come," the very same thing my friend is denying here.

Then they had a company that dwelt with the Lord, traveled with the Lord, during His personal ministry. In Acts 1:21 it says that one must be chosen to succeed Judas "who has companied with us all the time the Lord Jesus went in and out among us beginning from the baptism of John until that same day he was taken up from us." There was a company of baptized believers associated in the faith and fellowship of the Gospel and I went to the first chapter of John and read the five names of the members that constituted that company. My friend has never replied to that to this good day.

And the bride had the bridegroom before Pentecost, John 3:28-29.

And then again in John 13:3-4 it says that all things have been given unto Christ. That was a way yonder before Pentecost. "All things." If that is so, nothing was given to them on the day of Pentecost.

But what good will it do you to prove the church of our Lord began on the day of Pentecost, when you cannot reach Pentecost by 1800 years, when your church started with a man in 1827? You cannot find its beginning in the Bible. You cannot find its name in the Bible. "The Church of Christ." You cannot find a general name, "The Church of Christ." You cannot find a name for a local congregation called "The Church of Christ." All you can do is find the "churches of Christ," meaning churches that belong to Christ. And in the very same chapter, Romans 16:16, where it says the churches of Christ salute you, in the fourth verse it says "the churches of the Gentiles." Is churches of the Gentiles the name? And in Gal. 1:22 it says the churches of Judea. Is that the name? The churches of Christ, is that the name? No, it only expresses ownership and you cannot find the name as you claim anywhere in the lids of the Bible, and therefore you go down in utter failure.

I have one more thing that I want to present—not because it needs to be done, for my friend made no reply. I said that he teaches that his church, the so-called Church of Christ that by rights ought to be called the Campbellite Church, teaches that nobody can love God until after he is baptized. Now, you get up here and say you can love God before you are baptized. Then I quote I John 4 where it says "He that loveth is born of God and knoweth God." I put that to you this afternoon and you made no reply. If you say you can love God before you are baptized then you are saved before you are baptized. If you say you cannot love God until after you are baptized then it takes a dip in the water to make a man love God. Here is a man that has enmity against God, carnal minded, enmity against God. That man in enmity against God goes to the water a hater of God and is baptized and that changes him into a lover of God. He does not do it willingly.

Now, one more thought right here. Instead of people being baptized by him and his people in the so-called church of Christ that ought to be called the Campbellite Church, (I do not want to hurt your feelings. I am telling you what it ought to be.) instead of your coming into the church because you love the Lord, you come in because you are hell scared. You are forced. Suppose I were to take a pistol and lay it right down in front of a young man and say, "You come up here now and let me baptize you or I will blow your brains out," and he comes. Would that be any good? No, not a bit. He would come because he was pistol scared. Suppose I would stand up and preach that you would go to hell straight if you were not baptized. He comes up here and is baptized because he is hell scared. One is pistol scared and the other is hell scared.

Another thing, my friend has a shot gun salvation. One time I married a couple. Maybe I ought not to have done it. I was called down to the Marion Hotel to marry a couple. When I got there, the lawyer they had in charge said, "This is a forced wedding, Mr. Bogard." And I thought a while, "Shall I perform the ceremony?" Well, I did. And before I said the ceremony the old man got up and blessed that young fellow out who had ruined his daughter. He said, "You good for nothing scoundrel," cursed him out with the worst oath I ever heard, "You ruined my daughter and now you are going to marry her or I will blow your brains out. And not only that but you are going to marry her and live with her or I will blow your brains out. You are going to be good to her or I will blow your brains out." He married the girl not because he loved her but because he was afraid he would get his brains blown out, just like you are afraid you will go to hell if you are not baptized. Then he said, "You have got to be good to her. I am going to keep up with you and if you do not treat her right I am going to blow your brains out. You are not going to send her back on me and my wife after you take her." Well all right, I imagine the fellow was good to her. I imagine he tried his best for he was afraid he would get his brains blown out if he did not.

Now here is what you do. If you are hell scared and you come up and are baptized to keep from going to hell, then you try to live right to keep from going to hell. You take the Lord's supper every Sunday to keep from going to hell. You pay your debts to keep from going to hell. And you are hell scared all the way through and the love of God is not in you. The love of God has not been shed abroad in your heart by the Holy Ghost that is given unto us. Now, just wrestle that all you please now, there it is. You have a shot gun salvation, a forced salvation, a hell scared salvation, and you dare not say you love God or that you are baptized because you love God. If so, then you are born of Him before you are baptized.

And then you cannot find the name of your church in the Bible, either general or local. And you have a forced salvation. And by the way, you teach that leaving off baptism is *the sin against the Holy Ghost.* There is only one sin for which there is no forgiveness. If a man is a liar, a thief, a murderer, or a whoremonger, he gets forgiveness, but if he leaves off baptism there is no forgiveness for it. So that makes leaving off baptism worse than lying, worse than murder, worse than stealing, worse than adultery and all that. Had you ever stopped to think about the absurdity of your position? Had you thought anything about these things? Lord, I have been a thief; I have been a liar; I have been a whoremonger. "I will forgive you for all that," says the Lord, "But if you leave off baptism to hell you go." That is the size of your doctrine. Now wrestle with it. Try to look like you want to say something about it whether you want to or not. I will hear what you have to say about it. Then I will have some more to say along the same line.

Third Day

PORTER'S FOURTH AFFIRMATIVE

Gentleman Moderators, Mr. Bogard, Ladies and Gentlemen:

While it is fresh on your minds I shall deal with the last first. My opponent said that, according to what you teach, you folks advocate that leaving off baptism is the sin against the Holy Ghost. There is not a word of truth in it. He said a man may come up before God and say, "I was a murderer, I was a whoremonger; I was an idolater; I was a thief; and I was a liar; but I left off baptism." And the Lord tells him to go to hell then because he left off baptism, and that was the sin against the Holy Ghost. Well, take Bogard's side of it. Then the fellow comes up and says, "Lord, I was a thief; I was a murderer; I was a whoremonger; I was an idolater; and I was a liar." The Lord says, "I can forgive you for all of that, but you left off faith. And when you left off faith, you can't get any forgiveness." Therefore, leaving off faith is the sin against the Holy Ghost. Sauce for the goose is sauce for the gander. (Laughter)

I got shot by a shot gun, but only one barrel was fired. The other barrel is loaded, and I am going to turn it back to Mr. Bogard. (Laughter) This shot-gun wedding that he told about, and this hell-scared religion that he talked about. He said, "Why, you fellows are just hell-scared—just like this shot-gun wedding, you have shot-gun salvation. The fellow was forced to marry the girl because he was afraid his brains would be blown out; and you teach that you will go to hell if you are not baptized, and men are baptized because they are afraid they will go to hell. And it is just like being forced to marry a girl against your will." Shot-gun salvation—shot-gun wedding. Well, Mr. Bogard, I wonder if you had never thought about that other barrel—that it may be loaded too. Mr. Bogard preaches all over this country that if you don't believe in Christ, you will go to hell. Therefore, if somebody believes in Christ, he is hell-scared; and he has shot-gun salvation, because Bogard told him he would go to hell if he didn't believe. Better hunt you up another pistol, Mr. Bogard.

Now, he said, "You fellows ought to be called Campbellites." Well, maybe so. If that is so, I suspect you fellows ought to called Smithites (Laughter) because the first Baptist church of which we have any record was founded by John Smith, as we are told in Benedict's History, page 304, in 1607. Mr. Bogard said, "Oh, that was the General Baptists." Well, that just proves the General Baptists are older than you are. That's all. You cannot go as far back as the General Baptists then—that is all it proves. And that is the first one we have any record of. Now, then, back to some other matters.

I lacked a little getting to my condensed notes on his last speech this afternoon, because I wanted to get my affirmatives in. He came along and did a lot of blowing that I hadn't paid any attention to the argument he made about loving God—going into the water hating God and coming out loving God. He said, "I made that argument this afternoon, and you didn't pay any attention to it." Well, maybe I did like you did, Mr. Bogard—I didn't need to kill my time. That's the way you dispose of my Scriptures. All the passages I gave, except just a few, are so unimportant in this discussion that Mr. Bogard can't afford to waste his time fooling with them. What if I would deal that way with the arguments he gives. "Yes, that's all right, but I can't fool away my time with them—I've got something else." Why, it is your obligation, Mr. Bogard, as the negative, to pay attention to what I say and reply to the arguments I make. You are fooling away your time when you don't, and the audience sees it. Now, about this fellow—he says if he loves God before baptism, he is already saved. Therefore, he goes into the water hating God. Mr. Bogard, put this down. When a man goes to the altar to pray for salvation and prays for God to save him, is he hating God or loving him? Put it down. Well, put it down, Mr. Bogard. According to Mr. Bogard's idea, that man prays to God at the mourner's bench while hating God, because if he already loves God, he can't pray for salvation for he is saved just as soon as he loves God. So either that man that he prays for to be saved, or that he has to pray for himself that he might be saved, is hating God while he prays, or he is already saved and didn't know it. One or the other. That's another that works both ways.

Now, then, back to a few condensed notes on the other speech. I introduced Mark 9:1 in which we have the statement that the kingdom would come with power. And I showed this afternoon that Jesus said there were some standing there that would not taste of death till they "see the kingdom come with power." I showed from Acts 1:8 that the power would come with the Holy Spirit. And I showed from Acts 2:1-4 that the Spirit came "when the day of Pentecost was fully come." Consequently, the kingdom came with power "when the day of Pentecost was fully come." Mr. Bogard came up and replied, "No, that was fulfilled when the Lord gave the great commission in Matt. 28:18, 19 and said 'all authority,' or all power, 'is given unto me.' 'Go and preach the gospel—go and teach all nations.' There it was fulfilled." I hate to do this. But on page 201 of the Hardeman-Bogard Debate Mr. Bogard says, regarding that very same passage, "It means he was not given as the administrator, he hadn't become administrator, he hadn't come in baptismal power, and that was fulfilled on the day of Pentecost. He came on the day of Pentecost in baptismal power, the thing we don't have now; but he baptized the church that day in the Holy Spirit, that's what is meant when it says the kingdom should come with power." Bogard versus Ben M. Bogard. In the Hardeman debate he said the kingdom coming with power, in Mark 9:1, referred to the baptism of the Holy Spirit coming on the day of Pentecost. In this debate he said it was fulfilled when the Lord gave the great commission, before he left the earth, in Matt. 28:19. He's traveling in a circle again.

Another thing my friend said was that we do not accept Matthew, Mark, Luke and John as a rule of faith and practice. Mr. Bogard, do you accept *all of it?* Will you accept all of Matthew, Mark, Luke and John as a rule of faith for the Baptist Church? I challenge you to say "yes." Write your answer down on a little slip and let your moderator hand it up to me. You don't have to say anything audibly—

just say "yes"—just write "yes" on it and hand it up to me, or "no"—whichever it is. I don't see the paper. Why, the fact is in Matt. 23, verses 2 and 3, Jesus said to his disciples that "the scribes and Pharisees sit in Moses' seat: all therefore whatsoever they bid you observe, that observe and do." Will you take that as a rule of faith and practice for the Baptist Church today? Watch and see what he says about it.

When you came to that charter of the movement, and so on, quoting from a Christian Church authority, he is just about as far from the truth as Mr. Bogard is. I would about as soon take one of them as the other.

Another point was that he said we deny heartfelt salvation. He gave Rom. 5:1 and 1 John 5:10 along that line. And Acts 3:19, I believe. "You folks deny heartfelt salvation. You make fun of feelings." No, we don't. That's another misrepresentation. My brethren have just as good feelings as anybody and rejoice as much as anybody. But the thing, Mr. Bogard, that we affirm is that you *cannot depend upon your feelings as evidence of your salvation.* Will you say you can? I know that Baptists generally do, but I don't believe Mr. Bogard will say it. I don't believe that he will say he depends on his feelings as *evidence* of his salvation. We wait to see if he will.

Then once more to the ruling elders; he said something about them this afternoon—the ruling elders. I asked him, in that connection, Mr. Bogard, who ruled for the Baptist Church in Damascus in regard to this debate? He never did tell me. Who were the elders that ruled for the Baptist Church in Damascus concerning the holding of this debate? Let us see who has ruling elders and where they are.

Another statement that he made in his recklessness and in his condition, rattled and confused as he was, is that "you people are wrong on everything." You heard him this afternoon. "You people are wrong on everything." A man must be beside himself who would make a statement like that. Mr. Bogard, we believe that the sabbath of the Old Testament was abolished at the cross of Jesus Christ. Do you believe it too? *Are we wrong on that?* I have been writing some replies in the Gospel Pilot to some Adventist questions coming from a friend up in Missouri. Mr. Bogard commended me this afternoon for those articles and the way I dealt with that matter. He agrees perfectly with me regarding that Adventist's questions—that the sabbath was abolished at the cross of Jesus Christ. *Bogard and I both believe that.* If we are wrong on everything, then Bogard, you are wrong on that, because you agree with me. Not only so, but we believe that the only Scriptural mode of baptism is immersion. Mr. Bogard believes the same thing. If we are *wrong on everything, then immersion is not the Scriptural baptism.* We believe that Jesus Christ is the Son of God. But Mr. Bogard says we are wrong on everything. If so, then Jesus Christ is not the Son of God, and Mr. Bogard is wrong too, or he doesn't believe it. Now, that is just a starter. I can give you one after one, one after another, for a whole list of them, that Mr. Bogard and I agree on. Yet he says we are wrong on everything. Well, if we are, you are wrong on a lot of things, Mr. Bogard, because we stand exactly agreed on many of these things. Did you forget—or what was the matter with you? Were you so rattled you didn't know what you were saying?

He said, "For a thing to be Scriptural it must be named in the Bible," or at least made that concession. And then he said, "Well, but that isn't true, because immersion is not in the Bible." Well, that depends on what translation you read. Get your Baptist translation that was made some few years ago and see if you can't find the word "immersion" in it. And "immerse" and those things. The Bible Union Version—you know about it, don't you, Mr. Bogard? Now, you can certainly find it in it—it depends on what translation of the Bible you use, as to whether you find the word "immerse" or "immersion."

CHART NO. 1

Church of Christ	Baptist Church
Churches of Christ	**Baptist Churches**
— Rom. 16:16	———————

He said also that he would quit the debate now for the passage that says "the church of Christ." I have shown all along that Rom. 16:16 mentions "the churches of Christ," and if any man has any sense at all, he can see that if a number of them were called "the churches of Christ," one of them would be "the church of Christ" in any given community. If his reasoning powers are not long-legged enough to step from the plural to the singular, maybe God will take care of him anyway. But I am going two to your one, Mr. Bogard. I am going to give you ten dollars, and I am going to quit the debate, if you will find "Baptist Church" or "the Baptist Church" in the singular number in the Bible. That's parallel with this over here, isn't it? According to you? All right. I'll also give you another ten dollars, and I'll quit the debate also, if you will find "Baptist Churches" in the plural number in the Bible. I find "churches of Christ" in the plural number. Just write the passage down on a little slip of paper. You don't have to get up. Just write the passage down on a little slip of paper and hand it to your moderator, and he'll hand it to me, that mentions either "Baptist Church" or "Baptist Churches." We have a passage that does say "churches of Christ." You don't have one that says either. And if you will hand me one that says either, I'll quit the debate right now, and I'll never enter the pulpit again, and I'll go home and give you the credit for winning a great victory in this debate. *Don't you want it?* Write it down and let your moderator hand it to me. *Won't you do it?* We have one of them here; you don't have either of them. But suppose it does denote ownership—I agree that it denotes ownership—I have never said otherwise. Let it denote ownership. You can't find "Baptist Church" or "Baptist Churches" in either form in the Bible *denoting anything.* Now, if you can find either "Baptist Church" or "Baptist Churches" in the Bible, denoting anything, whether it is ownership or what not, you write that reference on a piece of paper, let your moderator hand it to me, and I'll say the debate is over right now. Do you know of them, Mr. Bogard? You folks see we are not in the same predicament. We have the passage that says "churches of Christ." He does not have the passage that says either on his side. *He can't produce them.* Shall we call the debate off, Mr. Bogard? Are you going to admit that you can't find either?

Well, he said, "In the Searchlight when I said 'the church of Christ' I didn't mean it was a name but it was owned." Well, you have been arguing all the time that the idea is not even Scriptural. That "the church of Christ" is not even a Scriptural idea, and therefore it isn't Scriptural; but now you have said it in your paper. Consequently, you stand on that as you have on all the others.

Then he came to one argument I made about the body of Christ as the church of Christ, and to be in the body is to be in Christ. He said, according to that, Christ is the church and the church is Christ; and if you are the church that meets here from time to time, why, you are Christ. You are confusing the personal body of Christ with his spiritual body—that's all. You are not in the personal body of Christ, are you, Mr. Bogard? What body are you in? You say you believe a man has to be in the body of Christ to be saved. In what body? That body that is up in heaven? That personal body of Jesus Christ? Is that the one you are in? Now, you are confusing the personal body with that spiritual body on earth. That's the trouble with you. Now, that upsets the whole argument you made on it.

Matt. 16:18. He said, "Yes, I have backed up to the apostolic age and have my hitching post up." I'll tell you what I am going to do, friends. I am just going to agree, for the sake of argument (I don't believe a word of it—but I am just going to agree, for the sake of argument) that Mr. Bogard has succeeded in tracing Baptist Churches in every age to the first century. There isn't a word of it so, but just to give him that much advantage in the case, I am going to say that's so, for the sake of argument. All right, Mr. Bogard. You have traced them back now through every century to the first age—to the apostolic age.

CHART NO. 1-A

Church of Christ	**Baptist Church**
Churches of Christ	**Baptist Churches**
— Rom. 16:16	**— Religious Encyclopedia, p. 796**

Now, then, where are you going to hitch on? It won't do any good to rattle the chain back through the centuries if you can't fasten the other end of it. You have to have some place to attach that chain when you get there. The only place you have attached it is the Religious Encyclopedia, page 796. Find in the book of God a reference that mentions either the "Baptist Church" or "Baptist Churches"—*either of them,* Mr. Bogard—that you might have a place to hitch on when you get back there. It doesn't do any good to go back if you can't find a place to land when you get there. You haven't found it.

Did you notice what he said about Saul's persecution—the persecution of the disciples, the saints, the believers, and all of that, and then persecuting the church? All of those were used interchangeably. What did he say about it? The only thing he said—"Well, I don't believe the church is Christ." *That's all he said.* Why not meet the arguments, Mr. Bogard? Why not come up and face them? Just because you cannot—that's why.

"Well, but in this age, Porter said—in this age." Then he said, "When did this age begin?" He went to Hebrews, about God's speaking in the last days unto us by his Son. Well, while he is in Hebrews we might find out what the Bible says about when this age began—or when that age ended—or what age it was—and so on. Heb. 9:26 tells us that Christ appeared in the end of the world to put away sin by the sacrifice of himself. "In the end of the world" in some translations and in the original indicates age. In the end of the age—Jesus died. Did this age begin before the other ended? *Did this age begin before the other age ended? Did it?* Did Jesus die in the end of the age? Was that the Christian age, Mr. Bogard? You said the Christian age began back over here before he died. Let us just make a cross here to represent the death of Christ. (Draws cross on the board). Now, you say that the Christian age began over here (pointing to place before the cross) before Jesus died. Well, Paul said that Jesus died in the end of the age. According to you, he died in the beginning of the age, and not in the end of the age. Paul said he died in the end of the age. All right, if the Christian age began back there, the Christian age began before the Jewish age ended. You want to try it over?

But he said that salvation has been the same in all ages, but Porter said that salvation in this age is in the church but not in ages before. But salvation has been the same in all ages—that God has had the same plan of salvation. Yes, God has always required obedience, if that is what you mean. But God hasn't always required the same things. I want to turn to another passage and read it for you—I know what it says—but I want to read it. This also is in the Hebrew letter. We want to see if the plan has been the same in all ages or not. Hebrews the tenth chapter, verses 19 and 20. And here the inspired writer says, "Having therefore, brethren, boldness to enter into the holiest by the blood of Jesus, by a new and living way, which he hath consecrated for us, through the veil, that is to say, his flesh." Paul declares that we enter in by the blood of Jesus Christ "by a new and living way." I want to know if it is the same old way that existed from the days of Adam down, how can it be a "new and living way," Mr. Bogard? Tell us how the way can be new. You said that it is the same old plan—the same old way—in all ages. Paul said this plan now, by the blood of Jesus, is *a new and living way*. A new way-N-E-W, new. You may take Bogard if you want to—I am going to take Paul.

Then regarding his answer to the arguments—he said, "That's all—I am not going to answer myself." He didn't answer Porter either. We will have more about that later on.

I made the statement that Campbell never belonged to the Baptist Church. He said, "No, but he belonged to the Association." Well, he was working in an Association. They were simply working together—cooperating in a way—but he was not a member of the Baptist Church. If he was, he didn't know it and didn't intend to be, for he said he had no intention of it. He had no idea of uniting with the Baptists. I read it from his own words. Furthermore, he said he was not a member during the time he was preaching with them — or for them — in countries round about. Many churches—miles around—he preached for them, but he was not a member of them, he said. So if he got into the Baptist Church, he didn't know it. He didn't intend to. Mr. Bogard says he wouldn't take one in today like that. But he says he got in by pretense—or through false pretense. Mr.

Bogard, tell me *what pretense he made upon which he got in. Put it down and tell me.* You said he got into the Baptist Church under false pretense. Now, I want to know what pretense he made. I want to know what scheme he worked in order to get into the Baptist Church. He got in through false pretense. Tell us what the pretense was! You watch how he deals with that. *He'll be just as silent as the tomb.*

Then he says, "I gave seventeen passages that prove the church before Pentecost." And they were all dealt with in the few days before—every one of them. They have been brought up a number of times, and I have spent just as much time replying to them as you spent making the argument on them. Why, he just gave them in running fashion. Just said this, and gave a reference; just said this, and gave a reference; he didn't make any argument on them at all. But one of them said that "all things were given into his hands," and Mr. Bogard says, "There couldn't be anything given to him on Pentecost, because all things had been given to him." Mr. Bogard, did he receive the throne of David during that time? Had Jesus already received the throne of David? You said that this means there was not *one thing* left to be given to him *at any other time.* In Luke 1:32,33 God said, "I will give unto him the throne of his father David." Now, you say that nothing could be given to him as late as Pentecost, and as he was to be given the throne of David, I want to know, Mr. Bogard, when Jesus received the throne of David. *God said he would give it to him.* When did he receive it? *Is he on it now?* I think Mr. Bogard will tell you that he will not be on it till he comes again, but we will wait and see. If he will not be on it till he comes again, then I wonder how he is going to get it there if he couldn't receive something at Pentecost. How could he receive something some two thousand years later? And that covers the matter.

I am going back now, for the few minutes I have left, to reemphasize some arguments I made this afternoon which Mr. Bogard hasn't had the courage to deal with. This is going to look bad on the record. He passed by these things so silently; he made no effort to answer them. And this one on the board stands out in all of its force and power. Mr. Bogard can't touch it. 1 Tim. 3:15, which Mr. Bogard and I agree refers to the house of God, which is the church of the living God. He said, "Well, yesterday he denied that the house is the church." No, I didn't. I said that Jesus left the material, of which the house was being constructed, when he went to heaven. In that sense it may be called a house. But we agree that here is the house of God in its completed form. Here's the building. And, consequently, the house of God is the church.

CHART NO. 7

The house of God	**Them that obey not**
Us	**The ungodly**
The Righteous	**The sinner**

In 1 Peter 4:17,18 Peter said, "The time is come that judgment must begin at the house of God." The time is come that judgment must begin at the church of God then. All right. "And if it first begin at us." "Us" means the church of God—the church of God means "us." All those who are included in the expression, "us," were those in the house of God. Those in the house of God simply embraces those that Peter mentioned as "us." All right, let us see it now. "The time is come that judgment must begin at the house of God: and if it first begin at us, what shall the end be of them that obey not the gospel of God? And if the righteous scarcely be saved, where shall the ungodly and the sinner appear?" Peter draws a contrast between two classes of people—those in the house of God and those out of the house of God. Those in the house of God are said to be "us" and "the righteous." And all of those who are out of the house of God—over on this other side—belong to "them that obey not the gospel of God." They belong to "the ungodly" and "the sinner." Now, if men can be saved out of the house of God, they can be saved while disobeying the gospel—they can be saved in their ungodly and sinful condition. Because all those who are not in the house of God, nor belong to the class on this side (pointing to the board), belong to the class over here. Peter just drew the distinction between two classes of people. And what has he said about it? Nothing. The only reply he made this afternoon was, "Does that mean the house of God began there?" No, I wasn't trying to prove where the house of God began with that. I was simply show-

ing that salvation in this age *is in the house of God,* in the church. And Mr. Bogard can't touch it. He has manifested his utter inability to even try to do so. The house of God, the church of God, us and the righteous—all are the same people on the one side; over here in contrast with the church (pointing to board) are those that obey not, the ungodly and the sinner. And if these over here are saved, then they are saved in that condition. But these over here (pointing to left side of board) are the saved ones—they are saved in the house of God. They are righteous—they are the ones Peter referred to as "us." These others are lost. They obey not the gospel—they are ungodly—and they are sinners. He doesn't have time to fool with that—he hates to kill his time. Well, I don't blame him. If I were in the predicament he is in, I wouldn't want to kill my time either. I would try to find some other way to put it in rather than to deal with an argument like that, because this audience knows that Mr. Ben M. Bogard can't touch it. He can't even make a reasonable effort—he can't even make an attempt to do so. He can't even have an expression on his face that looks like he thinks he can. He looks like he wants to, but he certainly cannot look like he thinks he can answer it—he knows he can't. If that were the only passage in all of of God's Book, I would be willing to stake the whole thing on it, for the simple fact that it cannot be met.

And then I gave "the Savior of the church." Eph. 5:23. "Christ is the head of the body, and he is the savior of the church." I showed, that being true, he saves those who are in the church. If he saves every body before he gets into the church, he is not the Savior of the church, unless they get lost after they get in. Mr. Bogard says they can't get lost once they have been saved. So if he ever saves the church, he will have to save them in the church, and not out of it. That reminds me too of that little quibble he made about being reconciled in one body. It didn't mean *by being in one body.* Well, why didn't you tell us about the fellow getting drowned in the river—whether that meant he got drowned *by being in the river* or he got drowned out on the dry ground and was thrown in. Now, you have a parallel. Deal with it.

I showed also from Acts 2:47 that the church comprises the saved. "The Lord added to the church daily such as should be saved." And if any body in Jerusalem was saved before he entered the church, he was saved when he should not be. That means either that they were saved *when they were added to the church* or they were saved *before they were added to the church.* If they were saved before they were added to the church, then the Lord is not the *Savior of the church.* If the Lord is the Savior of the church—and the Bible says he is—then they were saved when they were added to the church, and not before.

I showed also that we are redeemed by the blood of Christ. 1 Peter 1:19. Also that we were bought by the blood of Christ. Eph. 5:25; Acts 20:28. "Purchased with his blood." The Lord purchased the church with his blood. If you ever get any benefit from the blood, you must get it out of the institution that was bought with his blood. That's the church. And if you can't be saved without the blood of Jesus Christ, you can't be saved out of the institution that was purchased with that blood.

Likewise, I showed that they are written in heaven—the church in this age are those who are written in heaven. I asked Mr. Bogard to show somebody besides the church that are written in heaven in this age. He went back to Luke 10:20, but that was back over here (pointing to space on board before the cross) before Jesus died on the cross. And Jesus died in the end of that age—not the beginning of this one. So that age didn't end till the cross, and *that wasn't in this age,* Mr. Bogard. That was back there under the age that hadn't yet ended—and didn't end till Jesus died. But come this side of the cross and find where somebody has his name written in heaven who was not a member of the church. *Can you do it?* No, he can't do it. Unless they have their names written in heaven, Jesus said, in Rev. 21:27, they cannot enter the city. And Rev. 20:15 says they "will be cast into the lake of fire and brimstone, which is the second death." I believe my time is so near up—(time called).

Third Day

BOGARD'S FOURTH NEGATIVE

Gentlemen Moderators, Ladies and Gentlemen:

We are making wonderful progress in this debate by thrashing out everything for two or three days to get things in your minds so you will really understand what is being said. And the further we go the clearer it will be. I will begin right where my friend began and go straight through.

I called his attention to the fact that his doctrine taught that to leave off baptism was a sin against the Holy Ghost. He comes and says, "Well then, you say that you have got to have faith and so leave off faith and that is a sin against the Holy Ghost." Here is a man with faith. He already has faith; he has repented of his sins; he wants to be saved. He has the faith. He comes and says, "Lord, I want salvation. I have repented, I have believed, and I have the love of God in my heart. I have everything." And the Lord says, "To hell with you. You have not been baptized." That is the point. Without faith it is impossible to please God. But here is a man with faith. You say he has to have faith before he is baptized. Here he comes now with everything. God is willing to save. The Holy Spirit is willing to save. Jesus Christ is willing to save. The man wants to be saved. But one thing he has left out that he cannot get forgiveness for—that is leaving out baptism. That makes it worse than murder, worse than lying, worse than stealing, the worst thing in the world.

I get very much amused. He comes here and says the house of God is the church. When did the house of God begin? In Mark 13 that he is seemingly paralyzed over, Jesus left His house and left His servants with authority and a work to do and commanded them to watch for you know not when the master of the house returns. Now, the house is the church, my friend said. And I showed that the Lord left His house when He left the world. You cannot leave a thing that is not in existence. You cannot leave this house here tonight if there is no house here to leave. It does not take a scholar to see that. You can make wise-cracks and talk about hitching posts and getting a man up a tree and laugh and giggle, but you cannot meet that. *The Lord left something.* What did He leave? The Masonic Lodge? No, sir. The Farmers Union? No, sir. The Lord left something when He left the earth. He said He did. What did He leave? He left His house and gave His servants authority and a work to do and commanded them to watch for you not when the master of the house will return. *He was leaving something and He was coming back to it.* And He told them to watch as good servants for He was coming back again. My friend says that the house of God is the church of God. That part is settled. I do not have to go any further on that. If he says the thing was not complete then Jesus left an incomplete something and promised to come back to that incomplete something and gave an incomplete something authority and a work to do.

You do not like that idea about hell scare. You have not answered me yet. I will let you write it on a piece of paper and hand it up here. Did you *love God* before you were baptized or were you baptized just because you were *hell scared?* If you will write on a piece of paper, "I loved God before I was baptized," then I will quote I John 4:7, "He that loveth is born of God and knoweth God." Now, you have gotten your salvation before baptism. It does not take a scholar to see that. He said, "I did not love God before I was baptized." Then with enmity in your heart, you were baptized in order to get to love God. That made a magic difference. Here is a man with enmity in his heart against God when he walks into the water, up to his ankles he is still hating God, knee deep he is still hating God, waist deep he is still hating God. And you put him under the water all except his nose with him still hating God. Now when that priest you make yourself into dips him clear under and brings him up—presto, change! The love of God is in his heart. Do you believe that? If so, if I believed that, that you had to get folk who had enmity in their hearts against God and by baptizing them you could make them love God, I would grab every man I could get hold of by the nape of the neck and the seat of the britches and put him under. (Laughter) You say that would not be any good. It is just as much good to do him that way as it is to scare him with hell. You do not have the love of God in your heart.

"Well," he says, "do you not come to the mourner's bench hating God?" I rather think so, as a hater of God. I come to God and say, "Lord, I am sorry I have been hating you all along. I would like to get reconciled to you. We have been enemies up till now and you prayed that in Christ Jesus we would be reconciled to God. And I come as a hater of God for reconciliation asking forgiveness for my former hatred. God, have mercy on my poor wicked soul." And the Bible says He will have mercy and abundantly pardon. It seems to me that ought to be perfectly easy.

He comes back to John Smith founding the Baptist Church. My friend Porter knows I know he knows that he knows I know he knows that he knows better than that. On page 304 of Benedict's History it says under the head of *English Baptists* that John Smith established the first one the world knew anything about in 1607.It is headed "English Baptists." On page 343 of the same Benedict's History, the very book you quoted from and you know I know that you know I know you know, it says *a Baptist Church was old in the year 595* and divided. The old or Baptist Church divided in the year 595. And here you have the effrontery, the face, to come up here and try to pawn that thing off on us. If you have your book I will show it to you. If you do not have your book then you are quoting purposely wrong. If you have Benedict there hand it to me. (Mr. Porter: "It is out in the car; I will bring it tomorrow.) Well, I dare you to produce Benedict. I dog dare you and double dare you to do it. (Laughter) You bring Benedict here to me tomorrow and I will turn there and read just what I told you. I dare you to face it. You cannot put this kind of stuff over on me. I know Benedict's History from beginning to end. Now, before I would misrepresent, stand up before people who do not know and try to put off such false-hood as that, I would rather have my arm cut off at the shoulder. And you know you did it. Bring the book here tomorrow and I will show you that you did. Pass it around and let everybody read it, where the church was old, old enough to divide, in the year 595 and you know it is there. Then try to palm off the John Smith General Church, *General Baptist Church in England,* as the first Baptist Church in the world.

Now, comes my friend and quotes what I said in the Hardeman-Bogard Debate about the Spirit coming on the day of Pentecost as an administrator. I have told you three times in this debate already, you did not have to read Hardeman, that the Spirit came as an administrator on the day of Pentecost but did come to do His office work in salvation before the day of Pentecost. I have told you three times already. The kingdom came with power on the day of Pentecost, power of the baptism of the Holy Ghost, but it did *not come into existence on the day of Pentecost.* There is quite a difference between a man coming into existence and coming into power. So the power of the Holy Ghost came on the day of Pentecost. The church already existed and was endued with power from on high at Pentecost. It had to be there to be endued with power from on high. How in the world are you going to give a man power if the man does not exist? How are you going to give a church power if the church does not exist? How are you going to give a kingdom power if a kingdom does not exist? The kingdom came in power, not in existence. And I showed you when the Lord left the earth He left His church and gave His servants authority and a work to do.

On *heart felt salvation,* I will take it up just as he said it, he said they did not depend on their feelings. Nobody else does, that I know. If anybody depends on his feelings for salvation I am sorry for him. But you do not know you are saved unless you do have a feeling, for the love of God is shed abroad *in the heart* by the Holy Ghost. And you tell me you can love and not feel it? Did you have that love before you were baptized? If so, you were saved before you were baptized.

Now, we are coming back to the name. *He dies hard, but die he must.* Give me the passage of scripture where it says "The Church of Christ" in *any sense* at all and I will quit the debate. It is not in the Bible. You have harped and harped on the name. *"The Church of Christ."* Do you call that the name? I will quit the debate if you will give me the passage. You know it is not there. And you know I know you know that it is not there. Then why do you stand up here and keep on palavering about the name "The Church of Christ" and you cannot find it in the lids of the Bible. I ask you again to find one local congregation, just one—the seven churches of Asia, the church at Thessalonica, the church at Colosse, the churches of Judea, the churches of the Gentiles—show just one time when they were called churches or church of Christ in any local community. You cannot find it in the general sense; you cannot find it in the local sense; yet you harp around about the name.

Well, he says, "Why do you not find where the Baptist Churches are named?" I told you *the Lord did not name the church at all.* He left it nameless and gave a *description* of it. And the reason why the "Missionary Baptist Church" is a scriptural name is because *the scriptural idea is there.* You cannot find the idea of your shebang nor the name either. (Laughter) The name is scriptural in idea. Why should we say Missionary Baptist Church? Because that is what the Lord describes. He gave the doctrines and practices of the Missionary Baptist Church and anybody can read that description and see that is what it ought to be called. The Bible does not call it anything. It does not call any church by name except the local church like the church at Colosse. That is a local name, but it does not say "The church of Christ at Colosse." The Lord left it nameless on purpose. I am sure if He had put down in the Bible that this is the Missionary Baptist Church then every false creed, every false organization, would have adopted that name and tried to put it over on the world. The Lord describes it so they cannot possibly make the grade unless they meet the description. Scriptural in name? Yes sir, the scriptural idea is there.

If I make a picture of a cat on the board I do not have to write on it, "This is a cat." If I make a good picture everybody can see it is a cat. If I make a picture of a horse, I do not have to write under it,"This is a horse." Anybody who knows what a horse looks like could tell it is a horse. You cannot get the folks to believe the church you are in is the church of our Lord unless you tell them it is so. Name it. This is a cat. Before God, if I could not give a description of my church I would give it up as a bad job.

On the question of ruling elders, what has he said in

reply? Four times I brought it up. He replied by saying, "Who are the ruling elders in Damascus about this debate?" Bless your soul, they have *no ruling elders* in Damascus or anywhere else among Baptists, for the Bible says, "It shall not be so among you." Matt. 20:25, 26 says, "Ye know that the princes of the Gentiles exercise dominion over them, and they that are great exercise authority over them. But it shall not be so among you." If anybody in Damascus had told me I could not come I would have come in spite of high water. You can put the other word in front of it if you want to. (Laughter) I am not going to be ruled by any bunch of ruling elders. Who are the ruling elders in Damascus? We have none. Bless your soul, we are all free. And if a bunch of fellows got together and said they were the ruling elders in the Baptist Church in Damascus I would say, "You can go hang. I will come if I want to." And I expect the church would tell them to go hang too if they would undertake to rule as elders here in this church.

Now what are you going to do? You have ruling elders. They meet inside these walls. They tell the church, your church, what to do. If a new roof is to go on the house the ruling elders decide. If a new preacher is to be called the ruling elders decide. If somebody gets out of order and needs discipline, the ruling elders discipline. They are in control. Who appoints the elders? The evangelist that comes along, like my friend Blue, here. He will not object if I call his name. He is an evangelist. He can come here and if he wants to he can appoint elders. He can oust the last one of the elders here and appoint new ones, and you know it is so. Then after he gets the elders appointed then *those elders rule the church* while the Lord claims, "It shall not be so among you."

We come to the name again. We find "churches of Christ." He says, "I always did say that meant ownership." He did not say it day before yesterday nor yesterday. He said that is the name. Everybody knows he said it. Now he says *it means ownership*—the churches that belong to the Lord, not name at all. Thank you, sir, for coming around after I have whipped you all over the place on the subject, and you had to.

He says if we have a plural we are bound to have a singular. He comes back to that same old gag again. He cannot have a plural without a singular. When I say "the men of Arkansas," it means there is *the man of Arkansas embracing all the little men of Arkansas.* When I say "the houses of Damascus" there must be a singular, *the house of Damascus embracing all the little houses.* For the trees of the forest there must be *a great big tree that includes all the little trees of the forest.* The husband is the head of the wife. What kind of wife? *A great big wife that includes all the little wives?* Would she not be a whopper? If the church means a great big organization or institution that includes all the small churches, then the wife means a great big wife that includes all the little wives, or language means nothing. There is no such thing as "The Church of Christ" *in name or in fact.* You cannot find the idea in the Bible; you cannot find the name in the Bible. It is not there.

He wants me to find the name "Baptist Church." I told you to start with, I have told you three times already and this makes the fourth time, *the Lord did not name the church. He described it,* so that if anybody came along claiming the name he would have to prove that he is what the Bible teaches concerning the church and he would not get by with it. If the Lord had given the name "The Missionary Baptist Church," then all on earth, or a bunch of heretics like what you belong to, would come along and say, "We are the Missionary Baptist Church," like a polecat coming along and saying, "I am a nice little rabbit," but it did not take the stink off. A polecat calls himself a rabbit. Would that take the stink off? Here comes a non-scriptural organization and says, "We are that church. The Lord named it and we are going to claim that name." Do you not see that is why the Lord gave the description rather than give the name so that anybody would know how to name it if they saw what the description calls for?

Now about the body, he asks what body I am a member of. Missionary Baptist Body. Whose body is that? It belongs to the Lord. I am on a farm out here, Mr. Jones' farm. Whose farm? Mr. Jones' farm. What is the church? It is a body. Whom does it belong to? It belongs to Jesus Christ.

I am a member of that. He said, "You do not belong to that *'mystical' body*, that spiritual body?" *There is no such thing.* I will give you ten dollars to find it. Take all night. Sit up tonight and read and find anything about a *"mystical" body of Christ,* a spiritual body of Christ, in the sense you used that term. It is not there. You just invent ideas and try to put it over and say the same thing over and over and over again until people think you have scripture for it. You cannot find a thing about it in the Bible to save your life.

I read how we were saved just like Abraham was saved. I read how we were saved just like David was saved in the fourth chapter of Romans. What did he do with it? He went over to Hebrews and talked about the new and living way instead of answering what I put up. We are saved like Abraham. We are saved like David. They were saved by faith looking forward to Christ. *Christ is the new and living way.* But they were saved by that new and living way just like we are saved. For He stood as a lamb slain from the foundation of the world. Say that is not in the Bible and I will eat it. That new and living way has been *all the way along,* salvation by grace through faith in the Lord Jesus Christ.

Well, now let me see what else. I want everything, do not want to miss anything. He wants to know when Jesus got on David's throne. When He comes back to the earth again and goes back to Jerusalem, the thing he says He never will do. I have told you that four times now and this makes the fifth time. *You do not believe Jesus Christ ever will sit on David's throne.* You do not believe He is ever coming back to this earth to rule on the earth. You do not believe in the millennial reign of Christ at all. I will dare you to say so. And if you will come and say so we will have the biggest time of our lives tomorrow. You will go back on all your brethren if you say that is so. Very well.

Now, just a little more exposure. My friend and his church which by rights ought to be called the Campbellite Church, (I have abstained from saying you are a "Campbellite," for that would be personal. You get mad when you do it. You know if you call a negro a negro he gets mad. He does not like to be called what he is. And I could throw all that kind of stuff at you but I prefer not to do it.) *they deny the work of the Holy Spirit before Pentecost.* They harp it all over. He said it, denied that the Holy Spirit began His work before the day of Pentecost. Now, listen here. I read to you from II Peter 1:21. "For the prophecy came not in old time by the will of man but holy men of God spake as they were moved by the Holy Ghost." The Holy Spirit has been working *in all ages.* Mark 12:26, "David himself said by the Holy Ghost." That was back yonder in the Old Testament. Luke 1:41, "Elizabeth was filled with the Holy Ghost." That was before Pentecost. Luke 1:67, "Zacharias was filled with the Holy Ghost." And Luke 1:15, speaking of the birth of John the Baptist, said, "He shall be filled with the Holy Ghost from his mother's womb." Luke 2:25-26, Simeon spoke with the Holy Ghost upon him. Matt. 3:16 says, "Jesus, when he was baptized, went up straightway out of the water: and, lo, the heavens were opened unto him and he saw the Spirit of God descending upon him and lighting upon him." Matt. 12:28, "If I cast out devils by the Spirit of God, then the kingdom of God is come unto you." John 4:23, "The hour cometh and now is," not will be after Pentecost, "and now is when true worshippers shall worship the Father in spirit and in truth." John 20:22, "He breathed on them and said unto them, Receive ye the Holy Ghost." And they actually preach all over the country that the Holy Spirit did not begin His work until the day of Pentecost.

The Holy Spirit began His *administration* over the church on the day of Pentecost. The Lord organized the church, established it, gave it its doctrines and practices, and told it to go teach all nations baptizing in the name of the Father, the Son and the Holy Spirit, "And lo, I am with you always even unto the end of the world." Tarry in Jerusalem. Who? He told the church to tarry in Jerusalem till the power of the Holy Ghost came upon it in the administrative sense. That is what began on the day of Pentecost. And that is as plain as the word of God can make it.

Now, you deny all the time the doctrine of salvation by grace through faith and *make your preacher a priest and a mediator between God and man.* The Bible says there is one mediator between God and man and that is the man

Christ Jesus. According to your doctrine no man can be saved unless he has the sacred hands of one of your preachers laid upon him and is put under the water by your hands. And you decide who is to be baptized. Therefore, you decide who shall be saved. My friend right over here, Brother Joe Blue, a woman came up to the altar and made the good confession and somebody came to Blue and said, "That woman is a bad woman." She had made a bet with some sawmill men that, "I can join that Campbellite Church down there just like I am and they will take me in." They bet her five dollars she could not do it, and she came up there and offered herself to Blue as he was preaching and Blue said, "Thank God for this good confession. We will baptize this afternoon." Somebody at the noon hour came and said, "Blue, that woman is a strumpet and she has a bet on with the boys down at the mill," and Blue refused to baptize her. Well, you say he had a right to. I think so too. And so does the Missionary Baptist Church have a right to refuse to baptize a person, and that is why we vote. *Our whole membership votes.* Romans 14:1 "Him that is weak in the faith receive ye," but in your outfit just one of you does the voting. Since we do not think salvation depends on baptism, we are not voting on their salvation. But when you refuse to baptize a man why you decide whether or not that man shall be saved. By the way, since baptism washes away all sin, I would like to know why baptism would not wash away that gamble that woman made. She could join Joe Blue's church without any change whatever.

Very well, there is no time to make a new argument. I have replied to all my friend has said. Now come back tomorrow at two o'clock and we will go on with this and have more good times than you ever saw.

Fourth Day

PORTER'S FIFTH AFFIRMATIVE

Gentlemen Moderators, Mr. Bogard, Ladies and Gentlemen:

We are entering now on the closing day of this discussion. There will be two hours this afternoon and two hours tonight, and then the debate will be history. The subject for investigation today is the same one we had under study yesterday—that "the church known as the Church of Christ is Scriptural in origin, doctrine, practice and name." Since, of course, it is a general church question, there are different questions within it being discussed. While some of the things discussed yesterday will be repeated to some extent, of course, today, we will go along some new lines. Some new thoughts, some new arguments, of course, pertaining to other matters, will be introduced.

Before I introduce some affirmatives, which I wish to introduce at this time, I want to pay attention to some things said by my opponent in the closing speech last night. And the first thing I want to talk about is that woman that brother Joe Blue refused to baptize. Now, Mr. Bogard told you last night that brother Blue was conducting a meeting at some place and some lady came forward at the invitation and made the good confession, and brother Blue said, "Thank God for that good confession." But before baptizing time he learned that this woman had gambled, or made a bet with somebody of about five dollars, that she could join the Campbellite church, or something to that effect. I don't know where Mr. Bogard got all of his information along this line, but he said concerning the matter that "I believe that Joe Blue did right." Well, just granting him that the whole story he told was true, and he admits that Joe Blue did right, then Joe Blue did right *without consulting the church,* and the church didn't have to vote on it, even according to Mr. Bogard, because he said "Joe Blue did right." But the fact is, Mr. Bogard misrepresented the whole story—almost. The simple fact is that Joe Blue *never did see* the woman in question at all. She *did not attend any meeting* that he was conducting and *made no confession* whatsoever. And there was *no gambling* or betting about joining what he called the Campbellite church, as far as Joe Blue ever knew anything about. So with these exceptions, perhaps the story is true. Now, the fact is, this woman—and it was more than fifty years ago—came from West Plains down to Williford. She was a lewd woman, and located in an old barn and carried on her nefarious work. Some one out in the territory took her to his home, and then sent Joe Blue word to come and baptize this woman. Joe Blue sent word back that you can baptize her as well as I can—so go ahead. And that's all there is to it. Mr. Bogard has been harping on that matter through the years. He has been telling it for the last thirty years—in fact, for the last forty years, and he has every right to know that the representation he made of it is not true. And so you have now the facts concerning the woman that he has been talking about that Joe Blue refused to baptize and how the circumstances were.

Another thing now as we proceed with the speech last night. He talked again about haters of God—that we teach that men hate God until they are baptized. They go down into the water up to their waists, hating God. Then the preacher starts putting them under the water—up to their necks—and they are still haters of God, and up to and until finally their noses are out, and they are still haters of God. And finally we get their noses under, and we bring them up, and they are lovers of God. "Presto—and the change is made." Well, we might just talk about Bogard's side of that. You know he claims that the Baptist Church is the bride, or will be the bride after a while. But you can't be a part of the bride of Christ unless you belong to the Missionary Baptist Church, and, therefore, it takes the sacred hands of a Baptist preacher to put you under the water. Not only up to the waist, and up to the neck, and up to the nose, but you have got to get your nose under too, and the whole man has to go under, and then you come out, at the sacred hands of a Baptist preacher, before you have any right to be any part of the bride of Jesus Christ. Now, that's Bogard's theory.

Besides I asked him, you will remember, about this matter of hating God—what about the man who is praying to God at the altar—at the mourner's bench—for salvation? Is that man hating God while he is praying and while he is in that penitent state? What did my friend say? He said, "Why, yes, I come to God, and I say I have been hating you. I am sorry for all of my former hatred" and all of that. Yes, Mr. Bogard, but I wasn't talking about your *former hatred.* You dodged the question entirely. You knew that wasn't what I asked you. I am willing to admit that there was former hatred, that you had been hating, and all of that, but that isn't the question. I didn't ask you if you had been hating God before you prayed. Or if there was some former hatred toward God on the part of the man who was praying to be saved. I asked you: Is that man who comes to the altar to pray to be saved, in that state of penitence, a hater of God *while he is praying?* And before he obtains salvation? Now, that's the question, Bogard; you haven't touched it. Come back up here and try it again. Not his former hatred. Was he hating God *while he prayed?* You say he wasn't saved yet—he hadn't yet put his trust in the Lord. He hadn't yet obtained the forgiveness of his sins. He is in a state of penitence, which you say comes before faith. And so in that state of penitence he prays to God and says, "Lord, save me." But he hasn't reached salvation yet. I want to know: During that exercise is he hating God? Not what he did back yonder before he came to the altar to pray. But while engaged in the prayer, is he hating God? Now, you put it down and tell us. You are not deaf. That puts him in the hole where he thinks he has me.

Well, in 1 John 5:3 the apostle said that "this is the love of God that we keep his commandments." And certainly there must be some obedience to the commandments along the line.

Then to Benedict. Regarding Benedict he said that Porter knows, in the year 595, that Benedict referred to some Baptist Church as being old in that day. Well, yes, I know about Benedict's statement on page 343. And I know what Benedict meant when he referred to matters of that kind, because I know what Benedict said concerning such matters. The very context from which Bogard gave his quotations shows that the contrast was between those who held to infant baptism and those who held to the baptism of believers, or adults. And, in that sense, he referred to them as "baptists." But what does Mr. Benedict mean by referring to people that way? Here it is. In History of All Religions, page 198 (and this was the very same Benedict) —and here he said:

"The peculiar sentiments of this denomination having spread so much among people of all opinions, to *affirm that a man is a Baptist, proves nothing more than that he rejects infant baptism, and holds to believers' baptism, by immersion*; he may be a Calvinist or Arminian, a Trinitarian or Unitarian, a Universalist or Swedenborgian, for some of all these classes come under *the broad distinction of Baptists.*"

So he found somebody in the sixth century back there who held to believers' baptism by immersion, opposed to infant baptism, and therefore referred to them as "baptists." Certainly so, Mr. Bogard. He says that is what he means by referring to matters of that kind.

And I have here a little pamphlet—some of you have been buying them—"Baptist Churches In All Ages." And the author is Mr. Ben M. Bogard. On page 15 of this Mr. Bogard shows you can't tell what a man is because you find him referred to as a Baptist. He says:

"There were irregularities among these ancient people. But there are irregularities among the Baptists today. Some of them practiced sprinkling. *Yes, and some bearing the name of Baptists today practice sprinkling.* This is common in England. The local independence of Baptist churches permits a church to go *very far wrong* and *still wear the name of Baptist.*"

So just to find somebody referred to as a Baptist doesn't prove anything so far as he is concerned, because he has admitted in his own book that it doesn't.

And then I was amused at what he said about Mark 9:1 —"come with power." Jesus said the kingdom would come with power. Mr. Bogard said, "Yes, it comes with power, but that doesn't mean that it comes into existence." Well, where did it come? Usually, Mr. Bogard says when we came over here we came with power, but we didn't come into existence. No, but we were not here before we came. I didn't come into existence when I came to Damascus, but I wasn't in Damascus until I came. I came from some other place to here. And I wasn't here till I came. And then on the day of Pentecost the kingdom came with power. If the kingdom existed, it was somewhere else. Where did it come from? It wasn't on the earth till then, because it came with power then. And if it didn't come into existence, it came from some other place. Tell us where it came from, Mr. Bogard.

He says, "We Baptists don't depend on our feelings as evidence of salvation, but we don't know we are saved unless we feel it." Now, if you can distinguish between that, help yourself. "No, we don't depend on our feelings as evidence of our salvation, but you can't tell you are saved unless you feel it." (Porter laughs) I think everybody can see the contradiction in that.

And then regarding the "ruling elders." The statement he made regarding the "ruling elders" and that we teach that evangelists should come into the community and depose the elders and put somebody else in is not true. We teach no such thing. Mr. Bogard knows that those things he said about that are misrepresentations about what we teach. He simply puts out his misrepresentation and expects you to believe it. I asked him who ruled for the Baptists in this debate, and he said, "Well, we have no ruling elders. And there didn't anybody." Well, somebody decided. Somebody decided for the Baptists here about this debate, and the Baptists in Damascus didn't decide it. Who was it? Or did Mr. Bogard overrule them? Who was it that decided for him to come here and hold this debate? Somebody made the decision.

Regarding the argument made on 2 Sam. 7:12, he said, "Christ isn't on David's throne. He'll receive David's throne when he comes back." But yesterday he made the argument that he couldn't *even receive anything* on Pentecost because *he received everything* before Pentecost. Well, if he couldn't receive anything on Pentecost because he received everything before Pentecost, how could he receive David's throne two thousand years this side of Pentecost, or maybe four thousand years this side? Bogard meets himself coming back again.

Another misreprsentation was that we deny the work

of the Holy Spirit before Pentecost. There is not a word of truth in it. We have always taught that men of past ages "spoke as they were moved by the Holy Ghost." We have always taught these things. And that is another misrepresentation that Mr. Bogard has made.

That replies to the speech of last night, except things that have already been thoroughly discussed, and I pass on now to some affirmative arguments.

The next line of thought I am going to take up is that we believe and teach, and we are just sure of the fact that it is taught in the Bible, that baptism to a penitent believer is in order to obtain the remission of his sins. So for this session we are going to discuss more fully the subject of baptism.

My first argument is based upon a statement made by the apostle Paul in 1 Cor. 1:12,13. Here the apostle said, "Every one of you saith, I am of Paul; and I of Apollos; and I of Cephas; and I of Christ. Is Christ divided? Was Paul crucified for you? Or were you baptized in the name of Paul?" Now, in this statement Paul refers to certan people in Corinth who were saying, "I am of Paul," or "I belong to Paul," as some translations give it. "I am of Apollos," or "I belong to Apollos." "I am of Cephas," or "I belong to Cephas." And "I am of Christ," or "I belong to Christ." Paul went on to show that in order for that thing to be true there were two things that had to exist. Paul said, "Is Christ divided? Was Paul crucified for you? Or were you baptized in the name of Paul?" In other words, in order for a man to be "of Paul," or to "belong to Paul," these two things must be true. In the first place, Paul must be crucified for him; and in the second place, he must be baptized in the name of Paul. It is not enough for Paul to be crucified for him. That could be true, and still he wouldn't belong to Paul. But in order for that man to be "of Paul" and to "belong to Paul," Paul would have to be crucified for him, in the first place; and in the second place, he would have to be baptized in Paul's name. Just so with respect to those who said, "I am of Apollos." In order for them to belong to Apollos, Apollos must be crucified for them, and they must be baptized in the name of Apollos. And so with those who said, "I am of Cephas." In order to belong to Cephas, they must first have Cephas crucified for them, and then they must be baptized in the name of Cephas. Those two things are necessary to make men "of Paul" or "of Apollos" or "of Cephas." The same thing is true with those who said, "I am of Christ," for he lays down a principle here that governs the whole thing. "I am of Paul; I of Apollos; I of Cephas; and I of Christ." Therefore, when a man says "I am of Christ," in order for that man to belong to Christ, Paul says there are two things that must be true. In the first place, Christ must be crucified for him, and in the second place, he must be baptized in the name of Christ. If it holds true with respect to Paul, Apollos and Cephas, it holds true with respect to Jesus Christ. And so Paul declares that a man is not "of Christ"—he does not "belong to Christ"—unless, in the first place, Christ has been crucified for him, and in the second place, unless he has been baptized in the name of Christ. It is not enough for Jesus to be crucified for him. That is only one of them. In addition to that, he must also be baptized in the name of Christ, or he is not "of Christ"—he does not "belong to Christ." And, therefore, he is not saved. I have tried that on Baptist preachers, and other preachers, all over the country, and to this good day no man has even looked like he thought he could answer it. I want Mr. Bogard to try his hand on it.

And the second argument will be based upon the statement of the great commission, recorded by Mark in Mark 16, verses 15 and 16. Here the Lord said, "Go into all the world, and preach the gospel to every creature. He that believeth and is baptized shall be saved; but he that believeth not shall be damned." Now, notice that commission as the Lord gave it. "Go ye into all the world, and preach the gospel to every creature. He that *believeth and is baptized shall be saved.*" Notice where the Lord placed salvation. He did not say, "He that believeth and is saved can be baptized if he wants to, and the church votes that it is all right." But he said, "He that believeth and is baptized shall be saved." First, belief; second, baptism; third, salvation. All right. Just as certainly as that makes belief necessary to salvation, it makes baptism necessary to salvation. The Lord conditioned salvation on both belief and baptism—"he that *believeth and is baptized* shall be saved." He didn't say merely, "He that believeth shall be saved." But "he that believeth" *and does something else*—"he that believeth and is baptized shall be saved." Thus the Lord's own words put salvation after both belief and baptism and make both belief and baptism necessary to that salvation. That is the very thing that we teach, and we are Scriptural in that teaching, because it is in the language that fell from the lips of the Son of God himself.

Next I come to a statement made by the apostle Peter in the second chapter of Acts and verse 38. Here on the day of Pentecost we find the apostle Peter preaching under that commission the Lord had just given them a short time before. He had proclaimed the death, the burial, the resurrection, the ascension and the coronation of Jesus Christ, and those who heard were pricked in the heart. He told them that they stood as murderers of the Son of God—that their hands were dripping, as it were, with his innocent blood. And being pricked in the heart, they cried out and said, "Men and brethren, what shall we do?" Were they wanting to know what shall we do because we are saved already? No, *they were not saved.* They realized that they were not saved. Peter had condemned them as murderers of the Son of God, and they realized that the condemnation of heaven rested upon them, because of their sins. So they cried out and said, "Men and brethren, what shall we do?" What did Peter tell them? The 38th verse tells us that Peter said to them, "Repent, and be baptized every one of you in the name of Jesus Christ for the remission of sins." All right. There is the statement. "Repent, and be baptized every one of you in the name of Jesus Christ for the remission of sins." He did not merely say, "Repent and you will be saved." But he said, "Repent and do something else." "Repent, *and be baptized* in the name of Jesus Christ *for the remission of sins.*" Well, if he had said nothing more than just "repent and be baptized," that would have been sufficient. When they cried, "Men and brethren, what shall we do?" they realized their guilt, they realized their condemnation, and if he had only said "repent and be baptized," and stopped right there, it would still prove both repentance and baptism as conditions of salvation. But Peter made it more emphatic by going on to say, "Repent, and be baptized *for the remission of sins.*"

I want to give you a few translations—a few New Testament translations—on that particular expression, "for the remission of sins." I am reading from the King James Version. That is the one I ordinarily use in my preaching, because I started with that long ago.

The King James Version says, "For the remission of sins."

The Catholic Revised Version reads, "For the forgiveness of your sins."

John Wesley's translation reads, "For the remission of sins."

Moffatt's translation says, "For the remission of your sins."

Wilson's Emphatic Diaglott says, "For the forgiveness of your sins."

Weymouth's translation says, "For the forgiveness of your sins."

The Revised Standard Version, which came out only about two years ago, says, "For the forgiveness of your sins."

The American Bible Union says, "Unto remission of sins."

The American Revised Version says, "Unto the remission of your sins."

Charles Foster Kent says, "That your sins may be forgiven."

Goodspeed's translation says, "In order to have your sins forgiven."

Charles B. Williams' translation says, "That you may have your sins forgiven."

And Thayer, in his translation of it, says, "To obtain the forgiveness of sins."

Now, you remember these translations of that expression, and they say, "for the remission of sins," "unto the remission of sins," "that you may have your sins forgiven," "in order to obtain the remission of sins," and matters like that. So I am sure of the fact that I am upon safe ground when I say that Peter commanded men to be baptized for, unto, or in order to have, the remission of their sins. Besides I wonder if in fact many of us can't understand Mr. Bogard himself. I have here the Bogard-McPherson Debate. In the Bogard-McPherson Debate, on page 61, Mr. Bogard said,

"The promise in Acts 2:38"—Now, that is the passage I am discussing here.

"The promise in Acts 2:38 is not the baptism of the Holy Ghost but it is remission of sins. The promise to all them that are 'afar off' is that when they repent they will be saved, *they will obtain the remission of their sins.*"

All right, there is Mr. Bogard's statement about it, when he meets Aimee in debate—in discussing the baptism of the Holy Spirit. He said the promise in Acts 2:38 concerns obtaining the remission of sins. And the only thing in Acts 2:38 that says anything about remission of sins is this statement, "for the remission of sins." That is the only thing in Acts 2:38 that is said about it. And Mr. Bogard said that the promise in Acts 2:38 is, concerning that, that "they *will obtain* the remission of sins." So Mr. Bogard, when he was debating with Aimee, said that it means "to obtain the remission of sins."

We noticed in these translations that a number of them said, "unto the remission of sins," "unto the remission of your sins," and things of that kind. The little word "unto." We are told in Acts 11:18 that God hath to the Gentiles "granted repentance *unto* life." That means repentance first, followed by the life. "Repentance unto life." In Rom. 10:10 we are told that "with the heart man believeth unto righteousness; and with the mouth confession is made *unto* salvation." All right, we have there three expressions in which the same word is used—"repentance unto life;" "believe unto righteousness;" and "confession unto salvation." If "repentance unto life" means repentance followed by life, and "belief unto righteousness" means righteousness after belief, and "confession unto salvation" means salvation after confession, then what about "baptism unto remission of sins" just mentioned in these translations I have used today—"to be baptized unto the remission of your sins"? The word "unto" means "toward," or "in the direction of," and consequently, my friends, it puts the remission of sins after baptism, just as the things which I have explained that God put on that side.

We come next to 1 Peter 3, verse 21. Peter says, "The like figure whereunto baptism doth also now save us." I want to write that down here. (Porter writes on blackboard, "Baptism doth now save us.") "Baptism doth also *now save us.*" "The like figure whereunto baptism doth also now save us (not the putting away of the filth of the flesh, but the answer of a good conscience toward God) by the resurrection of Jesus Christ." You wouldn't have to make much change in that to make it read like Mr. Bogard wants it to read. Not much. Now, Peter said, "Baptism doth now save us." How much change shall we make? Just a very little. Take the word "now" and erase that "w" and put a "t" in its place, (Porter changes the word on the board) and you will have exactly the teaching of Mr. Bogard. "Baptism doth *not* save us." But that isn't what Peter said. Nobody has the right to make that change. I am going to put it back like it was. (Rewrites the word "now") "Baptism doth *now save us.*" I don't care how men were saved back in the days of Abraham, or back in the days of Moses, or back in the days of David, for the fact is that Peter says *now* baptism saves us.

CHART NO. 8

Baptism doth now save us

Baptism doth not save us

Then next to Galatians, the third chapter, and verse 27. Here the apostle says, "For as many of you as have been baptized into Christ have put on Christ." Beginning with verse 26, "For ye are all the children of God by faith in Christ Jesus. For as many of you as have been baptized into Christ have put on Christ." Now, notice the statement. "Ye are all the children of God by faith in Christ Jesus, *for—*" We have the little word "for" there. It is not the same one we have over here, however. (Referring to Acts 2:38) It is an entirely different word, coming from an entirely different original term—the original term being "g-a-r." And the word means, according to Greek lexicographers, "to introduce the reason." "To introduce the reason." All right. Now, then, keep that in mind—that Paul introduces here the reason and let us see what it is. "Ye are all the children of God by faith in Christ Jesus, *for*" (or the reason of it is) that "as many of you as have been baptized into Christ have put on Christ." Now, the word shows that those who have not been baptized into Christ and have not put on Christ are not the children of God by faith in Jesus Christ. If so, then the "reason" is no reason at all. Paul used the word to introduce the reason—"ye are God's children by faith." Why? Why are you the children of God by faith? Well, the reason is, Paul says, "as many of you as have been baptized into Christ have put on Christ." All right, then, the reason for their being God's children by faith is the fact that they had been baptized into Christ. And faith alone did not put them into Christ—faith alone did not make them children of God. But they became God's children *by faith because they were baptized into Christ.* That's the reason that Paul assigned—"for as many as have been baptized into Christ have put on Christ."

Can men be saved out of Christ? If they cannot, they cannot be saved without baptism, because Paul said men are "baptized *into* Christ." If you are saved before you are baptized, you are saved on the outside of Christ—you are saved without getting into him. Yet we are told that salvation is in him, and all spiritual blessings are in him. And you can be saved without salvation; you can be saved without any spiritual blessings—if you can be saved out of Christ, for the simple fact that Paul says you are baptized *into* Christ.

Then to Rom. 6, verses 3 and 4. Here Paul made a similar statement. He said, "Know ye not, that so many of us as were baptized into Jesus Christ were baptized into his death? Therefore we are buried with him by baptism into death: that like as Christ was raised up from the dead by the glory of the Father, even so we also should walk in newness of life." Note, in the first place, that Paul declared that we are "baptized into Jesus Christ" and we are "baptized into his death." All right—"baptized into Christ." If you can't be saved out of Christ, you can't be saved without being baptized, for Paul said you are "baptized into Christ." Secondly, we are "baptized into his death." Can you be saved out of the death of Christ? If you can, you can be saved without reaching the blood, and you can be saved without baptism. But if you cannot be saved out of the death of Christ, you cannot be saved without baptism, because Paul said we are "baptized into his death."

He went on to say "that like as Christ was raised up from the dead, even so we also should walk in newness of life." Where does the new life begin? Paul says "we are raised in baptism"—"we are raised to walk in newness of life." Mr. Bogard says, "No, you have got to walk in the newness of life first. Or you have got to have that journey in progress first, and then you are baptized *because you are walking* in newness of life." But the apostle Paul said, "We are raised in baptism to walk in newness of life." "N-e-w-n-e-s-s"—newness of life. Back in the days when I went to school we would have spelled it "N-e-w-n-e double s," but they don't double those letters any more these days. It is "N-e-w-n-e-s-s." And so "in the newness of life." And that walk in newness of life comes after baptism—"buried with him—raised to walk in newness of life." Thus we find all of these statements clearly show that men are not saved before they are baptized in this age. I don't care how Abraham was saved—Isaac or Jacob or men of that time. Peter says "now"—in this age, in this time—"baptism saves us." And he doesn't say that "baptism alone saves us." We don't believe that baptism alone saves us. No, we don't believe it is any more important than some other conditions—we believe it is just as important as some of the others. And that all of them must be met. I see my time is just about gone. I haven't time for another argument.

Moderator Joe Blue says: "You have about forty seconds."

About forty seconds? I haven't time to introduce the next argument. So I want you to think about these things closely and see how Mr. Bogard deals with them and how he endeavors to set them aside. And I thank you very kindly.

Fourth Day

BOGARD'S FIFTH NEGATIVE

Gentlemen Moderators, Ladies and Gentlemen:

I am delighted to reply to my good friend, and if I ever had an easy job on earth, I have got it right now.

I am starting in at the beginning, being very deliberate about it, so all of you will get exactly what is said. My friend explained about Mr. Blue's woman that he refused to baptize. No matter whether she came up to him or not, Blue said, "Somebody else can baptize her as good as I can." And he had the right to refuse to baptize that woman or any other woman he wanted to. If he did not, then he violated the law in not baptizing her. Here is the point. I think Blue did right.

(Joe Blue speaks: "Thank you.")

Yes, sir. You do right when you refuse to baptize somebody that you think is a hypocrite. Therefore a Missionary Baptist Church does right when they vote not to have one baptized who is unworthy. That is the point. Rom. 14:1: Him that is weak in the faith, let the preacher take him in, or refuse to take him in? No, the whole church is to do it. That is the difference between the Baptists and my friend's people.

Coming now to the question I asked him, "Did you love God before you were baptized?" What did he say? Well, he said, "Did you love God before you asked the Lord to forgive your sins?" No, sir, I was a hater of God. Being an alien from God, I came and asked for reconciliation. Then being born again, I had the love of God shed abroad in my heart by the Holy Ghost, and having the love of God shed abroad in my heart by the Holy Ghost, then I was baptized. Did you have the love of God in your heart before you were baptized? Say "yes" or "no." You have only got just a short time now before you. If you say you did, no matter how that love got there, "He that loveth is born of God and knoweth God." If you say you did not, then you remained a hater of God until a man put you under the water, or till he pulled you out, and of course that *made* you love God.

My friend tried to get out of the force of my reply to

him on the kingdom coming with power. I made the statement—and everybody with any sense knows what it means—that there is a difference between coming into *existence* and coming into *power*. Now, the kingdom was already in existence, came into power—power of the baptism of the Holy Ghost, on the day of Pentecost. He said, "Where did it come from?" I have given you that about fifteen times already. Mark 13—Jesus when He left His house, and gave His servants authority and work to do, and commanded them to watch for ye know not when the Master of the house returns — there is the house. And it came over on Pentecost, on the day of Pentecost, sometime after that, to be endued with power from on high. What is the matter with the man? That is where it came from. The Lord left His church when He left the world and told it to tarry in Jerusalem till endued with power from on high. What did He leave? What did He promise to come back to? That is the thing that got the power on the day of Pentecost. It did not come into existence on the day of Pentecost.

Well, now, take it up just one thing at a time. About his "ruling elders": He asked what elders decided my coming to Damascus. You challenged the whole American Baptist Association, and I am here representing them, thank you, sir. And no matter who decided it, I am here, and I whipped the socks off you after I got here. (Laughter) There is quite a difference between that and having a bunch of elders to control the church.

Now, *he says they do not deny the work of the Holy Spirit before Pentecost.* When this goes into the book, I am determined, if not forbidden by somebody that has power over me, to underscore that—that *they do not deny the work of the Holy Spirit before Pentecost.* Then when we get up here and say that the Holy Spirit works upon a sinner, and he is saved by the work of the Holy Spirit bringing him to Christ, and all that, and that all took place before Pentecost, you agree to it. *You agree with us* on the question of the Spirit working before Pentecost. So the Holy Spirit did not begin His work of salvation on the day of Pentecost. Get that down, put it in your memory, in your tablet. Very well. Take it easy now.

We come to baptism. That is a new argument. I began to think he was not going to come to it. It would have been good for him if he had not. (Laughter) He quoted what Paul said in I Corinthians, that he baptized none of them. And that if so, then it might have been that somebody would be of Paul, somebody of Apollos, or somebody of Cephas. But Paul did say, "I have *begotten* you *through the gospel,* though I *baptized none of you.*" How did he beget them by the gospel without baptizing them, you being judge? All right, take it easy now.

He comes to his translations. Wonderful man to quote translations! All right. He did not find a single one of the translations that said "baptism is in order to obtain salvation." And if he had, he would have had a false translation, for that is not so.

He takes up the Bogard-McPherson Debate where I said the promise there was salvation. Sure, it was. The promise was "to you and your children, and to all that are afar off." Certainly, it was. But how did they obtain salvation? By baptism? I Pet. 3:21 says that we are saved by baptism just like Noah was saved by water. How was Noah saved by water? How was he saved by water? By staying out of it—*not by getting in it.* (Laughter) Noah was a saved man and a preacher of righteousness 120 years before the water came. And we are saved by baptism just the same way. How was Noah saved by water? It was a figurative expression—"the like figure whereunto even baptism doth also now save us." What did the figure prove? It proved that he was saved—did not save him. If Noah had gone into the ark, and the ark had been sealed, and stayed there the same length of time without any water to come, he would have been a laughing stock. But when the water came it did not save him, but it proved he was a saved man. So we are *first saved,* and *then prove it* by baptism.

Come to Gal. 3:27. "As many as have been baptized into Jesus Christ have put on Christ." Now, listen. You have got another speech, and please put this down: Does everybody who puts on Christ become a Christian by putting Him on? Come on. I will give you time to write it down. If so, there was not a saved one in the church at Rome. Read

Rom. 13:14, where Paul told them, "Put ye on the Lord Jesus Christ." Persons *already saved—already baptized.* So "putting on Christ" does not mean to become a Christian. What does it mean? It comes from the Greek word "enduo"—means to "imitate." "As many of you as have been baptized with reference to Jesus Christ have imitated Christ." That is all. That is all Paul told those who were already baptized, already in the church. "Put ye on the Lord Jesus"—*imitate* the Lord Jesus Christ. *Follow* Christ. Follow in His steps.

We come to Acts 2:38. "Repent, and be baptized every one of you in the name of Jesus Christ for the remission of sins." I was afraid my friend was not going to bring it in, but he did. About repentance being unto life, "repent"—but what does that do? It brings you to life. And you who have "repented and been brought to life be baptized for the remission of sins." What does the word "for" mean? Does it mean "in order to obtain?" All right, when a man goes to the penitentiary for stealing, he goes to the penitentiary in order that he may steal. A man is put in the electric chair for murder; he goes to the electric chair in order that he may murder. Isn't that rich? (Laughter) "Be baptized for the remission of sins" in the same sense you go to the electric chair for murder. Now, since repentance is "unto life," as my friend kindly read, having reached life, then we are baptized on account of that. I want to give you a rule. Now, we have two, three, four or a half dozen Greek scholars sitting around here. And I will give you a rule and dare you to contract it. Thayer, the greatest Greek lexicon on earth, says that the preposition 'e-i-s," sometimes called "ace"—sometimes called "ice," when it refers to *place* means *into,* like coming into a house, going into heaven, into hell, into a country, into water. But when it has reference to *relationship,* it means *"with reference to."* Now, does Acts 2:38, "be baptized for remission of sins"—that is the Greek word "e-i-s", "eis," translated "for"—does that mean change of place or a change of relation? If it means a change of relation, then it means "with reference to.' Now, let us read it that way. I have got the best Greek scholar in America lying right before me here to quote in a minute. Let us read it that way. *"Repent unto life, and having obtained life, be baptized with reference to the life, or the remission of sins you already obtained."* I want that to go down good and plenty in the book.

The greatest Greek scholar who has lived during the last 100 years, *Dr. A. T. Robertson,* who wrote the great grammar, Greek grammar, what does he say about it? Here is exactly what he says in his book on "Epochs in the Life of Peter," page 137. He says: *"Acts 2:38. It means repent and be baptized upon the basis of the remission of your sins."* Now, you cannot laugh that scholar out. Every college in the world that uses Greek uses that grammar. And there it is. "Repent to life, and upon that basis, be baptized," because you have obtained life, already obtained it, are already saved, have already obtained forgiveness of sins.

Now, coming to Mark 16:16, "He that believeth and is baptized shall be saved." That amuses me. Take that out of the Bible and they are stranded. But what does it really mean? "He that believeth on the Son hath everlasting life." Who said that? John the Baptist. What did Jesus say in John 5:24? "He that heareth my words, and believeth on him that sent me, hath everlasting life." I could quote a dozen passages of Scripture that say when you believe you have everlasting life. Very well, then. If you cannot be saved without baptism, you get yourself in a dilemma. "He that believeth on the Son of God hath everlasting life." You cannot go to hell, but you have not been baptized—*cannot go to heaven.* And here is a believer who has everlasting life—*cannot go to hell,* because he believes. He cannot go to heaven, because he has not been baptized. What is the poor fellow going to do? Sit down on a stump half way between heaven and hell? (Laughter) What is he going to do?

Now, the truth about it is that "he that believeth and is baptized shall be saved" is like this: Get on the train and be seated and go to Little Rock. Getting on the train is necessary to go—or some other conveyance; being seated is a matter of convenience. In other words, it just means that *men and women who have believed and been baptized are certain of eternal glory,* a thing you do not believe—and you would not get up here and say so. *You do not believe that passage.* He that believeth and is baptized will *certainly* be saved. You say, "He *may* be saved *if* he does not fall from grace." But believers who have been baptized are perfectly safe and will be carried home to heaven. You deny it.

But is the baptism necessary to the salvation? If so, you flatly contradict the passages that say you get salvation at the point of faith. "He that heareth my words, and believeth on him that sent me, hath everlasting life, and shall not come into condemnation, but is passed from death unto life." He is already saved, then baptized in order to manifest it, in order to prove it. As Peter said, like it was in the case of Noah, the water came a long time after he had been saved. He was God's man, a saved man, and the water proved it. I was baptized for identically the same reason that Jesus Christ was baptized. Christ was already the Son of God. Being baptized did not make Him the Son of God, did not cause Him to be the Son of God. But John said, "I came baptizing that he might be made manifest as the Son of God." So I was *already* a child of God by faith and was baptized in order to be made *manifest* as a child of God. That harmonizes the Scripture. If you are going to make Mark 16:16 contradict all these other passages, you would just as well throw all the other passages in the junk heap. But you have got to harmonize Mark 16:16 with the others or you will have the Scripture contradicting itself.

Then come to Romans 6, "As many as have been baptized into Jesus Christ have been baptized into his death." What is the rule? Thayer says that "when it has reference to place it means into," like coming into a house, into a town, into heaven, into hell, into the water, into anything with reference to a place. But if it has reference to relationship it means "with reference to." So "as many of you as have been baptized with reference to Jesus Christ have been baptized with reference to his death." Why am I baptized? Now, stop and think a minute. Why, baptism is just a picture of the burial and resurrection of Jesus Christ. "Therefore we are buried with him by baptism into death, that like as Christ was raised up from the dead by the glory of the Father, even so we also should walk in newness of life."

Certainly, it is a *picture of the burial and resurrection of Jesus Christ.* And that is what Peter said. "The like figure whereunto even baptism doth also now save us." What is our baptism? It has reference to the death, burial and resurrection of Jesus Christ. How are we saved? Read 1 Corinthians 15, the first five verses. This says we are *saved by the gospel.* What is the gospel? The death, burial and resurrection of Jesus Christ. What is baptism? A picture of the death, burial and resurrection of Jesus Christ. And so we are baptized with reference to the death of Christ, and that is all it means. "As many as have been baptized with reference to Jesus Christ have been baptized with reference to his death." What does baptism refer to? To the death, burial and resurrection of the Lord Jesus Christ. It does not say you obtain salvation by it.

Now, having noticed that, I come to something else, and if I have failed to notice anything my friend said along that line, if he will call my attention to it in his next speech, I will take it up in my next speech.

Now, I come to something that I want my friend to take particular pains to answer if he can. My friend and his people deny the right of sinners to pray, and if they do pray, it will not do them any good. And they prove it, they think, by the language of the man who was born blind, who said, "We know that God heareth not sinners." All right, now let us look at that. There was Cornelius and his household in the tenth chapter of Acts. Here came the word to Cornelius: "Thy prayers and thine alms have come up as a memorial before God." *God heard Cornelius pray before he was baptized.* Now, take any position you please. God either heard Cornelius pray before he was saved, before he was baptized, or else he did not—one of the two. If he heard him pray before he was baptized, then you have got, according to your doctrine, an unsaved man praying. But you say, "No, God will not hear an unsaved man pray." Then Cornelius was saved before he was baptized. Take either horn of that dilemma you please. *Either God heard a sinner pray, or else Cornelius was a saved man when he prayed.* Take any position you please—one or the other; you cannot hold to both. If he were saved before he was baptized, that knocks you in the head. If the Lord heard him pray before he was baptized, that knocks you in the head, any way you want to turn.

Then take the ninth chapter of the Acts of the Apostles where Saul of Tarsus was praying. And the Spirit said to the preacher, "Go up there and see him, for behold he prayeth." And when Ananias came and saw him, he said, "Brother Saul, I have been sent to you that you might obtain your eyesight (blinded from the bright light that had shined), and *receive the Holy Spirit.*" Who can receive the Holy Spirit? John 14:17—"*Him the world cannot receive.*" Then when it says, "Arise and be baptized and wash away thy sins," what does it mean? Literal? If so, then here is a man qualified to receive the Holy Spirit and yet in his sins. If figurative—that is exactly the thing I am telling you about, first saved, then in a figure wash away his sins—do you mean to tell me that the water literally washes away sins? If so, then it is like sins are on the outside of the body and are to be washed off like dirt. That is absurd. What does it do? It figuratively washes away sins. That is precisely what I was talking about. "The blood of Christ cleanseth us from all sins." Then comes the water—*a figure of what has been done.* "The like figure whereunto even baptism doth also now save us (not the putting away of the filth of the flesh, but the answer of a good conscience toward God)."

Now, having noticed what my friend has said, I will come with one that I want you to wrestle with. *According to your doctrine, the church on the day of Pentecost was not a true church of the Lord Jesus Christ.* Why? Because you say the church should bear the name or else it is not a true church. They were not even called Christians for *twelve years after* that. Acts 11:26 says, "They were called Christians *first* at Antioch." There you have got a church—you say it was established on the day of Pentecost—and it is not called Christian. I dare you to say it was called Christian. If you say it was called Christian, the book will flatly contradict you. They were "first called Christians at Antioch" twelve years after that. So, according to your theory, you have knocked out the church on the day of Pentecost. That is what you harp on.

We have made some wonderful progress in this debate. The record will show we have whipped them clear off of the name. I come back again and say, "Give me the chapter and verse where it says the Lord's people, the family of God, was called 'The Church of Christ'." It is not in the Bible. Then I challenge you again to show where any local congregation in the New Testament was called "The Church of Jesus Christ." It is not there. I went to every one of the local congregations—the church at Thessalonica, the seven churches of Asia, the churches of Galatia, and the Churches of the Gentiles, mentioned in Rom. 16:4. Not a one is said to be "The Church of Jesus Christ." And they have been harping on the name—the name—the name—the name. I have driven them away from it. There is *no such an expression in the Bible* as "The Church of Christ." And there is no such a thing as "The Church of Christ" locally. If so, name the verse and the passage of Scripture.

We have made splendid progress up to date when my friend has wrestled with these arguments, not just wisecracks. The first day my friend spent his time on wisecracks. He had the folks laughing. The laugh is on the other side of the mouth now. (Laughter) When we come to the plain arguments from God's book the laugh's on the other side of the mouth now.

Salvation is "by grace through faith, and that not of yourselves; it is the gift of God, lest any man should boast." If salvation comes by the hands of a preacher, then it is not as this passage suggests. Now, my friend makes a statement that I was about to forget. I am trying to collect my mind on that point. He said, "Salvation comes by baptism. Of course, we acknowledge *we put the man into Christ by baptism.*" But he says, "You do the same thing, because a man cannot be a member of the bride of Christ unless he has been baptized. And you say the church is the bride." That is true. That is all true. But being in the bride does not exclude all others. There are plenty of Christian people outside of the bride of Christ. And in the last chapter of the book of Revelation, seventeenth verse, "The Spirit and the bride say,

Come. And let him that heareth say, Come." There are others who are not a part of the bride of Christ. And our putting into the bride of Christ, or their getting into the church, *does not have anything to do with their salvation,* for they are already saved. And being saved, they are baptized into the church, and that puts them into the bride of Christ. Stay out and you will be one of the guests at the wedding at the great day in the nineteenth chapter of the book of Revelation, one of the guests at the wedding. So that is not a parallel case at all. *Salvation comes by grace through faith; becoming a member of the bride of Christ is like becoming a member of the church of the Lord Jesus Christ.* And that is all there is to it. My friend is so confused that he does not know the difference between being a member of the bride of Christ and being saved.

There are thousands of people who are not in the bride of Christ that are saved. All babies that are saved are not in the bride of Christ for they are not in the church. All the righteous clear on back to Adam are saved but not in the bride of Christ. To be in the bride of Christ is a *special honor* given to those who come into the church of the Lord Jesus Christ. What *an honor to be married to Christ!* And come back to reign on the earth with the Lord Jesus Christ —He as king, and the church as queen! This is a great honor to the saved, *but you do not become saved by becoming a member of the bride of Christ.* That is sufficient on that.

And everything is perfectly clear, and why continue the argument? We will hear what my friend has to say. And then I will make my final speech, go home, rest, and come back and wind up the debate tonight. Thank you.

Fourth Day

PORTER'S SIXTH AFFIRMATIVE

Gentlemen Moderators, Respected Opponent, Ladies and Gentlemen:

My opponent was talking here at the close of his speech about somebody being confused. If I ever saw a man so confused he could hardly ramble, I saw him then. As far as his whipping all the socks off me after he got here, I have not only taken his theological socks off but all the rest of his clothes too. (Laughter)

Now, back to the beginning of the speech which my opponent has just made. He told you what an easy job he had before him this afternoon, and I am certain of the fact if he hadn't told you about it, you would have never discovered it. It's a little bit like the picture of the cat he would draw on the board—it looks so unlike a cat he would have to say, "This is a cat." In order for you to know that he has such an easy job, he has to get up and tell you about it, because otherwise you would never discover it. I am willing to let you decide whether the road is easy for him or not.

He says that brother Blue had a perfect right to refuse to baptize that woman. All right, then, the course we follow is *perfectly right,* Mr. Bogard, without consulting the church, because you said he had a perfect right to do it. Even if he did it as you said he did it, why, you still say he had a perfect right to do it. Joe Blue had a perfect right to do that. And that being so, then we can proceed without taking the vote of the church to see about the matter, according to Mr. Bogard himself.

He finally came back to the matter of loving God before baptism. All the arguments he makes upon that passage—1 John 4:7—is a misapplication of the passage. John declared that whosoever "loveth is born of God and knoweth God." And Mr. Bogard takes that as an indication that the very instant a man has any love for God that proves he is already saved. Well, there are three passages along that line. 1 John 5:1 says, "Whosoever believeth that Jesus is the Christ is born of God." 1 John 4:7 says, "Every one that loveth is born of God." And 1 John 2:29 says, "Every one that doeth righteousness is born of him." Now, I wonder if the man is born of God three times—once when he has faith, once when he loves, and once when he does righteousness. Or does it take all three of these to bring him to the one birth?

Does a man love God before he believes, Mr. Bogard? If he does, then he is saved before he believes, because he is born of God when he loves God. Or does he believe God before he loves God? If so, he is saved, because as soon as he believes he is saved. So that gets you going and coming. Your application of it is entirely wrong.

But Mr. Bogard did say this, "Yes, when I prayed, and when the sinner prays, to God, he is hating God while he prays." Now, you imagine that. A man realizing the condemnation of his sins, coming to God to pray, bowing before the Most High in prayer in a penitent state, wanting to be saved, and while actually engaged in that prayer in the penitence of his soul, the man is still actually hating God. He says, "Lord, have mercy upon me; I have sinned against you; Lord save me," and all the time a *hater of God.* Mr. Bogard said so. Can you imagine a man's coming to God and praying to God to save him while he is hating God from the very depths of his heart? Is that silly or is that brilliant?

I was amused when he came back to the matter of the kingdom "coming with power." He said, "Yes, the kingdom didn't come into existence—it was the coming into power." Mr. Bogard, that isn't what the passage says. You are changing it entirely—you are perverting the word of God. Jesus did not say, "There be some of them that stand here which shall not taste of death until they have seen the kingdom of God coming *into power.*" He didn't say it. That isn't the passage. You have misinterpreted it—you have perverted it—you have made it say what it doesn't say. Jesus said, "There be some of them that stand here, which shall not taste of death, till they have seen the kingdom of God *come with power.*" Mark 9:1. He didn't say "coming *into* power."

"But Porter wanted to know where it came from." Oh, he said, "That's easy. Over here in Mark 13 Jesus 'left his house.' That was the kingdom, and that moved over to Jerusalem on the day of Pentecost and came into power." When did it move to Jerusalem, Mr. Bogard? When did they move over to Jerusalem? Huh? Why, in the 24th chapter of Luke we are told about the matter. The Lord said to them, "You tarry in the city of Jerusalem until you are endued with power from on high," and they went back to Jerusalem and waited about ten days before Pentecost. They got to Jerusalem, then, ten days before the power came. I want to know how they "came with power" when they beat the power there by ten days. Mr. Bogard, I'm ashamed of you, and I think your brethren are too.

"Coming *into* power." Why, he said that church over there that was with the Lord simply moved over to Jerusalem, and that's the coming with power. Why, the power didn't come for several days after they arrived at Jerusalem, Mr. Bogard. How, then, did they *come with power?* If somebody came here *with* Mr. Bogard, would you understand that Mr. Bogard got here ten days before he did? Or that the other fellow got here ten days before Mr. Bogard did? Or would you understand that they came together—at the same time? So "coming with power" doesn't mean that a part of it came ten days before Pentecost and the other came on Pentecost, or whatever number of days you want to count it—I don't care. If one came at one time and the other came at another time, one did not come *with* the other. Jesus said the kingdom would "come with power." What quibbles a man will make to try to sustain a false theory!

Well, who ruled for him in this debate? He said, "The Baptist Association sent me over here." I thought the Baptists were democratic bodies and every body decided for itself. He told us that in the first day of this debate—that the Baptists are democratic bodies, and every one of them made its own decision. They officiate as democratic bodies. But now Mr. Bogard tells us that that is not true in this case. The democratic body in Damascus did not make the decision—the Association sent him here over the protest of the Baptist Church in Damascus. They were not allowed to exercise their democratic rights in Damascus. The Association sent Mr. Bogard over here, regardless of what the democratic Baptist body in Damascus thought about it. Is that what you call "Scriptural in government"?

He did with 1 Cor. 1:12,13 as all others have done—he just shied away from it as far as he could. He said just as little about it as he possibly could say. He has not touched it, and he cannot touch it. And you know that he cannot touch it, and he knows that he can't. And I know that he knows that he can't. (Laughter) And if I wanted to take it a little further like he did, I know that he knows that I know that he knows that he can't touch it. (Laughter)

1 Cor. 1:12,13. Paul said they were saying, "I am of Paul; I of Apollos; I of Cephas; and I of Christ." "Was Paul crucified for you? Or were you baptized in the name of Paul?" Thus Paul showed that in order for them to belong to him, he must, in the first place, be crucified for them, and in the second place, they must be baptized in his name. And since *that had not* occurred, *they did not belong to Paul.* Just so with Apollos and with Cephas. For men to belong to Apollos, Apollos must be crucified for them, and they must be baptized in his name; for them to belong to Cephas, Cephas must be crucified for them, and they must be baptized in his name. And so to "belong to Christ" —to be "of Christ"—Christ must be crucified for them, and they must be baptized in his name. They do not belong to Christ, then, until both of those things have occurred. And Mr. Bogard hasn't touched it, and he's not going to. *He'll not.* Don't you worry. He talks about these things becoming clearer. You see how they are getting. They may become clearer, but Mr. Bogard is becoming more confused all the time.

Yes, sir, you cannot be "of Christ" unless Christ has been crucified for you, and unless you have been baptized in the name of Christ. That's the argument of the apostle Paul. The only thing he said about it was that Paul said he had begotten them through the gospel, but he hadn't baptized but a few of them. Well, begotten is one thing—but that doesn't take in the whole proposition. Certainly, men are begotten through the gospel. When the gospel is preached to them, they are begotten through the gospel, and they are led by that to further obedience to the gospel.

And when that is completed, one of which is to be baptized in the name of Jesus Christ, then they become God's children. Then they are saved. Then they "belong to Christ." Then they are "of Christ."

Then to Acts 2:38. He said there wasn't one of those translations that said "in order to obtain." I read them to you awhile ago. Notice these:

Here is the translation by Charles Foster Kent, and he says, "That your sins may be forgiven." What's the difference between that and "in order to obtain"? "That your sins may be forgiven."

Goodspeed's translation, and incidentally Goodspeed is a Baptist, says, "In order to have your sins forgiven."

Charles B. William's translation, and he's a Baptist too, says, "That you may have your sins forgiven."

Bogard says there didn't any of them say that, and if they did, they were all wrong. Bogard knows more about it than the Greek scholars know.

In fact a number of those other translations say, "Unto the remission of sins." I'm asking my friend to produce the translation that translates Acts 2:38 "because of the remission of sins." Let him produce one—I want to see it.

Well, that promise in Acts 2:38, that he spoke of in the McPherson Debate, was the promise of salvation. He said, "Yes." And you said it meant that "they will obtain the remission of their sins." And the only thing that is said in Acts 2:38 is the expression, "for the remission of sins"; that is, the only thing about remission is the expression, "for the remission of sins," and you say it means that "they will obtain the remission of sins." So Bogard got back on the side of the truth—he had to when he met Aimee McPherson. So he had to get on the side of truth to do that.

1 Peter 3:21. "Noah was saved by water." But he said, "How was Noah saved by water?" Why, he said, "Noah was saved by water by staying out of the water." It is like the little boy's composition on pins. He said, "Pins have saved thousands of lives." The teacher said, "Why, Johnnie, how have pins saved thousands of lives?" He said, "Because they didn't swallow them." That's the way Noah was "saved by water"—by staying out of the water. Then Mr. Bogard,

why did you get into it? Noah never did get into the water. Why did you get into the water then, if Noah was saved by staying out of it?

He said it was only a figure, and that it didn't save him but simply proved his salvation. Well, let's revise the apostle Peter's statement then. Peter said, "The like figure whereunto even—" Well, getting back to the verses before, it speaks of the ark "wherein few, that is, eight souls were saved by staying out of the water." "The like figure whereunto even baptism doth also now prove that we are saved." Noah was "saved by water," Peter said; but Mr. Bogard said, "No, he wasn't saved by water—that simply proved his salvation." Therefore, the passage should read, "Wherein few, that is, eight souls were by water proved to be already saved." Is that what it says in your Book? You go home today and get your Bible and turn to 1 Peter 3:21 and see if Peter says that the water proved that Noah was already saved. "The like figure whereunto even baptism proves that we are already saved," said Peter. No, that's what Bogard says. Peter didn't say it. Peter said that Noah was "saved by water" and "the like figure whereunto baptism also now saves us." Bogard says it doesn't do it. Well, it's between him and Peter then. Peter said it does. Peter says "baptism saves us." Bogard says "it doesn't." "It doesn't save us—it just proves we are saved." Well, that's between you and Peter. I'm not concerned about that. I just believe that Peter told the truth about it, and if you want to fight it out with him, that is up to you. Bogard says it doesn't save us; Peter says it does. "Baptism doth also now s-a-v-e, save, u-s, us." That's what Peter said. But Bogard says it's not so. Bogard says, "Peter, you're wrong about it—it doesn't save us. You are mistaken about the whole thing. It just proves we are saved already." Too bad he wasn't there to correct Peter when he wrote that, isn't it? (Laughter) We would have had a different kind of Bible if Bogard could have had hold of it.

Oh, but he said, "Noah was God's man a long time before the ark was prepared." That's not the salvation he is talking about here, Mr. Bogard. He is talking about salvation from that destruction in the flood. He was not saved with the salvation spoken of here before the water came and before he got into the ark. In Heb. 11:7 Paul said, "By faith Noah prepared an ark to the saving of his house." And Peter, in 1 Peter 3:20, said that the eight souls were saved in the ark by water. Saved where? *In the ark.* Bogard says, "No, they were *saved before they got into the ark.*" Peter says they were *saved in the ark.* What salvation was he talking about? He was talking about salvation from that destruction that came upon the rest of the world by the flood. And their salvation from that destruction is a picture of our salvation, or a type of our salvation, by baptism. There is where the figure is. Some of the translations say, "After a true likeness baptism saves us." Or "in the antitype baptism saves us." Noah and his family were saved in the ark by water. They were borne from the old world to the new world, and thus saved by water. And in the same way, we are translated from a state of condemnation to a state of justification. And therefore baptism saves us like the water saved Noah. His was physical, material—ours is spiritual. But one is a true likeness of the other. That's where the figure is. He didn't say it is a figure of our salvation. That's what Baptist preachers say, but Peter wasn't a Baptist preacher, and *he didn't say it.*

Gal. 3:27 is next. Here Paul said, "As many of you as have been baptized into Christ have put on Christ." What did Mr. Bogard do about this little word "for" over here—the word that meant "to introduce the reason"? Paul said, "Ye are all the children of God by faith in Christ Jesus, *for* (the reason is) as many of you as have been baptized into Christ have put on Christ." Those, therefore, who had not been baptized into Christ had not become God's children by faith. Only those who had been baptized into Christ had become God's children by faith, said Paul. "For"—the reason is— that means the reason, Mr. Bogard. Why don't you grapple with it? You know what it is. There it is. You know it is the original word "gar," and you know that lexicon you introduced awhile ago says it means "to introduce a reason." All right, Paul says the reason you are God's children by faith in Christ is that you have been baptized into Christ. He can't touch it. He knows he can't.

But he wants to know if everybody who puts on Christ becomes baptized. Everybody who puts on Christ in the sense that this passage speaks of it—yes, sir. Because that is the very thing Paul is talking about. He went back to Rom. 13 where Paul told the Roman brethren to put on Christ. That had no reference to baptism, but this does, because Paul said so. And those Roman brethren had already been baptized, according to Rom. 6:3,4. They had already put on Christ in the sense mentioned here. And so Paul says you are "baptized into Christ" and you "put on Christ" and that's the reason you are God's children by faith.

But he says, "That means to imitate Christ." All right, we will just read it that way. That won't help you any. Let us read it that way. "Ye are all the children of God by faith in Christ Jesus, for as many of you as have been baptized to imitate Christ have imitated him." Does that help you any? That's still baptism, isn't it? And the little word "for" is still between them. Let it mean "to imitate Christ" if you want to, the little word "for" is still there. And then Paul would be saying, "You are God's children because you have been baptized to imitate Christ." Those who haven't been baptized to imitate Christ then are not God's children by faith. So that doesn' help you any. The word "baptism" is still there, and between it and the children of God the little word "for" is there, introducing the reason, just like it was before you tried to twist it around. "You are God's children by faith, for (the reason is) you have been baptized to imitate Christ." So if you haven't been baptized to imitate Christ, you don't have the reason, and therefore you are not God's children. Don't you see? That little twist doesn't help him any—just keeps him right in the same hole. Oh, what an easy job Mr. Bogard has! I would hate to have to hoe that row of stumps though.

Now back to Acts 2:38. He said, "I was afraid he wasn't going to bring up that repentance unto life—I was just afraid he wasn't going to mention it." Well, now you will wish I hadn't. "Repentance unto life." And he said the word "unto" means they were brought to life. Upon the basis of life already received then they are baptized because of it. Now notice that. Repentance ——— unto ——— life. (Porter writes on the board.) And baptism ——— unto ——— remission. (The blackboard appeared as follows):

Repentance *unto* life
Baptism *unto* remission

"Repentance unto life," and you reach the life after repentance; and then you are baptized "unto remission" because you have already reached remission. "Unto" here (pointing to first statement) looks forward—"unto" here (pointing to second statement) looks back, according to Bogard. It's the same word. Exactly the same word. If "repentance unto life" means you reach the life after you repent, then "baptism unto remission" means you reach the remission after you are baptized. Mr. Bogard says "baptism unto remission" means you reach the remission first, and then you are baptized because you have already reached it. Then "repentance unto life" means you reach the life first, and then you repent because you already have it. And so his argument saves men before repentance. The same thing is true about faith and many other things we might bring up along that line.

Then he said, "A man is put into the penitentiary *for* stealing, and he is hanged *for* murder. That doesn't mean he is put in the penitentiary in order to steal or that he is hanged in order to commit murder. But it means 'because of'." Certainly so, Mr. Bogard. But those are not parallel with Acts 2:38. The English word "for" sometimes means "because of" and sometimes it means "in order to." Here is one place (referring to Gal. 3:27) where even the Greek word meant "because of" but it is a different word. We have just one little word "for" for all these words in the Greek. And sometimes the English word "for" means "because of." Sometimes it means "in order to." So a man is "hanged for murder" or he is "put in the penitentiary for stealing." Certainly, the word "for" means "because of." But "the man works *for* his salary"—does that mean he has his salary already. The man worked *for* a salary—the man worked *for* money—does that mean he had the money before he worked? You see the English word "for" has two different meanings—sometimes it means one and sometimes it means the other. But now, Mr. Bogard, tell me where there is a Greek scholar on earth, if he were translating that statement you have given—"hanged for murder"—into the Greek, who would translate that little preposition into the same preposition that is translated "for" in Acts 2:38. Scholars don't do that. They know that it is an entirely different word—that you wouldn't translate that, if you were translating into Greek language, into the word that is found in Acs 2:38. So it is not a parallel case at all.

But Mr. Thayer said that this little word "eis" when it refers to relation means "with reference to" and when it refers to place it means "into." All right, let us get that now. "When it refers to relation it means with reference to." "Be baptized 'eis' the remission of sins," or "for the remission of sins." He says in this case remission of sins means relation, and so it means "be baptized with reference to remission" and that means you already have it. A while back I wrote Mr. Bogard "with reference to" this debate, but we hadn't had it yet. I wrote him with reference to this debate, but the debate hadn't occurred yet. All right, "Be baptized 'eis' remission" or "into remission" means with reference to remission which you have already. All right, take another passage. "Repentance 'eis' life." Is that relation or place, Mr. Bogard? You made the argument from Thayer that if it refers to relation it means "with reference to" and that means you have it already. All right, "repentance unto life"—"repentance 'eis' life." Is that place or relationship? If it's relationship, your argument says it means "with reference to"; and if it means "with reference to," you have it already. So you have life before you repent, according to Mr. Bogard's application of it. I agree with Thayer, but he didn't say "with reference to" means you have it already. That's Bogard's interpretation of it. It gets him into trouble.

Then he came to A. T. Robertson's foot note concerning this matter in which he said "on the basis of." But A. T. Robertson was a Baptist trying to prove his Baptist theology when he put that note in there. And therefore it isn't worth anything.

Now Mark 16:16. What does it mean? Yes, what does it mean? Why, he said, "Here is what it means. John 5:24 says that the believer has life." And he said, "You get on a train, and you're seated, and you go to Little Rock. The essential thing is to get on the train. You don't have to sit down. You can go to Little Rock whether you sit down or not." And so a man believes—"he that believeth and is baptized shall be saved." And there's the point. "He that believeth and is baptized shall be saved." All right, he makes this parallel. "Get on the train ____ and is seated ____ go to Little Rock." (Writes on the blackboard)

CHART NO. 9

Get on the train	—	**Be seated**	—	**Go to Little Rock**
Believe	—	**Be baptized**	—	**Shall be saved**

It is necessary to get on the train, he says, to go to Little Rock, but it is not necessary to be seated. And so it is necessary to believe in order to reach salvation, but it is not necessary to be baptized. He makes them parallel, you see. All right. Now, then, according to Mr. Bogard, "He that gets on the train is already in Little Rock before he has time to sit down." (Laughter) That's what he says about this (pointing to second sentence). "He that believeth is already saved before he has time to be baptized." So "he that gets on the train is already in Little Rock before he has time to sit down." Besides, Mr. Bogard, let us look at it from another angle. "Getting on the train," he says is essential because it is parallel to faith. "Sitting down" is not essential, and baptism being parallel to that, then baptism is not essential. So the essential this is here (pointing to first column), this is the non-essential (pointing to second column), and here is the destination (pointing to third column). All right. Since a man can get to Little Rock without sitting down, sitting down is not essential. And baptism, he says, is parallel with that. Then it is not essential to being saved. All right. Did you know, Mr. Bogard, that it is not necessary to get on a train to go to Little Rock? You're mistaken about that. There are a dozen ways I can go to Little Rock without getting on the train. So "getting on the train" is not essential to going to Little Rock. And you made that parallel with faith, and since I can go to Little Rock without getting on the train, then, according to your illustration, I can reach salvation without believing, for you made them parallel. That cuts out faith and baptism both.

He said he was baptized for the same reason that Jesus was baptized. Well, one reason that Jesus was baptized was to manifest him as the one who baptizes men with the Holy Ghost. Was that the reason you were baptized? Do you baptize men with the Holy Ghost?

Rom. 6—"with reference to" again. Rom. 6:3,4. "Baptized into Christ—baptized into his death." He says it means "with reference to." Well, let it mean that. It still says you walk the new life *after* you are baptized. So you are "baptized with reference to Christ," and then you are raised "to walk the new life." And so that still puts the new life after it. "With reference to" doesn't help you any.

But "it's a picture of the burial and resurrection of Christ." Yes, and when did Christ walk his new life—after his resurrection or before? If it's a picture of it, then we walk ours after we are raised and not before we are buried.

Then he came to "denying sinners the right to pray." "Cornelius," he says "was heard before he was baptized." Yes, and he was heard before he even believed in Jesus Christ, Mr. Bogard. If that proves he was saved, he was saved without belief, because he hadn't even heard the story of Jesus—it hadn't been preached to him. His prayer was heard before he was even told to send to Joppa and call for Peter—that he would come and tell him what he ought to do or words by which he would be saved.

Then he came to "Saul's praying." He said Saul was praying when Aananias came to him and said, "Brother Saul" so and so. Yes, and what else did he say? He came to him and he found him down praying. Acts 22:16. And what did he say? He said to him, "Just keep on praying. You're doing the right thing. You are on the right road. Just pray right on through to salvation. That's the thing to do." No, he didn't tell him that. He came to him and found him down praying, and he said, "And now why tarriest thou? Arise, and be baptized." Why do you stay down here? "Arise, and be baptized, and wash away thy sins, calling on the name of the Lord." So he didn't tell him *to keep on praying*—he told him *to quit praying*—to get up and be baptized and wash away his sins.

"Oh," but Mr. Bogard says, "does baptism literally wash away sins?" Well, sins are not *literal,* in the first place, if that is the way you are looking at it. They are not *material* things that can be washed away like dirt from your body. Certainly, baptism doesn't, and the blood of Jesus Christ doesn't wash them away that way either. Sins are not literal, material stuff like dirt is. It is a different proposition altogether. It simply means forgiveness—that's all. And that forgiveness which is accomplished by the blood of Jesus Christ is conditioned on baptism along with faith.

"According to Porter," he says, "the church at Pentecost wasn't a true church, because they didn't bear the name, and didn't even wear the name 'Christian' till twelve years later." Well, they *never did* wear the name "Baptist." Not throughout all the years of the New Testament age, from the day of Pentecost to the closing of it, did they ever wear the name "Baptist." He said, "We whipped them on the name." It looks like "we whipped them on the name."

CHART NO. 1-A

Church of Christ	**Baptist Church**
Churches of Christ	**Baptist Churches**
— Rom. 16:16	**— Religious Encyclopedia Page 796**

Right here Rom. 16:16 says, "The churches of Christ salute you." And the plural comprehends the singular. And over here (pointing to board) we have "Baptist Church" and "Baptist Churches" and the only place you found it was in Religious Encyclopedia, page 796. He never gave a Scripture reference, and yet he says, "We whipped them on the name." I would say "whipped them on the name"! You haven't touched the matter.

He talked about the "wise-cracks" and the laughing.

I wonder what that was last night about that "high water" and that other stuff that went with it that you could put in it if you wanted to. Was that a wise-crack?

"Salvation," he says, "is a gift. And if it is a gift, it can't depend on the preacher." Well, then , dispense with your preaching. What are you preaching for if people can be saved without it? Why are you preaching?

"Being in the bride," he says, "is not necessary to be saved." No, but you can't be in the bride without being baptized, and Mr. Bogard said, "The greatest honor that can come to a child of God is to be a part of the bride." And you can't become a part of the bride without being dipped in the water at the hands of Bogard or his brethren. Can't do it. They are always talking about being dipped—you've got to be dipped in the water, dipped in a mudhole and things of that kind, but it comes right back on him that you can't belong to Christ as a part of the bride—you can't be the bride of Christ—until you are dipped in a pond of water at the hands of a Baptist preacher.

Fourth Day

BOGARD'S SIXTH NEGATIVE

Gentlemen Moderators, Ladies, and Gentlemen:

We have learned that our friends believe that a preacher has the right to refuse to baptize a man, but a church does not have that right. That is rich! The point to bring up Mr. Blue's woman's baptism was, they tell us that we have no right for a church to decide whether a person is to be baptized or not. In rebuttal I say to you, as individual preachers decide who shall be baptized and who shall not be baptized, wherein is it right for one man to decide but a whole church cannot decide? So Romans 14:1 says, "Him that is weak in the faith receive ye." The *church* does the deciding as to who shall be baptized.

Then he comes and says, "In order to be in the bride of Christ someone has to baptize them." Certainly. That is a privilege that a child of God has, to become a part of the bride of Christ. All members of the family of God are not members of the bride of Christ, but it is the privilege of every one to be. But when you refuse to baptize some man, you refuse him salvation. When one comes and wants to be a member of the bride of Christ we will gladly take him in, and we decide to baptize him according to the Scriptures. "Him that is weak in the faith receive ye, but not to doubtful disputations."

Now my friend says, "Now Mr. Bogard found where the believer is born of God." Yes, certainly. "And he finds where one who loves is born of Gcd." Yes, sir. Is that two births? No, sir. Both are evidence of salvation, and a half dozen other things can be put in as evidence of salvation, but not in order to obtain salvation. You do not love God in order to get salvation. You love Him because you are saved. Then you love Him before you are baptized, therefore saved before you are baptized. "He that loveth is born of God and knoweth God, for God is love."

Now my friend speaks on the question of prayer. "Why," he said, "I do not dispute that the sinner can pray, but it will not do him any good. He has to get to the water first." Romans 10:13 says, "Whosoever shall call upon the name of the Lord shall be saved." There is a man calling on God. The Greek word is "epikaleo," and according to Thayer means "whoever invokes the name of God in prayer" shall be saved.

Now, my friend quibbles around—it is nothing but quibbling—on the question of the kingdom coming with power. He said the kingdom came with the power. Where was the power? Over on the right hand or left side of the kingdom? They came together—side by side—according to your doctrine. Get the point. "The kingdom came with power." That means the power is over here and the kingdom is over here, and the two come walking up together, and that is absurd. The kingdom came into *existence* during the personal ministry of Christ, and I have proved it to you by the fact that the Lord had His church, had His house. He left His house and told the servants to watch for He was coming back to His house again. That same house got the commission to "go teach all nations, baptizing them." And that same house was endued with power from on high for they were told to tarry at Jerusalem "until ye be endued with power." Who did the tarrying? The church. Nothing there, no church there, and yet the Lord told something to tarry till they be endued with power. He asked, "When did they move into Jerusalem?" They did not have to move in there. They just stayed there till the power came. They were already there. Right there in Jerusalem the Lord gave the great commission, "Ge ye therefore and teach all nations, baptizing them." "You stay here now till the power comes upon you." What power? The baptism of the Holy Ghost. They were already in existence and were waiting there for ten days for that special enduement of power. Yet my friend says the church did not come into existence until the day of Pentecost. It seems to me that anybody can see that. No use to stand here and waste time on a thing that is that simple and easy. If I were to tell my friend to tarry here till supper time, there would not be any Porter to stay till supper time. He would come into existence at supper time. Mr. Porter, stay right here till supper is brought to you. Why, he is not in existence till the supper comes. How ridiculous!

Now, I want to call attention to a thing that I have asked him again and again. What good will it do you and your people if you prove that the church began on the day of Pentecost when you cannot back up to Pentecost and reach it by 1800 years? If you prove the church began on the day of Pentecost, it would not prove that the one you are in began on that day. I can find Baptists who foolishly believe that the church began on the day of Pentecost. Does that prove that the Baptists are right when the Baptists believe that? Suppose you convince me, Mr. Porter, that the church began on the day of Pentecost. I get up here and say, "I now stand convinced that the church began on the day of Pentecost." Presto—change! Bogard will be in the church that started on Pentecost because I believe it. Is not that absurd? Convince a Mexican that the United States Government began on the fourth day of July, 1776, and that makes that Mexican a citizen of the United States. And to convince one of us Americans that the United States Government did not begin at that time would knock us out of citizenship. Why, it does not take a scholar to see that. The idea! What good would it do you when your church began with Alexander Campbell in 1827? What good would it do you? You can stand here and argue and argue and argue till your face gets red. I do not mean any reflections. You cannot help that physical defect. But if you get red and excited over the church beginning on the day of Pentecost, what *good* will it do you if you prove it? Your church does not reach Pentecost by 1800 years.

Now my friend made a statement that has nothing in the world to do with the merits of this debate. It was purely a personal thrust, unworthy of you. He said I came here under the protest of this church, it protested against my coming. That is not true. Whoever told you that told an absolute falsehood. This church is paying my expenses here and paying me mighty well to lick you. I have the money in my pocket right now, and the church protesting against my coming here to meet you in debate! What did you say that for? Purely a personal thrust. I am welcomed into Damascus, being nicely entertained, being well paid for my service, and no protest about it. He said, "Well, the association."

The association did not send me here at all. I came because I wanted to, and I will go anywhere in the world to get to whip one of you Campbellites any time I get a chance. (Laughter) What in the world is there in that on the merits of the debate? What has that got to do with the subject under discussion? Suppose I did come here under the protest of the church. I have licked you just the same.

Now, on Acts 2:38, my friend dies hard on it, but die he must. He ridiculed—well, he hardly ridiculed, he was ashamed to do that—the greatest Greek scholar that has lived in the last hundred years, Dr. A. T. Robertson, who wrote the greatest Greek grammar that has ever been published. He is recognized by scholars all over the world, and his grammar is used in the theological seminaries, colleges, and everywhere where they teach Greek. He said, "Well, he was a Baptist." What has that got to do with it? Well, all of your schools, your theological schools, your colleges, use that grammar because he was a scholar. What did Mr. Robertson say? He said, "Be baptized 'eis' the remission of sins means be baptized *upon the basis* of the remission of your sins." Why? Because he read in the eleventh chapter of Acts where it says we "repented unto life." *You reach life by repentance.* You must not make Scripture contradict Scripture.

Now let me call your attention to another thing right here. The very same preacher who said "repent and baptized for the remission of sins" is the one who is preaching in the tenth chapter of Acts where Cornelius and his household were saved. And there he said, "Can any man forbid water, that these should not be baptized, which have received the Holy Ghost as well as we?" Who can receive the Holy Ghost? Jesus said, "Him the world cannot receive." But Peter in Acts the tenth chapter said these folks should be baptized because they had received the Holy Ghost. Are you going to make Peter contradict Peter? Will you make Peter say in Acts 2:38 you have got to be baptized in order to be saved, then right over just eight chapters further on in the same book make him say you are baptized because you have been saved? You are making Peter contradict himself, Scripture contradicting Scripture. You cannot establish your position except by making one passage contradict the other passage.

Now, let me give you another one—about that "baptized 'eis' remission of sins," "baptized 'eis' repentance," and all of that. Go to Matthew 3:11 where they had "baptism 'eis' repentance." "E-i-s, eis, repentance." There is the very same word "eis" you have in Acts 2:38. *Were they baptized in order to repent?* Mark you, John "baptized with the baptism 'eis' repentance." Were they baptized in order to repent? Now, everybody knows better than that. And so since they were "baptized 'eis' repentance" the word is bound to mean "because of repentance," or "*with reference to repentance*." I just want to get the matter before you so you can see.

Here is the question of Noah being saved by water. Now, we are saved by baptism exactly like Noah was saved by water. Everybody knows that Noah was a preacher of righteousness one hundred and twenty years before the water came. What did the water come for? To convince the world, to convince those who saw, that he was a child of God—a proof of it. A like figure—l-i-k-e, like. Now a thing cannot be like something else unless that something else is like it. "A like figure." Then Noah's being saved was a figure, and in the like figure we are saved by baptism. Just like he was saved by water, in the very same way we are saved by baptism. He was a child of God first, and the water came and proved the fact that he was a child of God. I made the statement a while ago, and I think you will remember it, Noah was a child of God already. And he would have been a child of God if the water had never come. What did the water do? The water *demonstrated*—the water *proved*—his salvation. I am a child of God already. What did the water do when the water of baptism came? It proved or demonstrated that I was a child of God.

What did he say in reply about Jesus being baptized? Why was He baptized? Jesus was baptized because He was already the Son of God. And John said he baptized Him that he might make Him manifest to Israel as the Son of God. I am a child of God—baptized just like Jesus was, and therefore designated in Galatians 3:26-27. "As many as have been baptized into Christ have put on Christ," imitated Christ. The Greek word is "enduo," and the exact form of the word in that place is "enedusasthe," meaning to *imitate* Christ. What did Christ do? He was baptized, not to make Him the Son of God, but because He was the Son of God. And I could not imitate Christ by being baptized in order to become the son of God. There is no imitation of Christ about it. That word "enduo" there undoubtedly means to imitate.

Now he says, "The Bible says the water did save Noah. Bogard says it did not." I never said it awake or asleep, drunk or sober. *It did save him in a figure,* like the Bible says, but not in reality. That is what I said. Well, "Bogard says that baptism does not save us, but the Bible says it does." Bogard never said anything of the kind. Bogard does say baptism saves. How? In a figure. "The like figure whereunto even baptism saves," just like the water saved Noah. That is what I said. Now, my friend said that expression "the like figure" means "a true likeness." All right then. It is a true likeness. We know that Noah was saved before the water came. In a true likeness we are saved before the water comes. In both cases it demonstrates the fact that we have been saved.

Coming now to Mr. Thayer again, he cannot get up and say Thayer was a Baptist. He was a Lutheran. Thayer said with reference to, or when the 'eis' respects place or position it means into. You can remember that. So when we go into a house, that is a place. Into the water, that is a place. Into heaven, that is a place. Into hell, that is a place. But he said when it means relationship it means *"with reference to."* Do you change places, locations, when you are saved? Or do you change your relationship to God? Why anybody knows you do not move from one place to another in order to be saved, but you merely change your relationship to God. Then that being true, "repent and be baptized every one of you in the name of Jesus Christ with reference to the remission of your sins." You have not changed places. If it was "into" that would mean you would have to go to another place, go into another position. You merely change your relationship and remain right exactly where you are. So Robertson was right. Not that I could pronounce Robertson right, for he could have taught me Greek for fifty years. I could sit under him all the time. But his book says that after you have gotten the life by repentance unto life, then you are baptized upon that basis—"upon the basis of the remission of your sins."

I come to Cornelius. Listen. Cornelius prayed. God heard him. My friend says according to that he prayed before he even heard the word. I'll declare! In that very same chapter Peter said, "That word ye know that was preached throughout all Galilee, beginning with Christ's ministry." Sit right here and read it. Heard—prayed—before he even heard the word. Well, well, well! Look up right here and see. He had not even heard the word, had not heard of Christ, had not heard anything about it. We will just see now. I have my Bible open before me. Do you have one please? Read it. "Then Peter opened his mouth, and said, of a truth I perceive that God is no respecter of persons: but in every nation he that feareth him, and worketh righteousness, is accepted with him. The word which God sent unto the children of Israel, preaching peace by Jesus Christ: (he is Lord of all:) that word, I say, ye know, which was published throughout all Judea, and began from Galilee, after the baptism which John preached." My friend said he prayed before he even heard the word. Peter said he knew the word, and that it was the word that had been preached after the baptism which John preached. "How God anointed Jesus of Nazareth with the Holy Ghost and with power: who went about doing good, and healing all that were oppressed of the devil; for God was with him. And we are witnesses of all things which he did both in the land of the Jews and in Jerusalem; whom they slew and hanged on a tree. Him God raised up the third day, and shewed him openly; not to all the people . . .", and so on. "That word ye know." My friend got up here and said a while ago that he prayed even before he heard the word. It does not matter when he heard it—*he heard it before he was baptized.* That is the point. Can that go through your thick skull? (Laughter) The Lord heard a man pray *before* he was baptized. And if God will not hear anybody but a child of God pray, Cornelius was a child of God, you being judge, before he was baptized, and if he was not a child of God, then you are wrong on sinners praying.

Now coming to the Pentecost church, that church, even if it was established on the day of Pentecost, will not do you any good, for you cannot back up and hitch on to Pentecost. But *that church did not wear the name "Christian."* Let that go in. For the name "Christian" was never heard of till *twelve years afterwards.* Acts 11:26 says, "The disciples were called Christians first at Antioch." Very well. Then there is a scriptural church, God's church. You and I both agree that it was God's church. Both agree that it was a church established to the honor and glory of God. And it did not wear the name "Christian" for "the disciples were called Christians first at Antioch."

Now, what was his answer to that? They were not called "Baptists" either. Why of course they were not called "Baptists." I have told you about twenty-five times in this debate, and the record will show it, that *the Lord never named His church.* The Lord left it with a description so anybody who could read the description in the Bible could tell what the church was by the description. And I even gave you the reason why the Lord did that. If he had named it "Missionary Baptist," all imposters, like you fellows, would come along and claim the name and try to get by on the name. But when God put the description of the church in the Bible, put the doctrine and practices of the church in the Bible, then you cannot have your name and get by with it. You have to have the right description or you must come down as hard as you Campbellites are coming down in this debate. (Laughter)

Now it is established beyond question that a church can be a church of the Lord Jesus Christ *without wearing the name of Christ,* the thing you have been harping on all these years. And he necessarily goes down in confusion now.

What good would it do you if you proved the church began on Pentecost? You cannot back up and hitch on it by any sort of means. I will come right back and refresh this in the minds of the people here, and some have not been here before. Ziegler, in History of Religious Denominations, page twenty-five, said, "The Christian or Campbellite Church was *founded by Alexander Campbell* in Virginia in 1827."

Charles V. Seeger, in Life of Campbell, page twenty-five, said, "Alexander Campbell soon became chiefly and prominently known as the *recognized head of a new religious movement,* the purpose of which was to restore primitive Christianity in all of its simplicity and beauty. Out of this movement has grown a people who choose to call themselves Christians or Disciples, now numbering about five hundred thousand in the United States."

Richardson's Memoirs of Alexander Campbell, and Richardson was the son-in-law of Alexander Campbell, in the very family, in Volume II, page 548, quotes a letter from Henry Clay that was given to Campbell to travel on in Europe, and here is what is said of Campbell: "Dr. Campbell is among the most eminent citizens of the United States, distinguished for his great learning and ability, for his successful devotion to the education of youth, for his piety, and as the *head and founder* of one of the most important and respectable religious communities in the United States."

There is where you started—1800 years after Pentecost. Now, you started with a bunch of excluded Baptists 1800 years after Pentecost. What good would it do you to prove the church started on Pentecost when you cannot back up to Pentecost? Let me prove by Campbell himself on page 465 of Religious Encyclopedia: "After the Baptists had in the 1827 declared non-fellowship with the brethren of the reformation, thus by constraint, and not by choice, they were obliged to form societies of their own."

What did Campbell say? After the Baptists turned them out, a bunch of excluded Baptists got together 1800 years after Christ and then claim to go back to Pentecost! What good would it do you if you proved the Pentecost theory? Suppose the church did start on Pentecost, *it will not do you any good.* The only people in the world who can back up to Pentecost are the Missionary Baptists, and I gave you the history that proved it, a line of Baptist Churches, a succession, I ran back twice during this debate. It is on the record to go down in the book. He made no reply to it except to get up here and say, "Well, it did not mean what the historians said it meant; it did not mean what Bogard said." Well, bless your soul, I read the passages from history, gave you the chapter and page and verse in the history, and showed you they had men of our sort, churches of our sort, running all the way back to Jesus Christ. You cannot go one church beyond Alexander Campbell. I challenged him in the early part of this debate to show just one congregation on earth anywhere like the one that meets within the walls of this building, just one that taught and practiced the doctrines you teach, back of the time of Alexander Campbell. You cannot find it. And you cannot find it anywhere in history, for it did not exist back there. If it did not exist back there, how in the name of heaven did it go back to Pentecost? What good would it do you to prove Pentecost when *you cannot reach Pentecost by 1800 years?*

Now I showed from the International Centennial Celebration of the Disciples of Christ, page forty-seven, where it says they began the Restoration in the Pittsburg district in a log cabin and wrote up a charter that was the basis of their movement. Then coming on over I showed that this movement beginning back a little over a hundred years ago, is what is now called the Disciples or Church of Christ, Christian Church, and all that. What did he say in reply? He said that was just the Christian Church folks who got that up. Are they a bunch of liars? They started the same time you did. You just split off from them. You split over the organ question. They all used instruments of music back there until you fellows were kicked out. And so it started back there with this movement a little over a hundred years ago, 1800 years after Pentecost. And you are still of a *later date than that.* Why, I can go right down here to Texas and show you where the split first took place. You folks walked out and left the Christian Church. That is a fact too. Now, what good would it do you to prove the church began on the day of Pentecost when you cannot back up to Pentecost at all? You cannot get anyway near Pentecost, not within 1800 years of Pentecost. So instead of you being called the Church of Christ, you ought to be called Campbellites. If you started with Christ—you could not even find the name "The Church of Christ" there, but suppose you could—you ought to be called what you are. You started with Alexander Campbell, and you ought to be called for the fellow that started you. You ought not to be ashamed of your daddy. Therefore, we ought to dub you as Campbellites, the last one of you. You cannot get out of it. I have stamped that on you. There it is by the scriptures and by history.

Right now I have two or three minutes left. If you will write down on a piece of paper and hand it up to me, the chapter and verse where it says "The Church of Christ," I I will not come back tonight. I will give it up and walk off. Or if you will write down on a piece of paper the chapter and verse where any local congregation in the Bible was called "The Church of Christ," I will go out of this back door and never come back in here again, and leave it with you. It is not there. You cannot find it as a general name and you cannot find it as a local name for any church in the New Testament, not one. And yet they harp around here about being "The Church of Christ" and "The Churches of Christ" and all that. And yet after two days of diagramming on the board, trying to prove that the name was "The Church of Christ," I drove him yesterday, when he said, "I know it just means ownership. I said that all the time." You did not. You argued two days it meant the name.

And that telegram that came from Harding College knocked you cold, for it says *"Christ" there was genitive, singular, meaning possessive.* He owns something. What did Christ own? He owned churches. "The churches of Jesus Christ" means the churches owned by Jesus Christ and not the name at all. And in the same chapter, the fourth verse, it says "the churches of the Gentiles." Is that the name? And in Galatians 1:22 it says "the churches of Galilee, of Judea." Is that the name? No. It only denotes ownership, that is all. And my friend shelled down the corn last night and said, "I know it just means *ownership.*" He spent two days arguing for the name and gave it up as a bad job. And so the whole thing rests in my hands. And I thank you. Tonight I sure will ride you, and you do not forget it. (Laughter).

Fourth Day

PORTER'S SEVENTH AFFIRMATIVE

Gentlemen Moderators, Respected Opponent, Ladies and Gentlemen:

I wish to pay some attention to a few things said by my opponent in his closing speech this afternoon before going on with the affirmative arguments.

We discussed this afternoon, for the major part of the time, the subject of baptism—whether it's a condition of salvation to the sinner or whether he is saved before and without it. Some of the arguments which I introduced Mr. Bogard barely mentioned, and to most of them he paid but very little attention. He spent a great deal of his time otherwise. Well, he can just do as he pleases about that. He can come up and face the arguments and try to answer them —say something about them—or he can just spend his time otherwise as he sees fit. I intend to make the arguments. It's his duty in the negative to reply to those arguments instead of just rambling everywhere and ignoring them, but I leave that matter entirely with him. The record may not look so good—when it has gone to record.

One thing in particular my opponent said was: "The believer has everlasting life." He found some statements in which salvation is promised to the believer. But he said, "According to Porter, the man cannot go to heaven because he hasn't been baptized. Here is the man who believes—he can't go to hell, because he believes, and he can't go to heaven, because he hasn't been baptized. What will you do with him? Just set him out on a stump somewhere and let him whistle eternity away" or something of that kind? But all such efforts by my opponent can be turned back upon him with the same degree of force. Take his man, for example. We read in 2 Peter 3:9 that repentance will keep a man from perishing, and that God is "not willing that any should perish, but that all should come to repentance." But my opponent says that repentance comes before faith. All right, then, take the man who has repented, who yet hasn't reached faith. He can't go to hell, because he has repented, and yet he can't go to heaven, because he hasn't believed. So we will just put him out on the same stump and let him spend eternity with the other fellow.

Then I was really amazed and amused at Mr. Bogard concerning what he said about being born of God. The man that loveth is born of God, and the man who believes is born of God. He said, "No, that doesn't mean two births—that's all the one birth, but," he said, "that's the evidence of salvation." Now, a man is not born of God by love, or he doesn't love in order to be born of God, but when he loves that's evidence of his salvation. In other words, he is saved before he loves God; therefore, saved while he is a hater of God. And as soon as he is saved, why, then he begins to love God, and that becomes the evidence of it. And besides all that, there were two passages there, and it does look to me like Mr. Bogard could see two inches past his nose, so to speak, because he used the two passages concerning both belief and love. "He that loveth is born of God." "He that believeth is born of God." All right, Mr. Bogard says, "This means that a man is not born of God by loving—he doesn't love in order to be born of God, but the love is evidence that he is already born of God." Well, if it works on one passage, it works the same way on the other. The other says that the man who "believeth is born of God," and that means that he doesn't believe in order to be born of God, but he believes and that's evidence that he is already born of God. And so that cuts out love, and that cuts out faith, and that cuts out everything as conditions of salvation.

And then to the statement made by Jesus in Mark 9:1 that "there be some standing here that shall not taste of death till they see the kingdom of God come with power." I asked Mr. Bogard where they came from. Where did the kingdom come from? And he made a statement about it, and then came up in his next speech and said, "Now, they didn't come from anywhere. They were already waiting in Jerusalem." Well, the passage says "come." Yes, Mark 9:1 says they would see the kingdom "come," but you said the kingdom was already there and didn't have to come. You or the Lord one was mistaken about it. The Lord said they would see it "come," but you said, "No, it didn't have to come at all—it was already there—there waiting for the power." Well, the Lord said it would "come with power." Mr. Bogard says, "No, it didn't come at all." Just take whichever you want. I believe the Lord was right about it and Mr. Bogard was wrong.

Then regarding the matter of who sent him here, he wonders why this was brought up in the discussion, and so on. Simply because you have been referring to the local congregation of the church of Christ in Damascus, pertaining to their eldership, and trying to prove their form of government was altogether wrong. So I just paralleled it by using his brethren in Damascus too. And regardless of what Mr. Bogard said about it this afternoon, *everybody who knows anything about it knows that the Baptist Church in Damascus is not sponsoring this debate.* And the support and cooperation that Mr. Bogard has received in this debate among Baptists have come mostly from Baptists outside of Damascus. Everybody knows that, and Mr. Bogard knows it too. So we'll just let that pass and go on to other matters.

From Gal. 3:27 I made the argument to you that the apostle Paul said, "Ye are all the children of God by faith in Christ Jesus, *for* as many of you as have been baptized into Christ have put on Christ." I showed the word "for" is from the original word "gar" which means "to introduce a reason." In two speeches I have emphasized that fact prior to this one, and to this good hour Bogard hasn't even looked at it. *He hasn't even said one word about it.* Not a word. Oh, he said a little about Gal. 3:27, but he didn't say anything about the argument. He didn't say anything about the thing on which the argument was based. Here is the reason which the apostle Paul introduced. "Ye are all the children of God by faith in Christ." Why? What's the reason? Here it is. *"For* as many of you as have been baptized into Christ have put on Christ." So those *who had not been baptized* into Christ *did not have the reason,* and therefore, they were not the children of God by faith in Christ Jesus.

And then to Cornelius—I want to notice that. He endeavored to prove that Porter was altogether wrong about that. I said if Cornelius was saved when his prayer was heard, he was saved in unbelief, because he hadn't yet heard that word by which he was to be saved. Mr. Bogard undertook to prove that I was wrong about it. Well, I'll just see if I am wrong about it. He went over there to "that word ye know" and he said that meant that he already knew the word all back there—that he had already heard the gospel of Jesus Christ, even before his prayer was heard. Well, we'll see.

The tenth chapter of Acts. Turning to it now, we will read it. I know what it says, but I'm going to read it for you. Beginning with verse 1: "There was a certain man in Caesarea called Cornelius, a centurion of the band called the Italian band, a devout man, and one that feared God with all his house, which gave much alms to the people, and prayed to God alway. He saw in a vision evidently about the ninth hour of the day an angel of God coming in to him, and saying unto him, Cornelius. And when he looked on him, he was afraid, and said, What is it, Lord? And he said unto him, Thy prayers and thine alms are come up for a memorial before God." The same reading in chapter eleven says, "Thy prayers are heard." All right. "And now"—notice this. The angel said already "your prayers and your alms are come up for a memorial before God." "And now send men to Joppa, and call for one Simon, whose surname is Peter: he lodgeth with one Simon a tanner, whose house is by the sea side: he shall tell thee what thou oughtest to do." Why, his prayer was heard before the angel appeared, and the angel said, "You send for Peter over yonder, and he'll come and tell you words whereby you and your house shall be saved." He hadn't heard those words when that prayer was answered—or heard—when that prayer was heard, and when the angel said "your prayer was heard." No, he had not yet heard the word from the mouth of the apostle Peter. But he was to hear words by his mouth and believe, the Book says. And so if he was saved when his prayer was heard, he was saved without believing.

"Noah was a preacher for 120 years," my opponent said, "before the flood came—a preacher of righteousness." Yes, and that salvation mentioned there had nothing to do with his becoming a child of God. I have shown all the time that the salvation involved in 1 Peter 3:20,21 concerning Noah, was not a matter of his becoming a child of God, but it was salvation from the flood— from that destruction that came upon the rest of the world through the flood. He was saved from that. *And that salvation did not occur before the flood came.* And that's what the Book says he was saved by and saved from. He was saved in the ark. "Saved in the ark." Mr. Bogard tell us: Was Noah saved *in the ark?* You said he was saved before he entered the ark. Now, the salvation talked about here was not reached before he got into the ark, because it says, "Wherein"—that is, in the ark—"eight souls were saved by water." And so they were "saved in the ark."

Mr. Bogard said, "No, they were not saved by water; it just *proved their salvation.*" Then he came up in his next speech and said, "I never said it, sober or drunk, sleep or awake," or something like that. Well, if you'll just play the record back you'll find he did the same thing he did the other time on that other deal. *He did say it too. And the record will show that he said it when it comes into print*—that he did say that "Noah was not saved by water—it simply proved his salvation."

Then to Matt. 3:11—"baptism unto repentance." And he says that's the same word that is in Acts 2:38. Yes, Mr. Bogard, and it's the very same word that is in Acts 11:18 that says "repentance *unto life.*" If it proves then that remission comes before baptism, it proves that life comes before repentance.

And all that we have in history that he brought this afternoon; we have gone over that a number of times during the first few days of this debate. It's not necessary to just go back over and over that same thing again. He is simply doing it for the purpose of evading the arguments that I am making. Let him come up and meet the arguments.

And all that he said: "Well, suppose that so and so it true. Suppose the church was founded back there, suppose the church did begin on Pentecost, what good would that do you?" It would do me a lot more good than it will do Bogard if it was established back in the personal ministry of Christ, or in the days of John, or on Pentecost, or anywhere in the days of the New Testament's making, because he cannot find anywhere any reference to a Baptist Church in all the divine record.

CHART NO. 1-A

Church of Christ	Baptist Churches
Churches of Christ	Baptist Church
— Rom. 16:16	— Religious Encyclopedia Page 796

At least we have found Rom. 16:16 which says, "The churches of Christ salute you." He hasn't found "Baptist Church" in the singular, "Baptist Churches" in the plural, referring to local congregations anywhere, referring to it in a general sense, or in any other sense. Then get up here and say the Baptists are the only one who can back up and hitch on. The Baptists can't hitch on anywhere *and he knows it.* That is just a lot of stuff to try to keep people's minds blinded, to keep prejudice up, and to keep them from seeing the truth. The fact is, that he knows good and well, the *only place* he has found *any hitching post* is in "Religious Encyclopedia," page 796. But he cannot find any reference in God's Book. Now, then, to some other matters.

Well, this one thing before we go. All this charge he makes about Campbellism, and Campbell is your daddy, and stuff of that kind, and you ought not to be ashamed of your daddy, was just so much stuff put in to fill up. That's all. Because I do not preach or teach anything that originated with Alexander Campbell. I regard him no more as a leader in things divine—as authority in that matter—than I would Ben M. Bogard. Not a bit. I'm not following Campbell. I don't preach anything that originated with Alexander Campbell.

All right, now then, to another line of thought. We believe and teach that a child of God may so conduct himself, after he has become one, as to be lost in hell at last. Baptists teach, and Mr. Bogard contends, that it makes no difference what a child of God does after he is saved, that he will go to heaven anyway. I want to read you again a little quotation I read the other day from Sam Morris. It's "good reading"—presents Baptist doctrine. So I am just going to read this. This is a little pamphlet entitled, "Do A Christian's Sins Damn His Soul?" On page 1 Sam Morris said:

"We take the position that a Christian's sins do not damn his soul. The way a Christian lives, what he says. his conduct, or his attitude toward other people have nothing whatever to do with the salvation of his soul . . . All the prayers a man may pray, all the Bibles he may read, all the churches he may belong to, all the services he may attend, all the sermons he may practice, all the debts he may pay, all the ordinances he may observe, all the laws he may keep, all the benevolent acts he may perform, will not make his soul one whit safer; and all the sins he may commit from idolatry to murder will not make his soul in any more danger."

That's Baptist doctrine. I call upon Mr. Bogard again: Tell me, Mr. Bogard, do you indorse what Sam Morris said? That's what you have been saying. You said that a child of God can get drunk, and he can commit murder, but you say if he dies in that state, he will go to hell. But you say he can't go to hell.

And now we have some questions here that I asked him the other day. I want to call attention to one or two of them in this connection.

Question "No. 28," which I asked my friend, is this: "Is it possible for a child of God to lie and call his brother a fool?" He said, "Yes, and if he does, he'll be in danger of hell fire." But he said, "The blood protects him and he can't go to hell." All right, he says it is possible for a child of God to lie and call his brother a fool, and he will be in danger of hell fire. I want to know how he will be in danger if the blood won't let him go. Is there danger of the blood's failing someway and the man will go in spite of it? How could there be any danger of hell fire, Mr. Bogard, according to your position?

Now, then, get this. In Rev. 21:8 we have the statement made that "all liars shall have their part in the lake which burneth with fire and brimstone." All right, "all liars shall have their part in the lake of fire and brimstone." I would like to have some papers out of that (pointing to handbag)—I forgot to get one that I want. I don't know whether that is it—no, that is not it. Hand me up the bundle down under there, please. Now, notice that they'll "have their part in the lake that burneth with fire and brimstone." Just hand me up the whole bundle, and I'll—(Joe Blue hands bundle of papers to Porter). I think we have it here. Right here we have it. Now, I want to call your attention to a statement made here by Mr. Bogard. On page 5 of the Orthodox Baptist Searchlight of February 10, 1948, we have printed a letter which Mr. Bogard received from a certain lady concerning something that a Free Will Baptist told regarding what he had heard Mr. Bogard preach. And Mr. Bogard, replying to that, said:

"The fact that he deliberately LIED to you when he said that 'Baptists teach that there are infants in hell not a span long,' shows he is a liar. The fact that he said that 'MISSIONARY BAPTISTS TEACH THAT A COUPLE IS LIVING IN ADULTERY UNLESS THEY WERE MARRIED BY A BAPTIST PREACHER,' shows he deliberately lied. The Bible says: 'All liars shall have their part in the lake of fire.' That is where the poor deluded man is headed."

Now notice that. A Free Will Baptist liar will go to hell, but a Missionary Baptist liar won't. A Free Will Baptist liar will go to hell. Here is one—and he told a lie—and Mr. Bogard quoted a Scripture that says, "All liars will have their part in the lake of fire and brimstone."

And then another statement here he makes regarding another. Right in this paper here. This is one of April 25, 1941. We have reference made here to J. Frank Norris. And here is what Mr. Bogard said about him:

"Wish Dr. Norris and those who are working with him would quit exaggerating so much. It is BIG ENOUGH to tell it like it is without so much exaggeration."

And down here he says:

"When I get to heaven I expect to find Frank Norris there in spite of that wicked streak that now runs through him . . . I expect to ask Norris why he sought to ruin Bob White all because White would not submit to his dictation, and then when he practically destroyed White and White sued him at the law and got a judgment of TWENTY-FIVE THOUSAND DOLLARS DAMAGES and the COURT called it MALICIOUS LIBEL, why then did Norris PUBLICLY DENY THAT ANYTHING LIKE THAT EVER HAPPENED? SELAH! My! how the grace of God is magnified when we think of how it takes all THREE OF US TO HEAVEN in spite of our devilment.

"Peter, the apostle, cursed and swore and even denied the Lord and Paul withstood him to the face because he was to blame and if Peter got by with all that and went home to glory, I think it likely that Norris will also."

Now, he says that Norris was "sued at court" and was "charged with libel," and "twenty-five thousand dollars damage" was obtained, and then "denied the thing had ever happened." But in spite of it all he expects to meet Norris in heaven. I suppose that kind of liar won't go to hell, but a Free Will Baptist liar is doomed. That's all. Any other kind, perhaps, would not. J. Frank Norris and Missionary Baptist liars wouldn't go to hell, but a Free Will Baptist liar is doomed for hell—he is on his road there.

Now, Mr. Bogard, since you quoted that passage that says "all liars shall have their part in the lake that burneth with fire and brimstone," I want to know: Does that mean "all liars"? Or does it just mean "all unregenerated liars"? Which does it mean?

I pass on next to the fact that a child of God may get drunk and commit murder. Here we have it in questions No. 19 and 20, which I asked Mr. Bogard the other day.

"No. 19. Is it possible for a child of God to get drunk and commit murder?" And he said, "Yes."

"No. 20. If he should die while drunk and in the act of murder, will he go to heaven?" He said, "He'd go to hell." All right, but he said a child of God cannot go to hell, but he can get drunk; and if he should die while he is drunk, he would go to hell. *But he can't go to hell.* Therefore, he can't die while he is drunk. And I'm still saying, according to Bogard's doctrine, if you want to be safe from the atomic bomb, so that you won't need any bomb shelter during the next war that is threatening, just get drunk and stay drunk.

And the bomb can't kill you, because God won't let you die while you are drunk.

Another question I would like to ask Mr. Bogard is this: What is to be the eternal destiny of all drunkards? Put it down, Mr. Bogard. What is to be the eternal destiny of all drunkards? In Gal. 5:19-21 the apostle Paul declared that drunkards, along with every worker of the flesh as listed there, has no inheritance in the kingdom—"they shall not inherit the kingdom of God." In Eph. 5:5 he declares the same class—fornicators, the covetous, the idolaters, and men of that kind—have no "inheritance in the kingdom of Christ and of God." In 1 Cor. 6:9,10 he makes the same statement—that those guilty of those sins—as fornication, and covetousness, and idolatry, and murder, and drunkenness, and matters of that kind, "shall not inherit the kingdom of God." I want to know, Mr. Bogard, if this is true? You say a child of God can do all of these things—that a child of God can commit any sin in the catalog of sin. But you say, if he should die, he'll go to heaven—or go to hell, whichever it is. And if he can't go to hell, that means he can't die in that condition. Either he'll die in that condition and go to heaven as a result of it, or he just can't die in that condition, one or the other. Let Mr. Bogard clear that up and tell us which it is.

I turn to Luke 12, verses 45 and 46, and here we have a statement made by the Lord concerning that servant who began to say the Lord "delayed his coming" and "began to beat his menservants and his maidens" and "began to eat and drink, and to be drunken." Jesus said, "The Lord of that servant will come at a time he is not aware, and will cut him in sunder, and will appoint him his portion with the unbelievers." All right, notice the fact, now. Here is one of the Lord's servants going to be given his "portion with the unbelievers." He is not an unbeliever, Mr. Bogard—he is contrasted with the unbeliever. He is one of the Lord's servants. The Lord says he will be given "his portion with the unbelievers." What is the portion of the unbelievers? Rev. 21, and verse 8, says the "unbelieving . . . shall have his part in the lake of fire and brimstone." Hell, then, is the portion of the unbelievers. Jesus said this servant who begins to beat his menservants and his maidens, and to be drunken, "will have his portion with the unbelievers," which means he will have his portion in hell.

Then to Gal. 5 and verse 4. Paul said, "Whosoever of you are justified by the law; ye are fallen from grace." He is talking about men who are already made free. If you will drop back to the first of that chapter you will find it addressed to men who were standing in the liberty of Jesus Christ. And he said "if ye be justified by the law, ye are fallen from grace."

We pass on from that to 2 Peter 2, verses 20 and 21. Here we have another statement made. The apostle Peter said, "For if after they have escaped the pollutions of the world through the knowledge of the Lord and Savior Jesus Christ, they are again entangled therein, and overcome, the latter end is worse with them than the beginning. For it had been better for them not to have known the way of righteousness, than, after they have known it, to turn from the holy commandment delivered unto them." Now, note the fact that here are men who "have escaped the pollutions of the world" and "become entangled" therein "again." I want to know if a man can "become entangled *again*" in something that he has never been freed from. Could a man become "entangled again" in a barbed wire fence if he had been in a barbed wire fence all of his life? If he had never been freed from such, could he become "entangled again"? All right, the pollutions of the world is sin, and here the apostle Peter says, "He has escaped the pollutions of the world through the knowledge of the Lord Jesus Christ" and is "become entangled therein again," and that for that man, when thus overcome, "the latter end is worse with him than the beginning." If in the beginning he was lost, does that sound like heaven? If the latter end is worse than the beginning? I'll leave that dog and sow for you to talk about, Mr. Bogard, and then I'll attend to you.

We turn to Heb. 3 and verse 12. In Heb. 3:12 the apostle Paul says, "Take heed, brethren, lest there be in any of you an evil heart of unbelief, in departing from the living God." Paul is writing to "brethren" and Paul said, "Take heed, brethren, lest there be in any of you an evil heart of unbelief, in departing from the living God." Thus Paul shows that brethren can depart from the living God because of an evil heart of unbelief. If they depart from the living God, will God save them anyway in spite of all of that?

And then again I pass. I call your attention to a statement made in Rev. 22:14. This statement says, "Blesed are they that do his commandment, that they may have right to the tree of life, and may enter in through the gates into the city." Or the American Revised Version reads: "Blessed are they that wash their robes, that they may have the right to come to the tree of life, and may enter in by the gates into the city." Now, note that here are men who "washed their robes" that they may have the right to the tree of life. There are two things that they will have the right to: tree of life (Porter writes on blackboard) and to enter the city. (The blackboard chart appeared as follows):

CHART NO. 10
To tree of life
To enter the city

"Blessed are they that wash their robes, that they may have the right to come to the tree of life, and may enter in by the gates into the city." All right, now, in order to have the right to the tree of life, in order to have the right to enter that celestial city, one must have his robes washed. I turn to Rev. 7, verses 13 and 14. There I read about those whose robes are washed in the blood of the Lamb. All right, then, they have their robes washed in the blood of the Lamb in order that they might have the right to the tree of life and to enter in through the gates into the city. Can they ever lose that right? Can they ever lose that privilege that they have there? Can they ever lose their part in those matters? Well, all we have to do is just drop down to verse 19 of the 22nd chapter, and the Book of God declares very plainly concerning matters along that line. "If any man shall take away from the words of the book of this prophecy, God shall take away his part from the tree of life, and out of the holy city, which are written in this book." Now, note this fact. In order to have a right to the tree of life our robes must be washed; in order to have a right to enter that city our robes must be washed. They must be made clean in the blood of the Lamb, and that means we are saved. We must become saved—we must become God's children—before we have a right to the tree of life and before we have a right to enter that city. And the Book of God declares that "if we take away from the words of the prophecy of this book, God will take away our part from the tree of life and out of the holy city." All right, then, if our part to the tree of life is taken away, and if our right to enter that holy city is taken away, how are we going to enter heaven? How are we going to be saved eternally with that right—with that part—taken away? I would be willing to risk the whole thing on that passage. I am certain of the fact that it will stand when the world is on fire.

But there are many others. I think we will have time for about one more. I want to turn and read this one. I know what it says, but I want to turn and read this passage this time. Oftentimes I like to read because it helps to impress the thought upon your minds. I'm going to John, the fifteenth chapter and get some statements there from the Lord Jesus Christ. John, the 15th chapter, beginning with verse 1, the Lord says, "I am the true vine, and my Father is the husbandman. Every branch in me that beareth not fruit he taketh away: and every branch that beareth fruit, he purgeth it, that it may bring forth more fruit. Now ye are clean through the word which I have spoken unto you. Abide in me, and I in you. As the branch cannot bear fruit of itself, except it abide in the vine; no more can ye, except ye abide in me. I am the vine, ye are the branches: he that abideth in me, and I in him, the same bringeth forth much fruit: for without me ye can do nothing. If a man abide not in me, he is cast forth as a branch, and is withered; and men gather them, and cast them into the fire, and they are burned."

All right, there's the statement made by the Lord pointing out the fact that men in him may be taken away—that they may fail to bring forth fruit, and like the branch taken from the vine, so they'll be taken away and withered and burned, just as the branch that fails to bear fruit in the vine. Certainly, that refers to those who are in Christ, because Jesus said, "Abide *in me*, and I in you." They certainly could not "abide in him" if they were not "in him." And if they were "in him," then they were God's children, and consequently, being his children, they were in a state of safety, according to Mr. Bogard. They couldn't possibly be taken away. But this declares very plainly if he fails to bring forth fruit, that he'll be taken away. Unless you "abide in him," he'll take you away. Yes, sir, that's exactly what the Lord said. "Every branch *in me* that beareth not fruit he taketh away." I want Mr. Bogard to tell me, when he comes up here, just how Jesus Christ can "take away" a branch which was never in the vine. I would just like for him to illustrate it—just draw a little picture of a branch up here on the board, away from that vine that never had any connection with it. When you do that then we'll have something to say about it. But I want you to do that. Cerainly, you cannot do it. If the branch is in the vine, it is in the vine, it has a connection with the vine. And, consequently, I know that in order for him to prove his theory—to sustain Baptist doctrine along this line—he'll have to get rid of these plain statements in God's eternal truth. How much time do I have?

Moderator Blue speaks: "One minute and three quarters."

One minute and three quarters? All right, one minute and three quarters. Now, then, I want to get back to this just here. When my opponent comes up here again and begins to talk about these things, I want to leave "the tree of life" and "the city" there that he may deal with it. Otherwise we have these things for you on the board that we have had before.

CHART NO. 1-A

Church of Christ	**Baptist Church**
Churches of Christ	**Baptist Churches**
— Rom. 16:16	**— Religious Encyclopedia Pape 796**

And remember when my opponent comes and begins to blow and brag and bluff and do all of those things, and talk about "you can't find 'the Church of Christ' in the Bible," remember here's the passage that contains the plural number. And I have sense enough to know that if a plural number is "churches of Christ," one would be "church of Christ." If a plural number would be "the churches of Christ," then the singular would be "the church of Christ." I have enough sense to know that. And so Rom. 16:16. We have that passage in God's Book. Rom. 16:16 says, "The churches of Christ salute you." Over here on this side, the only "Baptist Church" or "Baptist Churches" that my opponent has been able to find is somewhere in some Religious Encyclopedia or something of that kind. Nowhere in all of God's Book can he find them. So when he makes his palaver about that just keep in mind the fact that he has failed to write the reference up here. Until he erases that and puts the Scripure reference in its place, he is gone, he is hopelessly gone. And all the boasts that he makes, and all the brags that he puts up, during the closing hours of this debate will not atone for the fact that he has failed, miserably failed, to write his reference on the board. I thank you, Ladies and Gentlemen.

Fourth Day

BOGARD'S SEVENTH NEGATIVE

Gentlemen Moderators, Ladies and Gentlemen:

I am glad to respond to this speech that has just been made, for my friend did the very best he could do; and if after doing the very best he could do, he has failed, then the best they can do is a failure.

I am beginning right where my friend left off, about the vine and branches. My friend makes a parable go on all fours—makes every detail work out. Now, here is the vine and the branches. Where does the branch get its power to bear fruit? From the vine. If the branch fails to bring forth fruit, why does it fail? Because the vine does not give it power to bring forth fruit. Who is the vine? Jesus Christ. Then that makes Jesus Christ the cause of every one who apostatizes if he apostatizes. That branch cannot bring forth fruit except as the vine forces the fruit on it. Again, what did that branch have to do with getting in the vine in the first place? It had nothing. All right then, it got in there without any means or instrumentality, so it was not to blame for getting in, and takes no credit for getting in—kicked out because it could not help itself. Why? Because if the vine had furnished power to bring forth fruit, the vine could not have helped, the branch *could not have helped* but bring forth fruit. The vine did not bring forth fruit because it wanted to but because it had to. And if it quit bringing forth fruit, it did it because it had to and not because it wanted to. That forces the apostasy on Jesus Christ Himself; He is to blame for it.

Now, what is the parable? The only thing about the parable is to show that we get all our power to bring fruit from the vine. And if the vine does not furnish any power to bring forth fruit, then the branch has to stop. It never will stop until the vine fails to furnish the power to bring forth fruit. That branch is helpless. I have run into hard-shellism, absolutely. Now, the branch had nothing to do in getting in the vine. It had nothing to do in getting out of the vine because that branch cannot stop bringing forth fruit of itself. Now, any simpleton knows that. You think that branch could make up its mind to quit bringing forth fruit? Oh, well, you can grin at that but *you cannot grin it off*. (Laughter) Very well.

Now, my friend goes on to tell about falling from grace and cites the many bad things that Christians can do. They can lie; they can steal; they can get drunk, and all that, which is conceded. But he fails to note the fact that Psalm 37:23, 24 says, "The steps of a good man are ordered by the Lord: and he delighteth in his way, and though he fall," (goes into these bad things) *"he shall not be utterly cast down."* That answers every last one of those bad conduct cases. "He shall not be utterly cast down." He says, "But suppose he should die that way." Then he would be utterly cast down. But suppose he should die that way and was utterly cast down, what would happen? Why, the Bible would be a plain falsehood, for it said, "he shall not be utterly cast down." Of course, a Christian can sin; of course, a Christian can get drunk; of course, a Christian can lie. Certainly, he can do all—a Christian can even murder. Did not David? Certainly. Well, was he utterly cast down? No, sir, for in the penitential Psalm, the fifty-first Psalm, he said, "Restore unto me the joy of thy salvation. Then will I teach transgressors thy ways," and so on. He did not lose his salvation but lost his joy. "But now if that is the case, I will take my fill of sin." Well, wait awhile. "Whom the Lord loveth he chasteneth, and scourgeth every son whom he receiveth." The Lord punishes in the flesh for the sins of the flesh.

In the 89th Psalm it says if His people forsake His ways, and keep not His commandments, walk not in His statutes, "I will let them fall from grace and die and go to hell." No, sir. But it says, "I will visit their transgression with the rod, and their iniquity with stripes. Nevertheless I *will not suffer* my loving kindness to fail." That answers every one of his misconduct problems; everything he said about the bad conduct of a Christian is covered right there. We all do wrong, and we all sin in one way or another, but we "shall not be utterly cast down." And if we are—if we die that way—then we would be utterly cast down, flatly contradicting the word of God.

Now, he brought up the case about as many as are justified by law "ye are fallen from grace." Exactly. How many are justified by law? How many? "But that no man is justified by law is evident, for the just shall live by faith." That is in the very same chapter where he found his "falling from grace." Who falls from grace? Those who are justified by law. Who is justified by law? "But that no man is justified by law is manifest, for the just shall live by faith." That takes away absolutely all that my friend said except one thing.

He said, "If any man takes away from the words of the book of this prophecy, God will take his part out of the tree of life." Who would take away the words of the book of this prophecy? Nobody but a wicked man. And if a wicked man would do that he would forfeit his right to salvation. That is all. What part had he? Out here in Oklahoma years ago every man who had any Indian blood in him had a right to a part of the land in Oklahoma. All right. If he went by the limit he forfeited his right—his right was taken away from him. Now, that answers all my friend said on falling from grace.

I do not care if he offers seventy-five or a hundred or five hundred cases of bad conduct—liars, thieves, and murderers. Did not Peter lie? Yes, sir. Did not Peter swear—curse and swear? Yes, sir. Was he utterly cast down? No, sir. You have got to show where, when a man does these things he will be utterly cast down, else you have not got your doctrine of falling from grace.

Now, coming to the arguments today—some of them on baptism. Gal. 3:26, 27. "As many as you children of God as were baptized into Jesus Christ have put on Christ." He made an argument on "gar." He wrote it out here: "g-a-r, gar." (Writes on the board.) I will try to write this so you can see it. Now, he said, "Mr. Bogard, that is the word used." Yes, sir. And I happen to know that no Greek scholar in the world would use that to express the idea of a reason. Why? Because "gar" is a conjunction and not a preposition. If you did not have sense enough to know that, why, you do not know much about Greek. Using a conjunction as a reason—if that is not rich! Won't that look pretty in the record? Very well.

I called to your attention today that "as many as have been baptized into Christ have put on Christ." In Rom. 13:14 it said, "Put ye on the Lord Jesus Christ." Those are already Christians; those are already church members, already baptized church members. They were told to put on Christ. So "put on Christ" does not mean to become a Christian. But the Greek word is "enduo" which means to *imitate*. "*As* many as have been baptized into Christ have imitated Christ." What did Christ do? He was already the Son of God. He was not baptized to make Him the Son of God. Then if you are baptized to make you the son of God, you have not imitated Christ. "As many as have put on Christ have imitated Christ." Baptism is merely an expression of the fact that we are children of God, just like Jesus was God's Son and was baptized to make it manifest that He was God's Son.

We now come to Cornelius. He said, "Cornelius' prayer was heard before he ever even heard the preaching." Then good night nurse! If his prayer was heard before he ever heard the preaching, certainly it was heard before he was baptized. You say God will not hear a sinner pray. And therefore he—well, I'll declare!! (Laughter) I am ashamed of him. You get up here in one breath and say, "God will not hear a sinner pray," and here is a man that God heard "who had not even heard the word preached," much less been baptized and saved. Now one of two things: Either Cornelius was heard while he was a sinner, and if so, then your doctrine of prayer goes down, or he was a child of God when he was heard, and then he was a child of God before he was baptized, and that in spite of high water—and you can put the other word in front of it if you want to.

Now coming to Noah: He says, "Noah was not saved *by* water but saved *from* it." He certainly did. You need not shake your head down there. You have been doing that all through the debate. He said he was saved from the flood. That is what he said. All right. "The like figure whereunto baptism saves us." So we are saved from baptism, from the water, just like Noah was. Noah was God's man. Noah was saved, a preacher of righteousness, and the water simply proved his salvation. How was he saved by water? In a figure. Just like I Pet. 3:21 says, "The like figure whereunto even baptism doth also now save us." It saves in a figure. There is *real salvation* and a *figure of salvation.* Very well.

He read about the sow and the dog that turned to the vomit and to the wallowing in the mire. They were still a sow and still a dog. If they had had that nature changed, they would not have gone back to the wallow and to the vomit.

He told about Frank Norris exaggerating. That proves a man can fall from grace because Frank Norris exaggerated. I think Peter rather exaggerated when he said, "I do not even know the man." He cursed and swore to clinch it. But did he utterly go down? Was he destroyed? Psalm 37: 23, 24: "The steps of a good man are ordered by the Lord: and delighteth in his way. Though he fall, he shall not be utterly cast down."

Now—hand me the Bible please. My friend has utterly failed to prove his Pentecost theory. There is no use to go over all of that again. I showed very plainly and very emphatically by the word of God that Christ had His house, and Paul said the house "is the church of God, the pillar and ground of the truth." He had it before Pentecost. And then He gave His servants authority and a work to do before Pentecost. And that body, that organization, that house, was told to tarry in Jerusalem till they be endued with power. They could not have tarried if it had not been there. If I say to my friend, "I want you to stay right here till breakfast in the morning," he would say, "Why, I do not have any existence—I cannot stay anywhere." But there was something that could tarry, something that could wait for power, and that kingdom or church or house of God did tarry till the power came. My friend wants to make the impression that the power was something like a man, and that the kingdom is something like a man, and the two men came walking in together. Did you know that word "with" was "e-i-s, eis"? Come *into* power? If you do not know that you are mighty green. (Laughter) Very well.

Now, coming to the word of God. He failed to prove his Pentecost theory. And I am going back here in the Bible and show you where people were saved, gloriously saved, without baptism. I go here to the seventh chapter of Luke where the woman came and fell at His feet, washed His feet with tears, wiped them with her hair, and the Lord said, "Woman, get up and be baptized, and I will save you." No, sir. He said, "*Thy faith has saved thee,* go in peace." There is a case of salvation. Now my friend need not get up here and say that is before Pentecost; you will have to prove your Pentecost theory first. I have shown by the word of God that the church went right on back "beginning from the baptism of John." Now, he presumes to guess—and if you presume to guess with him that the plan of salvation did not begin until the day of Pentecost, until the church was organized, as he says—but he has failed to prove that. And now here comes case after case of salvation. "Thy faith hath saved thee; go in peace."

Look at Luke 23:42, 43, where the thief hanging on the cross said, "Lord, remember me when thou comest into thy kingdom." And the Lord said to the thief, "Get down off the cross, hunt up Peter and James and John—some of those men—and have them take you down to the river and baptize you, and you shall be saved." No, He did not say that. He said, "*Today shalt thou be with me in paradise.*" There is a man clear above high water mark, hanging to the cross. He could not do a thing in the world except exercise faith in the Lord Jesus Christ, which he did. And the Lord said, "Today shalt thou be with me in paradise." His only answer to that is: "That was before Pentecost." What has that got to do with it? Absolutely nothing because you have not proved your Pentecost theory. The very thing you are assuming is the thing on which you base your argument.

Then go to the 19th chapter of Luke where Zacchaeus saw the Lord. He said, "Zacchaeus, make haste, and come down; for I must abide in thy house today." And when He got there He said, "*This day is salvation come* to this house." And there is not one word about baptism. Over and over and over again!

I wonder why my friend has not brought up John 3:5? If you bring it up, you bring it up back yonder before Pentecost. I have whipped you off of that, undoubtedly. Very well.

I want to see if I have left anything out because I will not have a right to bring it up in my next speech if I have.

Oh! I made the point that when one believes he is saved; when one loves he is saved. He said, "Oh, there are two salvations." No. You have never found a man who is a believer that was not saved. You have not found a man who loves who was not saved, for "he that loveth is born of God." My friend says that makes unconditional salvation. No, sir. "*He that believeth* on the Son *hath everlasting life.*" There it is. You believe before you are baptized. John 5:24: "*He that heareth* my words, *and believeth* on him that sent me, *hath everlasting life,* and shall not come into condemnation." He is perfectly safe because he believes. I John 4:7 says, "He that loveth is born of God, and knoweth God." And I can cite you numerous evidences of salvation, and all of that, and whenever you find these evidences of salvation, certainly you do not have to get it after that.

Now, the kingdom "come with power." My friend came speaking, but he was in existence before he got here. The kingdom was in *existence* before the power came. Otherwise, the Lord would not have said, "Tarry ye in Jerusalem till ye be endued with power from on high." What stayed there in Jerusalem? Come up like a man and answer the question. What was in Jerusalem to tarry? If the church did not exist at that time, how could it tarry anywhere? How could it go anywhere? That is perfectly clear to me, and I think it is clear to everybody else.

Oh, he read about my man that is a liar who charged the Baptists with all kinds of false things. He read in Searchlight, and I said that was proof that the man was unsaved. It was proof that he was unsaved; it did not prove that he fell from grace. It proved he was an unsaved sinner lying on Baptists, like I am afraid a lot of you folks do. I wish you would quit it. And if he had sinned and lied on the Baptists, "the steps of a good man are ordered by the Lord;

and he delighteth in his way. And though he fall, he shall not be utterly cast down."

Then my friend seems to forget all about Rom. 8:28 where "we know that all things work together *for good* to them that love God, to them who are the called according to his purpose." If "all things work together for good to them that love God," and something comes to me and causes me to die and go to hell, would that be for my good? Why, you say, "No, of course not." Then it can not happen. Well, somebody says, "What about those sins?" The Lord overrules our sins for our good. Peter said, "I am better than my brethren. I am stronger than my brethren. All of these may forsake you, but I will not forsake you." When the Lord let him down, and he fell, he was not utterly cast down, but it did him good, because it taught him he was not better than his brethren. It took the conceit out of him. It took that vanity out of him. And in that way it did him good. Our sins are overruled for our good and for the honor and glory of God. And no matter how much sin we may commit the blood of Christ covers it.

He wants to know if I indorse Sam Morris. If I understand what Sam Morris means to be that all of our sins are covered by the blood of the Lord Jesus Christ, and if that is what he means, I indorse him. So I will turn right over here and read in Romans, the fourth chapter, "What shall we say then that Abraham our father, as pertaining to the flesh, hath found? For if Abraham were justified by works, he hath whereof to glory; but not before God. For what saith the Scripture? Abraham *believed* God, and it was *imputed* unto him for righteousness." Salvation is imputed, and righteousness is imputed. I do not work out my salvation, in the sense of obtaining it, but I get it through the merits of Jesus Christ. "Now, to him that worketh is the reward not reckoned of grace, but of debt. But to him that worketh not, but believeth on him that justifieth the ungodly, his *faith* is counted for righteousness. Even as David describeth the blessedness of the man, unto whom God imputeth righteousness without works, saying, Blessed are they whose iniquities are forgiven, and whose sins are covered." Our sins are covered by the blood of the Lord Jesus Christ, and the blood never takes a vacation. It is on all the time. My friend depends on himself for salvation. He depends on what he does for salvation. I am depending on the blood of Jesus Christ and the substitutionary righteousness of the Lord Jesus Christ for my eternal salvation. The difference between me and him is that I am trusting the Lord and he is trusting himself. He depends on what he does, and as they sang a while ago, "Hold to God's Unchanging Hand," you are doing the holding. I am not holding; God holds me. I am "kept by the power of God through faith unto salvation, ready to be revealed in the last time." And if I had to depend on myself, I would give it up as a bad job right now, for I am not able to keep myself. But the Lord keeps me, kept by His power, saved by His grace, covered by His blood, and His substitutionary righteousness is given to me. "He that knew no sin became sin for me that I might be made the righteousness of God in him." *His righteousness is imputed to me; my sins are all counted against Him.* Unless you get that thought in your mind, you are a lost sinner—unsaved—you are trusting in yourself, depending on what you do instead of depending on the Lord Jesus Christ for your eternal security.

Now, coming to Cornelius again, Cornelius was undoubtedly a saved man when he was baptized. How do I know? Peter said, "Can any man forbid water, that these should not be baptized, which have received the Holy Ghost as well as we?" They had already received the Holy Ghost. What did Jesus say? He said, "Him the world cannot receive." If the world cannot receive the Holy Spirit, then whoever does receive the Holy Spirit is already a child of God. As he is already a child of God he does not have to be baptized to become a child of God. I told you I was going to ring that change on you till the very last, and I am going to do it in my last speech. If Cornelius had the Holy Spirit, he was already saved. He had the Holy Spirit before he was baptized. And Peter said, "Can any man forbid water, that these should not be baptized," in order to get salvation? No, but because they have already received the Holy Spirit.

And in the case of Saul of Tarsus, the ninth chapter, he was praying. And when Ananias came he said, "Brother

Saul," already a brother, "The Lord has sent me to you that you may receive your eyesight and receive the Holy Ghost." Very Well. What was he to receive? The Holy Ghost. Who could receive the Holy Ghost? Nobody except a child of God, for "him the world cannot receive." So he did not say, "I have been sent up here to get you saved." And so when he said, "Arise, and be baptized, and wash away thy sins," it was not the real washing away but the figurative washing away. Evidently so, unless you have two salvations. Salvation is in reality and in a figure. Like I Pet. 3:21, "The like figure whereunto even baptism doth also save us." How does baptism save? It saves; sure it saves, but how? In a figure. What is a figure? If I make a picture of a house here on the board—I am no artist, but suppose I made a picture of a house. That is a figure of a house; that is not the house. "The like figure whereunto even baptism saves us." Baptism is a figure. Who said it? The word of God. It is the figure, but it is not the real thing. If it is the real thing, it is not the figure. "The like figure whereunto baptism doth also now save us." As Noah was saved by water—actually? Certainly not. He was already a saved man before the water came. Even so "in a like figure," a similar figure, we are saved by baptism. We are saved first. Baptism is a figure of it. You have your house first then have a picture taken of it. "The like figure whereunto even baptism doth also now save us, (not the putting away of the filth of the flesh, but the answer of a good conscience toward God)."

What has my friend said in reply to what I said this afternoon about Matt. 3:11, where it says, "John baptized with the baptism of repentance?" The Greek word is "e-i-s, eis," "into repentance." Is that it? No, sir. "With *reference* to repentance." In exactly the same way we are baptized into the remission of sins. What has he said in reply to the fact that when you have the remission of sins you are baptized to make a figure of it? For baptism is a figure. How are we saved? Saved by the gospel. How does the gospel save? By our believing the gospel. Then what is baptism? It is a figure. "The like figure whereunto even baptism now saves us."

In the fifteenth chapter of I Corinthians it says we are

saved by the gospel. What is the gospel? The death, burial and resurrection of the Lord Jesus Christ. Now come over to the fourth chapter and fifteenth verse of I Corinthians. Paul said, "I have begotten you through the gospel." "I have begotten you through the gospel." But he said, "I did not baptize any of you, except Gaius and Crispus." I *begot* all of you *through* the *gospel.* "Begetting" means the bringing into life. It is the very same word in the Greek where it says we are born of God. And my friend will not deny it. Very well then, "I have begotten you through the gospel." But I did not baptize any of you. If you cannot get the new life without baptism, then Paul could not have begotten those folks without baptism. But he says, "I have begotten you by the gospel, but I did not baptize any of you." That ought to be perfectly clear to all who are willing to take the truth, and I believe this congregation, most of them, are honest enough to want to take the truth of God instead of some man's saying.

And now I will introduce no further arguments. I have not time to go further. And in my next speech I will make a replication of what has been said during the debate, and that will close the debate, after hearing my friend Porter.

Fourth Day

PORTER'S EIGHTH AFFIMATIVE

Mr. Bogard, Ladies and Gentlemen:

I am before you now for my closing speech of this debate. The first thing to which I wish to call your attention is the statement made by Mr. Bogard relative to the "kingdom coming with power." I want to illustrate that, if I can, so you can all see it. I am just going to say that we'll draw a little figure of some kind here and let that indicate Jerusalem. (Draws circle on board) Mr. Bogard says that the church was there in Jerusalem waiting for the power. We'll let heaven be represented up here (drawing at the top of the board), and then the power is to come. He told them to "tarry in Jerusalem until they were endued with power from on high." Bogard said, "If the church didn't already exist, how could it tarry in Jerusalem?" Well, it doesn't say a word about *the church* tarrying in Jerusalem. You've got a passage that says nothing about "church." Now, you know Mr. Bogard the other day was always talking about finding

CHART NO. 11

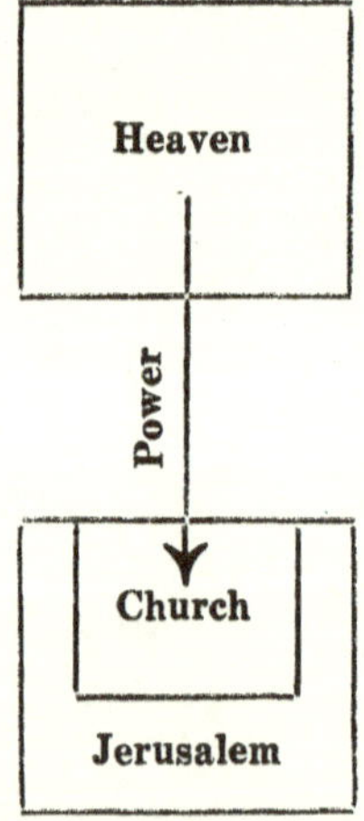

a passage that said nothing about "church" or finding a passage that said nothing about "Pentecost." Well, his passage that told them to "tarry in Jerusalem" doesn't say a word about "church." He just reads that into it. It didn't say the church tarried in Jerusalem. The apostles tarried in Jerusalem, but it didn't say a word about the church tarrying there.

Now notice. He said in that statement, "the kingdom will come with power," that that word "with" is from the Greek word "eis" and means "into." So the kingdom will "come into power." Now, if that is true, let us see what it has done for Mr. Bogard. Where is the church? Here's the church or the kingdom (pointing to "Jerusalem" on the board). The kingdom is here on Pentecost in the city of Jerusalem. And the passage, according to Bogard, says, "the kingdom will come *into* power." All right, the power comes from heaven, but the power comes *into the church,* and not the church *into the power.* So Mr. Bogard, you have the wrong passage. You have the wrong set-up there. The Holy Spirit came down from heaven and filled all of them. "They were all filled with the Holy Spirit, and began to speak with other tongues as the Spirit gave them utterance." So the power came "into the men," and you say they constituted the church or the kingdom there waiting for it—thus the power came "into the kingdom" and not the kingdom "into power." Didn't you have more judgment than to make a break like that, Mr. Bogard. You'll have to try that over. You've got the thing going the wrong direction there, as sure as you are here tonight. Yes, the power came "into the men." Therefore, the power came "into the church," but the passage, according to Bogard, says, "the kingdom or the church will *come into power.*" You've got the wrong one coming, Mr. Bogard—even the wrong Greek, for it doesn't say "eis."

Well, to get to the vine and the branches—he said, "Why, here's the vine and the branches." I asked Mr. Bogard to draw a picture here and illustrate how a branch could be taken away that had no connection there. Now, we've got these branches connected here to the vine. And here's the vine and here are the branches connected. Now then, Jesus said, "If a man bring not forth fruit, he is taken away"—"Every branch in me that beareth not fruit he taketh away." Mr. Bogard said, "That's impossible—the branch couldn't fail to bear fruit." Well, then, the Lord was talking silly stuff—he was talking nonsense. When he said "every branch that beareth not fruit he taketh away" he was simply filling space, because the very thing the Lord referred to was something that couldn't happen. Why did the Lord waste time and space talking about something that just couldn't possibly happen? Did you notice how he illustrated taking away a branch that had no connection with the vine? No. Mr. Bogard, I won't have any chance to reply, but I do wish in your last speech you would show me how to take away one of those branches that is not connected with the vine. Just show me how to take a branch away from a vine that has no connection with it. I would just like to see —even though I won't have any chance to reply to it, I would like to see how you do it.

"Well," but he said, "the branch has to bear fruit; and if the branch fails to bear fruit, then the Lord's to blame for it because he didn't furnish the power." And that takes away all of man's responsibility after conversion. After a man is converted he is not responsible for anything he does. Whatever he does, he does what the Lord *forces* him to do. And, therefore, he has no responsibility whatsoever. I guess that's why he can't fall from grace.

"Yes," he says, "I'll concede that a child of God can lie and steal and get drunk." You will? Why, you turned right around before you got through and said that Free Will Baptist liar over there proved he hadn't ever been saved, because he lied. Now, the very fact that he lied proves he had never been saved, you said. But now you say a child of God can lie. And a child of God can steal. And a child of God can get drunk. Well, if a child of God can lie and steal and get drunk, then how do you know that that Free Will Baptist had never been saved just because he lied? You say a child of God can do it. Bogard can make the most blunders of any man that I have ever seen who has had as many debates as Mr. Bogard has had. And the more debates he has the more blunders evidently he'll make.

But he said, "You failed to take into consideration Psalm 37:24 that says "the steps of a good man are ordered by the Lord: and he delighteth in his way. Though he fall, he shall not be utterly cast down: for the Lord upholdeth him with his hand." And you failed, Mr. Bogard, to read far enough to find in verse 27 that the promise of "dwelling forevermore" was to the man who would "do good" and "depart from evil." The 27th verse—just following that—shows the promise is to the man who "departs from evil" and "does good." He's the man that will "dwell for ever more." Mr. Bogard says, "No, he'll dwell forever more whether he does good or not."

"Yes," he says, "children of God can murder. David murdered, but he didn't got to hell." Well, did David die a murderer? Did David die in the act of murder? That's the thing I'm talking about. Certainly, a man who murders can repent of his crime and get forgiveness for it and not go to hell because he murdered. But did David die as a murderer? Now, Mr. Bogard, I have been begging you to tell me if it is possible for a child of God to die while he is drunk and in the act of murder. And you haven't said a word about it. I won't have any chance to reply, but I do wish you would tell us in your last speech whether it is possible for a child of God to die drunk or whether he can die in the act of murder. You say he can murder and get drunk. *Can he die in those acts?* Well, he said yesterday—I believe it was yesterday—that he "wouldn't stay drunk." Well, he'll have to stay drunk a while. If he got drunk, he would have to stay drunk a while—at least fifteen minutes. Well, if he stayed drunk just fifteen minutes, would it be possible to kill him during that fifteen minutes? If a railroad locomotive should run over him during that fifteen minutes that he is drunk, would it kill him? Would it be possible for him to die during the time he is drunk? Now, you haven't said one word about that, and I have been begging you ever since I introduced it to tell us something about it.

But he said, "The Lord will chasten every son whom he receiveth,"—the passage in Heb. 12. What does he chasten them for, Mr. Bogard? In the answers to these questions which I have given you prior to this time, you said that any man that is a child of God cannot possibly sin. You said that after conversion all the sin is committed by the outer man.

Now, I want to know what the Lord chastens for. Which man does he chasten—the inner man or the outer man? Well, if he chastens the inner man, he chastens him for what he didn't do, because Mr. Bogard says he can't possibly sin. Certainly, then, he isn't chastening the inner man. And if he chastens the outer man, and doesn't chasten the inner man, then the inner man is without chastisement. But the passage says, "If ye are without chastisement—then are ye bastards and not sons." Verse 8. And that proves the inner man is a bastard and not a son—if the Lord doesn't chasten him. But if the Lord does chasten the inner man, then the Lord chastens him for what he has never done but for what the outer man has done. There we have it.

Psalm 89. "He'll visit them with stripes." Well, but if the man *dies in the act of murder* and *dies while he is drunk,* when will he get his stripes? Luke 12 shows, which I gave awhile ago—incidentally, that's one of the passages he didn't even refer to—upon which I based a major argument. Luke 12:45 and 46. Jesus said that that servant who would say, "My Lord delays his coming; and begins to beat his menservants and maidens, and to eat and drink, and to be drunken. The Lord of that servant will come at a time that he is not aware, and will cut him asunder, and appoint him his portion with the unbelievers." And he went right on to say the "servant that knew his Lord's will, and prepared not himself, shall be beaten with many stripes." Referring to the day of judgment—so there'll be some stripes at the judgment day, Mr. Bogard. But this man wasn't an unbeliever, because he is used in contrast with the unbeliever.

Then, as we go along, I am wondering about this. Psalm 89 said he would visit them with stripes. But you gave Romans 4 to prove that the Lord didn't impute sin to them—the Lord doesn't charge sin against the child of God anymore. Well, then, why does he visit them with stripes? If their sins are not charged against them, why does the Lord whip them for it? Why does the Lord chasten them if their sins are not charged against them, Mr. Bogard? More and more and more Mr. Bogard becomes confused.

He came to Gal. 5 and verse 4 about "falling from grace." "Whosoever of you are justified by the law; ye are fallen from grace." Yes, but he said the same chapter said that "no man is justified by the law." Read it in the Revised Version. Gal. 5:4. "Ye who would be justified by the law; ye are fallen away from grace." All right, that simply shows if a man *makes an effort* to be justified by the law, he is fallen from grace. Can a man make an effort to do it, Mr. Bogard? If you "would be"—the Revised Version says. You'll accept the Revised Version reading, won't you? *Will you?* All right, if "*you would be* justified —you are fallen from grace." "If you would be justified by the law." And so *if a man seeks to be justified* by the law, Paul said he is "fallen from grace."

Who were these anyway? They were men who had been made free. I want to show you just what the passage says. Galatians, the fifth chapter. I want to begin reading with the first verse to show you just who these men were. "Stand fast therefore in the liberty wherewith Christ hath made us free." These are free men in Christ—in the liberty of Jesus Christ. "Stand fast therefore in the liberty wherewith Christ hath made us free, and be not entangled again with the yoke of bondage. Behold, I Paul say unto you, that if ye be circumcised, Christ shall profit you nothing. For I testify again to every man that is circumcised, that he is a debtor to do the whole law. Christ is become of no effect unto you, whosoever of you are justified by the law; ye are fallen from grace." Or as the Revised Version reads, "Whosoever *would be* justified by the law; ye are fallen away from grace." Who are these men? Men that stood in the liberty of Jesus Christ—free men in Christ—men who had been made free —saved men. And yet Christ may "become of no effect" unto them, and they "are fallen from grace."

CHART NO. 10
To tree of life
To enter the city

I was really amused at how my opponent dealt with this argument here—the tree of life and the city. Our robes must be washed to give us a right to the tree of life. "Blessed are they that do his commandments," the King James Version says, "that they may have right to the tree of life." The Revised Version reads, "Blessed are they that wash their robes that they may have the right to the tree of life, and may enter in by the gates into the city." All right, who has the right to the tree of life? Only those whose robes have been washed, Mr. Bogard. They are the only ones who even have a right to the tree of life. You can't forfeit something you don't have. He talked about the Indian forfeiting his right to land in Oklahoma. Yes, but if he never had the right to that—if he wasn't an Indian—he couldn't forfeit it, Mr. Bogard. And the man whose robes have not been washed has no right to it—he doesn't have any right to forfeit until his robes are washed, for the passage says, "Blessed are they that wash their robes that *they may have* the right to the tree of life." Not because they already have the right, but that "they may have the right." And so the man doesn't have the right to the tree of life *until his robes are washed.* He has no right to the tree of life to forfeit until he is saved. How is a man who has never been saved —who has no right to the tree of life and no right to enter that city—going to forfeit that right when he never had any? You haven't touched the argument, Mr. Bogard. This audience can see it, and you see it too.

Gal. 3:27. The word "gar." He said, "That 'gar' is a conjunction, but you said it is a preposition." Well, if I said it's a preposition, it was a slip of the tongue. I certainly know conjunctions from prepositions, Mr. Bogard. Maybe I said "preposition." I have had prepositions on my mind because I've been dealing with Acts 2:38. Maybe I said "preposition"—I don't know. If the record says I did, all right, but it was a slip of the tongue if I said it. I certainly know the difference between a conjunction and a preposition, Mr. Bogard. But the lexicons say that word "gar," though it is a conjunction, means "to introduce a reason." If you have Thayer, turn to it there, and hand it up here and I'll read it. We'll see whether Thayer says it or not. He's a scholar. If you have it there, open it and turn to where he says "gar." Hand it up to me and I'll read it, and we'll see whether he says that "gar," a conjunction, can mean "to introduce a reason" or not. You said it doesn't do it. *Thayer says it does.* And if you deny it, I'll call time and have them to hold my time, and I'll go out to my car and I'll get Thayer, and I'll prove it. I don't have it in my grip, but I do have it in my car.

Then back to Cornelius. His prayer was heard before he heard the preaching. Well, I have an idea his prayer was heard before he heard the preaching, but I have an idea God "heard" what Bogard said awhile ago about "high water and something," but that doesn't mean what Bogard might think it means. The mere fact that God heard his prayer doesn't mean that God answered his prayer and saved him in answer to prayer. That's an entirely different thing, Mr. Bogard.

He came to Noah. He said, "Porter said that Noah did not get saved by water but he got saved from the water." No, Porter didn't say that. Porter said that Noah was saved *by the water* in the sense that he was borne on the water in the ark and saved *from the destruction* which the water wrought—the destruction which the flood brought upon the rest of mankind. He was saved *from* that death, *in* the ark and *by* the water. That's the salvation that is being talked about—the salvation from that death that the others suffered. And the water and the ark saved him from that. *And he wasn't saved with that salvation before he got into the ark,* Mr. Bogard. That was the salvation that Peter was talking about, and that salvation from death on the part of Noah in the ark and by the water is a type of our salvation today. One is a true likeness of the other, and it doesn't have a thing to do about when Noah became a child of God. You're side-stepping the issue entirely, and you're getting entirely away from what the passage talks about.

He made just a little stab at the dog and the sow. I left him room to say something. In 2 Peter 2:20,21 Peter said, "If after they have escaped the pollutions of the world through the knowledge of the Lord and Savior Jesus Christ, they are again entangled therein, and overcome, the latter end is worse with them than the beginning. For it had been better for them not to have known the way of righteousness, than, after they have known it, to turn from the holy commandment delivered unto them." I was really amused at my opponent. This afternoon, you know, when I was discussing baptism, he didn't have time to fool with it. He wanted to discuss something else. And tonight when I got to discussing the possibility of apostasy, he didn't have time to fool with that—he wanted to go back and discuss baptism. So he almost skipped the arguments I gave, made a little stab here and there, and passed them by and went back and talked about the subject we discussed this afternoon. Therefore, it forces me back to reply to the things that he said. But when I was discussing baptism, he wanted to talk about something else; and now when I am talking about the possibility of apostasy, he wants to talk about baptism. Well, I'll take care of him, regardless of where he goes. "But it happened unto them," the passage says, "according to the true proverb. The dog is turned to his own vomit again; and the sow that was washed to her wallowing in the mire." He said, "Yes, but it was still the old sow and still the old dog. If you had changed the nature, they wouldn't have done that." Yes, Mr .Bogard, but you say that the nature is not changed in conversion. Don't forget that, Mr. Bogard. Here's the graft (writing on the board) and over here is the tree.

CHART NO. 6

Graft — Tree

My opponent has been up a tree for several days on that thing. He said the graft is the word of God. That graft had to be put into the tree, and it took the Holy Holy Spirit to put it in. Well, according to Bogard, the Holy Spirit doesn't put it in. According to him the Holy Spirit goes along to get the tree ready, and then steps aside and lets the word get in—lets the graft get in. He says the Holy Spirit prepares the tree to receive the graft. That's his argument—that's his doctrine.

But notice this. I have been begging him to tell me what the tree is. I first put "stump" up there. I had him treed on a stump for a good long while, and he said that he didn't mean "stump"—but that he meant "tree." So now he is stumped up the tree. And he never has been able to come back and say a word about it. What does the tree represent? The graft is the word of God. The tree is what? In his printed debates he has said it is the heart or soul. And you say that the tree is not changed when the graft is put into it. Therefore, the heart or the soul is not changed—the old nature is just the same. The old sinful nature of the heart is not in any way changed when a man is converted. And so, of course, the sow went back to her wallowing in the mire—she was still a sow. And the dog went back because he was still a dog. So the man still has the old depraved nature that he had before, according to Bogard, even of his heart. And so I guess he went back because his nature wasn't changed.

Then he came to just a few passages. About the woman —"Thy faith hath saved thee." And the thief on the cross and Zacchaeus. And he insisted that these were saved without baptism. There was nothing said about baptism. Well, I can find many passages that declare that men were saved and nothing said about baptism. He might as well to have gone to Abraham, Isaac and Jacob, as far as that is concerned. But the simple fact is that this great commission that concerns him and me today was not given when these things occurred, as the thief on the cross, the woman and Zacchaeus—that great commission had not even been given that embraces every creature in all the world today.

"Why didn't he bring up John 3:5?" Well, there are a lot of Scriptures that I could have brought up, but I couldn't bring them all up in one session. I just gave one session to the discussion of baptism. I certainly couldn't bring them all up in one session. If I had brought up any more, there would have just been that many more that you wouldn't have paid any attention to. And you didn't even get to a lot of those that I did bring up. So why bring up any more?

Finally, he came back to the believer and the lover again—the believer is born of God and the man who loves is born of God. And I showed, according to Bogard, that the man is saved unconditionally. He comes back and denies that, but that doesn't set aside the argument. For the simple fact that he says if a man loves God, he is born of God. "That doesn't mean that he loves to be born, or that he loves God in order to be born, but it means that love is an evidence that he is already born." Well, if that statement, "he that loveth God is born of God," means that he is already born, then the parallel statement, "he that believeth on Christ is born of God," means that belief is an evidence that he is already born. So he was born before he believes—he was born before he loves. That gets him back on the old Hardshell position—salvation without any conditions whatsoever.

He said, "Porter forgot about Rom. 8:28." "All things work together for good to them that love the Lord." And Bogard makes that mean the man's sins. Paul had no reference to the sins of man. He did not mean that man's sins would work out for his good when he said, "All things work together for good to them that love God." 1 John 5:3 says, "This is the love of God that we keep his commandments." The man who turns to sin, becomes drunk and turns to be a liar, a thief and a murderer, is not keeping God's commandments, Mr. Bogard, and *the promise is not to him.* But it is to a man who "loves God," to a man who keeps God's commandments. If a man keeps God's commandments, then all the surrounding circumstances will work out for his good, but it doesn't mean that if a man violates God's commandments, if he turns to sin, that that thing is going to work out for his good. If it does, then if Mr. Bogard should elope with some sixteen year old girl, that thing would work out for his good. I don't believe Bogard is going to stand on a thing of that kind.

Regarding Sam Morris, he said, "I indorse Sam Morris if I know what he means." Well, I have an idea that he meant what he said. I just feel sure that he meant what he said. And Morris said, "That all the sins we may commit from idolatry to murder will not make us in any more danger." You understand that, don't you, Mr. Bogard? Do you indorse that? I think you can understand what that means, and I told you that's Baptist doctrine. I want to picture Baptist doctrine to you again as I did before—just what the thing means.

Before conversion, according to Baptist doctrine, (you've heard it throughout these four days), everything a man does is a sin. If he tells the truth, it's a sin, and he will die and go to hell. But after he is converted he can tell a lie and go to heaven—he can die with a lie on his lips. Before conversion, if a man pays his debts, it's a sin; he'll die and go to hell. After conversion, if he fails to meet his obligations and beats every body out of everything he owes him, cheats him in every way possible, he'll still go to heaven. Before conversion, if he stays sober, it's a sin—he'll die and go to hell. But after he is converted, he can get drunk and stay drunk the rest of his life, but he'll die and go to heaven. Before conversion, if he loves his wife, it's a sin. After conversion, he can love every other man's wife and go to heaven. That's Baptist doctrine.

Then another thing—he said, "I'm not holding on to God." We sang that song about "Hold to God's Unchanging Hand." He says, "I'm not holding on to God—God is holding me." It looks like he lets his grip slip then if you fall and sin. "Though he fall, he shall not be utterly cast down." What is the matter? Did God's grip fail somehow and let you slip a little bit? But he finally got hold of you before you went too far? "God's holding me," Mr. Bogard said, "I'm not holding him." Well, that's the difference between you and Paul. I turn to Hebrews, the 6th chapter and verse 18—beginning with verse 17. "Wherein God, willing more abundantly to show unto the heirs of promise the immutability of his counsel, confirmed it by an oath: that by two immutable things, in which it was impossible for God to lie, we might have a strong consolation, who have fled for refuge to *lay hold* upon the hope set before us." Thus Paul said they had fled for refuge to *lay hold* on the hope. Bogard says, "I didn't lay hold on it—God laid hold on me; and I'm not holding to it—God's holding me." Well, that's between you and Paul.

Then to Cornelius. "As he began to speak." He mentioned the fact that Cornelius received the Holy Spirit, and he said he was already saved before he received the Spirit. I showed that before and I'm going to show it again. We'll let this mark the time when the Holy Spirit fell (Marks on the board). Bogard says he was already saved before the Spirit fell here (pointing to mark on the board). But Peter said in Acts 11:15: "As I began to speak the Spirit fell." All right, he was saved before the Spirit fell, but the Spirit fell "as he began to speak." Therefore he was saved before Peter "began to speak." And if he was saved before Peter "began to speak," then he was saved without faith, Mr. Bogard. Down goes your theory on it.

Back to "brother Saul." And he said he received the Holy Spirit before he was baptized, but the record doesn't say a word about it. I won't have time to discuss that because I'll have no further reply, but there is no passage that says he received the Holy Spirit before he was baptized.

Then to Matt. 3:11—he says, "What did he say about that 'eis'?" Why, I showed that it is the same thing in Acts 11:18. You said "eis—unto repentance" is the same thing in Acts 2:38. Well, it's the same thing in Acts 11:18—"repentance unto life." If that proves remission of sins before baptism, then it proves life before repentance, because it's the same word in both passages. That's what I said, and the record will show it.

Then those "begotten by Paul." He baptized a few. Bogard said that word "begotten" is the same word in the Greek that is used for "born." Yes, Mr. Bogard, and it is the same word that is used for "born" when it refers to the fleshly birth too. But the "begetting" in the fleshly relationship and the "birth" is not the same, though it is the same word used—in the Greek. That replies to what he said.

I have how much—about three minutes? Now, that brings us down to about the close of my part of this discussion. Mr. Bogard will come up in his last speech and he is going to have a great deal to say about this thing and that thing. He is going back and rehash a lot of stuff instead of meeting these arguments that I have brought out tonight. He is going to say, "Why, suppose it did happen on Pentecost, what good will that do him?" Well, suppose the church was established during the personal ministry of Christ, what good will that do Bogard? When my friend comes up and brings those things and talks about "what good will that do him—he can't back up and hitch on," I just want this audience to look up here at this passage.

CHART NO. 1-A

Church of Christ	Baptist Church
Churches of Christ	Baptist Churches
— Rom. 16:16	— Religious Encyclopedia Page 796

I believe in order to make it very simple for you, I am going to erase everything but that, so you'll be sure to see it. Look up here at this passage that says, "The churches of Christ salute you." And I don't have to find it in the singular number. If I find it in the plural number, it is just as well, because anybody knows who knows anything at all that if "churches of Christ" refers to a number of them, that "church of Christ" would refer to one of them, and that you can't have the plural without having the singular in that case. So if he comes up and says "the houses of Damascus-- you couldn't have a house, you couldn't have a singular number," you know better than that. Look over on this side and see the reference Mr. Bogard has where he can hook on. I have one to his nothing. He has neither of the terms he uses in the Bible, but we have the plural number here. It certainly embraces the singular—"the churches of Christ salute you." Oh, how much my friend would give if somewhere in God's Book he could just read a passage that says, "The Baptist churches salute you." Or just anything about the Baptist Churches. It's not there. I showed you from the history that the term "Baptist" when used back in history beyond that, as his own historians say, simply referred to those who practiced baptism by immersion and believed in believers' baptism, regardless of what other things they held. And to say that a man was a "baptist" in history proved nothing more than that. All right. And now let Mr. Bogard bring up and show his connection, where he can hitch on, in God's Book. No need to trace your histories--- no need to say "what good will that do you"—just put your reference up here and let it do you some good. That's the fact. The fact is it won't do you any good, regardless of where it was established, because you can't find the reference that mentions the "Baptist Church" as a local congregation, or "Baptist Churches" as local congregations, or

"Baptist Church" or "Baptist Churches" in the general sense anywhere—with any indication, with any meaning whatsoever. It's not in God's Book, and Mr. Bogard knows it's not in God's Book. I don't have to find the singular if I can find the plural, and he wouldn't have to find the singular if he could find the plural. He wouldn't have to find the plural if he could find the singular. Let him find either of them and I'll take both of them. *But he can't do it. We have* this plural number. We don't have to find the singular if we have the plural, because the plural comprehends the singular. You couldn't have a dozen "churches of Christ" without having one to save your life. But he'll never find it over here (pointing to other side of the board). So when he makes that final palaver about all of that, why, you just look up here at this line and see the reference on there. "Religious Encyclopedia, Page 796," is the only place he has found to hook on. And if he can find any other place, that mentions either "Baptist Church" or Baptist Churches" let him erase this and put it there. Though I won't have any chance to reply, I am willing for him to erase this and put a Scriptural reference there in his final speech. I thank you, Ladies and Gentlemen.

Fourth Day

BOGARD'S EIGHTH NEGATIVE

Gentlemen Moderators, Ladies and Gentlemen:

I will mention a few things before I begin my replication, bringing in all the things we have learned in this debate.

The vine and the branches in the 15th chapter of John, my friend says, teaches apostasy. If it does, it teaches unconditional salvation to start with, and it teaches that nobody falls from grace except Christ, the vine, falls down on the job and fails to furnish the power for the branch to bring forth fruit. That is perfectly evident. What does the vine and the branches teach? Simply this: *that all fruit bearing must be credited to the Lord Jesus Christ.* "I am the vine," furnishing the power to bring forth fruit, which cuts out every man who is not in Christ bringing forth any fruit whatever. That cuts out salvation by works. If you are going to bring forth any fruit, do any good works, you have got to be in connection with Jesus Christ. That is the one central thought, and that is all a parable is ever supposed to teach. If you want to make it go on all fours and get apostasy in it, then I will force you into unconditional salvation, for this branch here did not put itself into the vine. It had nothing to do with it. It did not even get its own consent to get in. It was there before it knew anything about it, and that is Hardshellism as sure as you are born. If it ever gets out, it has got to quit bearing fruit. How can it ever quit bearing fruit? It will not do it unless the vine fails to furnish the power to make the fruit. The branch is not responsible for bearing fruit. The branch cannot bear fruit of itself. It has got to be done by the power of the vine. That makes Christ the cause for every one who falls from grace, if anybody falls from grace.

Now come to my friend's "suppose you die." If - if - if - "suppose you die in sin." Well, sir, here would be two or three things. If a man dies in gross sin he goes to hell. That is number one. Number two is that if he does that he has been utterly cast down, and that flatly contradicts the Bible which says "he shall not be utterly cast down." Then, another thing would happen—God's word would fail where it says, "We know that all things work together for good to them that love God." Something evidently worked that was not for good if he fell from grace, died and went to hell.

Now, note the words of that last passage. To me it is the most wonderful passage in the Bible. Wake me up at midnight, no matter how sound asleep I am, and ask me, "What is your favorite passage of Scripture?" I would say, "Romans 8:28." "We know that *all things work together for good* to them that love God, to them who are called according to his purpose." If "all things work together for good to them that love God," well, I love God. That makes everything work for my good, everything. Not nearly everything, not 999 things out of a thousand, but all things—all things on earth, all things in heaven, all things in hell, including the devil himself.

But somebody says, "How can the devil work for good?" Let me show you, friend. The devil does not intend any good, but his devilish work is overruled for good. For instance, you could never have been saved if it were not for the devil. Why? You could not have been saved without the crucifixion of the Lord Jesus Christ, could you? Well, would good men have put Christ to death? No. Peter said, "Ye with wicked hands crucified the Lord." So the devil had the Lord crucified. The devil was intending to put the Lord out of business, but the very thing he did put the Lord into business, rather than put Him out. When the devil had Him persecuted, and finally tried and condemned, and later nailed Him to the cross, I can imagine I can hear the devil chuckle, "I have got Him now." And when he got Him in Joseph's new tomb, and sealed up with a Roman guard over Him, I can hear the devil, in my mind, chuckling, "I have got Him now." But He was doing the very thing that Jesus Christ came into the world to do and used the devil to carry out that purpose. And so when Christ arose from the dead the work of the devil was overruled for our good. And I feel like sometimes turning around and saying, "Thank you, Mr. Devil. I could not have been saved if it had not been for you. Christ would not have been crucified if it had not been for you. And if Christ had not been crucified, I could not have been saved." The very work of the devil is overruled for our good, or else "all things do not work together for good to them that love God." If that is true, falling from grace is out of the question, for that could *not* be for our good.

Now my friend comes to David. He said, "Did David die in the act of murder?" No, sir, because the Bible plainly says that they "shall not be utterly cast down." If he had died a murderer, he would have gone to hell. That is true. But what else would have happened? The failure of God's word to be true that "he shall not utterly be cast down." To fall from grace means to be "utterly cast down." When David sinned he suffered. He *sinned* in the *flesh* and *was punished* in the *flesh*. And war was brought on him, and bloodshed was brought unto his people, among his people. He suffered, suffered terribly, suffered agony. He said, "My soul got hold on hell." A little hell here on earth for him, and all of that. He was punished in the flesh for the sins of the flesh, for "*whom the Lord loveth, he chasteneth*, and scourgeth every son whom he received."

The 89th Psalm, as I just quoted a while ago, said, "If his children forsake his law, and obey not his commandments, I will let them die and go to hell, be utterly cast down." *No*. But, "I will visit their transgression with the rod and their iniquity with stripes but *I will not suffer my loving kindness to fail.*" That answers absolutely all his "ifs" and "ifs" and "ifs" and "what if they do this," and "what if they do that." If they do enough to send them to hell, you flatly contradict the word of God.

Then, in the 51st Psalm, as I quoted in my other speech, where David was praying for forgiveness, he said, "Against thee, thee only, have I sinned, and done this evil in thy sight.' Then he said, "Take not thy Holy Spirit from me." He had not lost the Spirit. I heard a preacher say once that "when sin comes into the front door, the Holy Spirit will go out at the back door." That is the very time we need the Holy Spirit most. Otherwise, we would not need Him at all. So when I sin I have the presence of the Holy Spirit to pick me up and "I shall not be utterly cast down, for *the Lord upholdeth me* with his hand."

Then my friend said, "Before we are saved, according to Baptist doctrine, all we do is a sin." That is correct: Now, let me give you the Scripture that he has utterly failed to answer up to this very minute, though it was brought in the very first day of the debate. I Cor. 10:30, 31. "Whether ye eat, or drink, or whatsoever you do, do all for the glory of God." *Do all.* Now, if you pay your debts, and do not do it for the glory of God, *the sin element is that you left the glory of God out.* Paying your debts is all right, but the sin element comes in by not doing it for the glory of God. If you eat—"whether you eat or drink or whatsoever you do"—eating is sin unless you do it for the glory of God. Taking a drink of water—I took it a while ago for the glory of God. Anything you do and leave God out, you are sinning. *The best deed of your life is a sin unless you do it for the glory of God.* And that shows that everything an unsaved man does is sin. The very best thing he can do is sin. Very well.

Now, he said, "After you have been saved, according to Baptist doctrine, nothing you do is sin." Well, who said that? Not Ben M. Bogard. No Baptist. Certainly we sin. And David said, "I have sinned against thee" and asked for forgiveness and said, "Restore unto me the joy of thy salvation." Certainly we sin, but we shall not so sin as to fall from grace and be lost and go to hell.

He read from Hebrews, the 6th chapter, about that hope—"lay hold on the hope set before us." I made the remark that I did not hold to God; God held me. If he did not quote this Scripture to say I was holding God! I laid hold on the hope, and God holds me, for it said "this hope is both sure and steadfast." My friend says it is not sure. A thing that is sure does not have any element of doubt in it. It is *"both sure and steadfast."* And if there is any possibility of losing that hope, then undoubtedly it is not sure and steadfast. That complements my friend's speech.

And now I am going to make a replication of all that has gone before. Beginning back yonder the very first day I showed the church began, "beginning from the baptism of John." In Acts 1:21 it says a company accompanied the Lord Jesus "all the time he went in and out among us, beginning from the baptism of John." Then in Mark 13 I showed that He had that company that He called His house and gave His servants authority and a work to do. And then He said, "Watch, for ye know not when the master of the house returneth." There He promised to come back to that house that He left. He gave them authority and a work to do, and then that company remained there till they received the power from on high. They had to be there or they could not have remained there. And they got that power on the day of Pentecost. And in I Tim. 3:15 Paul said that house is "the church of God, the pillar and the ground of the truth." That church was to tarry there to receive the power that was to come, and all that is as clear as can be.

Now, "coming *with* power" means "coming *into* power" for that is the very word used. "Coming into power." He seems to think the power is like a man here, and the kingdom is like another man, and the two walk in together—come together. Such sophistry as that! It certainly does not mean that or anything like it.

Now, we come to the name question. We have settled that forever and always. My friend says he finds it in the plural. He does not find any such thing in the plural. He finds that the churches belong to the Lord there in the plural, but not their name. He got that telegram from Harding College. It said that in "the churches of Christ salute you," that "Christ is in the genitive singular." That means the possessive case. What did Christ possess? He possessed the churches. He owns the churches, but what was their name? He said I cannot find "Baptist Church" in any sense, in the plural or singular. I have told you over and over again, I think this is about the sixteenth time, *you cannot find the name of the church in the Bible at all—anybody's name.* The Lord described the church and thought we would have sense enough to understand what it was when we saw it. He did not name it here; He said He owned it. "The Churches of Christ salute you." The churches that belong to Christ salute you. Now, you cannot find "The Church of Christ" in the Bible as a name. You cannot find it any other way. You cannot find "Churches of Christ" as a name. And I have defied him to do it, and I will quit the debate right now and cut my speech off right now, if you will tell me the verse of

Scripture that says "The Church of Christ." It is not there. I will quit the debate right now, walk out, and not finish the speech if you will hand me up the Scripture that names any local congregation in the Bible "Churches of Christ," any one. The church at Colosse, the church at Thessalonica, the seven churches of Asia—not one single time are they called "Churches of Christ." The expression here, "the churches of Christ," is no more the name than that in the 4th verse that says "the churches of the Gentiles." Is that the name? So he utterly whipped on the name. Completely whipped. You have been harping and harping and harping about the name—the name—the name. The Bible has left the church nameless, but gave the description that anybody can tell what it is by reading the description. If He had given a name, then every heretical sect on earth could have stolen that name and said, "We are it." But when the Lord gave a description of the church, then they cannot assume it unless they prove by the marks and characteristics of the Bible that the church they are in is the one found in the Bible.

Now, he argued two days that the name was "The Church of Christ." And he got the telegram from Harding College that said it was the possessive case, genitive case that denoted possession in it, and he came back today and said, "I have been saying it denoted possession all the time." He argued two days and gave diagrams on the board for it, and used a lot of time discussing grammar to prove it was a name. Now, you come and say *it just simply means possession*, ownership, like "the dogs of Johnson." (Laughter) "Dogs of Johnson." What are the names of those? He said he would not know what the names were if he had not been told. Neither would I know what the names of these churches are unless we are told, and the Bible does not tell. There you are—blank. You have been harping around about the name, and now you cannot find the name of the church in the Bible at all—either in the plural or singular. You find possession in the plural but not the name. It is nowhere called "The Church of Christ."

Now, coming to another feature. We have learned a whole lot going along. About the "ruling elders," they have "ruling elders"—this so-called Church of Christ. "Ruling elders." That means a bunch of men who control the church, have authority over the church. Matt. 20:25, 26 says, "The princes among the Gentiles exercise dominion over them, and they that are great exercise authority upon them, but it shall not be so among you." There must be *nobody in authority* over the church of the church of the Lord Jesus Christ. What does it mean then by "the elders that rule well"? Elders that lead well—that teach well—instruct well, and not by authority. So we have gained a wonderful headway on that statement.

Now I am coming down to what we argued today on baptism. My friend dies hard on it, but die he must. Acts 2:38, "Repent and be baptized every one of you in the name of Jesus Christ for the remission of sins." He says that means "in order to the remission of sins." In making that contention, and making that statement, he flatly contradicts the two greatest Greek scholars on God's green earth or that ever did live on God's green earth.

Thayer, who wrote the lexicon that is used in all the colleges, says that "eis" when used to denote position or location means *"into,"* and that "eis" when used to denote relationship means *"with reference to."* Now, when you are to become a Christian that changes your relation. It does not change your location. You still live right where you did before. Very well, then. "Repent and be baptized every one of you with reference to the remission of your sins." That is exactly what it means.

And then coming to the great grammarian, Dr. A. T. Robertson, whose grammar is used in all the colleges where the Bible is taught at all, he says that since salvation comes at the end of repentance—we *repent unto life*— therefore, in this passage, "baptized for the remission of sins" means "baptized upon the *basis of the remission* of your sins."

Now when he gets his position proved, if he thinks he has got it proved, he flatly contradicts the scholarship of the world, the greatest scholars on earth, Thayer and Robertson, the ones that are used in all the Colleges. But here comes Mr. Porter and says, "I know more than those great scholars. I know more than the man who wrote the lexicon. I know more than the man who wrote the great Greek grammar. I will tell you it means 'in order to'." These men both say it does not mean any such thing. What does the word "for" mean? That is the only question. As we "repented unto life," got that, then what does "for" mean? "Repent and be baptized every one of you in the name of Jesus Christ upon the basis of the remission of your sins" or "with reference to the remission of your sins," or something like that, not "in order to" the remission of sins. That is precisely what it means. Like when a man goes to the penitentiary *"for"* murder, did he go there *"in order to"* murder? Certainly not. He went there because he had murdered. And he goes to the electric chair "for" murder. "In order to" murder? Certainly not, but because he had murdered, or *with reference to the murder* he already has done. There it is in English and in Greek. So he has got nothing on that.

Gal. 3:27. "Put ye on the Lord Jesus Christ"—exactly the same expression there is in Rom. 13:14 where the church at Rome, Christian people, baptized people, already saved, already in the church, were told to "put ye on the Lord Jesus Christ." If it means to become a Christian when you put on the Lord Jesus Christ, then those Romans who were already Christians were to become Christians by putting on the Lord Jesus Christ. That is perfectly absurd. So it means to imitate Christ. How are you going to imitate Christ? By doing what Christ did. Why was Christ baptized? To manifest the fact that He was the Son of God. That is exactly what John said. "He sent me to baptize to manifest him to Israel." So then Christ was already the Son of God, baptized to show Himself to be the Son of God. And if I imitate Him—the greek word is "enduo"; you never have disputed it; it means to imitate—I am baptized in order to show that I am the son of God. Was Jesus Christ baptized to make Him become the Son of God? No. Well, I was not baptized to make me become the son of God. And if I imitate Jesus Christ I am baptized for the *very same reason* that Jesus Christ was. He was baptized to *manifest* Himself as the Son of God, and I was baptized to *manifest* myself as the son of God.

Rom. 6:1-4 speaks in the very same sort of language. "As many as have been baptized into Jesus have been baptized into his death." Now, if that means "into" in the literal sense, can you actually go "into Christ" *literally?* You know that is not so. It is always *relatively.* "As many as have been baptized into Jesus Christ have been baptized into his death." What does that mean? The Greek preposition "e-i-s, eis," according to Thayer and according to Robertson, the two greatest Greek scholars on earth, means *"with reference to."* How do I know what these words mean? Am I a native Greek? No, I know very little about it. How do I know? I get it out of the book. What book? The book that is used in the colleges. What book is used in the colleges? Thayer's Greek Lexicon and Robertson's great Greek Grammar. And they say that "eis" there means "with reference to" or "upon the basis of." So then "as many as have been baptized into Jesus Christ have been baptized into his death." "As many as have been *baptized with reference to Jesus Christ* have been *baptized with reference to his death."*

How does baptism refer to the death, burial and resurrection of Jesus Christ? What is the gospel? The fifteenth chapter of I Corinthians says that the gospel is the death, burial and resurrection of Jesus Christ. How does baptism refer to it? "We are buried with him by baptism—and like as Christ is raised up from the dead to the glory of the Father." We are buried with Him, with reference to Him. Here is a picture of the way by which we are saved. We are saved by the gospel and have baptism *as a picture of that.* I Pet. 3:21 says, "The like figure whereunto even baptism doth also now save us." A like figure. What figure? Like Noah was saved. How was he saved? He was saved before the water came. And as a similiar figure, a like figure, we are saved exactly the same way. We know that Noah was not saved—did not become a child of God—by the water. Neither are we. All right.

Now, coming to I Cor. 4:15. "I have begotten you by the gospel." Paul said he had "begotten" those Corinthians by the gospel. And that word "begotten" is the very same word that is used to express the new birth. And he correctly said it is the very same word that expresses our *coming into life naturally.* When a child is "begotten" it has *all* the life it is ever going to have. Any doctor will tell you so. And it does not come to life by any external birth, but when a child is begotten the life is in that child in his mother's womb, and if you kill that child in the mother's womb, they will put you in the penitentiary, or hang you. Everybody knows that. So "I brought you into life by the gospel." How did I bring into life? "By the gospel." Very well. But I did not baptize any of you. There you are. That plainly shows that *baptism is not necessary to salvation.*

Now, John 3:5. I brought it up yesterday or day before. My friend barely referred to it—afraid of it—walked away from it. But they preach it when there is nobody here to meet them. *They preach John 3:5 as meaning baptism* when there is nobody there to correct them, nobody to expose their heresy. They preach that John 3:5 means baptism, that you have got to be baptized to be saved. If so, you have got the plan of salvation before Pentecost. Therefore, you have the gospel preached before Pentecost. Now, you say it was not preached till Pentecost, but if John 3:5 is the gospel, the plan of salvation, you have it *before Pentecost.*

And let me show you what else you have got. Now, let me read to you. If the word "baptize" means "born again," and "born again" means "baptize," let us put the meaning of the word then instead of the word itself. Jesus said, "Verily, I say unto you, Except a man be baptized again, he cannot see the kingdom of God." Nicodemus said, "How can a man be *baptized* when he is old? Can he enter a second time into his mother's womb and be *baptized?* Jesus answered, Verily, verily, I say unto thee, Except a man be *baptized* of of water and *baptized* of the Spirit, he cannot enter the kingdom of God. That which is *baptized* of the flesh is flesh; and that which is *baptized* of the Spirit is spirit. Marvel not that I said unto thee, Ye must be *baptized* again." If the word "born" means "baptize" then before God, I will run you into Spirit baptism and turn you over to the Holy Rollers—Holy Ghost baptism. (Laughter)

And besides that, it is so absurd. No wonder he did not bring it up. No wonder he did not use it to try to prove his baptismal salvation. Because he knew exactly what I would do for him. But inasmuch as we both have referred to it,

I have a perfect right to make this explanation, and I think all of you see just where we are.

Now, he said I would ask the question: "What good would it do you?" I do ask that now in the closing part of my speech. Suppose you have proved the church began on the day of Pentecost, what good does it do you? Honestly, you cannot get in *1800 years* of Pentecost. What good does it do you? I read from the history, and he cannot deny it, that Alexander Campbell said that not until the Baptists had withdrawn fellowship from the brethren of the Reformation, "thus by constraint, and not by choice, they were compelled to organize societies of their own," and he said *that was done in 1827*. Alexander Campbell said you started up with a bunch of *excluded Baptists*. And from that day on down to the present most of your members are made up of excluded Baptists. I think nearly half the members of this church have been excluded from the Baptist Church. It has been that way all over the country. (Laughter) I think you can say that you will find that half the members right here in this church now were excluded from the Baptists. It started that way, with a bunch of excluded Baptists, and Alexander Campbell said it was—that "not until the Baptists had, in 1827, withdrawn fellowship from the brethren of the Reformation, thus by constraint, and not by choice, they were compelled to organize societies of their own." There you are. You started with a bunch of excluded Baptists, 1800 years after Pentecost. What good will it do you if you prove your Pentecost theory when you cannot back up and hitch on?

I can run a line of church succession and have done it; the record will show it. I have done it twice. So I have run a line of church succession from Arkansas clear on back to Jesus Christ the Son of God, without a broken link anywhere, and he knows I have. Before, he got up and said, "Well, that just meant those that believed in believer's baptism." Certainly. A believer has salvation, and when you believe in a thing and are baptized, that is a saved man baptized like Cornelius. Now, we have had that line of succession from the time of Christ on down to the present time.

If that is not hitching on, please tell me what it is to hitch on.

Now, we have had a very nice discussion. In the one minute that I have before me, I want to express my appreciation for the kindness of the people of this community. I have been so highly entertained, so well paid, and my friend and I are no enemies because we have debated. When I turn you over to Alexander Campbell as your father I am but doing you justice. If you started with Jesus Christ, you might be called Christians, but when you started with Alexander Campbell you ought to be called Campbellites. That is exactly what you are. A man-made institution. Organized by men in 1827 and run by men contrary to the leading of the Holy Spirit. I hope some of you will learn the truth and be saved. I am not your enemy because I tell you the truth.

Thank you, very much.

www.ingramcontent.com/pod-product-compliance
Lightning Source LLC
LaVergne TN
LVHW050918080826
845145LV00001B/127

* 9 7 8 1 5 8 4 2 7 0 4 3 0 *